The Lotus® Guide to Agenda®

THE LOTUS® GUIDE TO

AGENDA®

Robert H. Flast and
Lauren M. Flast

Lotus
Books™

ADDISON-WESLEY PUBLISHING COMPANY, INC.

Reading, Massachusetts Menlo Park, California New York
Don Mills, Ontario Wokingham, England Amsterdam Bonn
Sydney Singapore Tokyo Madrid San Juan

This book is part of the Lotus Learning Series.

Library of Congress Cataloging-in-Publication Data

Flast, Robert H.
The Lotus guide to Agenda.

(Lotus learning series)
Includes index.
1. Agenda (Computer program) 2. Business—Data processing.
I. Flast, Lauren, 1958- II. Title. III. Series.
HF5548.4.A35F53 1988 005.75'65 88-19252
ISBN 0-201-15786-1

ISBN 0-201-15786-1
ABCDEFGHIJ-AL-898
First printing, October 1988

To Drew and Lily,
who helped push their father
over the edge.

Acknowledgments

We would like to acknowledge the help, support, and unparalleled enthusiasm of two individuals without whom this project would have been impossible: Conall Ryan, who braved commercial air travel with a broken foot to share his vision with us; and Zyg Furmaniuk, whose zany and thoroughly professional commitment made E-Mail retrieval a task to be eagerly anticipated and who minimized the trials of these beta users.

Contents

Foreword

AGENDA: A PERSONAL VIEW

I write this foreword with particular pleasure because I knew Bob and Lauren Flast way back when … . Bob was spearheading new technologies (mostly expert systems) within American Express; Lauren was spearheading new life (and writing books on the side). Then they discovered Agenda, as you can read inside.

I also knew Agenda way back when … . Jerry Kaplan, a consultant who had earlier co-founded the AI firm Teknowledge, showed me a clumsy PC program that could look at little pieces of text and assign them to categories. Mitchell Kapor like the idea too, and the rest is history.

Since then Agenda has grown sleeker, more powerful, and prettier, and the world has grown ready for it. Agenda can do nothing without lots of information to chew up, and in a world of E-mail, word-processing, calendars and other texts, the need for an electronic junk-mail detector is immense. Most bits of information are fairly meaningless by themselves, and take on impact only in association with other information. At the lowest level, what good's a phone number unattached to a person's name? What good is an appointment without an address, or a date?

But that's the immediately useful part of Agenda. More interesting is the way it's going to change how we think about software and information—and perhaps about ourselves. Information will no longer seem lifeless and inert; it's active, capable of crystallizing and arranging itself—by itself.

Consider how exotic an internal combustion engine might have seemed to an eighteenth-century person: "It pushes things all by itself? But how does it do that? It's not alive!" Just as we have already come to terms with mechanical engines, we'll come to realize that data doesn't need to be alive to be active or even seem intelligent; it just needs the electronic/software engine of tools like Agenda.

Of course, even though a mechanical engine doesn't seem strange, you probably couldn't explain how it works; you're just reasonably satisfied that it's not alive and it's not magic. In the same way, people won't find software like Agenda mystical at all, whether or not they understand how it works. Just as I press on the gas pedal to go faster, so can I soup up my Agenda to make connections more rapidly—without any need to understand the underlying technology.

So, in a world of data engines, how will we live? Clearly, the basics of life—love and anger, pride and curiosity, food and sex—won't change any more than they changed with the arrival of the engine. But consider how casually we think of traveling from coast to coast.

In the same way, huge feats of organization will seem routine. How much more productive will this make us feel? Not very, because everyone around us will have access to those same capabilities (which may raise interesting sociological/political issues). People will take it for granted when they call you that you know who they are, what they called about last time, that you have their number, etc. Sure, we marvel at some people's strength, but generally it's not a very valuable commodity in this age of machinery and construction equipment. In the future, organization, time-management and memory abilities will be less prized, and leadership skills may be more so. We can be kept informed and coordinated by computers, but not motivated or uplifted by them. Agenda can find any links you can describe, but you've got to be explicit in specifying those links. Agenda can't make the kinds of creative jumps Einstein or Mozart or Tom Stoppard (or Mitch or Jerry) could.

As you work with Agenda, you may think you see its personality emerging, but that's deceptive. What's emerging is the automation of *your* personality—the connections *you* make, the way *you* categorize things. The only difference is that Agenda is probably more painstaking, more consistent, and more reliable in memory than you are. As you get more experienced, you'll know how to change its style, by slightly altering the rules, or changing its aggressiveness in making assumptions. Think of Agenda as the engine in a machine you can build to do your bidding.

So, I hope you enjoy this book, and that it helps you tune your engine to its peak performance.

Esther Dyson
Editor and Publisher
Release 1.0

How to Use This Guide

Lotus Agenda is a totally new concept in productivity tools for the IBM family of personal computers. As described by Lotus, Agenda is a dynamic, flexible tool for storing, organizing, and retrieving many forms of text-based information such as ideas, white papers, memos, status reports, speeches, news items, press releases, research abstracts, electronic mail, outlines, performance appraisals, tasks, people, projects, plans, and goals.

In more technical terms, which will become much clearer as you read this book, Agenda provides for:

the dynamic linking and multiple filing of text
the automatic parsing of dates
the automatic completion of typed input
the automatic categorization of text
the free-form entry of data
the ability to deal with randomly arriving and unstructured data.

What this really means is that Agenda can help you deal with the endless stream of information that you collect and organize daily. It provides:

- A means for recording the content of this information in a format referred to as *items* and *notes*.
- A way for you to discover, modify, or apply the structure for this information by identifying possibly overlapping groupings of related items referred to as *categories*.
- A way for you to display and modify this information from multiple perspectives in a format referred to as *views*.

Content or items, structure or categories, and displays or views are the three key concepts in Agenda, which will be thoroughly discussed in this guide.

As with any new tool, some of Agenda's uses were originally intended by its developers, and other uses will be created by its users. Due to its dynamic and flexible design, Agenda is more likely to be used in a broad range of applications than most PC tools. The purpose of this book is to help you become adept at using Agenda and find the ways that it can be most helpful to you.

WHO SHOULD USE THE GUIDE

We assume that you have purchased Agenda to run on your IBM Personal Computer or certified compatible, with a hard disk, a minimum of 640K, and MS-DOS version 2.0 or higher.

We strongly suggest that you install Agenda following the instructions in Chapter 2 of the Agenda *User's Guide* and that you use Agenda to actively follow the examples in this book. The examples should give you the additional hands-on experience that can help you become more comfortable, familiar, and confident with Agenda.

Although it is not essential, we also encourage you to read Chapter 1, Introducing Lotus Agenda, and Chapter 3, Thirty Minutes with Agenda, of the Agenda *User's Guide*. In addition, if you read and perform the Agenda *Tutorial* and *Sample Applications*, you will be in an even stronger position to gain the most from this guide.

ORGANIZATION OF THE GUIDE

The Lotus Guide to Agenda begins with Part I, Setting the Stage, which presents useful background material in Chapter 1 and covers some of the mechanics involved in getting around in Agenda in Chapter 2.

The guide continues with Part II Beginning Concepts, a thorough review of the beginning concepts of Agenda, namely, the content, structure, and display of information with Agenda. Examples are also given.

Part III Applications, presents a few powerful examples of Agenda at its best. Out of dozens of possibilities, we tried to select four examples that demonstrate Agenda's power, versatility, and flexibility. The first, the Personal Contacts File, is an example of a dynamic application where the items and categories can be added at any time. The second, a Quotations Reference, is also dynamic but introduces the use of the powerful text and profile conditions and profile actions features to automatically classify items. The third, Project Evaluation, is more of a static or one-time application whose value comes from Agenda's ability to help you view a set of objects from multiple perspectives and, in the process, to rank the objects in this multidimensional space. The fourth, an Executive Information System, is an example of how traditional, paper-based executive work can be transformed through the use of Agenda. A monthly reference document becomes a personalized tool that executives can use to annotate and classify the facts and figures concerned with the running of their business. In addition, this application demonstrates the importing of information from external sources.

Part IV Advanced Concepts, deals with higher level topics, such as printing and macros. As with Part II (which also deals with concepts), Part IV contains a number of examples that illustrate the points being made. After reading Part I, you can take either of two approaches to learning Agenda with this guide.

To concentrate on concepts, first read Part II, followed by Parts III and IV in any order.

To concentrate on applications, read Parts III, II, and IV, in that order.

SUGGESTIONS FOR BECOMING ADEPT WITH AGENDA

As part of our preparation for writing this book, we interviewed a number of early test users of Agenda, known as beta users, who shared their opinions on how to most effectively learn Agenda. Some of the suggestions they made were:

- Use Agenda to learn Agenda. As you read this book, which is based on the idea of teaching Agenda through the use of Agenda, put important facts or observations into Agenda as items. Assign them to as many categories as you can think of and when you have a question later, you can use Agenda as a reference. In fact, the tips and tricks and cross-referenced databases that are presented in Chapter 14 are based on this idea.

- Pick an application that is near and dear to your heart, and one that you understand well, to use on a daily basis in learning Agenda. This provides frequent practice, gives back something quickly, and closes the gap between the abstract definition of Agenda and its real-life uses.
- Think of Agenda as a note pad to jot down ideas with or without structure. Later when you have a collection of ideas, begin to organize them using the categories.

As you learn Agenda we encourage you to use it as often as possible. We have suggested many possible uses for Agenda, but because it is a very personal tool, you will discover many of your own applications. The hands-on development of these applications will ultimately expose and demonstrate the true power of Agenda.

CONVENTIONS USED IN THE GUIDE

Keystroke instructions appear throughout the book, either in paragraphs describing their functionality or in step lists using the following format:

Press: [F8] (VW MGR)
Move to: Initial View
Press: [F2] (EDIT)
Type: `Project Entry Screen`
Press: [↵]

Instructions in step lists such as **Press:** and **Type:** are printed in boldface type and followed by a colon. Key names are shown as keycaps and, where appropriate, such as with function keys, are followed by command descriptions in parentheses. Characters that you should type appear in `monospace type`.

When keystrokes are described in paragraphs, the first letters of the key names are capitalized. Screen prompts, such as *make backup copy:*, will appear in italics.

Be sure to follow the keystroke instructions carefully to ensure that your results match those in the book.

Part I: Setting the Stage

1

Introduction

''PC software that helps you think. . .it organizes data the way you—not the programmers—like it.''

Business Week, 11/2/87

''With Lotus Agenda, we're introducing a product that will help people manage textual data more intelligently.''

New York Times, 11/3/87

''Lotus unveiled a fascinating new program called Agenda. . .Agenda is a brilliant concept.''

New York Times, 11/10/87

''Simplicity and elegance''

PC Week, 3/15/88

''Agenda is both powerful and flexible—a good combination.''

Infoworld, 4/11/88

So now we know why Mitch Kapor was taking those courses at the Massachusetts Institute of Technology and attending American Association of Artificial Intelligence conferences. We also now understand why Kapor recruited Jerry Kaplan, a well-known expert in the field of artificial intelligence (AI), to join him at Lotus. The reason for these moves, and many others quietly made at Lotus over the last three years, was to develop Agenda. Lotus has brought its considerable skills in developing and marketing productivity software to the completion of this exciting project. For the first time, important and powerful techniques learned over the last thirty years in the study of human and machine intelligence have been incorporated in a commercial product targeted to millions of PC owners and users. In fact, this may be the first PC product since VisiCalc that provides solutions for a whole new class of personal computer users, in addition to satisfying the needs of millions of existing users.

WHY DO WE NEED AGENDA?

How We Work Today

If you're like us, keeping up with the constant flow of information can be a time-consuming and frustrating challenge. The tools you have at your disposal include a rotary card file, telephone message pads, incoming and outgoing mail boxes, Post-it notes, business card files, regular office files, microfilm cameras and readers, staplers and tape, maybe a PC, and certainly a trash basket. A typical day in the office involves employing these tools in the following way:

reading, prioritizing, and responding to telephone messages and correspondence from inside and outside the company

reading reports, newspapers, journals, magazines, and advertisements

producing reports and presentations

analyzing statistical and financial tables

organizing, leading, or attending meetings and conferences

interviewing candidates for open positions

talking with colleagues and subordinates about current issues.

Let's dissect each of these activities to see what is really involved.

First, with phone messages, we can typically sort them into a priority sequence with the most important messages on top of the stack. Frequently we need to do some research on a particular caller or writer to see what was proposed or agreed to in the last communication. This adds an element of delay to the seemingly simple task of answering dozens of phone messages, and yet it is an important part of ensuring that these calls and letters are productive. If we are lucky, we may have a secretary or assistant who understands enough about our business to do some of this sorting before we see the telephone messages or correspondence. This sorting might be by priority such as high, medium, and low; or by the source of the communication such as my boss, my boss' peers, others inside the company, and those outside the company; or by date received. Obviously, we can only choose one of these sorting rules because we only have single copies of the messages or correspondence.

Turning now to the reading tasks, whether we read word for word or skim, we are searching for pieces of information to which we want to respond or which we simply want to ''file away'' for future reference. We might write in the margins or use a highlighting pen, but then we have to keep the source documents and what's worse we have to flip through these documents to retrieve our notes or memorable passages.

Producing reports and presentations involves retrieving all kinds of relevant stored ideas, whether in our minds or in other reports, books, journals, newspapers, and magazines. Our task is to organize this information into a logical progression that communicates the points we are trying to make.

Analyzing statistical or financial tables may require us to do some calculations using a spreadsheet like 1-2-3. However, more often than not, we will be examining final results, searching for patterns of data or unusual items that we will want to note for follow-up or future reference. These reminders may take the form of marginal notes or Post-it notes pasted to the relevant sections of the tables.

Organizing meetings involves keeping track of myriad details concerning facilites, attendees, agenda, speakers, meals, transportation, and so on. We might keep all of these items in a special file with subfiles for each of these topics. Frequently, details change and they may affect the contents of one or more of these subfiles. For example, if the date of the meeting changes, you need to change reservations for facilities, transportation, speakers, and invitations to attendees. You may not even know where to find all the items that you need to reconsider in the event of a simple change such as the date of the meeting. Leading and attending meetings involve other sets of details such as transportation, lodging, and preparation for the meeting.

Interviewing candidates for open positions involves taking copious notes about an individual's qualifications. Ultimately the notes must be organized so that they can be compared across candidates competing for the same position and with the stated requirements of the position.

Finally, the impromptu and ad hoc discussions we frequently have with our colleagues and subordinates can produce all sorts of ideas requiring further discussion, decision making, or action.

The one thing that all these tasks have in common is that they require the collecting, organizing, storing, and retrieving of information coming from all kinds of sources and in all kinds of formats.

As the preceding examples demonstrate, anyone who deals with information by writing in pads or notebooks; on telephone messages; on Post-it notes; on napkins; in the margins of books, magazines, newspapers, or correspondence; or anywhere has the frustrating task of organizing this stream of information so that it can be retrieved for action or reference. Similarly, anyone who collects items of information such as newspaper or magazine clippings, memorable quotes, news items, theater playbills, restaurant reviews, recipes, or anything else also shares these frustrating tasks.

When the medium is strictly linear, for example, pads, notebooks, document margins, or stacks of papers, there is only one way to revisit the information: by a sequential search from beginning to end. However, examining every item is both precise and inefficient. Depending on the medium, you can trade off some precision for efficiency, for example, by flipping pages, when the medium is a book.

When the medium is fragmented, as in the case of telephone messages, index cards, Post-it notes, napkins, or file folders, you can sort any subset of the information to make it easier to retrieve. However, unless you create multiple copies of these items of information, you can only sort them into a single category, which may frustrate your attempts to retrieve them if you cannot remember the exact category where they are stored. If you duplicate them, they may be easier to find but harder to maintain.

Obviously, we want to organize this information, but often we are not quite sure how. Frequently a structure that suits one subset of items does not fit others. The fact is that items frequently fit into multiple categories, and it is hard to decide where to assign them if we are limited to single categories.

With this glimpse into how we deal with the constant flow of information today, let us look at Agenda and examine the ways in which this remarkable productivity tool can make this process more efficient and effective.

How We Might Work Tomorrow—With Agenda

Let's reexamine our daily tasks and see how Agenda might improve them or make them faster. Using Agenda, we can store telephone messages, summaries of correspondence, or even the complete correspondence, as items one time only and simultaneously assign them to multiple categories, such as priority, topic, source, and date received. This means that we can review the phone calls or correspondence from multiple perspectives or views. As we respond to and update the communications, the associated follow-up details simultaneously appear in all views of these communications.

In our reading tasks, instead of marginal notes and highlighting, we can enter important facts [or our thoughts and impressions] as items into Agenda, where they can be organized into categories and retrieved as views in any form that suits our purposes.

Using Agenda, the preparation of reports and presentations can be approached in a more creative way. We can throw lots of ideas down on "paper" and organize them after the fact into paragraphs or sections that make the most sense. We can use the categories we have set up to explore items of information that we may have filed away for some other purpose, but that may be relevant to the current report or presentation. Also, we can experiment with different sequences of ideas simply by setting up each sequence as a separate category and then viewing the items in category order in different views.

In analyzing financial and statistical tables, we can use Agenda to store our concerns or impressions about the numerical results. In fact, if we store the numeric table values in Agenda as text items, we can categorize them according to the people with whom we wish to discuss them, our specific concerns, and so on.

Agenda provides a number of planning features, which can be invaluable in organizing meetings. In addition to providing an automated scratchpad for storing the detailed items concerning facilities, attendees, speakers, meals, and transportation, Agenda provides a flexible means for categorizing these items by topic, party responsible, priority, due date, and so on. It also provides a mechanism for linking these details in prerequisite/dependent relationships so that you can identify all the tasks that depend on the completion of a particular task. As tasks are completed, they can be marked as "done" and, if desired, suppressed from future views of the items. Since you can categorize the items by the person who is responsible, you can create views of the items for each of these people and print out to-do lists that they can use to structure their efforts. Even though items can be multiply categorized and thus one item may be tracked on many lists, you only need to update an item in one of the lists. The change will automatically be reflected everywhere else the item is referenced.

In organizing the copious notes that you might collect during an interview, you can use Agenda's powerful categorizing features to both manually and automatically assign interview observations to categories of interest. These categories do not have to be decided on initially, as they would if you were using a database product for this purpose, but rather can evolve over time. Agenda automatically classifies observations in categories depending on the item text or other category assignments. As the structure evolves for one candidate, it can be exported as a template to be used for other candidates, so that you will have common dimensions with which to compare and contrast the candidates.

Finally, in day-to-day interactions with colleagues and subordinates, Agenda can help you store facts, opinions, decisions, events, commitments, and other information by person, by topic, by priority, and so on. You can then view these reminders according to these categories that makes them easier to locate, aggregate, and assign.

As you can see, Agenda makes it easy for you to store and retrieve your items of information in any number of categories. As a specific example, let's consider reminders to yourself to call Fred about the new fall line, to examine plans for the new fall line, and to review Fred's commissions, which can be assigned to categories called Fred and fall line, as shown in Figures 1-1 and 1-2.

Figure 1-1.

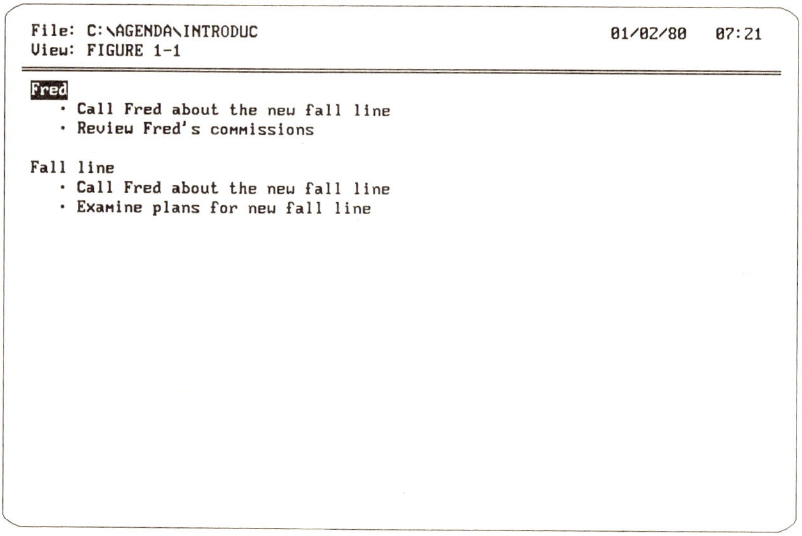

Figure 1-2.

```
File: C:\AGENDA\INTRODUC                                      01/02/80   07:20
View: FIGURE 1-2
==============================================================================
Tasks                                              Fred          Fall line
   · Call Fred about the new fall line               *               *
   · Examine plans for new fall line                                 *
   · Review Fred's commissions                       *
```

As shown in these figures, which are actual screens from Agenda, you can use the categories to label sections of related items or to simply display the relevant category information in columns adjacent to the items. The star(*) format is only one of the many formats available for displaying category membership.

As mentioned earlier, you do not have to determine your categories in advance, as you would with a typical database tool. You can create them as you think of them, before, during, or after you enter your items. In other words, since the structure can evolve, you do not have to tailor your data a priori to suit your structure. This is one important way that Agenda serves your individual and idiosyncratic information needs.

As shown in Figures 1-1 and 1-2, the categories can be used to separate related items into sections or simply to display the relevant category information in columns to the left or right of the items. Having assigned this item to these two categories, you will now be able to easily retrieve it along with other items relevant to Fred or along with other items relevant to the fall line, thus assuring that you will not lose track of it. Also, you can update or change the item in any section in which it appears, in this case, Fred or fall line, and that change will be reflected for that item in all the sections in which it appears.

In addition to supporting the manual assignment of items to categories, Agenda can further assist you by automatically assigning items to categories based on the item text or the previous assignments of the items to other categories. These features are referred to as conditions and actions and are attached to categories to enable this automatic matching. This powerful feature means that even if you are not familiar with a set of categories that someone has provided to you, or if you simply overlook a category in assigning items, Agenda may still correctly classify your items for you. Of course, just as you can assign items to multiple categories, Agenda can too.

Although Agenda is the flexible tool we have described, it is also a great deal more. For example, you can attach to the preceding item a date when you intend to make the call to Fred. This feature allows you to use Agenda as a personal planning tool to remind you of the tasks to be done on or by a certain date. When you make the call, you can mark this item as done and the appropriate date will be assigned to indicate that the call has been made. This feature makes it extremely easy to write status reports, to prepare invoices for work completed, or simply to remind yourself when you accomplished a particular task.

Also, you can create dependencies among your tasks or items such that calling Fred about the fall line is contingent upon first reviewing the plans for the fall line with your staff. Agenda has a feature for handling dependencies whereby you can identify the prerequisite items for a given item. With this feature you can retrieve an item along with the items on which it depends or the items that depend upon it. For example, suppose that you are looking at all your notes concerning Fred and you find the fall line item. You notice that it is marked as having prerequisites. You can use Agenda to identify those items that need to be completed before you make that call to Fred as well as those items that cannot be done until that call is made.

Finally, through a variety of file import and export capabilities, you can merge databases, eliminating duplication, and assigning new items to old categories, or vice versa.

Based on the preceding features, it is easy to see why Agenda has been used in many applications. For example, Agenda can be used to:

- maintain a keyword or lexical filing system
- recruit executives
- plan human resources
- appraise personnel and project performance
- analyze a document, e-mail, reports, memos, and so on
- manage PR media lists, executive briefings, and press releases
- solve a complex problem
- keep a to-do list
- build a creative platform
- manage advertising traffic
- develop a curriculum
- analyze a stock portfolio
- negotiate a contract
- sift through news for significant data
- brainstorm
- manage people
- organize information for a meeting or phone call
- write a brochure
- keep a self-sorting notebook
- consolidate notes from a meeting
- prepare a status report
- prepare a presentation
- write a speech, article, or outline
- write a marketing plan
- write a business plan
- manage a project
- manage a sales account

WHY ARE THESE AI TECHNIQUES SO IMPORTANT?

The important thing to keep in mind is that although Agenda uses some concepts that have been developed in the field of artificial intelligence (or AI), it is not a tool for doing AI research or systems development. The AI component by itself is mildly interesting, but the integration of AI concepts into a personal productivity tool for PC users is the real achievement of those associated with Agenda's design and development.

Artificial intelligence is an academic discipline that concerns itself with building automated models of what we would describe as intelligent behavior. The term artificial intelligence is said to have been used for the first time at a conference in New Hampshire in the late 1950s. For the last thirty years, AI has broadened into many subfields including robotics, vision systems, learning systems, ''natural'' language systems (an unnatural way to refer to processing the English language or any native language), and knowledge-based or expert systems. A central issue in AI is how to represent knowledge in a computer so that it can be processed in ways that mimic intelligent behavior.

Agenda incorporates a number of the knowledge representation concepts associated with language and knowledge-based systems. For example, Agenda parses or translates your typing to anticipate the words or concepts that you are entering. It suggests an automatic completion to your typing once it begins matching your entry to previously entered information. You can still type in the whole word or phrase that will override any automatic completion that Agenda is proposing. This contributes both to efficiency and consistency in assigning items to categories, creating new categories, and defining views. From an efficiency perspective, as you see the desired phrases being automatically displayed on the screen, you can truncate your typing by pressing the Enter key, and Agenda will accept the proposed completion of your typing. From a consistency perspective, it makes sense to pay close attention to the automatic completion feature and select completion suggestions that match your expectations.

In knowledge-based systems, knowledge is encoded or represented by two popular methods. The first technique uses rules, which appear in the form: If A, then B. An example of this if-then technique might be: If a child is Lauren's daughter, then the child is Bob's daughter. Agenda permits you to use rules in the Category Manager in the form of conditions and actions that govern how Agenda automatically assigns items to categories. In the preceding example, a condition could be attached to a category called Bob's daughter, so that when an item such as Lily was assigned to the category called Lauren's daughter, Lily would automatically be assigned to the Bob's daughter category, too. Also, when working with items, a limited form of rule-based processing is employed in the dependent/prerequisite features discussed earlier (more about this in Part II).

The second method of representing knowledge uses frames, or hierarchical, nested information structures, where concepts lower down in the hierarchy inherit the attributes of the concepts that are linked to and above them. This hierarchical structure supporting inheritance is built into Agenda's Category Manager (more about this in Part II). For example, if we have a restaurant database in Agenda with the attributes of restaurants as categories, one category could be American as a type of food served. Within American there could be additional categories such as Californian, Cajun, or Barbecue. Thanks to the inheritance feature of the hierarchically structured Category Manager, a specific restaurant item when assigned to Cajun can be found under Cajun or American or both.

The knowledge representation work in AI draws upon and contributes to the study of intelligence in general. Whether we are talking about infants, early civilizations, or modern business leaders, researchers have shown that classification, conceptualization, pattern recognition, and encoding are central tasks in intelligent behavior. Agenda is unique both in providing a medium in which we can perform these tasks as comfortably as we can manipulate numbers in a spreadsheet, and in directly helping its users perform these tasks.

HOW DOES AGENDA COMPARE WITH OTHER PC PRODUCTS?

Although Agenda's format can suggest the appearance of columns and rows, it is not a spreadsheet. Unlike a spreadsheet, Agenda treats all information, including numbers, as text. Therefore, it cannot perform any of the calculations normally associated with a spreadsheet. On the other hand, text information is often best presented in a tabular format for which a row and column orientation is particularly useful, as shown in Figure 1-3.

Agenda is unlike traditional database packages in that it permits a totally flexible structure to evolve and does not require the user to specify that structure in advance. In other words, you can set up a structure that uses items and categories as though they were records with fields, but you are not required to do so.

Figure 1-3.

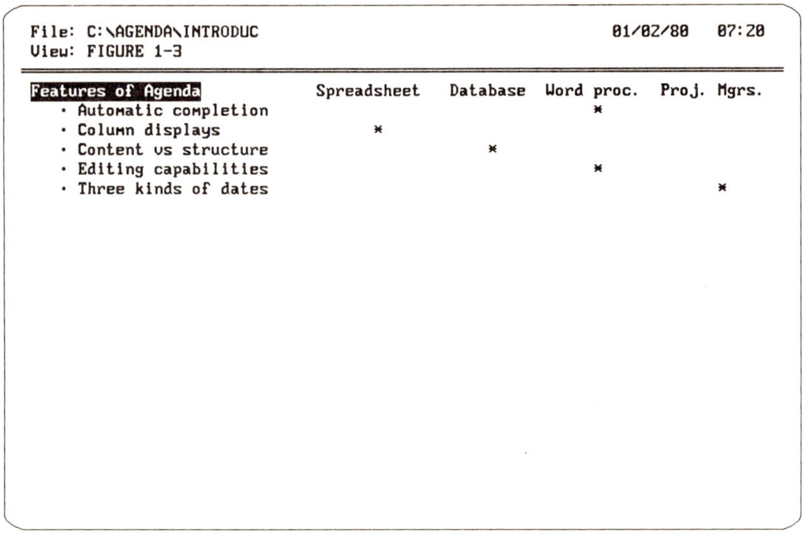

Agenda is also not a word processor, even though you can use it to compose a document, which in turn you can print directly or input to a word processor for more formal presentation. This idea of Agenda as a pre-processor is suggestive of thought processors or outlining packages. Once again, although Agenda can be used to create an outline as a first step in developing a document, it does not require the user to do so. Instead, you can jot down your thoughts and ideas at random, organize them in groups, whether linear or not, and then go on to write the document from any point in your outline you find comfortable.

Although Agenda is not a traditional project planning and management tool such as Pert chart or CPM network products, Agenda's date, condition/action, and dependency/prerequisite features enable you to build a project plan that you can use to schedule and track activities, resources, time, personnel, and so on. As with the traditional tools, you can prepare lists of activities by start dates, completion dates, priorities, dependencies, length of task, and personnel responsible for their completion.

What should be obvious now is that Agenda can be used to accomplish tasks normally associated with a variety of PC software products. In one sense, you can think of it as a common denominator among spreadsheets, databases, word processors, thought or outline processors, and project management products. The fact that you can use Agenda to accomplish all of these applications suggests that Agenda has captured the common information dimension of these various activities.

On the other hand, to say that Agenda represents some form of common denominator in the PC tools described above implies that it does not include many of the specific functionalities that make some spreadsheet, database, word processing, and project management packages truly great. And, in fact, Agenda does not attempt to duplicate or incorporate every feature of these traditional PC tools. For many of us, Agenda's functionality will be just fine, but even if you are a power user of these PC tools, you may still find Agenda to be of great help in preparing your ideas, data, text, and plans for use by these more sophisticated tools in their respective specialized areas.

IN CLOSING

Agenda is in a class by itself. Its unique contribution is its ability to support its users in either a structured or an unstructured fashion. This distinction is descriptive, not evaluative, in nature and has been recognized for some time. Seymour Papert, in his book *Mind-storms* (Basics Book, Inc, 1980), a history of the Logo programming language, identified *structured* and *unstructured* as the two principle styles used by children in mastering the computer. Sherry Turkle, in her book *The Second Self* (Simon & Schuster, Inc, 1985), brings this distinction up to date by contrasting hard, or structured, mastery of the computer with soft, or unstructured, mastery. Hard mastery is the style associated with scientists, mathematicians, engineers, and computer professionals. Soft mastery is the style associated with poets, musicians, and artists. Regardless of how or why these two styles have evolved, the important point is that until now, most computer software has been developed by and for the hard masters. Agenda is one of the first products that can and should appeal to the soft masters as well. This acknowledgment of individual differences or preferences is particularly rare in the software world.

Our goal in writing *The Lotus Guide to Agenda* was to demonstrate, through examples, large and small, the rich and varied possibilities for applying Agenda to help you solve a new class of problems as well as improve upon the solutions to some existing problems. We hope that with this book and through your own experimentation you will share our excitement for this important new PC product.

2

Getting Around Agenda

Before we delve into the content, structure, and display of information in Agenda, we will review briefly the flexible and varied methods for navigating within Agenda and managing your files. These consist of function keys, special keys, accelerator keys, and dialog and selection boxes. There are frequently multiple ways of accomplishing the same thing. Once you learn a technique that you find comfortable, you will probably forget the other five ways to perform the same function.

TYPES OF KEYS

Agenda, offers three types of keys—function keys, special keys, and accelerator keys—to help you efficiently guide Agenda.

Function Keys

Generally, to perform any function, you will use the menu system, a series of keystrokes, a dialog box, or some combination of these. On most screens, the available function keys are displayed in a function key map in the bottom row.

If the bottom row of the screen does not display the function key map, press Alt-K (press and hold the Alt key and then press the K key as well) to reveal the function key map. Alt-K is an example of the accelerator keys, which will be described later in this chapter.

The names that appear under the function key labels are brief mnemonics to remind you of the functions served by the keys. The two most frequently used function keys on every screen are F10(Menu) and F1(Help).

F10(Menu) displays a menu bar at the top of the screen with the available commands that are relevant to what you were doing when you pressed F10(Menu). You can move from choice to choice in the menu bar by pressing the right and left arrow keys, thus highlighting the various selections. As you highlight the selections, the submenus displayed on the second row from the top change, too. For example, when the File option is highlighted on the first row, the choices within the File option, namely, Open, Backup, Use-Backup, Copy, Delete, Transfer, Note, and Info, are displayed on the second row.

To select a menu option, move the highlight over the option and press Enter, or simply type the first letter of the menu option and the selection automatically takes place. The submenu now appears on the top row and additional information is displayed for each option on the second row. For example, if you press Enter when the highlight is on the File option, the choices within the File option will be listed on the first row, and the first one, Open, will be highlighted. If you move the highlight to the Transfer option, you will see three words—Import, Export, and Template—appear on the second row. This is reminding you that within the File commands, you can transfer files into Agenda by importing them, transfer files out of Agenda by exporting them, or transfer just the structure of your information out of Agenda by using the Template option.

F1(Help) displays the section of the help system that is most relevant to where you were when you pressed F1(Help). From any help screen you can access any other help screen by displaying the Help Index. On all help screens you will see the words Help Index, generally near the bottom of the screen. If you use the arrow keys to move the highlight to the words Help Index and then press Enter, the master index for the help system is displayed, as shown in Figure 2-1. From this point, you can look up any information that you want in the online help files by moving the highlight to the desired topic and pressing Enter. To return to Agenda from any help screen, just press Esc.

Esc is a very useful key because it generally permits you to back up or undo your last keystrokes. At the very least, it will back you out of the current function and return the system to where you were before you began the function from which you Esc-aped. This shift may not always be obvious, but you will learn over time what to expect from Esc. If you press Esc multiple times, it will continue to back up through your commands until it reaches the screen where you first started entering your commands. When you reach this screen, repeated Esc's will do nothing.

Figure 2-1.

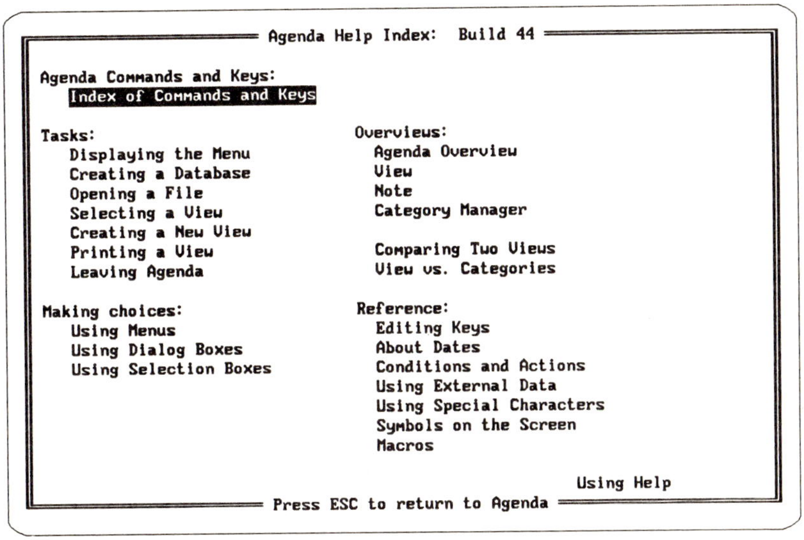

As you can see on the function key map at the bottom of the screen, there are a number of other function keys besides F1(Help) and F10(Menu). In fact, there is even another set of function keys you cannot see unless you press Alt. If you press Alt and hold it down, you will see the mnemonics under the function key labels change to new terms. These alternate function keys can be used by pressing and holding Alt and then pressing the function key while Alt is depressed. As you learn Agenda, the meanings of the function key mnemonics will become clear and useful. However, if you are ever confused about their functions, press F1(Help), go to the Help Index and, since the function and Alt function key maps are different depending upon whether you are in a view screen, a note screen, or the Category Manager screen, select the appropriate function keys section by highlighting it and pressing Enter. You will now see a list of the function and Alt function keys, an example of which is shown in Figure 2-2 for the view function keys.

Figure 2-2.

View Function Keys

F1 (HELP)	Display on-line Help
F2 (EDIT)	Edit item or category name
F3 (COPY)	Copy item(s) to another section
F4 (DONE)	Designate item(s) as done
F5 (NOTE)	Create or edit note for current item
F6 (MOVE)	Reassign item(s) to a different section
F7 (MARK)	Mark unmarked item; unmark marked item
F8 (VW MGR)	Switch, create, or modify view(s)
F9 (CAT MGR)	Go to the category manager
F10 (MENU)	Display the view menu
ALT F1 (COMPOSE)	Type special or international characters
ALT F2 (WHEN)	Set When date for item(s)
ALT F3 (DEPENDS)	Make current item depend on marked item(s)
ALT F4 (DISCARD)	Discard current or marked items to Trash
ALT F5 (SEARCH)	Search for a specific text string
ALT F6 (GOTO)	Move quickly to another section
ALT F7 (UNMARK)	Unmark all marked items in current view
ALT F8 (LAST VIEW)	Return to the last view you looked at
ALT F9 (PROFILE)	Display item assignment profile
ALT F10 (MACRO)	Create, edit, or execute a macro

View Overview | Help Index

Press ESC to return to Agenda

The function key labels, mnemonics, and short descriptions are provided to remind you of the behavior of these keys. Return to Agenda by pressing Esc, and you can proceed with whatever function you intended to perform.

Special Keys

The special keys include the arrows, PgUp (Page Up), PgDn (Page Down), Home, End, Ins (Insert), Del (Delete), Ctrl (Control) (together with one of the previously mentioned keys), Enter, Grey –, and Grey +. Generally speaking these keys perform the expected functions of moving you around a screen, line, word, or database, and experimenting will help you to quickly master them. However, if you are unsure about how Agenda will behave when you press one of these special keys, press F1(Help), go to the Help Index, and once again you can select the type of special key you need depending upon whether you are in a view, note, or Category Manager screen. An example of the View Special Keys screen in the help system is shown in Figure 2-3.

Figure 2-3.

View Special Keys

UP/DOWN	Move highlight up/down one item or category
PAGE UP/PAGE DOWN	Move highlight up/down one screen
HOME/END	Move highlight to beginning/end of section
CTRL HOME/CTRL END	Move highlight to top/bottom of view
RIGHT/LEFT	Move highlight one column to the right/left
CTRL RIGHT/CTRL LEFT	Move highlight to column at far right/left
INSERT	Insert item in section or category in column
DELETE	Remove item from current section and category; remove section or column from view; remove category or date from column
ENTER	Complete item or category you are entering or editing; move to next item or category
ESCAPE	Back out of current task
GREY +	Display category hierarchy to select a section or column head, to select column entry, or to change item assignments
SHIFT GREY -	Collapse current or all section(s)
SHIFT GREY +	Expand current or all section(s)

View Overview Help Index

Press ESC to return to Agenda

Accelerator Keys

The accelerator keys combine Alt with letter keys, for example, as Alt-K, to perform some function or to short cut the menu approach to guiding Agenda. Although the letters chosen for these keys are usually helpful reminders of their functions, it will probably take some time for you to feel completely comfortable using them. However, as their name suggests, accelerator keys can be very useful in speeding your work with Agenda. It is probably a good idea to get in the habit of using them. To be sure about how Agenda will behave when you press one of these accelerator keys, press F1(Help), go to the Help Index, and once again you can select the type of accelerator key you need depending upon whether you are in a view, note, or Category Manager screen. An example of the View Accelerator Keys screen in the help system is shown in Figure 2-4.

Figure 2-4.

View Accelerator Keys

Key	Use To...
ALT A	Assign current item or marked item(s) to another category
ALT D/U	Insert untitled section below/above current section (down/up)
ALT E	Execute all conditions for current item only
ALT F	Close current file and open last file
ALT H	Hop to next section in current (or next) view that contains current item
ALT I	Insert new item from anywhere in view
ALT J	Jump to next marked item in view
ALT K	Turn function key map on/off
ALT L/R	Insert untitled column to left/right of current position
ALT N/P	Go to next/previous view
ALT Q	Display Questions box to confirm/reject suggested assignments
ALT S	Sort section(s) according to current sort preferences
ALT V	Go to same item in same section in another view
ALT X	Execute all conditions for all items
ALT Y	Retrieve last removed from trash and insert it in current section
ALT Z	Run current macro

View Overview Help Index

Press ESC to return to Agenda

DIALOG BOXES

Agenda uses a format called dialog boxes to obtain information from you in order to properly follow your instructions. For example, when loading and converting a file into an Agenda database, Agenda needs to know the filename and whether or not you want the file to be erased after the transfer is completed. When you press F10(Menu), F for File, T for Transfer, and I for Import, Agenda responds by displaying the dialog box shown in Figure 2-5.

You can either change the fields shown in the dialog box or accept them as shown by leaving them alone. For any field, you can type your response, or for certain fields that have predetermined lists of available options, Agenda can help you select the desired option. Agenda always shows you the default options, which are either the default values assigned when Agenda was shipped or the most recent default selections you made.

To see the available options one at a time, place the highlight on the field and press the Spacebar multiple times to rotate through the options one by one. To select an option in this fashion, press the Spacebar until you find the desired option and then simply move the highlight to the next field in the dialog box where a choice is required.

Figure 2-5.

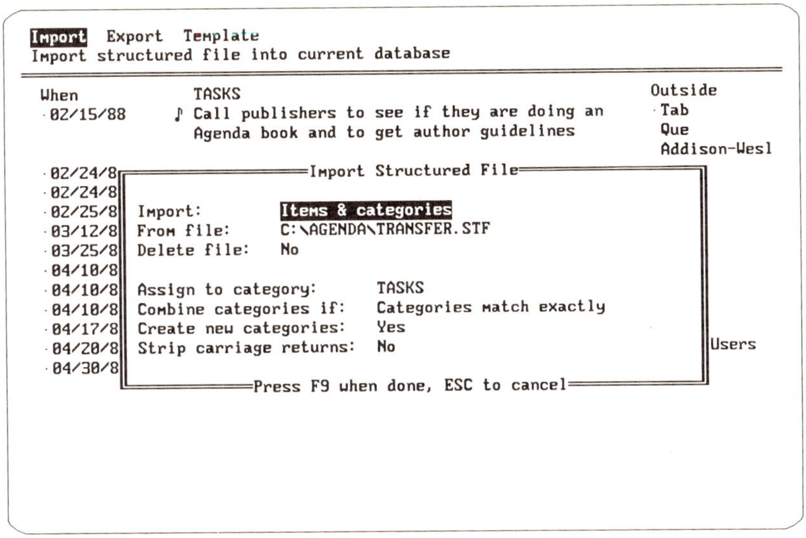

To see all of the available options at one time, press F2(Edit) or GREY +, and a window or selection box listing the available options will be shown. To select an option in this fashion, move the highlight to the desired option and press F9(Accept) or Enter. The window will be closed and the option will appear under the highlight in the dialog box. Then move the highlight to the next field in the dialog box where a choice is required.

To restore the default option for any field in a dialog box, move the highlight to the field and press F8(Default). To restore the default options for all of the fields in a dialog box, press Alt-F8(DfltAll).

By pressing F9(Accept) you indicate to Agenda that you are satisfied with the responses in the dialog box and are ready for Agenda to take the appropriate actions.

FILES IN AGENDA

Agenda uses several file types. They have new file extensions such as .AGA, .AGB, .BKA, .BKB, and .STF. The AGA and AGB files are the files in which your database is stored. The BKA and BKB files are files in which backup copies of your database, either created automatically by Agenda or manually by you, are stored. The STF files are used for importing and exporting information between Agenda databases and between Agenda and other PC programs as well as for saving items you have completed and marked as done. There is one other kind of file, the note file, which does not have a file extension and is used to store exported notes from your database.

If you are in an Agenda session and want to find out all the files that are being accessed by your database, you can turn on your printer, go to the Category Manager by pressing F9(Cat Mgr), and press F10(Menu) and P for Print. Agenda displays a Print dialog box, with the first prompt, *Print:*, already showing the default setting, Database info. If not, press the Spacebar to rotate through the options until Database info is displayed. Each time you press the Spacebar, a new option appears until you have exhausted all the possibilities. Then the first option appears again and so on. Having set the Database info option as the response to the *Print:* prompt, press F9(Accept) to begin the printing. Agenda will print out the database information, including the name and description of the file, all files associated with this file, and miscellaneous statistics about numbers of items, categories, assignments, and unused space.

Agenda provides two other methods for displaying information about your database or view, in this case as screens not in printed form. To see statistics about the file or database on any view screen, press F10(Menu), F for File, and I for Info. A File Information window will appear as shown in Figure 2-6.

With the exception of the Unused space term on the first line, the statistics shown are self-explanatory. Unused space refers to the space which Agenda reserves for data while you add items and categories that are no longer needed due to the discarding of items or categories. This space is still reserved but "unused." You can reclaim this space for use by pressing F10(Menu), U for Utility, and C for Compress.

Figure 2-6.

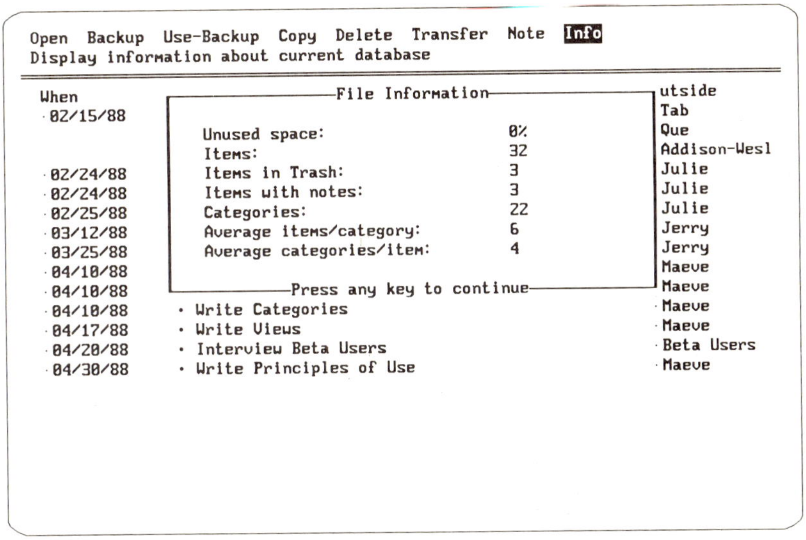

To see the other screen containing view statistics, press F10(Menu), V for View, and I for Info. A View Information window will be displayed as shown in Figure 2-7. While both information screens are accessed from a view screen, they display different statistics based on the file and view contents respectively.

Figure 2-7.

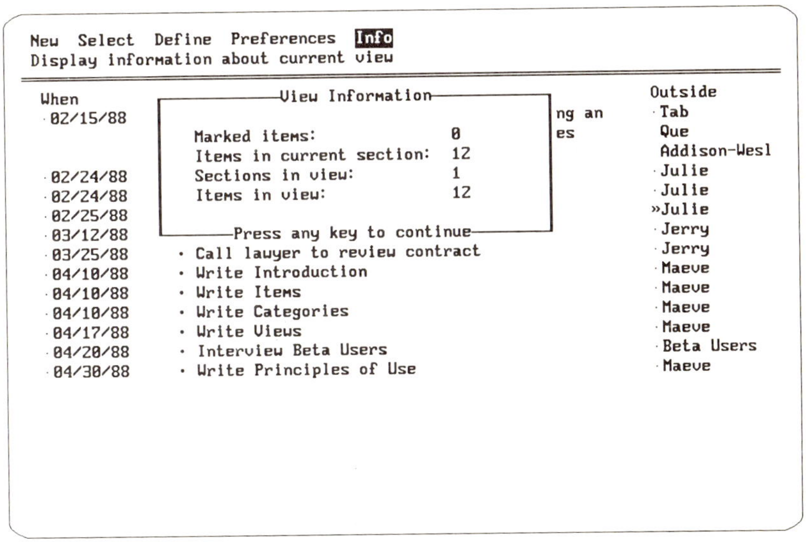

When you initiate a session with Agenda by typing the word Agenda at the DOS prompt, Agenda displays its startup screen with the last file on which you worked proposed as the file to access. If you want to access another file, type its name or press GREY + to see a list of the stored databases to date. You can move the highlight to the name of the database you want to access and press Enter to select it. Whether you type the name or select it from the list, you must press Enter again to accept the file, at which point Agenda will load it.

You may also open a database from within an Agenda session by pressing F10(Menu), F for File, and O for Open. Agenda displays a Select File window listing all the stored database filenames. You can either move the highlight to the desired filename or type in a name, and then press Enter or F9(Accept) to actually select the file. If you type in a name that is not already listed, Agenda displays a New Database dialog box where you can provide a description of the file and a password to prevent unauthorized access to the file. Press Enter after responding to each of these prompts. Press F9(Accept), and Agenda creates a new database with this name. In the Select File window, in addition to selecting the highlighted file by pressing Enter or F9(Accept), you can remove the file from the system by pressing F4(Delete), or change its name by pressing F6(Rename).

If you decide to copy a database to another file, either on your fixed drive or on a floppy, you can do this from DOS with the standard file copy instructions, as long as you copy at least the .AGA and .AGB files. From within Agenda, you can also copy files by pressing F10(Menu), F for File, and C for Copy. Agenda displays a Select File window listing all the stored database filenames. You can either move the highlight to the desired filename or type in the name, and then press Enter or F9(Accept). If you are using an existing file as the destination file, Agenda asks you to confirm whether you want to replace that file. If you answer yes, Agenda proceeds with the copying. If you answer no, Agenda returns you to the Select File window for another filename selection.

Finally, in addition to being able to add and copy database files, you can also delete them. To delete a database file from DOS, use the standard file erase commands and be sure to include the extensions .AGA, .AGB, .BKA, and .BKB. Alternatively, if you are in an Agenda session, you can press F10(Menu), F for File, and D for Delete. Once again,

Agenda displays a Select File window listing all the stored database filenames. You can move the highlight to the desired name or type in the name, followed by pressing Enter or F9(Accept). Agenda then prompts you to verify that you really want to delete the named file. If you answer yes, Agenda proceeds with the file deletion. If you answer no, Agenda returns you to the Select File window for another filename selection.

SAVING AND BACKING UP YOUR WORK

With all these filenames and types to worry about, you might think that it would be very difficult to protect your work by saving or backing up your files. Fortunately, because of the way Agenda has been designed, you are not required to back up or save your files unless a special situation requires it.

Periodically during your Agenda session, Agenda automatically saves your .AGA and .AGB database files. You can control this saving by using the Environment Preferences dialog box, which you access by pressing F10(Menu), U for Utility, P for Preferences, and E for Environment. The sixth prompt in the dialog box asks how often, in minutes, you want Agenda to perform the automatic saving. The default is zero, which means that Agenda will save the changes to your database files intermittently during your work and whenever you close your database. If you change this setting to a number ranging from 1 to 60 minutes, Agenda automatically saves your work whenever the amount of time you specified has passed without any activity on the keyboard.

Since your work is automatically saved, you cannot try out ideas on your database and expect to return to an earlier version if you should not be happy with the results. Therefore, Agenda provides a backup capability that you control by using the Other Preferences dialog box, which you access by pressing F10(Menu), U for Utility, P for Preferences, and O for Other. The third prompt, *Make backup copy:*, offers three options: On demand, when file is opened, and when file is closed. You can back up your files on demand, that is manually, or you can back them up when you open or close the database. You select the option you want by rotating through the options using the Spacebar and pressing Enter when your choice appears. For example if you selected On demand, you would press F10(Menu), F for File, and B for Backup to back up your files.

With backup files saved, whether for insurance or experimentation purposes, you can retrieve these files by pressing F10(Menu), F for File, and U for Use-Backup. You will be asked whether or not you want Agenda to revert to the backup version whose date is displayed. If you answer yes, Agenda replaces the current file with the backup. If you answer no, Agenda returns you to your current database display. If for any reason you cannot access your backups, perhaps due to some damage to your database, you can still recover the backup files. The way to do this is to exit to DOS, copy the .BKA and .BKB files to new files with .AGA and .AGB extensions, reenter Agenda, and load the new files.

OTHER CUSTOMIZING SETTINGS

In the previous section, you saw examples of how you can customize Agenda through the use of the Environment and Other Preferences menu commands. Using the Environment Preferences dialog box, you can also disable the automatic display of the function key map and the beep which sounds when Agenda is proposing auto-completion, or you can change the colors displayed on the screen, the character set used, or the suppression of snow (as described in Chapter 2 of the Agenda Users Guide).

Using the Other Preferences dialog box, you can change the defaults that Agenda uses to insert new columns, empty trash, make backup copies, process done items, and auto-import files. All of these modifications are described in the relevant sections of this book. In addition you can change tab sizes, hide carriage returns, and change the description or password associated with the current file.

If you change any settings in the Environment or Other Preferences dialog boxes, press F9(Accept) to store them and close the dialog box. To permanently change these settings, and the date settings that will be discussed later, press F10(Menu), U for Utility, P for Preferences, and U for Update.

EXITING TO DOS

You do not have to exit from or quit Agenda to execute certain DOS functions or even other programs. Agenda provides an option called System, which you can access by pressing F10(Menu) and S for System. Agenda prompts you for the program name you want to run. In response to the prompt, either type in a program name and press Enter twice or just press Enter once to activate the default name COMMAND.COM, which takes you back to DOS. In either case, Agenda closes the database in which you were working. If you entered a program name that program will be run. If you used the default, control will be returned to DOS. Any time you want to return to Agenda and resume where you left off, type EXIT and you are returned to Agenda with your database and screen restored.

QUITTING AGENDA

It is essential, especially due to the automatic saving feature, that you never turn off or reboot your computer until you have left the Agenda program by pressing F10(Menu) and Q for Quit. Unless you exit Agenda in this fashion, your database will probably be damaged. If you lose power, for example, you may not be able to recover your files through the normal Agenda startup or file open procedure. If you have saved backup (.BKA and .BKB) versions at any previous time, you will be able to recover their contents by copying them to files with .AGA and .AGB extensions and then loading them instead. Therefore, remember that there is only one proper way to leave Agenda: press F10(Menu) and Q for Quit.

SUMMARY

You should now have a sense of the flexibility that Agenda offers in moving around the screen, your database, your files, and even your system as well as in using the various Menu, Function Key, Special Key, and Accelerator Key options. Consistent with the general design of Agenda, the way you choose to operate is up to you. Some people like to see all their options and may prefer to use the menus, whereas others prefer to work expeditiously and may prefer to use accelerator keys. Regardless of which group you are in, the choice is yours.

Part II: Beginning Concepts

3

Items

Just as numbers are the fundamental units in a spreadsheet, records are the fundamental units in a database, and words are the fundamental units in a word processor, items are the fundamental units in Agenda. They represent the content dimension of your personal information.

The following pieces of text are examples of items:

- Call Joe to confirm lunch today
- Hold IBM until it reaches 140
- Now is the time for all good men to come to the aid of their party. The previous sentence is used as a standard for testing all the keys on a typewriter It is not a good sentence with which to test typing speed.
- Marylou's Southern Kitchen
- Robert H. Flast
- e=mc**2

In Agenda, these items would appear as shown in Figure 3-1.

Most simply, an item is any piece of information that is meaningful to the user. It can be a phrase, a sentence, a word, several sentences, or a paragraph. It can even be a number, although you cannot perform arithmetic functions on numbers represented as items. Finally, items can be about related or unrelated topics and can be similar or different in grammatical form. Perhaps the only limitation is that an item cannot be longer than 350 characters. On the other hand, it can be 0 characters long and used solely as a placemarker in an Agenda database.

Figure 3-1.

```
File: C:\AGENDA\ITEMS                                         05/13/88   12:45
View: Exhibit 3-1
================================================================================
Examples of items
   • Call Joe to confirm lunch today
   • Hold IBM until it reaches 140
   • Now is the time for all good men to come to the aid of their party.  The
     previous sentence is used as a standard for testing all the keys on a
     typewriter.  It is not a good sentence with which to test typing speed.
   • Marylou's Southern Kitchen
   • Robert H. Flast
   • e=mc**2
```

Items can come from a large variety of sources. They can be ideas you have on any topic. They can come from comments people have made to you, either directly or in quotes that you have read or heard. They can come from clippings in newspapers, magazines, books, or online services. They can come from things people send to or leave for you, such as letters, memoranda, or phone messages.

To provide some concrete examples, here are examples of items that could be found in the Agenda applications listed in Chapter 1:

Application	Item
Maintain a keyword or lexical filing system	Page numbers or paragraphs
Recruit executives	Names or positions
Plan human resources	Names or positions

Application	Item
Appraise personnel and project performance	Factual accounts of performance
Analyze a document, e-mail, reports, memos, and so on	Words, sentences and paragraphs
Manage PR media lists, executive briefings, and press releases	Individual media or events
Solve a complex problem	Facts
Keep a to-do list	Action items, reminders
Build a creative platform	Ideas
Manage advertising traffic	Tasks, people, and resources
Develop a curriculum	Subjects to cover
Analyze a stock portfolio	Facts and figures
Negotiate a contract	Goals or terms
Sift through news for significant data	Words, sentences, and paragraphs
Brainstorm	Ideas
Manage people	Names
Organize information for a meeting or phone call	Notes or ideas
Write a brochure	Outline
Keep a self-sorting notebook	Notes or ideas
Consolidate notes from a meeting	Notes or ideas
Prepare a status report	Status notes
Prepare a presentation	Key Concepts
Write a speech, article, or outline	Ideas
Write a marketing plan	Tasks and events
Write a business plan	Tasks and events
Manage a project	Tasks
Manage a sales account	Tasks

HOW DO ITEMS GET INTO AGENDA?

You can manually enter items into Agenda by typing them, or you can automatically transfer items stored as text files into Agenda using utility programs built for this purpose. These text files can come from anywhere, including other PC software such as word processors, spreadsheets, project management packages, communications packages, and other Agenda databases.

Manual Entry of Items

To enter items manually, the highlight must be positioned on the heading of, or on an item in, a section of your view. A section is a group of items that have been assigned to the same category name. If you are working in a section without a category name or heading, Agenda labels it Untitled. If there are two or more untitled sections or column headings, Agenda numbers them, for examples Untitled-2 and Untitled-3.

To enter the item, all you have to do is press Ins or Insert. Agenda will insert an item tag on the line below the current line and wait for you to enter the item text. An item tag is simply a dot to the left of the first word of the item that denotes the beginning of a new item. Other special characters are used as item tags to denote different attributes of an item, but these will be discussed later. If the Num Lock feature has previously been turned on, then, instead of Ins alone, you will have to press Shift-Ins together.

Although it is a bit more complicated, you can also use the menu approach by first pressing F10(Menu) to select the menu, then pressing I for Item and N for New, and finally typing the text when the item tag appears on the line below the current line. Use the Backspace key and the arrows to edit your item while you are typing it. When you are done, press Enter or F9(Accept) to enter the item and leave the highlight on it. If you press Ins, Insert, or Alt-I instead of Enter or F9(Accept), the item will be entered and the highlight will move to a new line, waiting for you to type your next item. If you have columns with category entries (see Chapter 4), pressing Tab or Shift-Tab instead of Enter or F9(Accept) will cause the item to be entered and the highlight to move to the right or left, respectively, waiting for you to enter the appropriate category in the adjacent column. If you have moved to a category column and want to enter a new item, press Alt-I and Agenda will move the highlight to a new line in the item column where you can type the next item.

For example, to write this book we used Agenda to organize our tasks. The first thing we did was to enter those tasks as items into Agenda as shown in Figure 3-2. Since this example will be used throughout the book to illustrate the various features of Agenda, enter these items now in a file called Items and in a view called To-do list.

Figure 3-2.

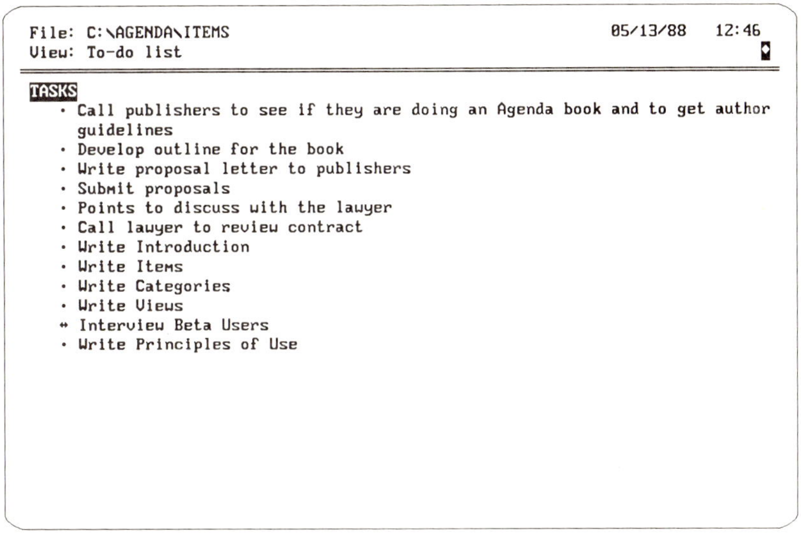

Begin by loading Agenda, and when it prompts you for a filename, type Items. Since this is a new filename, Agenda responds by creating an Items file and prompting you for a description of the file and a password to control access to the file. Type anything in the description line, and then press Enter and F9(Accept). Agenda opens the Items file and leaves you in an Initial view and on an Untitled section heading. Press F8(Vw Mgr) and Ins to identify a new view. Type To-do list following the *View Name:* prompt, and type TASKS following the *Category:* prompt. Press F9(Accept), and you will now be in the To-do list view on the section heading called TASKS.

To enter the items shown in Figure 3-2, press Ins and type the first item, Call publishers... Press Enter and the first item will appear highlighted. To enter the next item, press Ins again and type the second task on the to-do list, followed by Enter and so on, until you have reproduced Figure 3-2.

Notes Attached to Items

Since an item is limited in length to 350 characters, Agenda offers the option of annotating that item with up to ten pages of additional text, stored either in the database or in an external file. Press F5(Note) to access the note screen for an item, as shown in Figure 3-3.

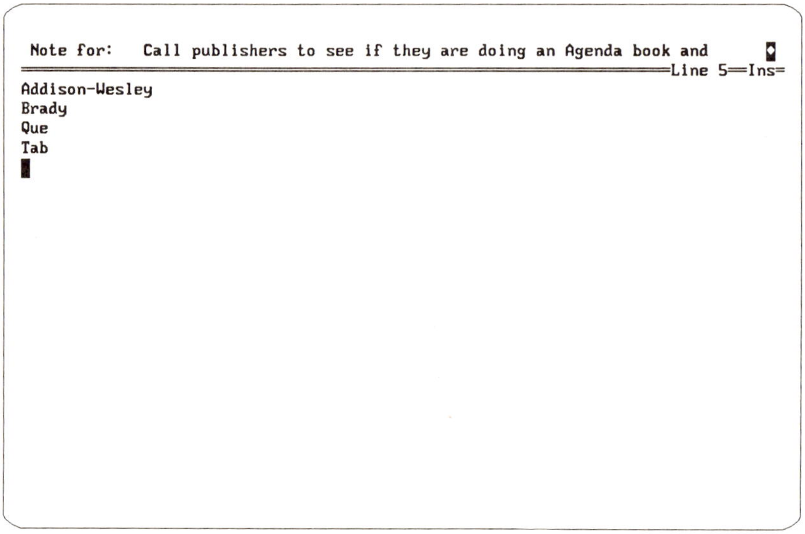

Figure 3-3.

Notice in Figure 3-3 that the top line of the screen begins with the words Note for: heading. This line can help you remember to which item this note is attached. You enter text in the note screen in the same way as you enter item text, using the Backspace, Enter, and various arrow keys. You can insert a "hard" carriage return to force Agenda to move to a new line by pressing Alt-M when the highlight is at the place you want to put the carriage return. To return to the item, press

F5(Return) again and, if you have entered any note text, you will see a musical note to the left of your item, replacing the original item tag, that indicates there is a note attached to it.

If you are working in a note screen and decide you want some piece of the note text to become an item, you must first mark the desired text. To mark the text, place the highlight over the first character of the text to be moved, press F7(Mark) to mark the text, and use the Arrows to move the highlight to the end of the text to be moved. The marked text is now shown in highlighted characters. To unmark the highlighted text, press F7(Mark) again. Now you can either insert the marked text as a new item just below the current item by pressing F8(MakeItm) or append it to the current item by pressing Alt-F8 (Append).

If you want a single word or line or the entire note text for an item to become an item, press F8(MakeItm) or Alt-F8(Append) without first using F7(Mark). You are then prompted in a dialog box for your choice of text to move. You can also change a single word or line, the entire text, or some marked portion to a category by pressing F6(MakeCat), but we will save the details of this procedure for later in this chapter.

Notes as External Files

If you have an external ASCII text file that contains your note text for a particular item, you can either import it into your database from the item's note screen, or attach it to the item from the item view screen without making it part of your database (thus saving space in the database.)

To import an external note text file, first be sure that you are in the item's note screen, and then press F10(Menu) and I for Import. Agenda displays a File dialog box, prompting you for a filename. If you are not sure of the filename, press Grey + to see a listing of all your files. To select a file move the highlight to it, and press Enter. If you know the filename, type it and press Enter. Agenda verifies that the file exists. If the file is found, the filename will be highlighted. You must then decide whether or not to remove carriage returns from the file as it is being imported. To close the dialog box and complete the note importing, press F9(Accept). The note text will appear on the note screen.

Any editing you now do to the note text is maintained in the database but not on the external file. Any time you want to refresh the external file, which you might be saving for some other purpose, simply return to the item's note screen and press F10(Menu) and E for Export. Agenda then prompts you for a filename. Once again, use Grey + to select a filename or simply type the name. Then press Enter and F9(Accept), and Agenda writes the note text to the external file. If the file already exists, Agenda gives you the option of appending the note text to the existing file or replacing the file with the note text. Choose the appropriate option with the Spacebar, F2(Edit), or Grey + and Agenda exports the note.

To attach an external note file to a highlighted item in the view screen without incorporating it into the database, press F10(Menu), F for File, and N for Note. If a note already exists for the item, Agenda asks whether you want to delete it. If you answer no, Agenda returns to the Item View screen. If there is no existing note or you answer yes, Agenda displays a File dialog box, prompting you for the name of the note text file. Type the filename and press Enter. Agenda verifies that the file exists. If the file is found, the name will be highlighted and you will have to press F9(Accept) to close the dialog box and attach the note. To see the note text, press F5(Note) and return to the item view screen by pressing F5(Return), just as you would for a note in the database. The only way you are assured that the note is being read from an external file is the appearance of the filename in the upper left-hand corner of the note screen. Since the note text remains as an external file, any changes you make to it are made directly to the file. Therefore, there is no reason to periodically export the note text to the external file, as there was when we imported the note text into the database from an external file.

Regardless of where you store your note text, either in the database or in an external file, Agenda keeps track of it, so that when you add, change, or delete note text, Agenda will know where to apply the modifications. However, it will not know whether the file from which you have imported note text needs to be updated or forgotten. This decision is understandably left to you.

Item Format

When typing text for items, you have limited flexibility over the format of the display, in both the note or view screens. However, you can insert hard carriage returns in your item text to force Agenda to skip to a new line and continue displaying the text. To insert hard carriage returns, simply press Alt-M, not Enter, at the appropriate places in your item text. This can be done when you are initially entering the item or later as an edit task. The reason that you cannot press Enter to insert these new lines is that Enter instructs Agenda to terminate the typing function and accept the item as complete.

File Transfer of Items

Items can be automatically entered from an ASCII text file previously saved in a special format (with an extension of .STF) or from the Clipboard in Lotus's accessory product called Metro. Both the saving of files in this special format and the use of the Metro Items Accessory are discussed in Chapter 13 of Part IV, Advanced Concepts.

Assuming that you have saved a file in the required format, to enter items automatically from this file, you must first access the menu for File commands by pressing F10(Menu) and F for File. Then you press T for Transfer and I for Import. You will be presented with an Import Structured File dialog box as shown in Figure 3-4.

The first prompt line, *Import:*, gives you the option of transferring items, categories, or both. Depending on the content of your text file, you can use the Spacebar to rotate through these choices, or you can press F2(Edit) or Grey + to see the choices all at once. F2(Edit) or Grey + always display a list of the options for a field where there is a predefined set of choices. Grey + always displays a list of the user-determined choices such as filenames or categories. If you press F2(Edit) or Grey +, you can use the arrows to move through the menu choices, or you can begin typing the name of your choice, and Agenda's automatic completion feature will begin searching for matching items in the menu. Once you have made your choice, use the Down arrow to move down to the next line in the dialog box.

Figure 3-4.

```
Import  Export  Template
Import structured file into current database
════════════════════════════════════════════════════════════════════════════
TASKS
   ♪ Call publishers to see if they are doing an Agenda book and to get author
     guidelines
   ♪ Develop outline for the book
   • Writ╔═══════════════Import Structured File══════════════════╗
   ** Subm║                                                        ║
   • Poin║ Import:        Items & categories                      ║
   • Call║ From file:     C:\AGENDA\EMAIL.STF                     ║
   • Writ║ Delete file:   No                                      ║
   • Writ║ New data only: Yes                                     ║
   • Writ║ Assign to category:        TASKS                       ║
   • Inte║ Combine categories if:     Categories match exactly    ║
   • Writ║ Create new categories:     Yes                         ║
   • who ║ Strip carriage returns:    No                          ║
   • who ║                                                        ║
         ╚══════════Press F9 when done, ESC to cancel══════════════╝
```

The second line prompts you for the filename of the file where your text is stored. It assumes that the extension is .STF and that the file is stored in the current directory. If necessary, you can edit the filename. Agenda checks to make sure the file is present. If it is not present, the *File does not exist* message will be displayed. Use F2(Edit) to edit the filename, just as you would any text field in Agenda. Alternatively, if you wish to select an existing file press Grey + to display a list of all filenames and move the highlight to the desired name. Press Enter to return to the dialog box.

The third prompt line asks whether or not you want to delete the text file after transferring it. The default is No, which is the safer choice until you are absolutely sure that you will have no further use for the text file. As with the first line in the dialog box, you can use the Spacebar, F2(Edit), or Grey +, to make your choice.

The fourth prompt line *New data only:* appears only when the file you are importing is the file you used the last time you imported information into this database. Agenda recognizes the file it last accessed and the data which it imported during the last session. The prompt asks if you wish to import only new data from that file (that is, items and categories) or everything including the data you imported during the previous session. The default is Yes, which is generally the correct choice. As with the first line in the dialog box, you can use the Spacebar, F2(Edit), or Grey + to make your choice.

The fifth line prompts you for the category to which you want the items assigned. The default is the category name of the current section heading. If you want to insert the transferred items into the current section, move to the next line; otherwise, enter a category name for the new section heading. Once again, you can use F2(Edit) or Grey + to display a menu window with all the category names. If you access this display, you will have to use the arrows to move to the desired category name and press F9(Accept).

The sixth line prompts you to determine your preferences concerning the combining of categories. For example, you can combine categories if they match exactly. You can also combine categories if any term in the new category can be found in an existing category or in just the first position of the existing category. You indicate your choice by using the Spacebar to rotate through the choices and moving down to the next line, or by pressing F2(Edit) or Grey + to select your choice from the menu.

If you chose the Items & categories option on the first line, a special prompt will be displayed in the seventh line asking whether or not you want Agenda to create new categories, if any are encountered. Use the Spacebar, F2(Edit) or Grey + to select your choice. If you chose only items or categories, but not both, on the first line, Agenda skips this special prompt and goes directly to the last line of the dialog box.

In the last line, you are asked whether or not you want carriage returns in the text removed as the items and/or categories are being transferred. Once again, use the Spacebar, F2(Edit), or Grey + to make your choice.

You can change your answers in the dialog box as many times as you want. When you are done answering the questions, press F9(Accept).

Agenda reads the text file and displays a small window continuously indicating how much of the structured text file has been imported. If you need to interrupt the transfer, you may do so by pressing the Ctrl and Break keys simultaneously. If you have to press Ctrl-Break, Agenda will remember where the process was interrupted, so that when you return to complete this transfer, Agenda will skip over the already imported information. When the transfer is complete, the new items will appear in the current view and the new categories can be found in the Category Manager.

HOW DO I USE ITEMS?

Once entered, items can be edited, moved, deleted, or annotated.

Editing

To edit an item you need to be in Edit mode. Place the highlight on the item and press F2(Edit). A full range of editing commands is shown in the function key map at the bottom of the screen. To change the item text, simply use the arrows to move to the first character you wish to change. You can use Backspace to erase a character including the invisible Alt-M (''hard'' carriage return) by backing over it or you can use Delete to erase the character under the highlight. The characters you type will be inserted to the right of the highlight as opposed to being typed over existing characters and spaces.

While in Edit mode, you can move to the next or previous item by pressing Alt-N or Alt-P, respectively, and still remain in Edit mode in the new item. Finally, to leave Edit mode, press F9(Accept).

Copy and Cut

In Edit mode you can copy or cut text from an item. This text can consist of a single word, the current line, the entire item, or a specially marked sequence of characters within the item. The first three choices are immediately available when you press F3(Copy) or F4(Cut). To use any of these three, move the highlight to the beginning of the word, line, or text and then press F3(Copy) or F4(Cut). You can use the Spacebar, F2(Edit), or Grey + to see the choices available. After you make your choice, press F9(Accept), and the identified text will be copied into the edit buffer.

Alternatively, if you are copying or cutting marked text, place the highlight over the first character to be marked, press F7(Mark), and use the arrows to highlight the remaining characters. Then press F3(Copy) or F4(Cut) and the highlighted text will be copied into the edit buffer.

If you are copying the selected or marked text, it will remain within the item. If you are cutting the selected or marked text, it will disappear. The highlight remains within the item you are editing so that you can continue your work.

Paste

Once you have text in the edit buffer, you can paste it into another item or into another location within the current item by using F2(Paste) and pressing Enter.

Split

Another feature available in Edit mode enables you to split an item to make two items from one. To do this, place the highlight on the first character of the portion of the item that is to become a new item. Press F8(Split) and the portion of the item on and to the right of the highlight becomes a new item inserted below.

Making Categories from Items

Another feature available in Edit mode permits you to create a new category from an item or a marked portion of an item. Categories will be thoroughly discussed in the next chapter, so we will save the review of F6(MakeCat) until then.

Delete

The last feature available in Edit Mode is the Alt-F4(Delete) key which permits you to remove a single word or line, the entire text, or some marked text from the current item entirely without storing it in the edit buffer as with the F4(Cut) command.

Finally, to leave Edit Mode, press F9(Accept).

Moving Items Within a Section

Items can be moved within a section by pressing F10(Menu), I for Item, and P for Position. Use the arrows to move the item. You can see the item change position as you press the arrows. When you are satisfied with the position, press Enter.

Moving or Copying Items Between Sections

Items can also be moved or copied from one section of a view to another. To move or copy a single item, first highlight the item, then press

F6(Move) or F3(Copy), and finally select the destination section by moving the highlight with the arrows. When you have found the desired section, press F9(Accept) to move or copy the item to the new section.

To move or copy a group of items, identify the items by moving the highlight to them and pressing F7(Mark). If all the items in a section are to be marked, highlight the section heading and press F7(Mark). The item tag appearing to the left of the item will change from a dot to a diamond shape to indicate that the item has been marked.

If you make a mistake while marking, you can unmark individual items by highlighting them and pressing F7(Mark) again, or you can unmark all of the marked items by pressing Alt-F7(UnmkAll).

Now press F3(Copy) or F6(Move) to copy or move the marked items. You will be asked whether you want to copy or move the marked items or just the current item. The default is Marked items, which you will select by pressing Enter.

Dates

Entry Dates

Agenda allows you to associate three kinds of dates with an item: the Entry, When, and Done dates. The Entry date is automatically set for an item when it is entered. You can instruct Agenda to reset an Entry date when you edit or reassign the item. This can be done using commands on the Utility/Preferences/Date menu, which is accessed from the item view screen by pressing F10(Menu), U for Utility, P for Preferences, and D for Date. Agenda displays a Date Preferences dialog box, prompting you for the default date format, the conditions under which the Entry date should be set or reset and under what circumstances to automatically set When dates.

With the highlight on the *Default date format:* prompt line, press F2(Edit) or Grey + to see the available date formats, for the Entry, When, and Done dates, displayed in a window. Use the arrows to move the highlight up and down through the choices. When you have found the format you prefer, press F9(Accept).

Now move the highlight down to the next prompt line, *Set Entry date:*. Here the options, which can be displayed by pressing F2(Edit) or Grey +, are to set the Entry date when items are reassigned, edited, or entered.

The way these choices work is as follows. If you choose the When item is entered option, the Entry date will only be set for new items. If you choose the When item is edited option, the Entry date will be set for new items and reset for edited items. If you choose the When item is reassigned option, the Entry date will be set for new items and reset for edited and reassigned items. The last option, Do not set, disables the automatic setting of Entry dates, thus allowing you the use of this date field for some other date-oriented purpose, in addition to the When and Done dates. For example, in project management applications, there is a concept of earliest and latest start dates. If you needed such an option, you could use the disabled Entry date field for the earliest start date, and the When date field for the latest start date. Choose whichever Set Entry date option you prefer by highlighting it and pressing Enter or F9(Accept).

The next two prompt lines ask questions that pertain to When dates, which we will cover after a discussion of Done dates. Therefore, press F9(Accept) to exit the dialog box and return to the view screen.

Done Dates

Agenda automatically sets a Done date when you press F4(Done) to indicate that the highlighted item or marked items have been completed. To identify a group of items as done, you may first mark them using F7(Mark) and designate them as done using F4(Done) and the Marked items option. When you mark an item as done, the item tag character to the left of the item changes from a dot (or the default character, if you have changed it) to a double exclamation point (!!).

Agenda uses today's date to assign the Done date. If you are marking an item as done after the fact and today's date is not the date you wish to use, you can create a view with Done date as one of the columns and make the change manually. (The procedures for creating columns and views are described in Chapters 4 and 5.)

If you make a mistake, you can correct it by pressing F4(Done) again, which removes the Done date(s). To see a listing of the items you have identified as done, press F10(Menu), U for Utility, S for Show, and I for ItemsDone. A special *Show view* will be created with a listing of the done items, as shown in Figure 3-5.

Figure 3-5.

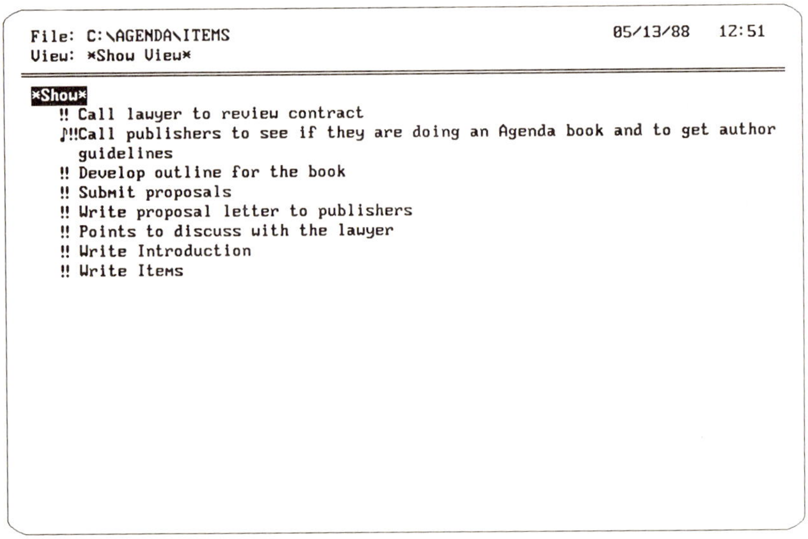

You can leave this view in your view manager or delete it by pressing F8(Vw Mgr), F4(Discard), Y for Yes, and Enter. To return to the previous view, simply press Alt-F8(Last Vw).

Items that have been marked as done can be left in the database or discarded in the Trash or exported to a Done file. To select one of these options, press F10(Menu), U for Utility, P for Preferences, and O for Other. Agenda displays an Other Preferences dialog box, whose fourth prompt asks how you want to treat done items. Highlight the fourth line and press F2(Edit) or Grey + to see the three options referred to above.

The Discard and Export to Done file options have suboptions, which are revealed when you select the main option. If you choose the Discard option, you then have to tell Agenda when to discard the done items. The choices are the Immediately, When file is closed, and End of day suboptions. You can use the Spacebar to rotate to your choice or F2(Edit) or Grey + and the arrows. Pressing F9(Accept) records your choice.

If you choose the Export to Done file option, you also have to tell Agenda when, as well as where, to export the items. The choices for when to export are the same as for when to discard. As for the Done file, either press Grey + to select an existing file name or type the filename, and Agenda will insert the path and extension (.STF) information and check to make sure that the file exists. Press F9(Accept) to close the dialog box, and from now on, at the time you have specified, done items will be discarded or exported to a file.

When Dates

You set a When date to indicate a date of significance associated with an item or a group of items. Under certain conditions, as specified in the Utility/Preferences/Date menu, Agenda can automatically set a When date. To assign a When date manually, first highlight the desired item or mark a group of items using F7(Mark) and press Alt-F2(When). Then you can either type the date directly at the top of the screen or you can select either the Current item or Marked items options in the dialog box (if it is presented), press Enter, and type the date directly at the top of the screen.

You may type a date using either numbers or words. For example, if today's date is 10/13, you can enter this as 10/13 or today or the thirteenth of October. To describe October 20, you might say next Sunday. If you enter a date as numbers, you should follow the default date format found on the Utility/Preferences/Date menu described earlier.

Agenda's powerful date interpretation capability enables it to correctly translate the words that you type into the default date format. Words used in dates that Agenda can understand are: first-tenth; today; to-night; tomorrow; yesterday; day, week, month; from, after, before; of and in; next and last; each and every; this; as well as and, beginning, and end. This flexibility in entering dates applies whether you are entering When dates, or editing When, Entry, or Done dates. To edit a highlighted date in the item view screen, simply press F2(Edit) and retype the date in numeric or relative format.

Agenda can also set When dates based on dates appearing in item text. For example, first display a When date column in an item view screen by highlighting the section heading in the item column and pressing Alt-R to insert a column to the right. Then start typing When over the Untitled column heading and Agenda will automatically suggest the completion of your typing as When date. Press Enter to insert the new column heading.

Now look at any items that have dates, either in numeric or word format, in the item text. Notice that Agenda has filled in the When date column with the appropriate date entries. If you edit an item and change the date, the entry in the When date column will change automatically, unless it had been set previously by using the Alt-F2(When) command. If for any reason you want to disable this automatic entry of new or edited dates in item text, you can do so in the Utility/Preferences/Date menu, which you access by pressing F10(Menu), U for Utility, P for Preferences, and D for Date. The third prompt in the Date Preferences dialog box asks you whether or not you want to set When dates from items. Answer yes or no and press F9(Accept) to exit the dialog box and return to your item view screen.

The last feature that Agenda offers concerning date processing is the ability to reset When dates automatically for items that recur on a periodic basis such as every Thursday or each Monday. In other words, as long as the item remains in the database, the When date will be reset automatically as the periodic date expression in the item text dictates. This feature, too, is governed by the Utility/Preferences/Date menu, through which you can have Agenda display the Date Preferences dialog box. The fourth prompt, *Redate recurring items:*, asks whether you want Agenda to perform this redating automatically when repetitive expressions are recognized in the item text. Type yes or no and press F9(Accept) to exit the dialog box and return to your item view screen.

Dependencies

Agenda provides a technique for identifying dependencies between and among items. In our example, before we could Submit proposals, we had to Call publishers. . . , Develop outline. . . and Write proposal. . . . Using F7(Mark), we marked these items in preparation for indicating that they were prerequisites for Submit proposals. We then moved the highlight to the dependent task, Submit proposals, and completed this action by pressing Alt-F3(DpndsOn). Agenda now recognized that Submit proposals depended on the three marked items, in this case Call publishers. . . , Develop outline. . . and Write proposal. . . , and the marked items were automatically unmarked. This dependencies/prerequisites feature can be useful in project management applications where task dependencies are critical to understanding what needs to be done at any given time. Once an item has been identified as depending on some one or more marked items, the item tag symbol to the left of the item will change to a double arrow, pointing left and right, to remind you of the dependency relationship.

To see what dependency relationships exist among items, you will need to press F10(Menu), U for Utility, and S for Show to access the menu where prerequisites and dependents can be requested. To begin, the highlight must be on an item that has prerequisites, as indicated by the item tag. After pressing F10(Menu), U for Utility, and S for Show, press P to see the prerequisites for the highlighted item. You will now be given the choice of seeing only one level of prerequisites, or all levels of prerequisites (item A depends on item B, which in turn depends on item C, is an example of two levels of prerequisites). There is also an option to see all items with prerequisites, which you might use to check on the population of dependent items. A special *Show view* is created to display the desired information. *Show view* is discussed in greater detail in Chapter 5. If a *Show view* already exists, you are asked whether or not you want to delete it. The *Show view* will appear, listing the items that satisfy your request, as shown in Figure 3-6. To return to the view which you left, press ALT-F8(Last Vw).

Agenda also lets you show all the items that depend on a given item. You place the highlight on the prerequisite item in which you are interested and press F10(Menu), U for Utility, S for Show, and D for Dependents. A menu is then presented from which you can choose to see the items that depend on this prerequisite item directly at the next level (one level) or indirectly over multiple levels (all levels). At this point you also can ask for a list of all the items that are prerequisites for other items, or, in other words, all items with dependencies. Once again, a *Show view* is created, if one does not already exist, and the desired items are listed. To return to the view you left, press Alt-F8(Last Vw). To select any other view, press F8(Vw Mgr) or F10(Menu), followed by V for View and S for Select.

Figure 3-6.

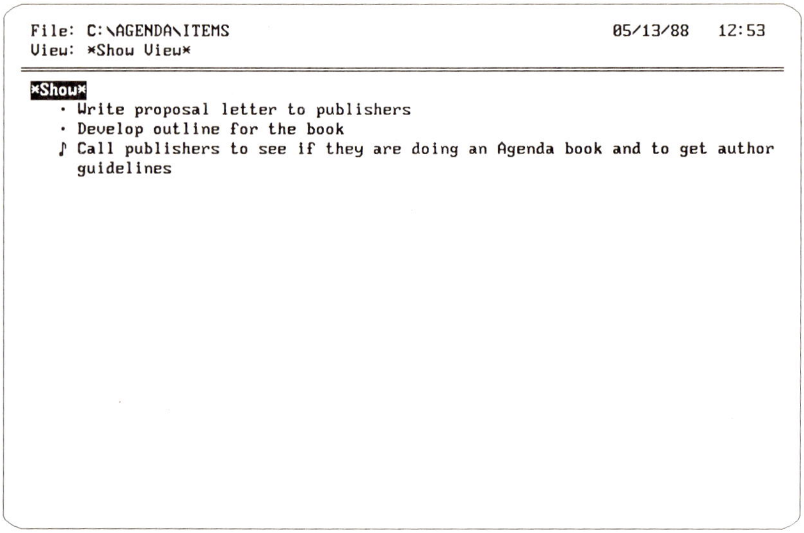

Searching for Item or Note Text

Agenda also allows you to search for an item based on some portion of its content or the content of its associated note. To do so, press Alt-F5(Search). A Search dialog box appears, as shown in Figure 3-7. You are prompted for the text on which you are searching. Type this in the highlighted area and press Enter. The next prompt, *Match on:*, permits you to search item text, note text, or both. Choose one and move down to the next prompt, which asks for the direction of the search. The options are to go forward or backward from your current position in the database. The last option allows you to ignore case (upper and lower) in conducting the search or to be sensitive to it. Press F9(Accept) when you have made your choices. The first item matching your criteria will be highlighted. If you want to continue the search, press Alt-F5(Search) and F9(Accept) to move to the next matching item.

Agenda provides an alternate method of searching for items, where you can simultaneously display all items matching your criteria in a special *Show view*. To use this search method, press F10(Menu), U for Utility, S for Show, and M for Match. A Show Match dialog box appears, and the first line prompts you for the specific word or phrase you are interested in locating, as shown in Figure 3-8.

Figure 3-7.

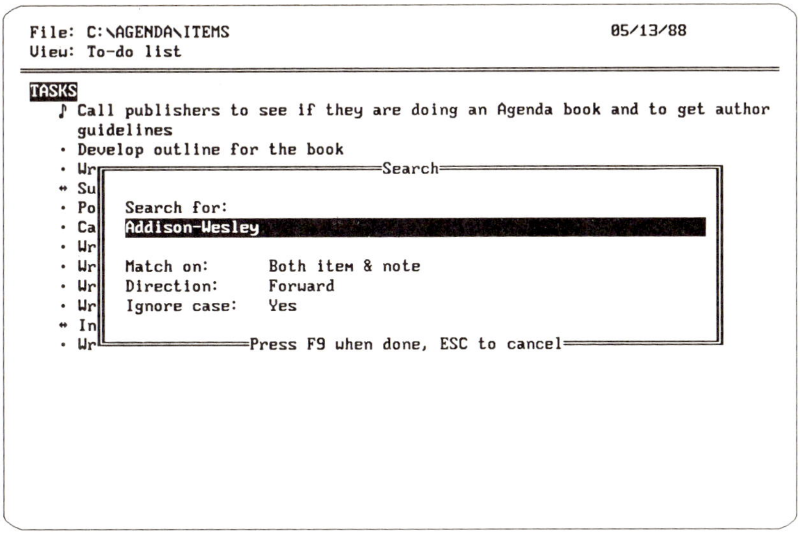

Figure 3-8.

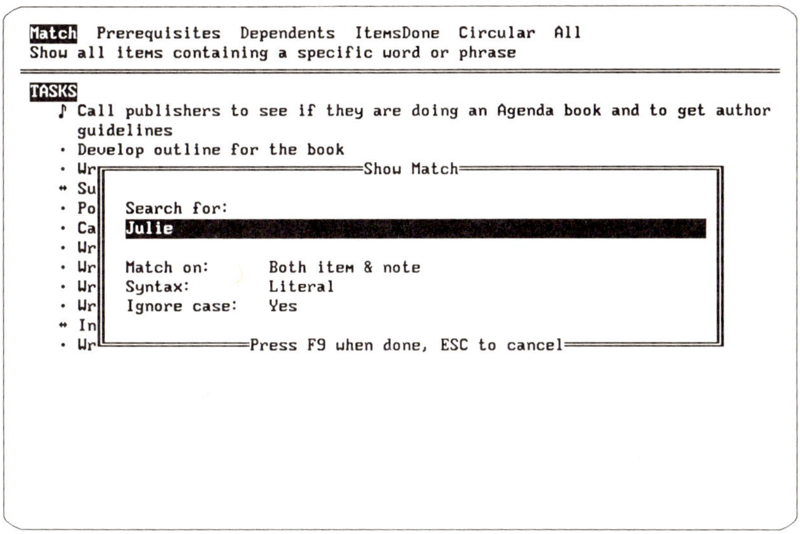

After typing in the desired word or phrase, press Enter and you will move to the next line, which gives you the option of matching on item text, note text, or both. This is followed by a prompt that asks whether or not you want to literally match on the identical word or phrase. If you answer yes, you will also be asked whether or not you want Agenda to ignore case (upper and lower) in performing the matching. In the *Syntax:* prompt, the alternative to the Literal option is the Text condition option, which refers to the appearance of the word or phrase in the Category Manager, with alternative or synonymous expressions. In other words, if you want to match on the name Dave and in the Category Manager you have defined a text condition that shows that in this database the word Father is synonymous with Dave, you can direct Agenda to match on Dave or Father by choosing the Text condition option. (Text conditions are discussed fully in Chapter 4.) Once again, to select these options, you can use the Spacebar to rotate through the available choices, or F2(Edit) or Grey + to display a menu of the available choices. After filling in the dialog box options, press F9(Accept) to instruct Agenda to proceed with the display of the *Show view*.

Removing Items from the Section or Database

As you would expect, Agenda provides the capability to remove a highlighted item from either the entire database or just the current section in which it is highlighted. To remove a highlighted item or a group of marked items from the database, you can either use Alt-F4 (Discard) or press F10(Menu), I for Items, and D for Discard. If you mark items to be discarded, you are presented a dialog box that gives you the option of discarding either the current item or all marked items. Select the appropriate option by using the Spacebar, F2(Edit), or Grey + and press Enter. Discarded items are stored in the Trash so they can be retrieved if necessary.

To conserve space, it is a good idea to empty the Trash from time to time by pressing F10(Menu), U for Utility, T for Trash, and Y for Yes. Alternatively, you can instruct Agenda to empty the Trash periodically by pressing F10(Menu), U for Utility, P for Preferences, and O for Other. Agenda displays an Other Preferences dialog box, where the second prompt, *Empty trash:*, has four options. By selecting one of these, using the space bar, F2(Edit) or Grey +, you can instruct Agenda to empty the Trash on demand (as just described), automatically when the file is closed, at the end of the day, or when an item is discarded.

As long as you have not emptied the Trash, you can retrieve discarded items from the Trash by pressing F10(Menu), followed by I for Item and U for Undiscard. You are presented a dialog box that gives you the option of retrieving the last item or all items in the Trash. An alternative approach to retrieving the last item is to press Alt-Y.

If you want to remove the highlighted item or a group of marked items from the section, press F10(Menu), I for Item, and R for Remove, or simply press Del or Delete. If the item is assigned to categories other than the section heading, it will be removed from the section heading category, and therefore from the item view screen, but not from the database. If the item is only assigned to the section heading category, not only will it be removed, but it will also be discarded from the database and can only be recovered from the Trash by using the undiscard commands mentioned earlier.

Notes Attached to Items

As a compromise between speed and storage, Agenda limits an item's length to 350 characters. But if you have more text to associate with a particular item, Agenda provides a feature called Note, which allows you to attach up to ten pages of additional text to a given item, stored either in the database or in an external file. Agenda keeps track of where the notes are stored and updates them appropriately so that you do not have to worry about these alternate locations. External note files were thoroughly reviewed in the subsection Notes as External Files, which appeared earlier in this chapter.

From the item view screen or while in item Edit mode, you can enter or edit a note for the highlighted item by pressing F5(Note). Assuming that you do not already have a note for the item, Agenda presents you with a blank screen into which you can type up to ten pages of text. To enter this additional text, place the highlight on the item you want to annotate and press F5(Note). As the function key map (if you have removed it by pressing Alt-K, you can retrieve the key map by pressing Alt-K again) at the bottom of the screen indicates, you have a full range of text editing features available to you, similar to those used in editing items, including F2(Paste), F3(Copy), F4(Cut), Alt-N, and Alt-P.

Making Note Text into Items and Categories

Some special features are available to you when you are using notes. For example, you might want to make some note text into an item using F8(MakeItm), or into a category using F6(MakeCat). In either case, the desired text can be marked using F7(Mark) and the right or left arrows to highlight the text. If you are making an item out of note text and no text is marked, Agenda gives you the choice of selecting the current word or line or the entire note text. You can view these choices by pressing the Spacebar to rotate through them or by pressing F2(Edit) or Grey + to see a menu of all the choices at once. If you are making a category from note text and no text is marked, Agenda uses the current word in which the highlighted character is located.

If you press F8(MakeItm), the selected text becomes a new item immediately following the item in whose note you are working, and the selected text is removed from the note. If you press F6(MakeCat), you are prompted for the name of the parent category, if any, to which you want the new category name assigned. Either enter the name of a parent category or press Enter to insert the new category in the top level as a parent category. If you are unsure about the potential parent category candidates, press F2(Edit) or Grey + to see a listing of the Category Manager, use the arrows to locate and highlight the desired parent category, and press F9(Accept) to select the parent. The parent category's name appears in the note screen dialog box, and you can press Enter or F9(Accept) to make the selected note text into the desired category. (Chapter 4 on Categories goes into greater detail about these features.)

Appending Note Text to an Item

If you do not want to create an entirely new item from some selected note text but rather append the text to the current item in whose note you are working, select and mark the text using F7(Mark) and the arrows, and then press Alt-F8(Append). The marked text is removed and appended to the current item. If you want to append the current word or line or the entire note text, press Alt-F8(Append) without pressing F7(Mark), and you will be given these options.

Other Note Functions

Additional functions that can be performed within a note screen include retrieving marked items and inserting them in the note, deleting or erasing some or all of the note, and searching for or replacing selected text within the note. There is also a menu of note specific functions, which is accessed by pressing F10(Menu) from within the note screen.

Retrieving Marked Items into a Note

To retrieve items that were marked in the view screen by using F7(Mark), press Alt-F3(GetItms). You are asked whether or not you want to discard the marked items after copying them into the note. After you answer, the items are copied into the note beginning at the spot where the highlighted character is located, and the original items are either removed from the view or left in it.

Deleting Marked Text from a Note

You can delete any note text you have highlighted using F7(Mark) and the right or left arrows. Press Alt-F4(Delete), and the highlighted text is erased. Alternatively, if you are interested in deleting the current word, line, or the entire text, you can press Alt-F4(Delete), without pressing F7(Mark), and you will be presented with these options. After using the Spacebar, F2(Edit) or Grey + to select the word, line, or text, press Enter to erase the desired text. You can also delete a note when you are in the note screen by pressing F10(Menu) and D for Delete. You are presented a dialog box asking you to confirm your request. Press Y for Yes, and the note disappears.

Searching for Text Within a Note

To search for text within a note, press Alt-F5(Search). A Search/Replace dialog box appears, prompting you for the text (one or more words or characters) to be found, as shown in Figure 3-9.

You are also asked whether or not you want to replace the selected text when found. If you answer no, you will have to provide just two more answers: the direction of the search (forward or backward from where the highlighted character is located in the note text) and whether or not Agenda should ignore case (upper or lower) in searching for the text. If you answer yes in response to the prompt concerning replacement text, besides providing the direction and case responses, you will also have to provide the text to be used in replacing the search text and indicate whether or not the replacement should be global and whether you want to confirm every replacement before it takes place or let Agenda automatically perform them all. Close the dialog box and begin the search by pressing F9(Accept). To repeat the search with the same parameters press Alt-S. To change the parameters press Alt-F5(Search).

Figure 3-9.

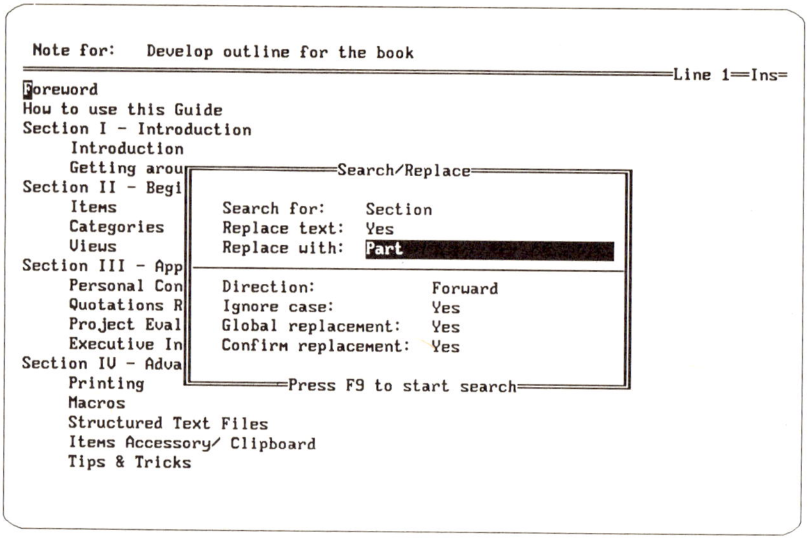

More About Notes

The note screen menu is selected by pressing F10(Menu). You have the option of printing a note by pressing P for Print. (Since this is another way of displaying information, this feature will be explained in Chapter 5 on Views.) You can also Import a text file into a note by typing I for import and entering the filename in the File dialog box that appears. You are then asked whether or not you want to eliminate carriage return characters from the text file as the text is being imported. Similarly, you can export a note to a text file by typing E for Export and entering the desired filename in the File dialog box that appears. You can delete all the text in the current note by pressing D for Delete and responding to the prompt that checks to make sure that you want to do this. Finally, you can return to the view screen you left to work on the note by pressing R for Return.

Assignment Profile

The item profile identifies the categories to which either a single highlighted item or a group of marked items have been assigned. In the view screen, this feature is accessed by pressing Alt-F9(Profile) after you have highlighted a particular item or marked a group of items using F7(Mark). A window appears called the Assignment Profile, which lists the Category Manager.

If you are checking on a single highlighted item, asterisks (*) appear to the left of the categories to which the item belongs. If you are checking on a group of marked items, the numbers to the left of the categories indicate how many of the marked items belong to each category. If you want to see the profile for the highlighted item, even though you have already marked a number of items, press Grey+ instead of Alt-F9 (Profile). In these profiles, a blank to the left of a category indicates that no items are assigned to that category. If you want to see a profile for all your items, assuming that all items in your database are displayed in the sections of the current view, place the highlight on each section heading in your view and press F7(Mark). In this fashion, all items will be marked, and you can press Alt-F9(Profile) to see the numbers of items that are assigned to the various categories in your database.

You can also use the Assignment Profile to assign a highlighted item or a group of marked items to new categories by moving the highlight to the desired categories in the Category Manager, and either pressing the Spacebar or F7 (Assign). The numbers to the left of the category names will be changed to reflect these new assignments. Similarly, you can unassign the marked items in a given category by moving to the category name and pressing the Spacebar or F7(Assign). The number to the left of the category will disappear, indicating that no more marked items are associated with this category.

Show All Items

The show all items feature displays all items in your database, regardless of whether they appear in any view. To see this listing, press F10(Menu), U for Utility, S for Show, and A for All. A special *Show view* will be created that lists all the items in the database. You can return to the previous view by pressing Alt-F8(Last Vw).

Sort Items in a Section

The sort feature is selected by pressing F10(Menu), C for Category, S for Section, and S for Sort. A Sort dialog box is displayed, giving you the option of sorting items in the current section or in all sections, by item text alphabetically, or by category, category note, entry date, when date, or done date.

Category and category note sorts can be in the order that the categories appear in the Category Manager or in alphabetical or numeric order. Categories and dates can also be sorted in chronological order. If you are sorting on category notes, you must specify which line number within the note is to be used for sorting. You can sort on both a primary or top-level key and a secondary key that sorts within the primary level. After selecting the desired options in the dialog box, press F9(Accept) and the items are sorted according to your preferences.

Another method for sorting items, according to the preferences you last entered in a sort dialog box, is by pressing Alt-S when your highlight is anywhere in a section. The items within the section will be sorted according to the stored preferences.

SUMMARY

The only constraints on your use of items in Agenda are the limits of your own imagination. Your use of items is linked to your individual needs. You can build things from them, create new ideas, and see things in a new way by sorting or grouping them differently. Moving items around in Agenda can show you ideas, structures, and relationships that you may not have seen before. Items can be stored or deleted. Items can be grouped together according to topic, time frame, who is responsible for them, geographical location, size, color, shape, national origin, age, cost, and so on. In other words, items can be grouped or sorted according to as many attributes as can apply to them. Any attribute of an item can be used to categorize it, which brings us to the next major concept of Agenda, namely, structure or categories.

4

Categories

Items represent the content of your personal information. Categories represent the structure of this information.

A category is a label that is used to represent an attribute or characteristic shared by a group of items. The following are categories:

- White-collar workers
  - Professional and technical
  - Managers and administrators
  - Salesworkers
  - Clerical workers
- Blue-collar workers
  - Craft and kindred workers
  - Operatives, excluding transport
  - Transport equipment operatives
  - Nonfarm laborers
- Service workers
- Farmworkers

In Agenda, these categories would be displayed in the Category Manager as shown in Figure 4-1.

These categories or occupational groups are one way that economists and government statisticians organize their knowledge of the labor force. Statistics about employment, turnover, and compensation can be organized by these categories. Facts concerning legislation affecting labor can be organized by these categories. Congressmen who are partial to certain labor groups can be organized by these categories.

Figure 4-1.

```
File: C:\AGENDA\WORKERS
Category Manager
════════════════════════════════════════════════════════════════════
MAIN
  White-collar workers
    Professional and technical
    Managers and administrators
    Salesworkers
    Clerical workers
  Blue-collar workers
    Craft and kindred workers
    Operatives, exc. transport
    Transport equip. operatives
    Nonfarm laborers
  Service workers
  Farmworkers
```

Although these terms may seem like obvious examples of categories, in other contexts, such as collecting lists of occupational group names from around the world, these same terms could alternatively be used as items of information.

It is important to understand the levels of categories, also known as the hierarchy, that are used in the preceding example. The major or top-level categories are as follows:

- White-collar workers
- Blue-collar workers
- Service workers
- Farmworkers

Important subdivisions within the white-collar and blue-collar categories such as Salesworkers and Nonfarm laborers are shown indented and beneath these headings. Of course, subcategories can be divided into further levels of subcategories, as in the following example:

- Professional and technical
    - Accountants
    - Computer specialists
    - Engineers
        - Civil
        - Electrical and electronic
        - Industrial
        - Mechanical

etc.

As expected, these additional levels are displayed in the Category Manager as shown in Figure 4-2. In other words, there can be multiple levels of categories, which, because they are typically displayed in a nested format, are referred to as a hierarchy.

Figure 4-2.

```
File: C:\AGENDA\WORKERS
Category Manager
================================================================
MAIN
  White-collar workers
    Professional and technical
      Accountants
      Computer Specialists
      Engineers
        Civil
        Electrical and electronic
        Industrial
        Mechanical
    Managers and administrators
    Salesworkers
    Clerical workers
  Blue-collar workers
    Craft and kindred workers
    Operatives, exc. transport
    Transport equip. operatives
    Nonfarm laborers
  Service workers
  Farmworkers
```

Categorization is the process of assigning items to categories according to rules that reflect your understanding of the content and concepts represented by your items. Although there are no universal or best methods for categorizing an arbitrary collection of items, it is useful to begin by stating the reasons you are analyzing these items so you can better plan how you are going to go about developing the structure. There are some principles of category construction that can help you develop both efficient and effective ways of categorizing your items.

First, categories should reflect the purpose of the analysis. In the preceding example, the purpose of the analysis is to understand something in terms of occupational groupings. The categories shown are the names of these groupings at various levels of generality. The top-level categories, which are not indented, are more general ones such as white-collar workers. Agenda uses the term *ancestor* to refer to these most general categories. Any category at this or any lower level that has subcategories is referred to as a *parent* category. Subcategories, which represent more specific groupings such as professional and technical, are indented and are referred to as *child* categories in Agenda. Still more specific subdivisions are possible, for example, civil engineers. Agenda does not have a special term for these children of child categories, even though they can be used.

Second, categories should represent valid and reliable groupings. That is, if you assign an item to a category, you want to be sure it is the correct category and that you would assign it to the same category if you encountered the item again. Also, you want to be sure that when you are looking for an item, you will be able to find it.

Third, you need to decide which groups of categories, if any, should be treated as mutually exclusive. Agenda provides the capability of defining a set of categories as mutually exclusive. What this means is that if you assign an item to one of the categories in this set, you cannot also assign it to any other category in the set.

Finally, the set of all categories should be exhaustive, or, in other words, all items should be capable of being assigned to at least one category. Sometimes there are naturally occurring exhaustive structures such as gender (male versus female).

The hierarchical organization of categories can help us to better understand and represent the underlying structure of the items. Agenda supports this feature in what it calls the Category Manager, which is the format it uses to display the categories without their associated items.

Categories that are shown in the Category Manager at the far left margin of the display are ancestor, and possibly parent, categories, and all categories that line up vertically with them are at the same, or highest, level in the hierarchy. This nesting permits you to locate an item either at the lowest level of categorization or at higher levels of aggregation, which in Agenda is a feature called inheritance. In other words, items assigned to a child category, inherit the category assignments of their parent, grandparent and so on to ancestor categories. The display of inherited items can be suppressed by use of the display preferences in the View Preferences dialog box, which will be discussed later. However, this does not change the inheritance relationships in the database. It just permits you to see only the items explicitly assigned to their categories.

The Category Manager can be up to twelve levels deep, in effect permitting you to have categories that are children of children, or grandchildren, and great-grandchildren, and so on. Of course, subdividing categories permits you to make more comparisons and test more theories about your items, but the costs of categorizing may increase, and the reliability of categorization may decrease. You certainly do not want to subdivide so much that you wind up with one category for every item because you will have then lost the grouping efficiencies made possible by categories.

Here are some concrete examples of categories that might be found in the Agenda applications listed in Chapter 1:

Application	Category
Maintain a keyword or lexical filing system	Keywords
Recruit executives	Open positions
Plan human resources	Divisions
Appraise personnel and project performance	Goals
Analyze a document, e-mail, reports, memos, and so on	Topics of interest
Manage PR media lists, executive briefings, and press releases	Products
Solve a complex problem	Subgoals

Application	Category
Keep a to-do list	Priority
Build a creative platform	Product features
Manage advertising traffic	Project
Develop a curriculum	Major topic
Analyze a stock portfolio	Industries
Negotiate a contract	Major sections
Sift through news for significant data	Topics of interest
Brainstorm	Goals
Manage people	Departments
Organize information for a meeting or phone call	Priority
Write a brochure	Major sections
Keep a self-sorting notebook	Topics of interest
Consolidate notes from a meeting	Priority
Prepare a status report	Priority
Prepare a presentation	Major sections
Write a speech, article, or outline	Major sections
Write a marketing plan	Major sections
Write a business plan	Major sections
Manage a project	Team members
Manage a sales account	Salespeople

Although the Category Manager displays the structure for information in Agenda, it is only when categories are applied to items that the structure of information in Agenda is made useful. (We referred to this process earlier as categorization.) Because of Agenda's design goal of flexibility, categories as applied to items can appear in three places. This is an obvious benefit in the expression of structure.

The three forms in which categories applied to items can appear are as section headings, column headings, and column entries. Category names as section headings divide the vertical, or sequential, display of items into groups whose member items share the same category assignments. However, do not think of this as simply a typical database style sort of the items. Since the same item can be assigned to multiple categories, it can appear in multiple sections. Category names as column headings provide horizontal opportunities for you to display category assignments, as in tables with rows and columns. Finally, since each item can be in a different category, Agenda provides a number of different formats for the display of category names within columns.

Since examples are excellent ways of clarifying these formats, Figure 4-3 shows the Category Manager that we developed for our to-do list application that was introduced in Chapter 3. When we assigned the items of our to-do list to these categories, we were able to display them as shown in Figure 4-4.

Figure 4-3.

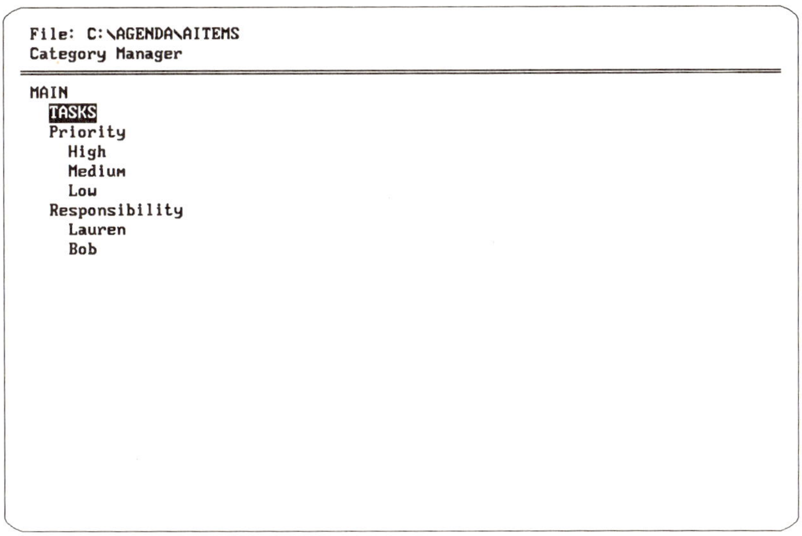

Figure 4-4.

```
File: C:\AGENDA\ITEMS                                          01/02/80    05:54
View: By responsibility                              When Date: 03/25/88

Lauren                                               When          Priority
    • Call lawyer to review contract                 »03/25/88     ·Medium
    • Points to discuss with the lawyer              ·03/12/88     ·Low
    ** Submit proposals                              ·02/25/88     ·High
    ♪ Call publishers to see if they are doing an    ·02/15/88     ·High
      Agenda book and to get author guidelines
    • Write Categories                               ·04/10/88     ·High
    • Write Views                                    ·04/10/88     ·High
    ♪ Write Application 1 - Exec Info System         ·04/10/88     ·High
    • Write Application 2 - Personal Contact File    ·04/10/88     ·High
    • Write Application 3 - ?                        ·04/10/88     ·High
    • Write Application 4 - ?                        ·04/10/88     ·High
    ** Interview Beta Users                          ·04/20/88     ·Medium
    • Write Principles of Use                        ·04/30/88     ·High

Bob                                                  When          Priority
    • Write Items                                    ·04/10/88     ·High
    • Write Principles of Use                        ·04/30/88     ·High
    • Write Views                                    ·04/10/88     ·High
    • Write Categories                               ·04/10/88     ·High
```

As you can see, and purely for this quick example, the various category names shown in the Category Manager of Figure 4-3 appear as section headings, column headings, and column entries in Figure 4-4. You decide whether a category should appear as a section heading, as a column heading, or as an entry in a column. In Figure 4-4, the category names Lauren and Bob appear as section headings; the category Priority appears as a column heading; and the categories High, Medium, and Low appear as entries within the Priority column. This decision about the display (or view) of categories does not restrict the way in which you enter them. In other words, you may use one of the category name formats for categorizing items and another for displaying groups of items in a view. In the remainder of this chapter, we will try to focus on the use of categories in developing structure for your items.

HOW DO CATEGORIES GET INTO AGENDA?

You can manually enter categories into Agenda by simply typing them, or you can automatically transfer categories stored in text files into Agenda using utility programs built for this purpose. As with items, these text files can come from anywhere, including other PC software such as word processors, spreadsheets, project management packages, communications packages, and other Agenda databases.

As explained earlier, categories appear in three places in a typical Agenda view, as well as in the Category Manager. Since there must always be at least one section in a view, the logical place to begin is with categories as section headings.

Categories as Section Headings

To enter a section head manually, press F10(Menu), C for Category, S for Section, and N for New, and you will be prompted with a New Section dialog box asking whether to position the new section above or below the current section and asking for the category name for the new section heading, as shown in Figure 4-5.

Figure 4-5.

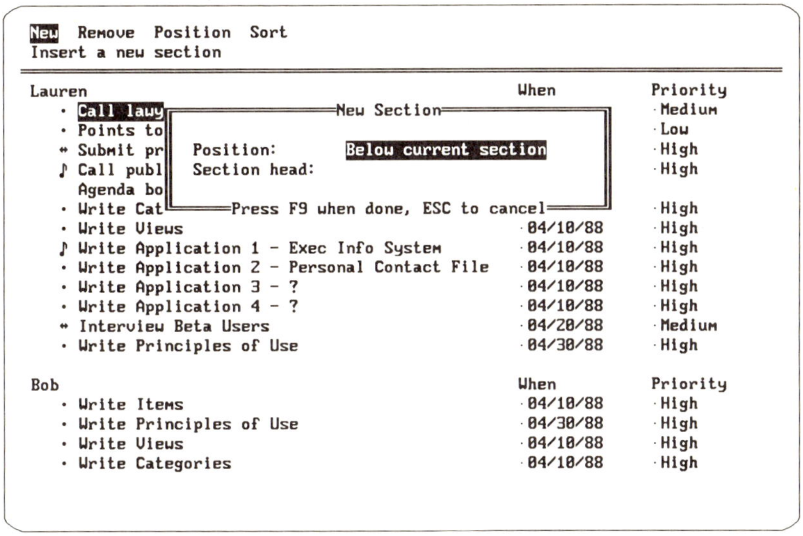

```
New  Remove  Position  Sort
Insert a new section

Lauren                                                  When          Priority
     • Call lawy ═══════════════New Section═════════════               Medium
     • Points to                                                       Low
     • Submit pr   Position:        Below current section              High
     ♪ Call publ   Section head:                                       High
       Agenda bo
     • Write Cat ══════Press F9 when done, ESC to cancel═══            High
     • Write Views                                        04/10/88     High
     ♪ Write Application 1 - Exec Info System             04/10/88     High
     • Write Application 2 - Personal Contact File        04/10/88     High
     • Write Application 3 - ?                            04/10/88     High
     • Write Application 4 - ?                            04/10/88     High
     • Interview Beta Users                               04/20/88     Medium
     • Write Principles of Use                            04/30/88     High

Bob                                                     When          Priority
     • Write Items                                        04/10/88     High
     • Write Principles of Use                            04/30/88     High
     • Write Views                                        04/10/88     High
     • Write Categories                                   04/10/88     High
```

For both of these options, if you press F2(Edit) or Grey +, you will see and be able to select from the available choices. If you do not type or select a category name, Agenda assigns the category name Untitled to the section heading. If there are two or more untitled section or column headings, Agenda numbers them, for example, Untitled-2 and Untitled-3. Enter the section head by typing in the highlighted space provided, using Backspace and the arrows to edit as you type.

As you type, (and this is true throughout the system) Agenda attempts to match your entry to existing category names using the automatic completion feature. If you hear a beep, you should look at the top of the screen to see the categories Agenda is proposing based on what you have typed so far. If a category appears that matches the category you intend to enter, simply press Enter to accept it.

Since Agenda is proposing automatic completions based on the characters typed so far, there may be more than one possible match, as noted at the top of the screen. Before continuing to type, you can view the alternate matches by pressing F8(NextSel) or Alt-N to see the next possible match, or F7(PrevSel) or Alt-P to see the previous possible match. To accept a proposed match, press Enter or F9(Accept). To override automatic completion, either continue typing or press F5(NewCat). Press F9(Accept) to close the dialog box and insert the new section heading.

The accelerator key method for inserting a new section uses Alt-U and Alt-D to insert Untitled sections above (Up) or below (Down) the current section. With the highlight on the Untitled heading, you can type a new category name, which will replace it. Agenda uses the automatic completion feature to help speed your typing. Press Enter to either accept a proposed completion or signal that your typing is finished.

Regardless of which method you used to insert a new section, from this point on you can either insert items following the procedures described in Chapter 3 or continue to insert section headings below or above the one you have just entered by repeating the procedures just described.

Categories as Column Headings

To enter categories as column headings, which may be inserted to the right or left of the column in which you are working, your highlight should be on an existing section heading or column heading. To enter a column heading, press F10(Menu), C for Category, C for Column, and N for New, and you will be prompted with a New Column dialog box, as shown in Figure 4-6.

Figure 4-6.

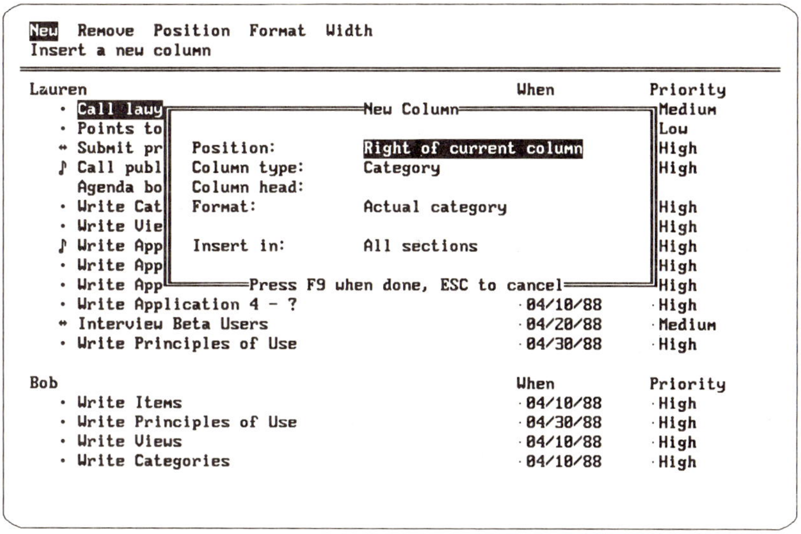

The first prompt line, *Position:*, gives you the option of inserting this new column to the left or right of the column in which you are working. Press the spacebar to rotate through the options or press F2(Edit) or Grey + to display a list of the available options. Use this method for selecting options on the remaining prompt lines. The second prompt line asks whether the *Column type:* will be a category name or one of the three date types.

If the column type is a category name, you will be prompted on the third and fourth lines for the *Column head:* category name and the *Format:*. As you type the column head category name, Agenda will beep to indicate that it is proposing automatic completions to your typing. You can save time by pressing Enter whenever you see the desired category proposed at the top of the screen. If you are not sure of the possibilities that already exist in the Category Manager, press F2(Edit) or Grey + to see the list of available category names and use the arrows to locate the one in which you are interested, and then press

F9(Accept) to select it and return to the dialog box. With respect to display formats for the categories that appear as entries in the column, you can choose

- the actual category for an item
- the actual category with its parent
- the ancestor of the actual category
- a star (*) to indicate that the item is assigned to the category
- a Y/N format as an alternative to the star format
- a category note format in which you can display a specific line, referred to by its number, from a note attached to the actual category.

If the column type is one of the three date types, you can use the Spacebar to rotate through the Entry, When, and Done date choices, or use F2(Edit) or Grey + to display and select one of these three. Notice that the *Column head*: prompt on the third line disappears and your next prompt is the *Format:*. By pressing F2(Edit) or Grey +, you can see a list of the available format choices for displaying dates in the column. Use the arrows to identify one, and press F9(Accept) to return to the New Column dialog box.

Regardless of column type, the last prompt in the dialog box asks whether you want this column inserted in all sections or only the current section. If you insert this column in the current section, the overall format for the current section will differ from that of any other sections in your view. In other words, Agenda does not insert compensating space in the other sections to match the column inserted in the current section. When you have finished responding to the prompts in the New Column dialog box, press F9(Accept) to close the box and return to the item view screen.

The default for the last prompt in the New Column dialog box can be altered by pressing F10(Menu), U for Utility, P for Preferences, and O for Other. Agenda then displays an Other Preferences dialog box, in which the first prompt, *Insert new columns in:*, has the same two options just discussed, namely, all sections or the current section. Your response to this prompt sets the default not only for future New Column dialog boxes, but also for the accelerator key methods discussed in the next paragraph. To exit from the Other Preferences dialog box, select your response to the first prompt by using the Spacebar, F2(Edit), or Grey +, and press F9(Accept) to close the dialog box.

The accelerator key method for inserting a new column uses the Alt-R and Alt-L keys. With your highlight positioned on a column or section heading, press Alt-R to insert a column to the right of the current column or press Alt-L to insert a column to the left of the current column. The new column will be inserted in all sections with an Untitled heading. With the highlight on Untitled, begin typing the desired column heading category name and, after either using automatic completion or typing the name yourself, press Enter to insert the desired category name in the column heading.

Categories as Column Entries

Finally, the third place that a category name can appear is as an entry within a column. At this point, you are ready to assign an item to a category by adding a category name entry for the item to the appropriate row in a column. Therefore, the first task is to make sure that your highlight is on the correct row, or item and column intersection. If you start in the column and move down the rows, you will notice that the item tags to the left of the items change from the default character (a dot, unless you changed it) to a >> to help you orient yourself and to ensure that you are on the desired row. With the highlight on the appropriate column entry position, press F10(Menu), I for Item, and A for Assign. You are then prompted for a category name at the top of the screen. As you type the desired name, Agenda will suggest automatic completions for you. Press Enter when you see the desired completion or when you are finished typing, and Agenda displays the category name as the entry in the column.

If you are assigning the item to an existing category, instead of typing the name, press Grey +. A Category Select box will appear. Move the highlight to the desired category name and press Enter or F9 (Accept) to assign the item to the highlighted category. The accelerator key method for assigning an item to a category uses the Alt-A key. With your highlight positioned on the column entry position where you want to assign the item, press Alt-A, and you will be prompted for the category name at the top of the screen. To complete the assignment, use the automatic completion feature or type the desired name completely and press Enter. As before, if you are assigning the item to an existing category you can press Grey + instead of typing the name and an Assign Box will appear. Move the highlight to the desired category and press Enter or F9(Accept) to assign the item to the highlighted category.

Since item assignment involves existing categories as well as new categories, and since it is the principal application of categories, we will return to it as a separate topic at the end of this chapter.

If, after entering a category name as a column heading or a column entry, you find that the column is not wide enough to display the contents satisfactorily, you can change the width by pressing F10(Menu), C for Catgeory, C for Column, and W for width. The current width is displayed on the second row at the top of the screen, and you may enter either a new column width number or use the arrows to adjust the width directly. If you use the arrows, the width number will change automatically. Press Enter to accept the new width. You can also let Agenda set the column width for you by typing a question mark (?) instead of a numeric column width.

The Category Manager

The last method of entering a category is directly into the Category Manager itself. Whenever you are in a view, press F9(Cat Mgr) to access and display the Category Manager. Similarly, whenever you are in the Category Manager and want to return to the view screen, press F9(To View). Once in the Category Manager, use the arrows to place the highlight on the category name below which you wish to insert the new category. Press Ins or Insert, and a line of dots appears in the place where the new name will be inserted at the same level as the category above it. Alternatively, if you want to insert a sibling category above (up from) or below (down from) the highlighted category, you can use the Alt-U or Alt-D (or Alt-I) accelerator keys, respectively. Instead, if you want to insert a child category below and to the right of the highlighted category, you can use the Alt-R accelerator key. Finally, if you want to insert a parent category below and to the left of the highlighted category, you can use the Alt-L accelerator key. Regardless of which insertion approach you use, you are prompted for the new category name at the top of the screen, where you can begin typing immediately, as shown in Figure 4-7. Note that Agenda does not use automatic completion while you are typing because it assumes that you are only going to add entirely new category names into the Category Manager.

Figure 4-7.

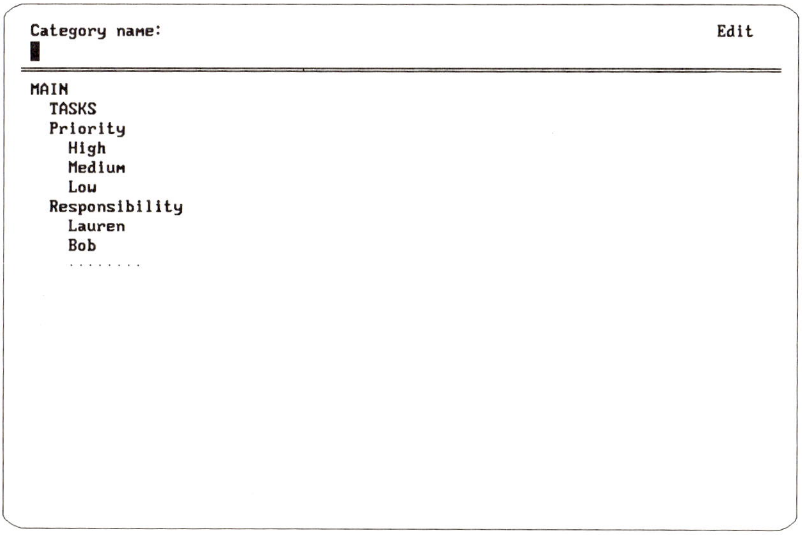

Notes in Categories

Since a category is even more limited in length (69 characters) than an item, Agenda offers the option of annotating that category with up to ten pages of additional text, either stored in the database or in an external file. Whenever you position the highlight on a category name—regardless of whether it is a section heading, a column heading, a column entry, or in the Category Manager—to access the note screen for that category, you press F5(Note). To return to the category from the note screen, press F5(Return) again and, if you have entered any note text, you will see a musical note displayed indicating that there is a note attached to it. This musical note is displayed to the left of section headings as well as in the upper-right hand corner of the screen, on the second row, for all three formats, and in the Category Manager.

Notes as External Files

If you have an external ASCII text file that contains your note text for a particular category, you can either import it into your database from the category's note screen, or attach it to the category from the item view screen without making it part of your database (thus saving space in the database).

To import an external note text file, first be sure that you are in the category's note screen and then press F10(Menu) and I for Import. Agenda displays a File dialog box, prompting you for a filename. If you are not sure of the filename, press Grey + to see a listing of all your files. Select a filename by moving the highlight to it. If you know the filename, type it and press Enter. Agenda verifies that the file exists. If the file is found, the filename will be highlighted. You must then decide whether or not to remove carriage returns from the file as it is being imported. To close the dialog box and complete the note importing, press F9(Accept). The note text will appear on the note screen.

Note that any editing you now do to the note text is maintained in the database but not on the external file. Any time you want to refresh the external file, which you might be saving for some other purpose, simply return to the category's note screen and press F10(Menu) and E for Export. Agenda then prompts you for a filename. Once again, use Grey + to select a filename or type the name directly. After selecting or typing the filename, press Enter and F9(Accept), and Agenda writes the note text to the external file. If the file already exists, Agenda gives you the option of appending the note text to the existing file or replacing the file with the note text. Choose the appropriate option with the Spacebar, F2(Edit), or Grey +, and Agenda exports the note.

From the item view screen only, you can attach an external note file to a highlighted category without incorporating it into the database by pressing F10(Menu), F for File, and N for Note. If a note exists for the category, Agenda asks whether you want to delete the existing note. If you answer No, Agenda returns to the item view screen. If there is no existing note for the category or you answer Yes, Agenda displays a File dialog box, prompting you for the name of the note text file. Type the filename and press Enter. Agenda verifies that the file exists. If the file is found, the name will be highlighted and you will have to press F9(Accept) to close the dialog box and attach the note. To see the note text, press F5(Note) and return to the category in the item view screen press F5(Return), just as you would for a note in the database. The only way you are assured that the note is being read from an external file is the appearance of the filename in the upper left-hand corner of the note screen. Since the note text remains as an external file, any changes you make to it are made directly to the file. Therefore, there is no reason to periodically export the note text to the external file, as there was when we imported the note text into the database from an external file.

Regardless of where you store your note text, either in the database or in an external file, Agenda keeps track of it, so that when you add, change, or delete note text, Agenda will know where to apply the modifications. However, it will not know whether the file from which you have imported note text needs to be updated or forgotten. Understandably this decision is left to you.

Making Note Text into a Category or an Item

If you are working in a note screen and decide that you want some piece of the note text to become a category or an item, you must first mark the desired text by placing the highlight over the first character of the text to be moved. Press F7(Mark) to mark the text and use the arrows to move the highlight to the end of the text to be moved. This will mark the text, which will now be shown in highlighted characters. To unmark the highlighted text, press F7(Mark) again. If you want the marked text to become a new item inserted below the current item and assigned to the category name of the section you are in, press F8(MakeItm). The text is then removed from the note and inserted as an item. If you want the marked text to become a new category, press F6(MakeCat). Agenda prompts you for the parent category to which you want the new category assigned, as shown in Figure 4-8.

You can press F2(Edit) or Grey + to see the current category names in the Category Manager, as shown in Figure 4-9. Use the arrows and F9(Accept) to move to and select the one you want. If, instead, you want the marked text appended to the category within whose note you are working, press Alt-F8(Append). The text is then removed from the note and appended to the current category.

Figure 4-8.

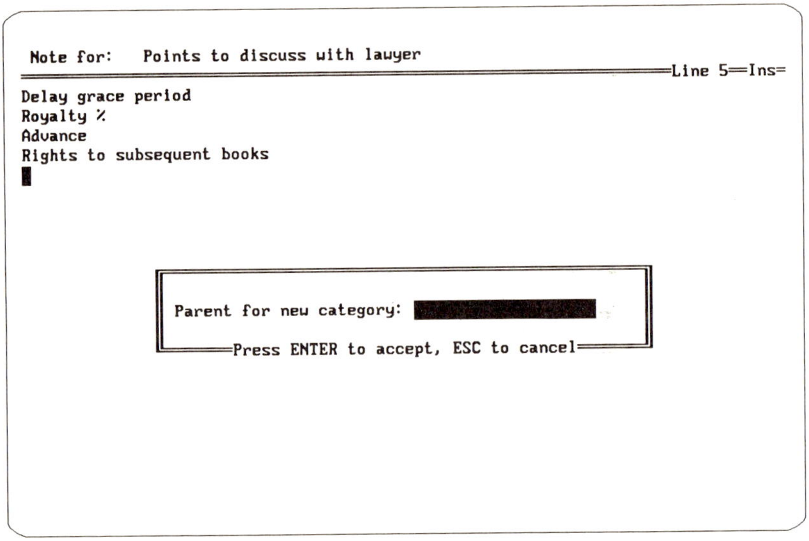

Figure 4-9.

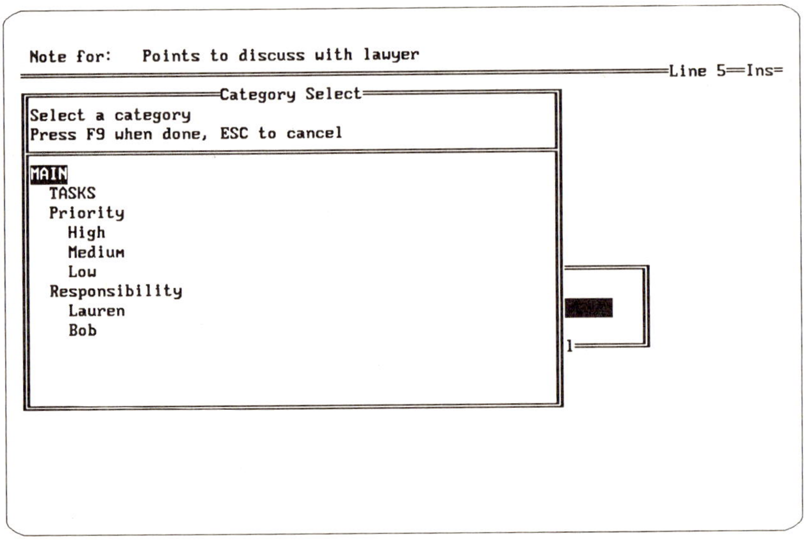

Alternatively, if you want to change a single word or line, or the entire note text for an item, press F8(MakeItm), F6(MakeCat), or Alt-F8 (Append), without first using F7(Mark). You will be prompted for your choice of the type of text to move, as shown in Figure 4-10.

Figure 4-10.

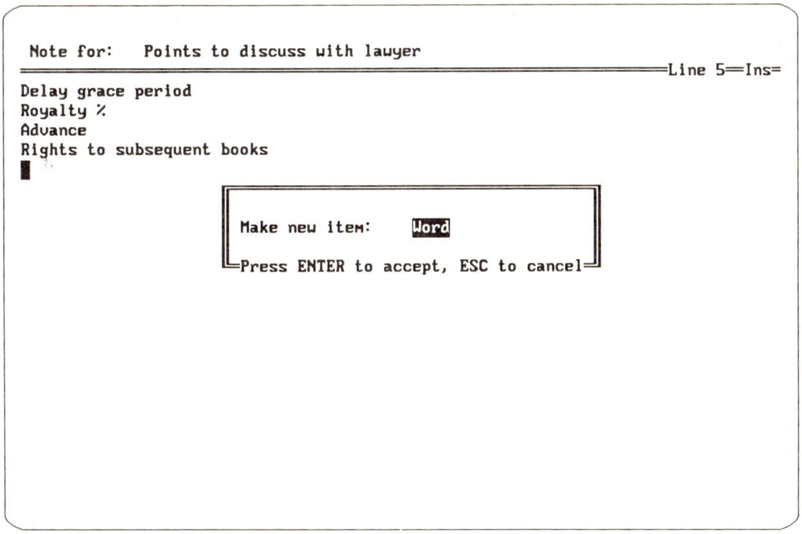

File Transfer of Categories

Categories can be automatically entered from an ASCII text file previously saved in a special format (with an extension of .STF) or from the Clipboard in Lotus's desk accessory product called Metro. Both the saving of files in this special format and the use of the Metro Clipboard Accessory are discussed in Chapters 12 and 13.

Assuming that you have saved a file in the required format, to enter categories automatically from this file, you must first access the menu for File commands by pressing F10(Menu) and F for File. Then you press T for Transfer and I for Import. You will be presented with an Import Structured File dialog box, as shown in Figure 4-11.

The first prompt line, *Import:*, gives you the option of transferring items, or categories, or both. Depending on the content of your text file, you can use the Spacebar to rotate through these choices or you can press F2(Edit) or Grey + to see the choices in a menu. If you press F2(Edit) or Grey +, you can use the arrows to move through the menu choices, or you can begin typing the name of your choice, and Agenda's automatic completion feature will begin searching for matching items in the menu. Once you have made your choice, use the Down arrow to move down to the next line in the dialog box.

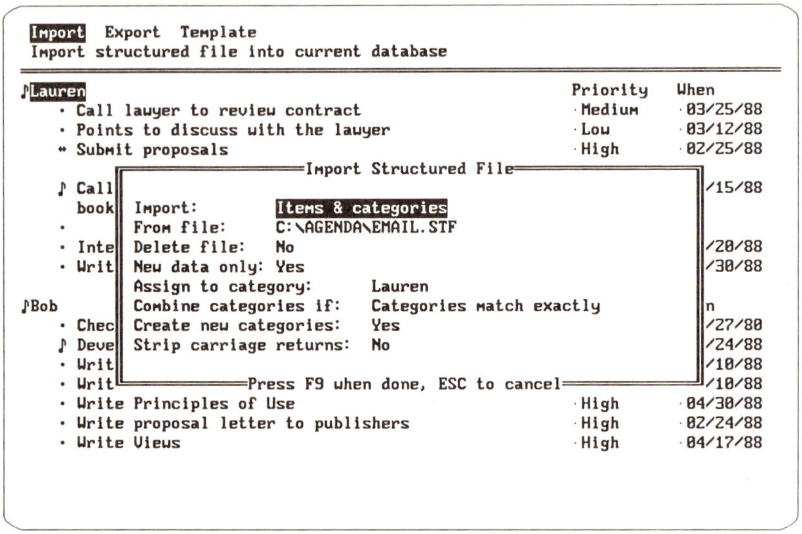

Figure 4-11.

The second line prompts you for the filename of the file where your text is stored. It assumes that the extension is .STF and that the file is stored in the current directory. If necessary, you can edit the filename. Agenda checks to make sure the file is present. If it is not present, the *File does not exist* message will be displayed. Use F2(Edit) to edit the filename, just as you would any text field in Agenda. Alternatively, if you wish to select an existing file, press Grey + to display a list of all files and move the highlight to the desired filename. Press Enter to return to the dialog box.

The third prompt line asks whether or not you want to delete the text file after transferring it. The default is No, which is the safer choice until you are absolutely sure that you will have no use for the text file. As with the first line in the dialog box, you can use the Spacebar, F2(Edit), or Grey + to make your choice.

The fourth prompt line *New data only:* appears only when the file you are importing is the file you used the last time you imported information into this database. Agenda recognizes the file it last accessed and the data which it imported during the last session. The prompt asks if you wish to import only new data from that file (that is, items and categories) or everything including the data you imported during the previous session. The default is Yes, which is generally the correct choice. As with the first line in the dialog box, you can use the Spacebar, F2(Edit), or Grey + to make your choice.

The fifth line prompts you for the category to which you want the items assigned, or below which you want the categories inserted in the Category Manager. The default is the category for the current section. To accept the current section, move to the next line; otherwise, enter a new category name. As with the first line in the dialog box, you can use F2(Edit) or Grey + to display a menu window with all the category names. If you access this display, you will have to use the arrows to move to the desired category name and press F9(Accept).

The sixth line prompts you to determine your preferences concerning the combining of categories. For example, you can combine categories if they match exactly. You can also combine categories if any term in the new category can be found in an existing category or in just the first position of the existing category. You indicate your choice by using the Spacebar to rotate through the choices and move down to the next line, or by pressing F2(Edit) or Grey + to select your choice from the menu.

If you chose the Items & categories option on the first line, a special prompt will be displayed in the seventh line asking whether or not you want Agenda to create new categories, if any are encountered. Use the Spacebar, F2(Edit) or Grey + to select your choice. If you chose only items or categories, but not both, on the first line, Agenda skips this special prompt and goes directly to the last line of the dialog box.

In the last line, you are asked whether or not you want carriage returns in the text removed as the items and/or categories are being transferred. Once again, use the Spacebar, F2(Edit), or Grey + to make your choice.

You can change your answers in the dialog box as many times as you want. When you are done answering the questions, press F9(Accept).

Agenda reads the text file and displays a small window continuously indicating how much of the structured text file has been imported. If you need to interrupt the transfer, you may do so by pressing the Ctrl and Break keys simultaneously. If you have to press Ctrl-Break, Agenda will remember where the process was interrupted so that when you return to complete this transfer, Agenda will skip over the already imported information. When the transfer is complete, the new items will appear in the current view and the new categories can be found in the Category Manager.

An alternative method of transferring only categories is the use of templates. In the F10(Menu), F for File sequence, the next choice is I for Import, E for Export, or T for Template. If you choose T for Template, Agenda copies the structure of your current database to a new file whose name you are prompted for immediately after pressing T. If you choose a filename that already exists, Agenda asks you whether or not you want to replace it. If you answer no, Agenda cancels the transfer. If you answer yes, the Template structure, including your Category Manager and the views that you have defined, but no items, will be transferred to this new filename. However, you will remain in the current file. To see the results of this template transfer, press F10(Menu), F for File, and O for Open, followed by the new filename and Enter.

HOW DO I USE CATEGORIES?

Once entered, categories can be edited, moved, deleted, or annotated.

Edit

To edit a category you need to be in Edit mode. Place the highlight on the category name, wherever it appears, and press F2(Edit). A full range of editing commands is shown in the function key map at the bottom of the screen, including F2(Paste), F3(Copy), F4(Cut), and F7(Mark).

To change the category text, simply use the arrows to move to the first character you wish to change. You can use Backspace to erase a character by backing over it or you can use Delete to erase the character under the highlight. The characters you type will be inserted before the highlight as opposed to being typed over existing characters and spaces.

Copy and Cut

In Edit mode you can copy or cut text from a category. This text can consist of a single word, the current line, the entire category, or a specially marked sequence of characters within the category. The first three choices are immediately available when you press F3(Copy) or F4(Cut). To use any of these three, move the highlight to the beginning of the word, line, or entire text, and then press F3(Copy) or F4(Cut). You can use the Spacebar, F2(Edit) or Grey + to see the choices available. After you make your choice, press F9(Accept), and the identified text will be copied or cut into the edit buffer.

Alternatively, if you are copying or cutting marked text, place the highlight over the first character to be marked, press F7(Mark), and use the arrows to highlight the remaining characters. Now press F3 (Copy) or F4(Cut) and the highlighted text will be copied into the edit buffer.

If you are copying the selected or marked text, it will remain within the category. If you are cutting the selected or marked text, it will disappear. The highlight remains within the category you are editing so that you can continue your work.

Paste

Once you have text in the edit buffer, you can paste it into another category or into another location within the current category by using F2(Paste) and pressing Enter.

Delete

The last feature available in Edit mode is the Alt-F4(Delete) key, which permits you to remove a single word or line, the entire text, or some marked text from the current category entirely, without storing it in the edit buffer as with the F4(Cut) command. Finally, to leave Edit mode, press F9(Accept).

The Category Manager

A category can be moved within the Category Manager by highlighting the category to be moved and pressing F6(Move). Use the arrows to move the highlight to the category above or below which you want to move the desired category. When you are satified with the position, press Enter to insert the category to be moved below the highlighted category, or Ctrl-Enter to insert the desired category above the highlighted category.

Sorting Categories in the Category Manager

Another way to move category names around in the Category Manager is by sorting them. The only sort sequence that is possible in the Category Manager is alphabetical. To sort categories at one level of indentation in the hierarchy, position the highlight on the parent category for the group of categories you wish to sort at the lower level. If you want to sort all the top level categories, place the highlight on the first row of the Category Manager. Press Alt-F9(Sort) and the categories at the desired level will be sorted. If there are unalphabetized subcategories within the categories being sorted, they will remain unalphabetized after the sort of their parent categories.

Promoting and Demoting Categories

A related feature in Agenda's Category Manager is the ability to change the hierarchical structure of the category names, not just by moving categories as just described, but also by promoting or demoting categories. Promoting a category means to change its level in the hierarchy, for example, from a child to a parent or from a grandchild to a child. In the Category Manager, this means to move an indented category name to the left. With the highlight on the category name you want to promote, press F7(Prm←) and the category name will be moved one level of indentation to the left. Demoting a category means to change its level in the hierarchy, for example, from a parent to a child or from a child to a grandchild. In the Category Manager, this means to move a category name to the right. With the highlight on the category name you want to demote, press F8(Dem →) and the category name will be moved one level of indentation to the right.

There are only two restrictions on your ability to promote or demote categories. The first is that you cannot promote or demote a category if doing so would cause you to skip a level in the hierarchy. For example, if you have a parent category immediately followed by one or more child categories, you cannot demote the first child to a grandchild because two levels would then separate the parent from this category being demoted. Similarly, you could not promote the parent in this example either.

The second restriction concerns existing item assignments and states that you cannot promote or demote categories if in doing so you would cause an item to be assigned to both a parent and one of its child categories. If this potential conflict is detected, Agenda displays either a Promote or a Demote dialog box asking you how you want to resolve the potential conflict. Your choice, which can be made with the Spacebar, F2(Edit), or Grey +, can be to remove the item(s) from the category you are promoting or demoting, in other words, the current category; to remove the item(s) from the conflicting or other category; or to move the item(s) to a totally different category, for example, one called: To Be Resolved.

Mutual Exclusivity

Agenda can help you assign items to categories when the categories represent mutually exclusive classes, for example, male versus female, by providing a way to indicate this in the Category Manager. With the highlight on a category that has subcategories within it, press F10(Menu) and E for Exclusive. Agenda attempts to make these subcategories mutually exclusive and displays this fact by connecting the subcategories with a line to the left of their names, as shown in Figure 4-12.

Figure 4-12.

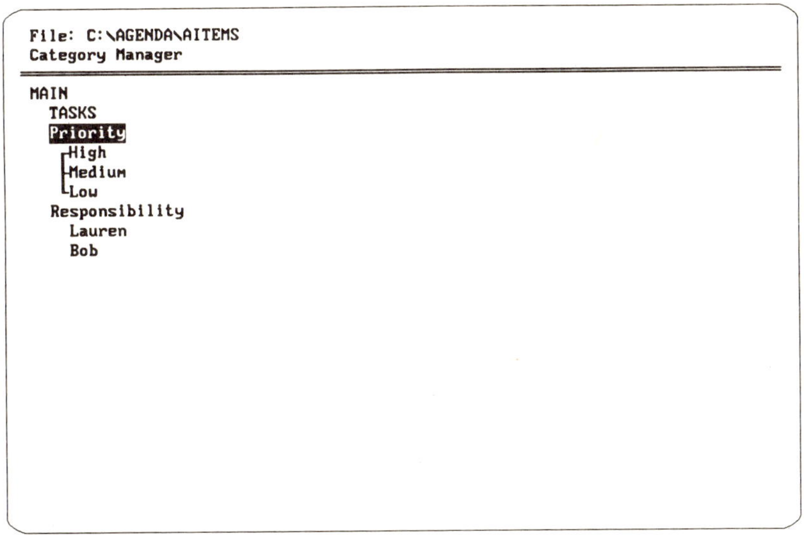

You can also make categories mutually exclusive from the item view screen by highlighting the parent category and pressing F10(Menu), C for Category, M for Management, and E for Exclusive.

If there are items that have already been assigned to two or more of the intended, mutually exclusive subcategories, Agenda does not automatically make the categories mutually exclusive. Instead, it displays an Exclusive dialog box alerting you to this conflict in the item assignments and giving you the options to assign the conflicting items to their parent category, to an existing category, or to a new category, for whose name you will be prompted, as shown in Figure 4-13.

Figure 4-13.

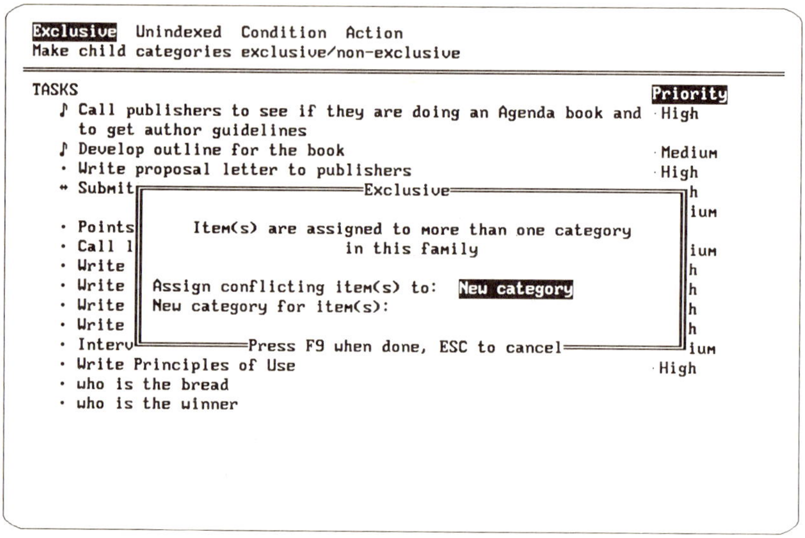

As with all other dialog boxes, you can use F2(Edit) or Grey + to see a window with all the available choices, including the Category Manager where appropriate, and use the arrows and F9(Accept) to identify and select an option. Agenda reassigns the conflicting items according to your instructions and then marks the categories in the Category Manager as mutually exclusive.

To reverse the process and make mutually exclusive categories not mutually exclusive, just perform the preceding operations a second time, either from the Category Manager or from an item view screen. Although there might seem to be simpler ways to accomplish this, repeating the mutually exclusive process removes the initial mutually exclusive condition.

Indexing Categories

Another feature of Agenda that can help you manage categories is the indexed/unindexed option. When you enter categories, Agenda indexes them so that it can apply the automatic completion feature and so that it can automatically apply them as section headings in a view. This indexing assumes that you will have many items per category, that you therefore might want to see them grouped vertically by section, and that automatic completion is a significant efficiency feature.

On the other hand, if in fact you have categories that contain only one or just a few items, which would make the preceding features unimportant to you, you can unindex the parent category within which these category names appear. Agenda notes this in the Category Manager with a small triangle symbol to the left of the parent category name, and the unindexed child category names will not appear. In views, when the unindexed parent's name is highlighted, the small triangle will appear at the top right of the screen as a reminder. The principal value in making a category unindexed is the space it conserves in the display of the Category Manager and the speed that it brings to certain operations. On the other hand, as mentioned earlier, if a category is unindexed, you cannot use it in section headings, Agenda will not use it in automatic completion of your typing, and you cannot promote or demote an unindexed parent category.

One other limitation to keep in mind is that when you unindex a category, you lose whatever conditions and actions were attached to that category. We will be describing conditions and actions a little later on in this chapter and will return to this issue.

Since Agenda starts out by indexing every category, your first encounter with this feature will likely be to unindex a category that meets the criteria just described. To unindex a category, highlight the category name, which is usually a column heading in a view, and press F10(Menu), C for Category, M for Management, and U for Unindexed. You will be asked whether or not you want to unindex this category, with Yes being the default. From the Category Manager, with the highlight on the desired category name, press F10(Menu) and U for Unindexed, and you will be presented with the same prompt.

To reverse the process and reindex a category, simply repeat the preceding procedures. In reindexing, Agenda does not prompt you to make sure that you really want to reindex the category; it simply reindexes it, removing the triangle symbol from the category name and redisplaying the child categories. Any conditions and actions that were lost in unindexing the category are not restored in reindexing.

Removing Categories

As you would expect, Agenda provides you the capability to remove a highlighted category, along with its child categories, either from the view or from the Category Manager and, therefore, the database. To remove a column from a view, highlight its heading and press F10(Menu), C for Category, C for Column, and R for Remove, or simply press Del or Delete. You are asked whether you want to have the column removed from all sections or just from the current section. This action does not affect the Category Manager or any of the items assigned to the categories in the column. Similarly, to remove a section from a view, highlight its heading and press F10(Menu), C for Category, S for Section, and R for Remove, or simply press Del or Delete. This action, too, does not affect the Category Manager or any of the items assigned to the category that was the section heading.

On the other hand, if you want to remove a category, along with its child categories, from the database, losing all the item assignments as well, place the highlight on the category name in the Category Manager, and press Alt-F4(Discard), Del, or Delete. If no items are assigned to the category, the category name is deleted. If items are assigned to the category, you are asked whether or not you still want to proceed. Answer yes or no, and Agenda responds accordingly. If some items are assigned only to the category being deleted, these items will be discarded along with the category. Unlike discarded categories, which cannot be automatically retrieved, these discarded items will be stored in the Trash, which, as long as it has not been emptied, can be used to recover the discarded items.

Notes in Categories

As we mentioned earlier, Agenda limits a category's length to 69 characters. If you would like to associate more text with a particular category, Agenda provides a feature called Note, which allows you to attach to a given category up to ten pages of additional text, stored either in the database or in an external file. Agenda keeps track of where notes are stored and updates them appropriately so that you do not have to worry about these alternate locations. External note files were thoroughly reviewed in the subsection Notes as External Files, which appeared earlier in this chapter.

From either the item view screen or Category Manager, with the highlight on a category name, you can enter or edit a note for the highlighted category by pressing F5(Note). Assuming that you do not already have a note for the category, Agenda presents you with a blank screen into which you can type up to ten pages of text. As the function key map (if you have removed it by pressing Alt-K, you can retrieve the key map by pressing Alt-K again) at the bottom of the screen indicates, you have a full range of text editing features available to you, similar to those used in editing categories, including F2(Paste), F3(Copy), and F4(Cut).

Making Note Text into Items and Categories

Some special features are available to you when you are using notes. For example, you might want to make some note text into an item using F8(MakeItm), or into a category using F6(MakeCat). In either case, the desired text can be marked using F7(Mark) and the right or left arrows to highlight the text. If you are making an item out of note text and no text is marked, Agenda gives you the choice of selecting the current word or line or the entire note text. You can view these choices by pressing the Spacebar to rotate through them or by pressing F2(Edit) or Grey + to see a menu of all the choices at once. If you are making a category from note text and no text is marked, Agenda uses the current word in which the highlighted character is located.

If you press F8(MakeItm), the selected text becomes a new item assigned to the category of the note you are working, and the selected text is removed from the note. If you press F6(MakeCat), you are prompted for the name of the parent category, if any, to which you want the new category name assigned. Either enter the name of a parent category or press Enter to insert the new category in the top level as a parent category. If you are unsure about the potential parent category candidates, press F2(Edit) or Grey + to see a listing of the Category Manager, use the arrows to locate and highlight the desired parent category, and press F9(Accept) to select the parent. The parent category's name appears in the dialog box, and you can press Enter or F9(Accept) to make the selected note text into the desired category.

Appending Note Text to a Category

If you do not want to create an entirely new category from some selected note text but rather append the text to the current category in whose note you are working, select and mark the text using F7(Mark) and the arrows, and then press Alt-F8(Append). The marked text is removed and appended to the current category. If you want to append the current word or line or the entire note text, press Alt-F8(Append) without pressing F7(Mark), and you will be given these options.

Other Note Functions

Additional functions that can be performed within a note screen include retrieving marked items and inserting them in the note, deleting or erasing some or all of the note, and searching for or replacing selected text within the note. There is also a menu of note specific functions, which is accessed by pressing F10(Menu) from within the note screen.

Retrieving Marked Items into a Note

To retrieve items that were marked in the view screen by using F7 (Mark), press Alt-F3(GetItms). You are asked whether or not you want to discard the marked items after copying them into the note. After you answer, the items are copied into the note beginning at the place where the highlight character is located, and the original items are either removed from the view or left in it.

Deleting Marked Text from a Note

You can delete any note text you have highlighted using F7(Mark) and the right or left arrows. Press Alt-F4(Delete), and the highlighted text is erased. Alternatively, if you are just interested in deleting the current word, line, or the entire text, you can press Alt-F4(Delete) without pressing F7(Mark), and you will be presented with these options. After using the Spacebar, F2(Edit), or Grey + to select the word, line, or text, press Enter to erase the desired text. You can also delete a note when you are in the note screen by pressing F10(Menu) and D for Delete. You are presented a dialog box asking you to confirm your request. Press Y for Yes, and the note disappears.

Searching for Text Within a Note

To search for text within a note, press Alt-F5(Search). A Search/Replace dialog box appears, prompting you for the text (one or more words or characters) to be found. You are also asked whether or not you want to replace the selected text when found. If you answer no, you will have to provide just two more answers: the direction of the search (forward or backward from where the highlighted character is located in the note text) and whether or not Agenda should ignore case (upper or lower) in searching for the text. If you answer yes in response to the prompt concerning replacement text, besides providing the direction and case responses, you will also have to provide the text to be used in replacing the search text and indicate whether or not the replacement should be global and whether you want to confirm every replacement before it takes place or let Agenda automatically perform them all.

Close the dialog box and begin the search by pressing F9(Accept). To repeat the search with the same parameters press Alt-S. To change the parameters press Alt-F5(Search).

More about Notes

The note screen menu is selected by pressing F10(Menu). You have the option of printing a note by pressing P for Print. (Since this is another way of displaying information, this feature will be explained in Chapter 5 on Views.) You also can import a text file into a note by typing I for Import and entering the filename in the File dialog box that appears. You are then asked whether or not you want to eliminate carriage return characters from the text file as the text is being imported. Similarly, you can export a note to a text file by typing E for Export and entering the desired filename in the File dialog box that appears. You can delete all the text in the current note by pressing D for Delete and responding to the prompt that checks to make sure that you want to do this. Finally, you can return to the view screen or Category Manager screen that you left to work on the note by pressing R for Return.

Category Info

The Category Info capability displays a window of category information for a selected category, including the number of items in the category; the number of child categories; and the number of section headings, view filters, conditions, and actions in which it is used. To access this display from an item view screen only, highlight the desired category name and press F10(Menu), C for Category, and I for Info, and you will see the display shown in Figure 4-14.

Figure 4-14.

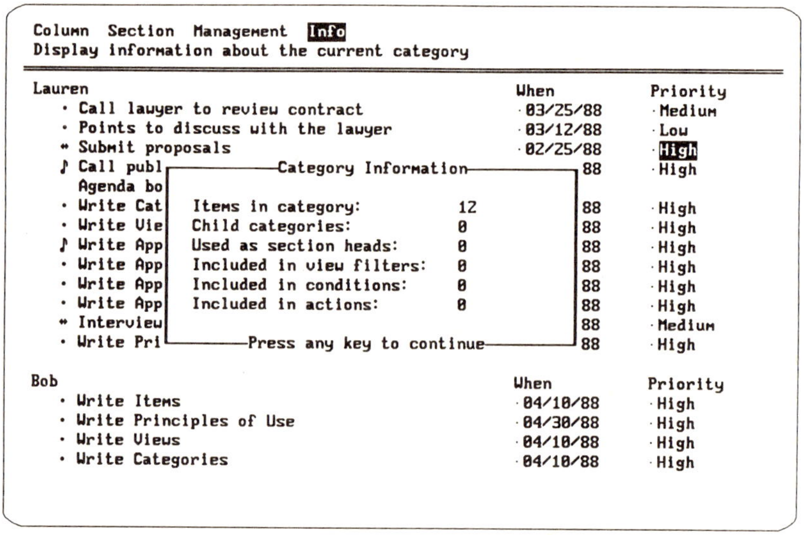

In Figure 4-14, the category on which we requested information was High. You can see there are 12 items in the category and that the answer is 0 for all the other pieces of information. When you are through with the display, press any key to return to the item view screen.

Hide Display of Child Categories

Another special feature is the ability to hide, or suppress, the display of child categories within any parent category in the Category Manager. To do this, place the highlight on a parent category with child categories and press Alt- (the Alt and minus keys together) or Shift Grey –. The child category display, not the child categories themselves, disappear from the screen, and the parent category will have three dots (. . .) appended to the end of its name to indicate that there are child categories within this category. Unlike unindexing, this procedure only changes the display of child categories. You can still use the child categories as section headings. The conditions and actions attached to the child categories are not disturbed, and Agenda uses the category names in the automatic completion of your typing. To hide the child categories for the entire Category Manager press Alt- a second time. To reverse the process, press Alt= (the Alt and = keys together) or Shift Grey +, anywhere in the Category Manager, and all of the hidden child categories, in all of the parent categories that had been collapsed, are redisplayed.

CONDITIONS AND ACTIONS

The conditions and actions capability lets Agenda help you automatically assign items to categories.

Conditions are statements attached to a category that instruct Agenda to assign items to the category if they meet certain criteria concerning 'their text, their other assignments, or their associated dates. Each of these criteria represent a different type of condition, with its own format in the Category Manager and its own method of input.

On the other hand, actions are statements attached to a category that instruct Agenda to do something with the items that are assigned to the category. This action can be an assignment to one or more other categories, the discarding of the item, the assignment of a When or Done date (including the marking of the item as done), or the exporting of the item to a structured file.

Text Condition

Let's begin with the first type of condition, the text condition, which Agenda uses to assign items to categories based on a match of the text contained in the items and/or their notes to the words and phrases in the text condition. Text conditions are like synonyms in that they represent different triggers for the same category, as far as assigning items to categories is concerned. In the Category Manager, the synonymous words and phrases are appended to the category name with semicolons (;), using the standard edit procedure.

Place the highlight on the category name to which you want to attach the text condition and press F2(Edit) and End to move the highlight to the right of the last character in the category name. Then type a semicolon (;) and the word or phrase which, in addition to the category name, you want Agenda to associate with this category when it finds it in the text of an item, note, or both. If you want a phrase matched word for word in the order that they are typed, enclose the phrase in parentheses. Otherwise, Agenda matches on the presence of one or more of the phrases' words, regardless of order, depending on the match strength parameter which you set in the Utility/Preferences/Auto-Assign menu, which will be described later.

After entering as many synonyms as you need separated by semicolons, simply press Enter or F9(Accept). You can see the category name, Bob, with its appended synonym, husband, displayed in the Category Manager, as shown in Figure 4-15.

Figure 4-15.

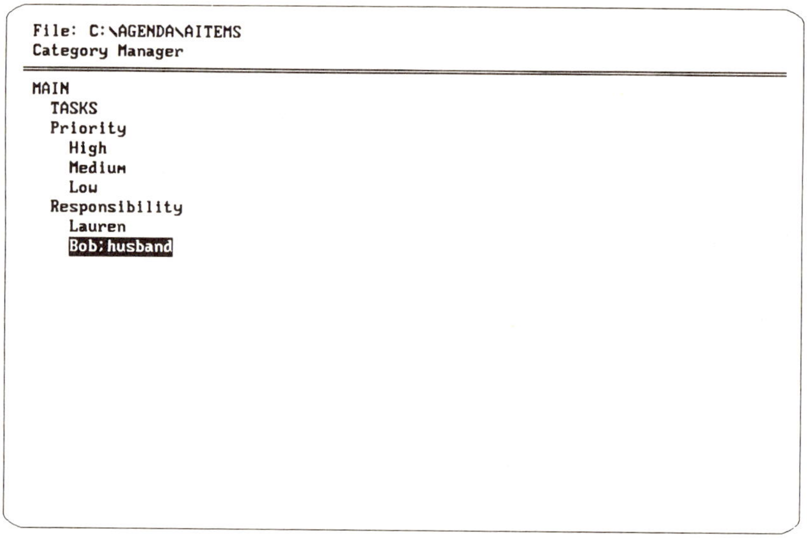

Agenda uses the first text condition after the category name as a replacement for the category name in column headings where the column width is too narrow for the column heading category name as entered, but it is wide enough for the first text condition. If you want to suppress this default alternative, separate the first text condition from the category name with two semicolons (;;), rather than the usual one.

The words and phrases that you use as text conditions can include a variety of special characters to control the matching. For example, enclosing text in the category name or text condition in double quotes (" ") suppresses the matching of the enclosed text with item and/or note text. This choice of double quotes can be changed, as you will see shortly. To use the rest of the special characters, both they and the words or phrases they appear in must be enclosed in parentheses when you add them as text conditions to the Category Manager.

The caret symbol, for example, in (^helps), suppresses Agenda's normal matching of words without regard to different suffixes (the words "helps" and "helpful" normally match). If you want to match on only the word "helps," use the caret symbol.

The tilde symbol, for example in (~Agenda), suppresses Agenda's normal matching of words without regard to case differences (the words "Agenda" and "agenda" normally match). If you want to match on only the word "Agenda," which could be the product name or the noun when used as the first word in a sentence, use the tilde symbol.

The exclamation point, for example, in (!Agenda), instructs Agenda to match successfully only if the item or note does not contain the word or phrase following the exclamation point.

Since special symbols may sometimes be important in matching, you can place a backslash in front of a special symbol to tell Agenda to ignore the symbol's usual meaning.

Wildcard symbols, the question mark (?), and the asterisk (*) are used to match words or phrases where one letter exactly or zero or more letters, respectively, can be different and you still want the match to take place. For example, (m?t) as a text condition would match with mit, met, mat, and even mot and mtt, if such three-letter combinations were found in your item or note text. On the other hand, (m*t) as a text condition would match with mt, mit, meet, moot, and even myghfgt, if such words, beginning with m and ending with t, were found in the item or note text.

Controlling Text Matching for All Categories

You can also control Agenda's text matching for all categories by using the Utility/Preferences/Auto-Assign options from the view menu. Press F10(Menu), U for Utility, P for Preferences, and A for Auto-Assign.

You will be presented with the Auto-Assignment Preferences dialog box shown in Figure 4-16. The dialog box asks you whether you want to enable the text (and other) conditions or not. If you answer yes (the default), you have six parameters to use in tailoring the text matching to your requirements.

Figure 4-16.

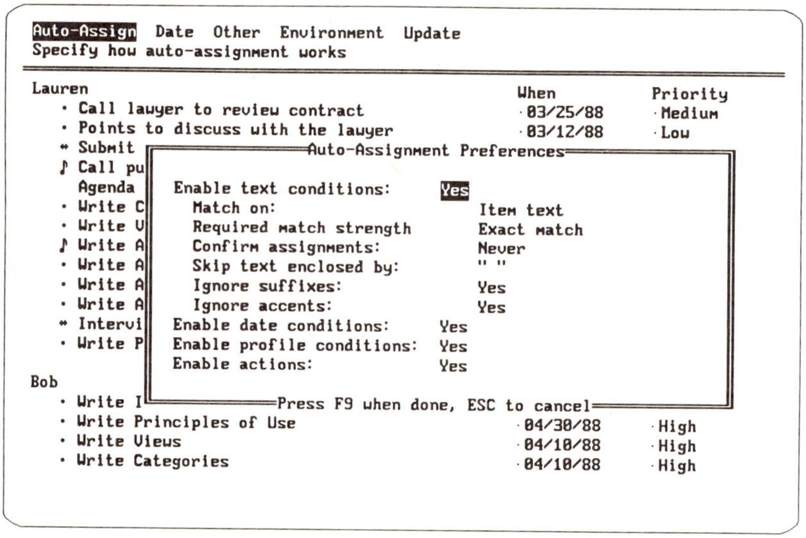

The first prompt asks whether you want to match text appearing in items or notes or both. With each of these prompt lines, you can use the Spacebar to rotate through the available choices, or press F2(Edit) or Grey + to see all the choices listed at once, and use the arrows and Enter to select your choice.

The second prompt asks how strong a match you want Agenda to apply. The responses range from Exact to Partial to Minimal. Exact means that all the words in the text condition are found in the item or note text. Partial means that at least half of the words in the text condition are found in the item or note. Minimal means that at least one word in the text condition is found in the item or note.

The third prompt asks you how often you want Agenda to check with you when it is assigning items to categories based on text conditions. The responses range from Always to Sometimes to Never. Always means that Agenda will validate its proposed assignments every time. Sometimes means that Agenda will automatically assign items if there is an Exact match; otherwise, it will verify the assignment. Never means that it will simply assign items automatically, without verifying the assignments with you.

When applying these text conditions, Agenda indicates that there are assignments to verify by displaying a question mark in the upper right-hand corner of the screen. You can respond to this question mark when it appears, or at any time, by pressing F10(Menu), U for Utility, and Q for Questions. (The accelerator key combination Alt-Q will accomplish the same purpose.) A Questions window will appear, displaying the first item for which Agenda is suggesting possible categories and the list of possible categories. You can move the highlight up and down the list, marking the appropriate categories by pressing the Spacebar, or if all the suggested categories apply, you can mark them by pressing Tab. After marking some or all of the suggestions, press F9(Accept). If there are more items to verify, Agenda repeats the preceding process by displaying a Questions window for the next item. After all questions have been resolved, Agenda returns you to the item view screen.

Back in the Auto-Assignment Preferences dialog box, the fourth prompt asks you whether you are including comments or terms in categories you do not want Agenda to attempt to match. You can enclose these terms in pairs of special characters (“ ”,< >,‘ ’,( ),/ /,# #,[ ],{ }), and this prompt asks which set of characters you want to use in categories to suppress text matching.

The fifth prompt asks you whether or not you want Agenda to ignore suffixes in matching the text conditions to text in the items and/or notes. Similarly, the last prompt relating to text conditions asks whether you want Agenda to ignore accents in matching text conditions to text in items and/or notes. The remaining three prompts deal with the other forms of conditions and actions, and they will be reviewed after we complete this discussion of text conditions.

After responding to the six text condition prompts, press F9(Accept). Now when you add items, Agenda applies the text conditions in the Category Manager according to your preferences. Agenda will not go back and reapply the text conditions to existing items. To reapply the text conditions (and all other conditions and actions as well) to a single item, highlight the item and press Alt-E. To reapply the conditions and actions to all items in your database, press Alt-X. Remember, that each time you change text conditions in the Category Manager, you must press Alt-E or Alt-X to apply the new conditions to existing items.

If you want to test the text conditions on a set of items other than the whole database or you want to test the text conditions in a family of categories that is smaller than the entire hierarchy, you will have to use the Utility/Execute commands from the main menu. This approach will be described in the section on Controlling Conditions.

Controlling Text Matching for a Single Category

If you want to control the text matching for a single category, for example, by turning off the matching applied to all categories as described earlier, you can do this in the Conditions Settings dialog box, which will also be described in the section on Controlling Conditions.

Profile Condition

The second type of condition is the profile condition, which is most easily understood if we recall the discussion of the item profile feature in Chapter 3. The item profile can be used to identify the categories to which a single highlighted item has been assigned. In the view screen, this feature is accessed by pressing Alt-F9(Profile) after you have highlighted the desired item. A window, called the Assignment Profile, appears and lists the Category Manager. Asterisks (*) appear to the left of the categories to which the item has been assigned. A blank to the left of a category indicates that the item has not been assigned to that category.

Now let us return to the profile condition, which, as defined earlier, assigns items to a category when it recognizes that the items have or have not been assigned to specific other categories. It does this by comparing the item profiles to the one specified in the profile condition. The profile condition is appended to the category name in the Category Manager, just like a text condition, and it has the following format:

```
{C= Item | Category 1, Category 2, . . .}
```

where Category 1, Category 2, and so on represent the categories to which the item must belong for the item to be assigned to the category to which this profile condition is appended. If an item is to be assigned to a category based on its absence from another category, the category to which it is not to belong is preceded by a Down arrow (to indicate the negative of the category) in the profile condition.

To develop a profile condition for a category, either highlight the desired category name in the Category Manager and then press F10(Menu), C for Condition, and P for Profile (or press Alt-C), or highlight the desired category name in an item view screen and press F10(Menu), C for Category, M for Management, C for Condition, and P for Profile. You will be presented with a Profile Condition dialog box, as shown in Figure 4-17.

Figure 4-17.

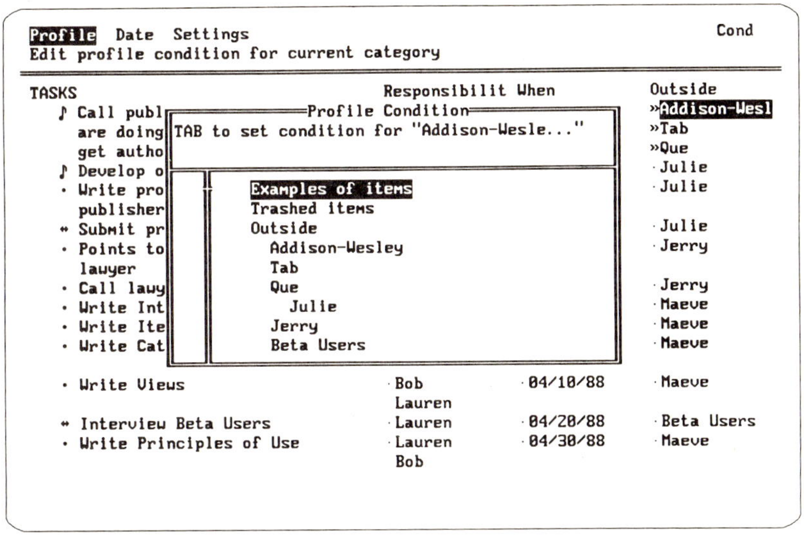

In the dialog box is a listing of the Category Manager. Move the highlight to the categories you want to use for matching. If an item must be present in a highlighted category for the match to be successful, press Tab or F3(InclCat). An up pointing arrow appears to the left of the category name to signify its inclusion in the profile condition and, if you can see the category to which this condition is being appended in the window, you will notice that the condition format has been used to reflect this profile condition. If the item must be absent from a highlighted category for the match to be successful, press Tab or F3(InclCat) twice. A down pointing arrow appears to the left of the category name to signify its exclusion from the profile condition and, if you can see the category to which this condition is being appended in the window, you will notice that the category name, preceded by a down pointing arrow, has been added to the condition format.

After highlighting and Tab-ing, once or twice for inclusion or exclusion, as many categories as you need for this profile condition, press F9 (Accept) to close the dialog box and return to the Category Manager. You will see the full profile condition appended to the category name, after any other conditions you previously developed and in the format shown in Figure 4-18.

Figure 4-18.

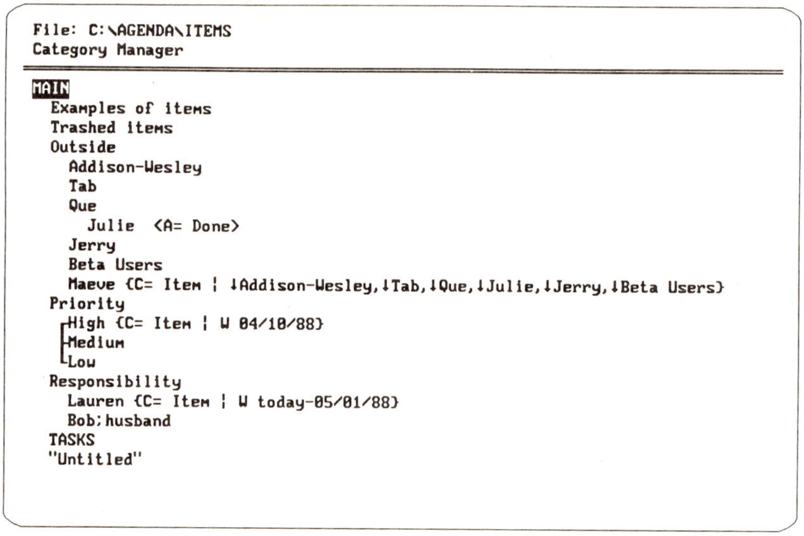

Now, whenever you assign items to categories or edit their category assignments, Agenda will match the item profiles to the profile conditions that have been set up in the Category Manager, and the items whose profiles match these profile conditions will be automatically assigned to these new categories as well.

It is important to understand how this profile matching works. All the categories that are marked for inclusion and exclusion (that is, with arrows in the profile condition dialog box or separated by commas in the Category Manager display) must be present or absent as specified for the match to complete successfully. The only exception to this and-ing of criteria is when the categories marked for inclusion are mutually exclusive subcategories of some category. Since an item can be assigned to only one of a group of mutually exclusive categories, the profile condition categories are interpreted as Category 1 or Category 2 or . . . , as opposed to Category 1 and Category 2 and . . . . This is unlike the text conditions, which apply if any condition is met, in other words, condition 1 or condition 2 or . . . .

There are three ways you can specify an or condition in a profile condition. First, if the categories that are being or-ed can be coded as mutually exclusive without conflicting with your item assignments, you can change them to a mutually exclusive state and use the profile condition to mark them for inclusion or exclusion. Since they are now coded as mutually exclusive, the profile condition treats them as or-ed conditions. The second approach is slightly more laborious, but will not conflict with your desires for assigning items to multiple, non-mutually exclusive categories. Basically, the trick is to exclude all categories except the ones you want to have or-ed for the purpose of the profile condition. In other words, if you exclude categories 1, 3, and 5 from a Category Manager listing with only five categories, Agenda matches items with this profile if they are assigned to categories 2 or 4 or both, but not 1, 3, and 5. The third approach avoids this constraint on conditions by using actions instead, the details of which will be covered shortly in the section on Actions.

To edit a profile condition, first highlight the category name in the Category Manager, and then press F10(Menu), C for Condition, and P for Profile. Use Tab or F3(InclCat) as before to change up pointing arrows to down, or vice versa, or to remove the arrows entirely. At any time, you can press F4(ClrCats) to clear all the inclusion and exclusion marks at once. Press F9(Accept) to close the dialog box and return to the Category Manager.

Date Condition

The third and last type of condition is the date condition. It assigns items to a category if the item's When, Entry, or Done dates are inside or outside specified ranges. To specify a date condition for a particular category, highlight the desired category name in the Category

Manager and then press F10(Menu), C for Condition, and D for Date, or highlight the desired category name in an item view screen and press F10(Menu), C for Category, M for Management, C for Condition, and D for Date. For example, to assign all items with a When date of April 10 to the high priority category, place the highlight on the category High in the item view screen, and then press F10(Menu), C for Category, M for Management, C for Condition, and D for Date. You are presented a Date Condition dialog box, as shown in Figure 4-19.

Figure 4-19.

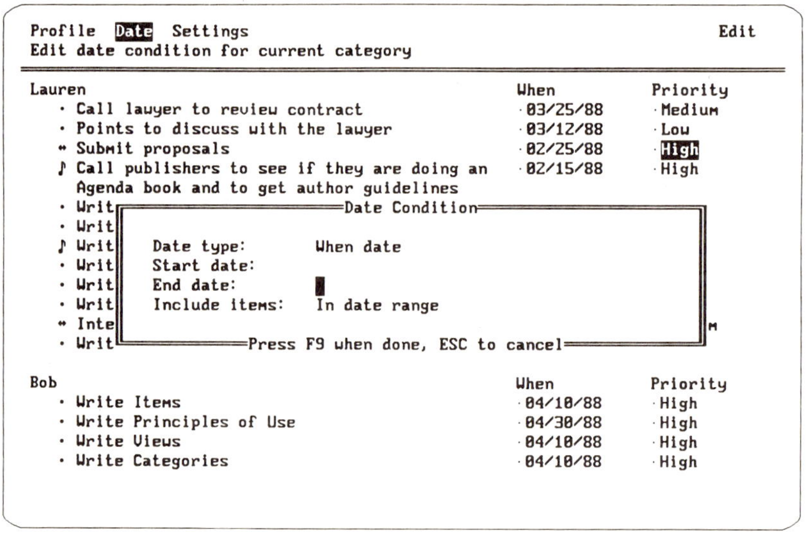

The first prompt line asks whether or not you want any date condition at all. If you respond that you do not want a date condition, you are returned to the Category Manager or item view. If you press F2(Edit) or Grey +, you will see the available options, which include the three types of dates that may be attached to items. Use the arrows to highlight the desired date or, if you have not pressed F2(Edit) or Grey +, use the Spacebar to rotate through the available choices. Press F9(Accept) or Enter to choose a particular type of date.

Having chosen a type of date, you will be presented two additional prompt lines requesting the beginning and ending dates of the range you wish to include or exclude. Either the beginning or end dates can be left blank, in which case the range will be open-ended. Enter these dates in any legitimate date format, including a relative format such as today. The dates you enter will appear on these prompt lines. One difference between how the relative dates appear in this dialog box versus elsewhere in Agenda is that the word "today" will appear in addition to the calculated month, day, and year format. Agenda does this because, armed with this relative date information, it can update these ranges on a daily basis, thus producing a useful and continuing date screen in, for example, an electronic mail monitoring application. This automatic feature can be suppressed by preceding the relative date with a dollar sign, for example, $today.

After entering the Start date, a fourth prompt appears asking whether to include or exclude items in this category, depending on whether the item dates fall inside or outside the date ranges. After choosing the appropriate options in the dialog box, press F9(Accept) and Agenda returns you to the Category Manager or view screen you left.

Controlling Conditions

You can control the way Agenda applies conditions to individual categories by using a combination of the Utility/Preferences/Auto-Assign global settings and the individual category Condition/Settings.

To access the global settings, press F10(Menu), U for Utility, P for Preferences, and A for Auto-Assign. The Auto-Assignment Preferences dialog box shown in Figure 4-16 is displayed, where the second and third enable prompts ask whether you want the date and profile conditions to be globally enabled or disabled.

You can access the settings for an individual category by highlighting that category in either the Category Manager or the item view screen. In the Category Manager, press F10(Menu), C for Condition, and S for Settings. In an item view screen, press F10(Menu), C for Category, M for Management, C for Condition, and S for Settings. In either case, Agenda displays the Condition Settings dialog box as shown in Figure 4-20.

The first prompt, *Evaluate:*, allows you to disable the conditions for this category; to have the conditions applied automatically when items are entered or changed; or to have the conditions applied on demand, when you either use the Utility/Execute command from the main menu or press the Alt-X or Alt-E accelerator keys. This last option improves performance because the condition testing only takes place when you want it to.

Figure 4-20.

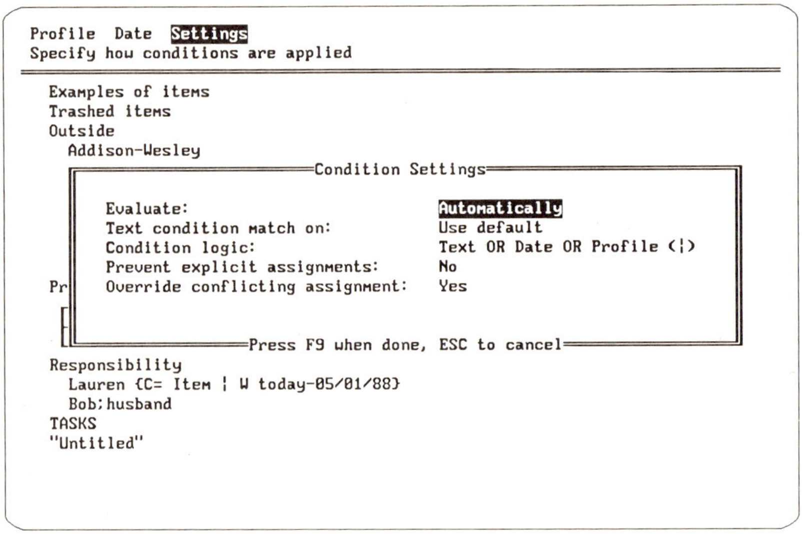

The second prompt, *Text condition match on:*, has four options that can be seen by rotating through them with the Spacebar or pressing F2(Edit) or Grey +. The first is the default setting, which says that you want the Utility/Preferences/Auto-Assign options to govern the matching. The second, third, and fourth options cause the matching to be done on item text, note text, or both item and note texts. For example, if the Utility/Preferences/Auto-Assign options specified matching on both item and note text, but you wanted this category matched on only item text, you could select the second option here. The fifth and last option disables the matching for the current category.

The third prompt, *Condition logic:*, specifies how you want Agenda to apply multiple types of conditions within a single category. If a given category contains any combination of text, date, and profile conditions, Agenda can either assign items based on all the conditions being met or based on any one condition being met. Appropriately, the two choices are OR and AND as ways of combining the testing of multiple types of conditions.

The fourth prompt, *Prevent explicit assignments:*, instructs Agenda to include only the items that meet the conditions attached to the category, regardless of whether there have been explicit assignments of items to this category or automatic assignments of items to this category based on profile actions. If you answer yes, Agenda applies this "if and only if" test to the assigning of items to the category based on conditions.

The fifth and last prompt, *Override conflicting assignments:*, instructs Agenda to remove items from categories to which they were explicitly assigned if assigning them to other categories based on condition statements would cause conflicts. For example, with mutually exclusive categories or when promoting or demoting categories, we saw earlier how certain conflicts could arise. In those cases, Agenda prompted us with dialog boxes to determine how we wanted to resolve these conflicts. In the *Condition settings:* prompt, we are instructing Agenda to resolve these conflicts without our intervention.

To exit the *Condition settings* dialog box, press F9(Accept), and you will be returned to either the Category Manager or the item view screen you left.

Actions

Actions, in some sense, are the opposite of conditions in that if an item is assigned to a specific category, you want it assigned to one or more other categories, or else you want some other special action taken. Assigning an item to one or more categories is like creating an item profile for the item, and, not surprisingly, this type of action is referred to as a profile action. Special actions, on the other hand, include discarding items, marking items as done, setting item when dates, and exporting items to files.

Profile Actions

To specify a profile action for a particular category, highlight the desired category name in the Category Manager, and then press F10(Menu), A for Action, and P for Profile (or press Alt-A), or highlight the desired category name in an item view screen and press F10(Menu), C for Category, M for Management, A for Action, and P for Profile. You will be presented the now familiar profile listing of the Category Manager, prompting you to identify categories to which items will be assigned or removed based on their inclusion in the highlighted category. Use the arrows and Tab or F3(InclCat) to identify and select categories to which items will be auto-assigned. Use Tab or F3(InclCat) a second time to select categories from which items will be removed. Note that pressing Tab or F3(InclCat) a third time removes the profile action from the category. At any time, you can press F4(ClrCats) to clear all the inclusion and exclusion marks at once. Finally, press F9(Accept) to exit the profile listing and return to the Category Manager or item view screen.

The profile action is the third way to overcome both the constraint mentioned earlier in connection with the profile condition and the fact that it requires the simultaneous presence or absence of all the profiled categories to assign an item to the category with the profile condition. If you want an item assigned to a target category (call it category A) because it is also assigned to at least one, but not necessarily all, of a group of other categories (call them X, Y, and Z), use the profile action feature with each of the categories X, Y, and Z to cause the item to be assigned to category A, if it happens also to be assigned to category X or category Y or category Z or any combination of them.

Special Actions

To specify a special action for a particular category, highlight the desired category name in the Category Manager and press F10(Menu), A for Action, and S for Special, or highlight the desired category name in an item view screen and press F10(Menu), C for Category, M for Management, A for Action, and S for Special. You will be presented a Special Action dialog box, asking you whether you want to return to the Category Manager or item view screens. If you respond No action to the first prompt line, you are returned. Otherwise, you can use the Spacebar, F2(Edit) or Grey + to reveal the other Special Action choices.

First, you can discard an item, if it happens to get classified in the category to which the Special Action is attached. Second, you can mark items as done, if they happen to get classified in this category. Third, you can set the when date for an item assigned to this category. If you choose this option, you will have to enter a date, which can be in absolute (3/31) or relative (today) format. Fourth, you can export items to files if they are assigned to the category where you are adding the Special Action. Here you will have two more fields to fill in, namely, File name and whether you want the items discarded after they are exported by this Special Action. Press F9(Accept) to close the dialog box. Agenda will be ready to apply the actions to new or edited items in your database.

Controlling Actions

You can influence the way Agenda uses actions by accessing the Utility/Preferences/Auto-Assign menu. In the item view screen, press F10(Menu), U for Utility, P for Preferences and A for Auto-Assign. You will see the now familiar Auto-Assignment Preferences dialog box, as shown in Figure 4-16. To enable or disable actions, answer the last Yes/No prompt, labeled Enable actions.

Other Processes with Conditions and Actions

In addition to these menu driven commands relating to conditions and actions, there are some function keys that can be used to hide or suppress the display of conditions and actions, copy a condition or action from one category to another, and clear all conditions and actions. If you press Alt-F3(HideC/A) to hide the conditions and actions, you can redisplay them by pressing Alt-F3(HideC/A) again.

To copy a condition or action attached to a highlighted category in the Category Manager, press F3(Cpy C/A) and use the arrows to move to and highlight the desired destination category. If conditions and actions are attached to the category, Agenda asks you if you want to copy conditions, actions, or both. After answering this question, if asked, press Enter to complete the copying or Esc to back out of it.

Finally, to erase or clear a condition or action attached to a highlighted category, press F4(Clr C/A).

Issues in the Use of Conditions and Actions

We have already discussed the relative merits of conditions versus actions with regard to the and-ing or or-ing of criteria for categorization. There is another case where profile conditions are more appropriate than profile actions. Profile conditions can assign items to their categories based on the items not being assigned to one or more other categories. On the other hand, a single profile action can be used to assign an item to many categories versus having to set up profile conditions in each of the destination categories. Also, only a profile action can remove an item from a category based on its assignment elsewhere.

Although these differences need to be considered in choosing profile conditions or actions, at times both can be used together to accomplish a specific goal in categorizing items. In the Introduction, we spoke about rule-based representation in the field of artificial intelligence. Rule-based representation is frequently referred to as if-then processing. When a condition and an action appear in the same category, a form of if-then processing can occur. If an item is assigned to category A, the profile condition attached to category B might also assign the item to category B. At the same time, the profile action attached to category B might assign all items that are assigned to category B to category C as well. Therefore, in this simple case, items assigned to category A get assigned to category C, but only because of the intermediary assignment to category B.

Another issue should be considered in working with profile conditions and actions, that is, the possibility of circular references. Circular references occur, for example, when a condition causes an assignment to take place to its category that contradicts the condition. This in turn causes the item to be removed from the category, which again causes the item to be assigned to the category, and so on. Agenda recognizes these situations and prevents the endless processing that would follow from these circular references. Agenda also displays a small circle in the upper-right hand corner of the screen to alert you to the existence of circular references in your categories. It assigns all the items involved in the circular references to a special category called !Circular Reference!, which can be displayed by pressing F10(Menu), U for Utility, S for Show, and C for Circular. The !Circular Reference! category will appear as a section in a special *Show view*. You may have to mark the items in this view and look at the assignment profile for them to see the categories that are causing the circular references.

Assigning Items to Categories

Before leaving the subject of categories, it is important to review the ways in which you can take maximum advantage of the powerful classification capabilities in Agenda. As we said earlier, when you add or modify conditions and actions for your categories, Agenda does not go back to reevaluate all the items that now should fall in the redefined categories. Agenda does apply the new conditions and actions when items are added or changed. Also, the only checking that Agenda performs in assigning items to categories is the identification of assignments requiring confirmation, circular references, and conflicts due to simultaneously trying to categorize an item either into two or more mutually exclusive categories or into a parent category and its child category. Methods for resolving these problems, which are identified either by a question mark or small circle in the upper right-hand corner of the screen, or by a Promote or Demote dialog box, have already been discussed.

Agenda does provide the capability of reevaluating either individual items or all the items in the database. To reevaluate a single highlighted item using all conditions and applying actions only if the item's assignments have changed because of the reevaluated conditions, press Alt-E. To reevaluate all the items using all conditions and applying actions only to those items whose assignments have changed because of the reevaluated conditions, press Alt-X. A window will appear continuously indicating how much of the database has been reevaluated.

If you want to test these new conditions and actions on a limited number of items or only want to test a single category's logic on one or more items, you need to use the Utility/Execute commands available from the main menu. In an item view screen, with one item highlighted or one or more items marked, press F10(Menu), U for Utility, and E for Execute. Agenda will display an Execute dialog box as shown in Figure 4-21.

The first prompt, *Evalute conditions for:*, gives you the choice of the current highlighted item, the marked items, the items in the current section, the items in the current view or the items in the database. The second prompt, *Categories to check:*, gives you the choice of the entire Category Manager or hierarchy, or a partial hierarchy. If you select partial, a new prompt, *Family:*, appears below *Categories to check:*. If you press F2(Edit) or Grey +, you will see a listing of the Category Manager you can use to select a category by moving the highlight to the desired category name and pressing F9(Accept). Alternatively, you can simply type the desired category name after the *Family:* prompt. This Family category can be at any level in the Category Manager, which means that you can temporarily move categories around in the Category Manager to facilitate testing only certain categories all at once, or you can test them one at a time. The third prompt in the Execute dialog box, *Perform actions:*, gives you the option of applying actions to only those items whose assignments have changed due to reevaluated conditions or applying actions to all items whether their assignments have changed or not.

Figure 4-21.

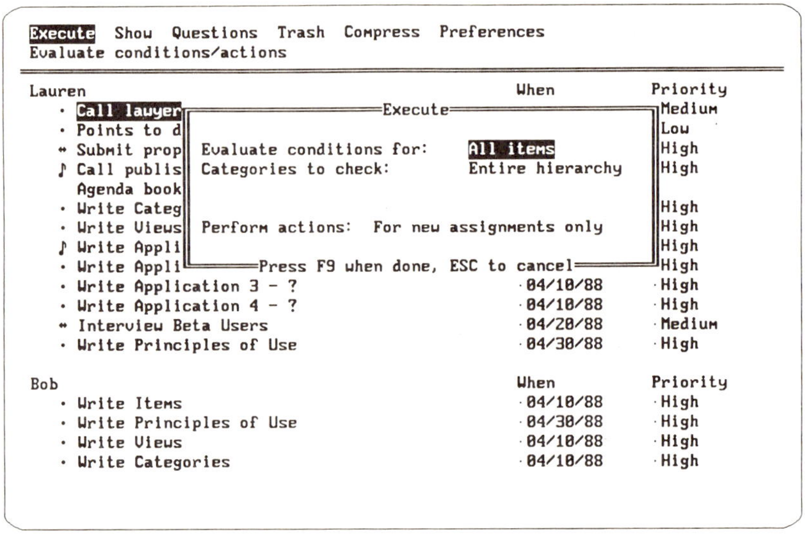

Item Profile

As mentioned in Chapter 3 and just reviewed here, another useful feature in connection with the assigning of items is the item profile. The item profile identifies the categories to which either a single highlighted item or a group of marked items have been assigned. In the view screen, this feature is accessed by pressing Alt-F9(Profile), after you have highlighted a particular item or marked a group of items using F7(Mark). A window called the Assignment Profile appears, which lists the Category Manager.

If you are checking on a single highlighted item, asterisks (*) appear to the left of the categories to which the item belongs. If you are checking on a group of marked items, the numbers to the left of the categories indicate how many of the marked items belong to each category. If you just want to see the profile for the highlighted item, even though you have already marked a number of items, press Grey + instead of Alt-F9(Profile).

In these profiles, a blank to the left of a category indicates that no items are assigned to that category. If you want to see a profile for all your items, assuming that all items in your database are displayed in the sections of the current view, place the highlight on each section heading in your view and press F7(Mark). In this fashion, all items will be marked, and you can press Alt-F9(Profile) to see the numbers of items that are assigned to the various categories in your database.

You can use the Assignment Profile to assign the marked items to new categories by moving the highlight to the desired categories in the category hierarchy and pressing either the Spacebar or F7(Assign). The numbers to the left of the category names will be changed to reflect these new assignments.

Similarly, you can unassign the marked items in a given category by moving to the category name and pressing either the Spacebar or F7 (Assign). The number to the left of the category will disappear, indicating that there are no more marked items associated with this category.

Manual Techniques for Assigning Items to Categories

In addition to the item profile method of assigning items to categories, several other manual techniques are available for you to use to assign items to categories. To start with, whenever you add or insert an item in a section, as described in Chapter 3, that item is automatically assigned to the category whose name is the section heading. Copying items from one section to another generally leaves the source or original category assignment unchanged and assigns the copied items to the new category whose name is the destination section heading as well. The only exception to this rule is when you are copying items from and to categories that are mutually exclusive child categories of a common parent category. In this case, the item is removed from the source category and added to the destination category.

As you would expect, moving an item within a section does not change its assignment to that section's category. However, moving an item from one section to another does change its category assignments. It is removed from the category name for the section it is being moved from and added to the category name for the section it is being moved to.

In addition to assigning items to categories through the use of sections, you can assign items to categories by using column entries, which can either be actual category names or codes (* or Y/N) to indicate membership in the category whose name is the column heading. With the highlight positioned under the desired column heading and in the desired item's row, you can begin typing a category name. Agenda matches your typing to the previously indexed names and suggests automatic completions for you at the top of the screen. By pressing Enter in response to its suggested category name or after you are finished typing a new name, you will be assigning the item to the typed category name. Instead of typing a name, you can press Grey + to see a listing of the child categories within the column heading category name, if any. Use the arrows to highlight the one to which you wish to assign the item, and press the Spacebar to select it.

With the highlight on the category column entry, you can remove the assignment by pressing Del or Delete or Alt-F4(Discard). The delete commands simply unassign the item, leaving the category in the Category Manager. Discarding the category unassigns the item and removes the category from the database, checking first with you to see if other items are also assigned to the category.

If you have formatted the column to be a * or Y/N format, simply press the Spacebar, and the * or Y code will appear to indicate that the item is a member of the category whose name is the column heading. Pressing the Spacebar again will remove the * or Y code, thereby unassigning the item.

SUMMARY

As with items, the only constraints on your use of categories in Agenda are the limits of your own imagination. Your use of categories is linked to your individual needs. You can build things from them, create new ideas, and see things in a new way by sorting or grouping them differently. Of course, you cannot see very much until you start building the personalized displays of your items and categories, called views, which is the subject of Chapter 5.

5

Views

Items represent the content of your personal information. Categories represent the structure of this information. Views represent the ways in which you can display your information, in either screen or print formats. After you have set up your Agenda database, you will want to look at different subsets of the items you have entered. In other words, you will want to view your information in different ways. By using Agenda's View feature, you can customize the displays of your data.

You have already seen many item view screens throughout the previous chapters, such as Figure 3-2, which is reprinted here as Figure 5-1.

Figure 5-1.

```
File: C:\AGENDA\ITEMS                                       01/02/80   06:42
View: To-do list
==============================================================================
TASKS
   ♪ Call publishers to see if they are doing an Agenda book and to get author
     guidelines
   ♪ Develop outline for the book
   • Write proposal letter to publishers
   •• Submit proposals
   • Points to discuss with the lawyer
   • Call lawyer to review contract
   • Write Introduction
   • Write Items
   • Write Categories
   • Write Views
   •• Interview Beta Users
   • Write Principles of Use
```

In fact, every screen on which items were displayed in previous chapters was a view of the database. These views were suited to whatever purposes were important at the time, for example, to facilitate the entry of item data or to show the result of a sort or search operation. Beyond the display of data, the view feature provides even more flexibility in the area of dynamic updating. This means that whenever you add or edit an item, regardless of which view you are in, that item will be updated in all views where it appears.

Here are some concrete examples of views that might be found in the Agenda applications listed in Chapter 1, Introduction:

Application	View
Maintain a keyword or lexical filing system	Alphabetical list
Recruit executives	Candidates by skill
Plan human resources	Open jobs by region
Appraise personnel and project performance	Achievements by goal
Analyze a document, e-mail, reports, memos, and so on	Items by topic
Manage PR media lists, executive briefings, and press releases	Releases by product
Solve a complex problem	Possible solutions
Keep a to-do list	High priority tasks
Build a creative platform	Possible products
Manage advertising traffic	Tasks by project
Develop a curriculum	Assignments by date
Analyze a stock portfolio	Stocks by industry
Negotiate a contract	Terms by section
Sift through news for significant data	News items by topic
Brainstorm	Ideas by goal
Manage people	List by department
Organize information for a meeting or phone call	Agenda by priority

Application	View
Write a brochure	Ideas by section
Keep a self-sorting notebook	Items by subject
Consolidate notes from a meeting	Items by priority
Prepare a status report	Items by priority
Prepare a presentation	Ideas by section
Write a speech, article, or outline	Ideas by section
Write a marketing plan	Ideas by section
Write a business plan	Ideas by section
Manage a project	People by function
Manage a sales account	Actions by customer

You create views to suit your information needs. Views are a product of your imagination. They are created to display the relationships between the items and categories you are entering or those that you have already entered into Agenda. Once you have a complete database of categorized items, you can create views to answer any question you might have about the items. In this chapter we will focus on the view feature itself, and how you can use it to develop flexible, dynamic displays of your data to meet your needs.

HOW DO VIEWS GET INTO AGENDA?

You select views by pressing F8(Vw Mgr), or F10(Menu), V for View, and S for Select. You are presented with a View Manager or View Select dialog box, where you have the option of creating a new view or looking at an existing view, as shown in Figure 5-2.

If you want to look at an existing view, move the highlight up or down to the desired view name by using the arrows. Then press F9(Accept) to select the highlighted view, and it will appear on the screen. If you are creating a new view, you use Insert or Ins. You will be presented with a New View dialog box as shown in Figure 5-3. Another way to get to the New View dialog box from the item view screen is to press F10(Menu), V for View, and N for New.

Figure 5-2.

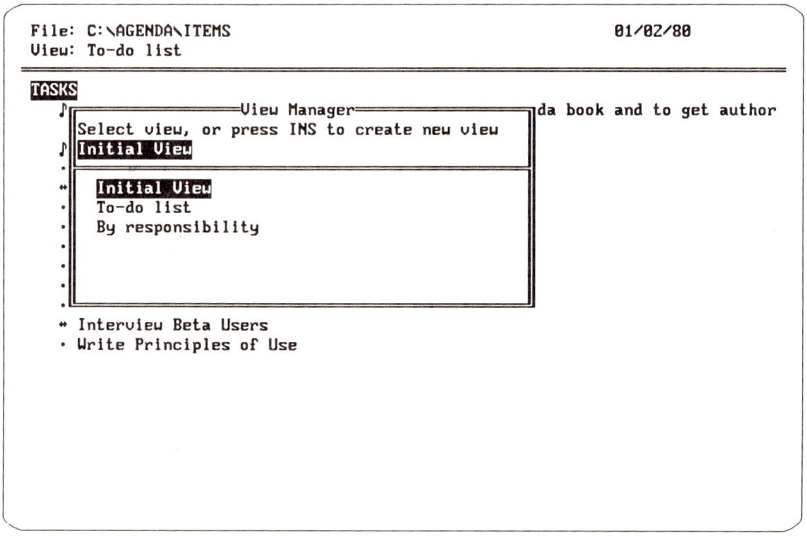

Figure 5-3.

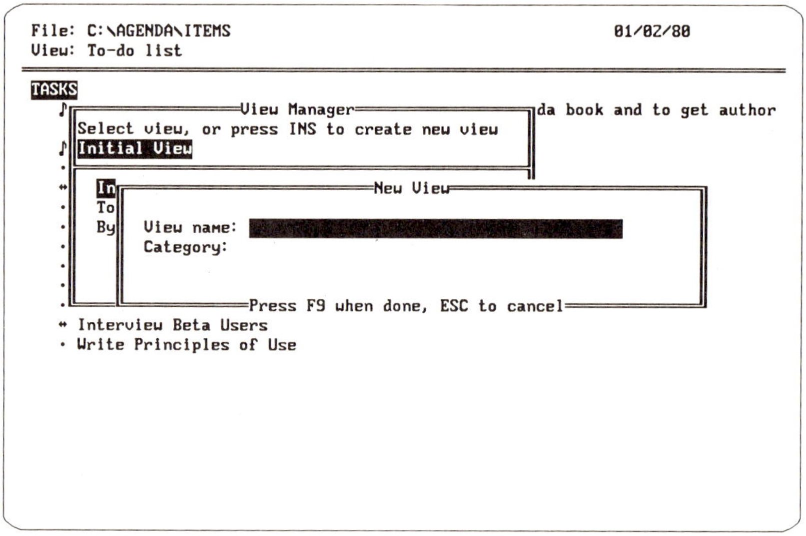

Once in the New View dialog box, you type the name for the view and the category whose items you wish to see displayed in the first, and perhaps only, section in the view. If you are not sure of the possible category names, move the highlight to the right of the *Category:* prompt and either press F2(Edit) or Grey + to see a list of the Category

Manager, or start typing a category name and Agenda will suggest automatic completions for you. If you press F2(Edit) or Grey +, you must move the highlight to the category names you want to select as sections, press the Spacebar after you highlight each name to select it. Then press F9(Accept).

The categories you select can be parent or child categories. If you choose a parent category, you have the option of seeing all the children within the parent section as sub-sections of the view. If you do not enter a category name, the section heading will be labeled Untitled.

You can include or exclude items or sets of items based on characteristics of those items by using a feature called a filter, which will be described later on in this chapter. Although the view feature is very flexible, the way in which you select your categories also contributes to determining which items will be included in the view.

HOW DO I USE VIEWS?

Once you have a view on the screen, regardless of whether you just retrieved or created it, there are a number of things you can do to tailor it to your needs. You can add, change, reposition, reformat, or delete individual item rows, sections or groups of item rows, or category columns. Also, you can sort items within sections. Finally, you can filter items in or out of your view, based on their category or date assignments.

Sections

Adding a Section to a View

Let's begin by adding a section to a view. First, you have to decide where to position the new section. Place the highlight in a section above or below the area where you want to insert the new section. Then press F10(Menu), C for Category, S for Section, and N for New. Agenda presents a New Section dialog box as shown in Figure 5-4.

Figure 5-4.

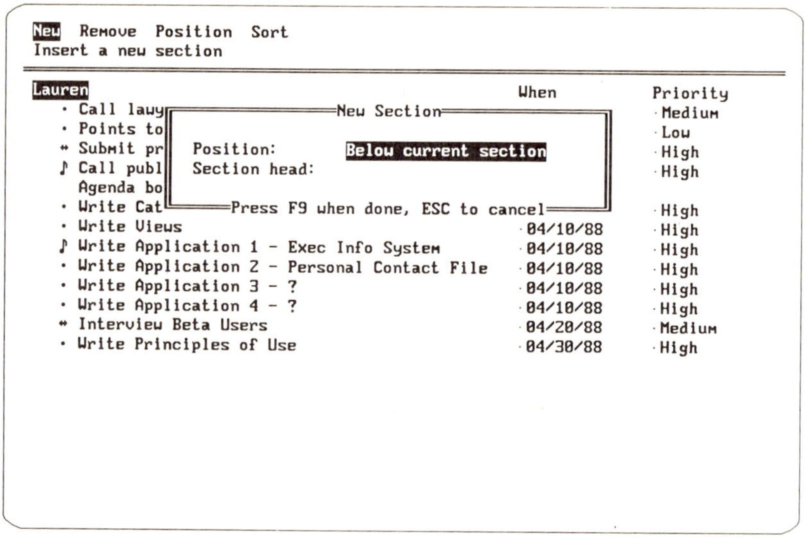

At the *Position:* prompt, answer whether you want to position the new section above or below the section that you are in by using the Spacebar to move between these two choices and press Enter. Then move the highlight down to the *Section head:* prompt and type the name of the category you want used for this section. If you are not sure which category names are available, press F2(Edit) or Grey + and a listing of the Category Manager will appear. Move the highlight to the desired category name and press Enter, followed by F9(Accept). The new section will be inserted either above or below the section in which you are located.

Alternatives to this procedure would be to press either Alt-U to insert a new section above (Up from) the current section, or Alt-D to insert a new section below (Down from) the current section. Using these accelerator keys inserts Untitled section headings only. To replace the Untitled section headings, place the highlight on the word Untitled and simply type the desired category name for the section heading over the word Untitled.

Once you have identified a group of sections for your view, you can change the member sections by using the View Define command. Access this command from the item view screen by pressing F10(Menu),

V for View, and D for Define or by pressing F8(Vw Mgr) and F8(Define). In either case, Agenda displays a View Define window listing the Category Manager with space provided for category selection and filtering as shown in Figure 5-5.

Figure 5-5.

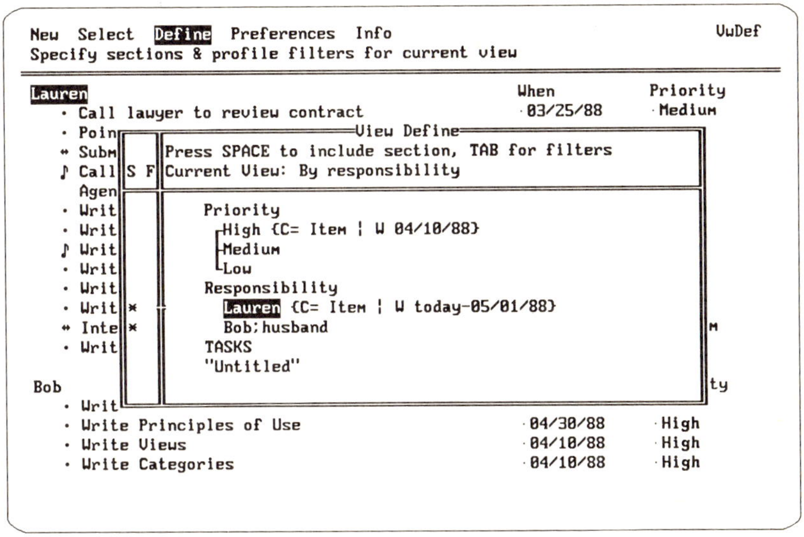

Asterisks (*) appear in a column labeled S for Section to the left of the categories that have been selected as sections. In Figure 5-5, the asterisks are next to Lauren and Bob, which are the two section headings in this view. To add a category as a section, move the highlight to the category name using the arrows and press the Spacebar or F7(Section). If you want to automatically select the children of some parent category as sections, place the highlight on the parent and press F8(Chldrn). Asterisks will appear next to the child categories, but not next to the parent category. For example, if you placed the highlight next to Priority in Figure 5-5 and pressed F8(Chldrn), asterisks would appear next to High, Medium, and Low, but not next to Priority. Pressing the Spacebar, F7(Section) or F8(Chldrn) a second time removes the asterisks and, therefore, the categories as section headings. In other words, pressing these keys toggles the selection of section headings on and off.

Removing Sections from a View

In addition to the View Define approach to removing sections from a view, there are three other methods you can use. To remove a section from within the item view screen, place the highlight anywhere in the section and press F10(Menu), C for Category, S for Section, and R to Remove. An alternative method for removing a section from a view is to place the highlight on the section heading and press Del or Delete. Both of these procedures simply remove the section from the view without changing the database.

If you want to remove a section heading category and its items from the database, place the highlight on the section heading and press Alt-F4(Discard). If the category has assigned to it items that are not assigned to any other categories, Agenda will ask whether or not you are sure you want to discard the items because they will be removed from the database and put in the Trash.

Collapsing a Section

You can collapse the section displays by hiding the items and leaving only the section headings as we have done in Figure 5-6. This will give you a better perspective on the overall organization of the sections within your view. To collapse the section in which the highlight appears, press Alt- or Shift Grey –. To collapse the rest of the sections, press Alt- or Shift Grey – again. To reverse the process and expand the sections to redisplay the items, press Alt= or Shift Grey +, either once or twice.

Repositioning a Section

Now that you have your sections set up, you may find that you would like to reorganize them, that is, change the sequence of sections from top to bottom in the view. To do this, place the highlight anywhere in one of the sections whose position you want to change, and then press F10(Menu), C for Category, S for Section, and P for Position. At this point, all the sections will be collapsed, leaving just the section headings to remind you of their order and the highlight on the section you want to reposition. Use the arrows to move the highlighted section up or down until it is in the desired location. Then press Enter and you will be returned to the item view screen with the sections and their items fully displayed. To reposition another section, move the highlight to the new section and repeat the procedure.

Figure 5-6.

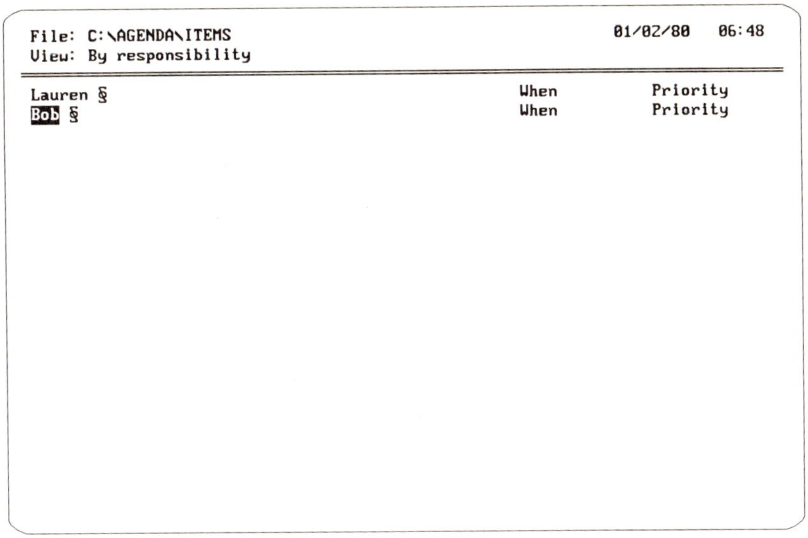

As with the previous menu-driven procedures, there is an accelerator method for repositioning sections. Place the highlight on a section heading you want to move, and then press F6(Move). The sections will be collapsed and the highlight will remain on the section heading to be moved. Use the arrows and Enter as just described to move the highlighted section.

Sorting Items in a Section

The last thing we can do with sections is to sort the items contained in a section based on some category, portion of a category note, or the item text. To initiate the sort procedure, press F10(Menu), C for Category, S for Section, and S for Sort. A Sort dialog box is displayed, as shown in Figure 5-7.

The first prompt, *Sort new items:* asks when you want the items to be sorted: on leaving a section, when an item is entered, or on demand. The rest of the dialog box gives you the option of sorting items in the current section or all sections by item text alphabetically or by category, category note, Entry date, When date, or Done date. Category and category note sorts can be in the order the categories appear in the Category Manager or in alphabetical or numeric order. Categories and dates can also be sorted in chronological order. If you are sorting on category notes, you must specify which line number within the note is to be used for sorting. You can sort on both a primary (or top-level) key and a secondary key, which sorts within the primary level.

Figure 5-7.

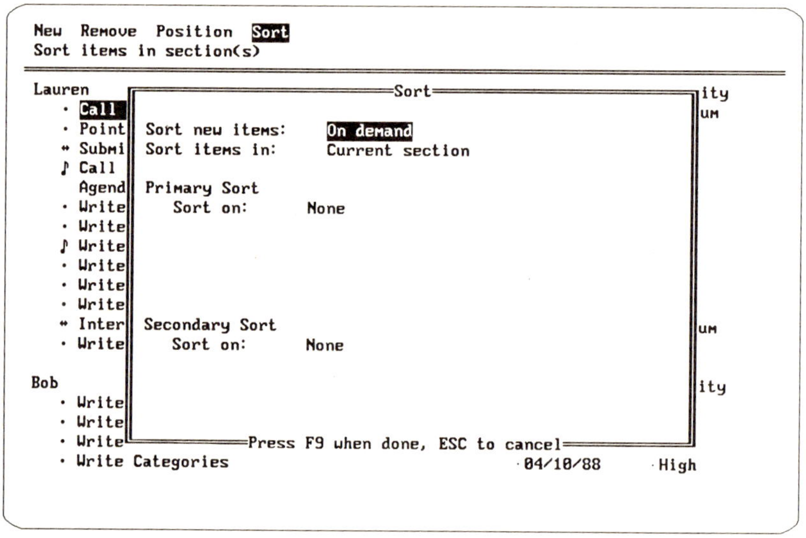

After you select the options in the dialog box, press F9(Accept) and the items will be sorted according to your preferences. From this point on, whenever you are in a section that you want to sort according to the criteria developed for the section as specified in the Sort dialog box, you can press Alt-S and the items will be sorted automatically.

Columns

Adding a Column to a View

Now that we have exhausted the vertical organization of views through the use of sections, let us turn to the horizontal organization of views through the use of columns. We have already discussed columns at some length in Chapter 4. However, we will review and supplement the essential material focusing on adding, positioning, formatting, and removing columns in a view.

To add a column, press F10(Menu), C for Category, C for Column and N for New, and a New Column dialog box will be displayed as in Figure 5-8. In the first line, the *Position:* prompt provides the option of inserting this new column to the left or right of the current column. The second line asks whether the column type will be a category name or one of the three date types.

Figure 5-8.

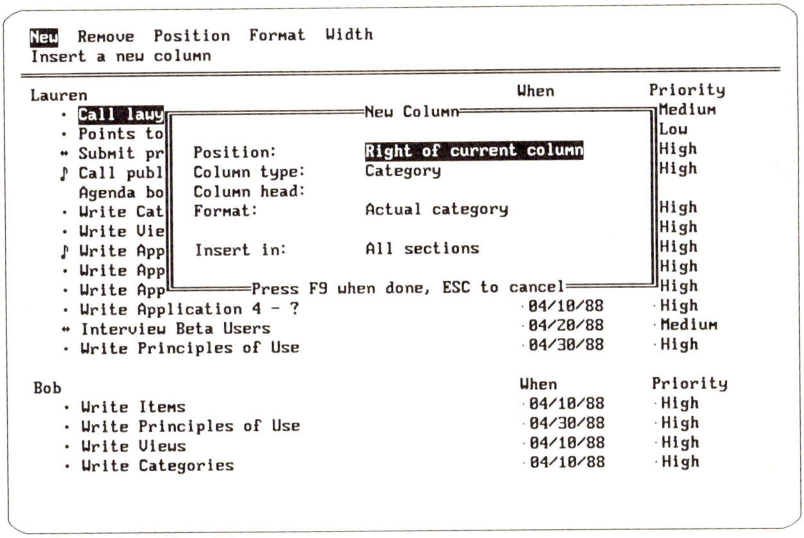

If the column type is category, you will be prompted on the third and fourth lines for the *Column head:* category name and the display *Format:*. As you type the column head category name, Agenda will beep at you to indicate that it is proposing automatic completions to your typing. Whenever you see the category you intend to enter proposed at the top of the screen, you can press Enter and Agenda will complete the category name for you. To see the list of possibilities that already exist, press F2(Edit) or Grey + and the Category Manager will appear, showing you all the current category options. Use the arrows to locate the one in which you are interested, and press F9 (Accept) to select it and return to the dialog box.

Agenda provides several choices for the display formats of the categories that appear as entries in a column. You may use the actual category for an item, the actual category with its parent, the ancestor of the actual category, an asterisk (*) to indicate that the item is assigned to the category, a Yes/No format as an alternative to the star format, or a category note format in which you can display a specific line, referred to by its number, from a note attached to the actual category column entry.

If the column type is one of the three date types, you can use F2(Edit) or Grey + to display the Entry, When, and Done date choices or the Spacebar to rotate through these options. Once you have made a choice, the *Column head:* prompt on the third line disappears and your next prompt is the display *Format:* on the fourth line. By pressing F2(Edit) or Grey +, you can see a list of the available format choices for displaying dates in the column. Use the arrows to identify one, and press F9 (Accept) to return to the New Column dialog box.

The last prompt in the dialog box asks whether you want this column inserted in all sections or only in the current section. If you insert this column in the current section, the overall format for the current section will differ from that of any other sections in your view. In other words, Agenda does not insert compensating space in the other sections to match the column inserted in the current section. Press F9 (Accept) to close the dialog box and insert the new column.

The default for the last prompt in the New Column dialog box can be altered from the item view screen by pressing F10(Menu), U for Utility, P for Preferences, and O for Other. Agenda then displays an Other Preferences dialog box as shown in Figure 5-9 in which the first prompt, *Insert new columns in:*, has the same two options just discussed, namely, all sections or the current section. Your response to this prompt sets the default not only for future New Column dialog boxes, but also for the accelerator key methods discussed in the next paragraph. To exit from the Other Preferences dialog box, select your response to the first prompt by using the Spacebar or F2(Edit) or Grey +, and press F9(Accept) to close the dialog box.

Of course, there is an accelerator key method for inserting a new column. With your highlight positioned on a column or section heading, press Alt-R to insert a column to the right of the current column or press Alt-L to insert a column to the left of the current column.

Depending on the Insert new column setting in the Utility/Preferences/Other menu, the new column will be inserted in either all sections, or just the current section, with an Untitled heading.

Figure 5-9.

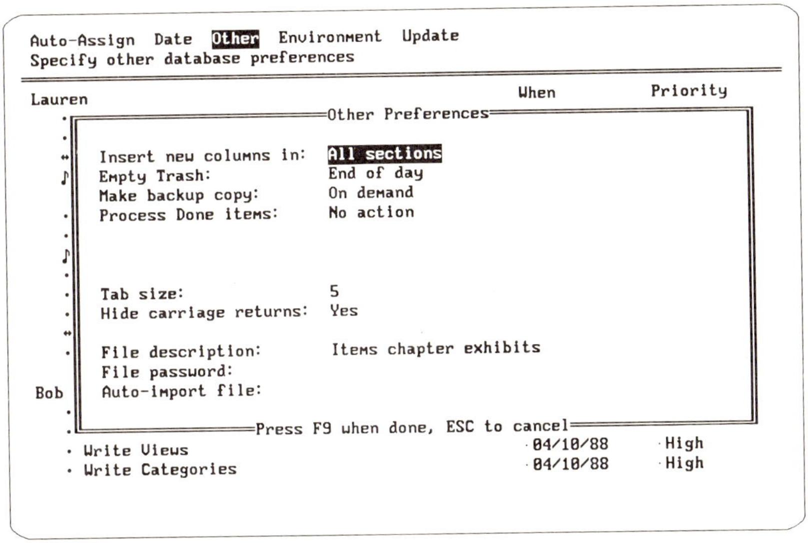

With the highlight on Untitled, begin typing the desired column heading category name or date type and, after either using automatic completion or typing the name yourself, press Enter to insert the desired category name or date type in the column heading.

Changing the Position of a Column

Having added columns, you might want to change the positions of one or more columns within a section (not all sections). To do this, highlight the heading of the column you wish to move, and press F10(Menu), C for Category, C for Column, and P for Position. Use the right and left arrows to move the column with the highlighted heading in either direction. You will see the other columns within the section adjusted to accommodate the movement of the highlighted column. Press Enter to accept the placement of the column.

Removing a Column from a View

Similarly, you might decide that you would prefer to remove a certain column from the section or the view. With the highlight on the column heading, press F10(Menu), C for Category, C for Column, and R for

Remove. You will be asked whether you want to have the column removed from all sections or just from the current one. Answer yes or no and press Enter. The column is automatically removed from the current or all sections. As an alternative, you can place the highlight on the column heading and press Del or Delete to remove the column from the view. Both of these methods result in the column being removed from the view, but nothing will happen to the categories in the Category Manager or to the items assigned to these categories. On the other hand, if you want to remove the column from the view and the database, highlight the column heading and press Alt-F4(Discard).

Other Column Functions

Changing Column Format

To change the column format, place the highlight on the column heading and press F10(Menu), C for Category, C for Column, and F for Format. Agenda displays a Column Format dialog box, prompting you for the new format and asking whether or not you want the new format to be applied globally. The available formats, which will be different depending on whether the column is a date column or a category column, can be seen by rotating through the choices using the Spacebar or by pressing F2(Edit) or Grey + as shown in Figure 5-10.

Use the arrows and F9(Accept) to identify your choice. If you choose the Category note format, an additional prompt will be added to the dialog box requesting the line number of the category note to be displayed as the column entry. After entering the line number, if called for, answer yes or no in response to the Link column globally prompt, and press F9(Accept) to format the column. If you link the column globally, any format change entered for the column in the current section will be applied to the same column in all sections. On the other hand, if your answer to the Link prompt was no, the format will only be applied to the column in the current section.

Figure 5-10.

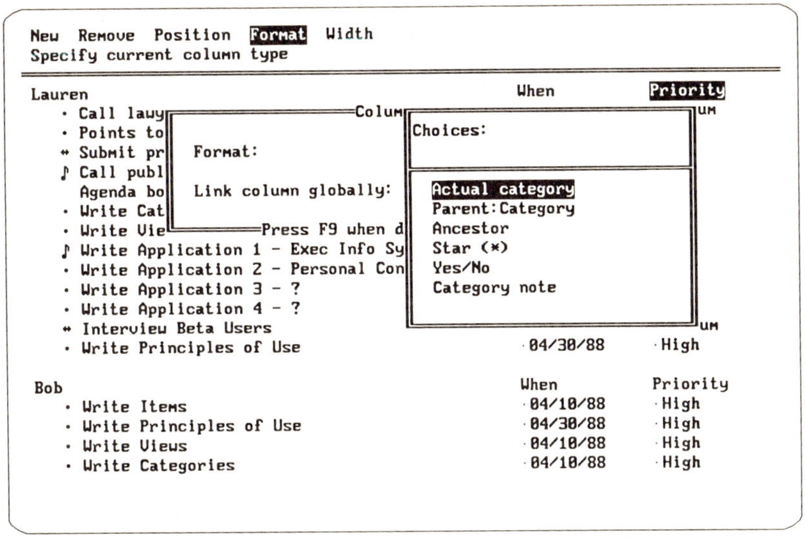

If you are using the category note line format, the text appearing in the selected line of the category note will be displayed instead of the actual category values for both the column heading and the column entries. Therefore, if you want the column heading for the parent category to describe the displayed line of the column entry child category notes, type the desired heading into the same line of the category note for the column heading parent category.

To change the width of the column with the highlight, press F10(Menu), C for Category, C for Column, and W for Width. If you now press ?, Agenda will set the column width to the minimum needed to display the column's headings and entries, including child categories of the column heading that have not yet been assigned to items. If you want to assign more space for the column than is needed by the actual or potential entries, you can enter a column width number instead of the ? and press Enter. Finally, if you do not know the specific column width you want, but you know you do not want to use the ? automatic setting, you can use the right and left arrows to adjust the width interactively. When the column width is satisfactory, press Enter to return to the item view screen.

So far, most of what we have discussed about views has been previously covered in Chapter 3 and 4 (Items and Categories). Now we are going to explore how you can customize your views by filtering their items by category assignments and dates. Filtering permits you to include or exclude items within a view based on their category assignments.

Filtering Items in a View

To filter items in a view, you need to access the View Define window by pressing F10(Menu), V for View, and D for Define, or F8(Vw Mgr) and F8(Define). Agenda will display the View Define window, which you saw earlier in Figure 5-5 when we were discussing adding and deleting categories as section headings. As you might have noticed, there are two columns to the left of the category names, one labeled S for Section and the other labeled F for Filter. To restrict items appearing in the view to only those that simultaneously are assigned to one or more categories, highlight each of those categories in turn, pressing Tab or F3(Filter) to select them. For each category you select, an up pointing arrow will appear in the F column to the left of the category name. On the other hand, if there are one or more categories whose items you wish excluded from the view, highlight them and press Tab or F3(Filter) twice to mark them with down pointing arrows in the F column. Any new items entered in the view will be automatically assigned by Agenda to the categories that define membership in the view, based on the filter settings.

The preceding discussion should seem similar to what we did in producing profile conditions for categories. In fact, one way to think about filtering by category is that we are producing a profile condition for a category, which we might call View This and which will never explicitly appear anywhere. Therefore, the same conjunction principles that we discussed concerning profile conditions apply to filters, both for inclusion and exclusion. In other words, imagine that the pattern of up and down pointing arrows is a template for the items that are present in some and absent from other categories. Unless an item is in fact present in and absent from all the specified categories, we are not interested in seeing it.

As with profile conditions, this and-ing of filters is sometimes superseded. This can happen, for example, when the categories that are being filtered are mutually exclusive, and an item cannot be simultaneously assigned to two or more filtered categories. Otherwise, the only way to get around this and-ing issue, is to set up special categories in the Category Manager for the sole purpose of specifying view preferences and then use a single filter on these special categories to include them in a view. In this appproach you can use profile actions as well as profile conditions to produce some very complex category assignments for the purposes of the view.

As you saw earlier, to clear the category filters you have assigned, all you have to do is highlight the specific categories in the View Define window and press Tab or F3(Filter) once or twice to make the arrows disappear. To remove all your filters simultaneously, press F4(ClrFltr), and all the arrows will disappear.

Date Filters

The other type of filter supported by Agenda is the date filter, which includes or excludes items based on their Entry, When, or Done dates, relative to date ranges that you supply. To enter a date filter from the item view screen, press F10(Menu), V for View, and P for Preferences; or press F8(Vw Mgr), move the highlight to the desired view name, and press F5(Prefs). Agenda displays a View Preferences dialog box as shown in Figure 5-11, where the second or middle section is labeled Date Filter. (We will return to the other sections later on in this chapter.)

Move the highlight to the *Type of date:* prompt and press either the Spacebar, or F2(Edit) or Grey + to identify the type of date with which you want to filter the items in the view. Regardless of the type of date, Agenda adds three new prompts to the Date Filter section. The first two will be the Start and End dates for the range for inclusion or exclusion. Entering these dates, which can be in numeric or word format and either absolute or relative, triggers one more prompt called *Include items:* on the last row of this Date Filter section. This last prompt asks whether the items to be included in the view fall inside or outside the range of dates beginning with the Start date and ending with the End date.

Figure 5-11.

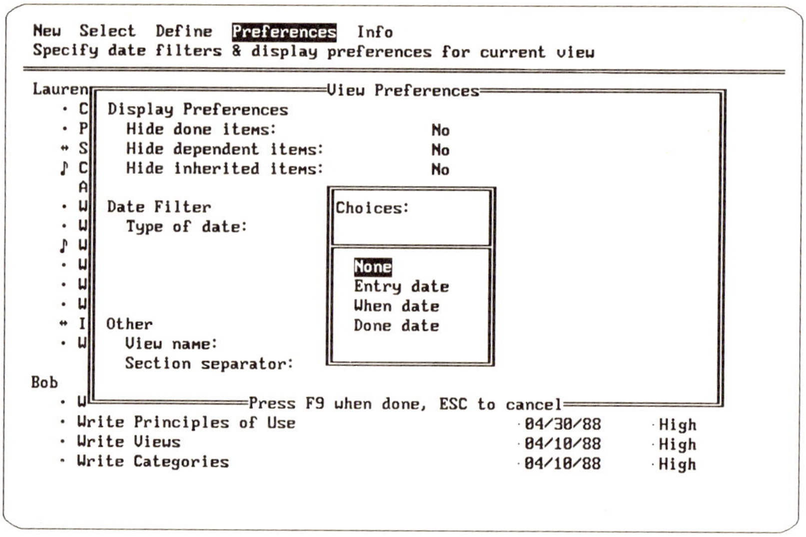

The next to the last prompt, *Display*, permits you to further refine the view by restricting the display to only those items that have date values for the type of date being filtered; or only those items that do not have date values for the type of date being filtered. The third option is to display all items, regardless of whether they are dated or undated with respect to the filter date type. Agenda always reinterprets the Start and End dates (if entered in relative terms such as next week or today) to be valid at the point in time when you are using the system, unless you precede them with a $ or absolute date indicator as in $Today. Therefore, next week will be reinterpreted each time you access the view in which it appears as a Start or End date for a date filter.

Finally, to clear a date filter, all you have to do is return to the View Preferences dialog box, move the highlight to the *Type of date:* prompt, and press the Spacebar until the option None appears, at which point the date filters will be removed.

Hiding Items

As mentioned earlier, in addition to the Date Filters options, other options for tailoring your views are available in the View Preferences dialog box, as you saw in Figure 5-11. The first section concerns hiding items that are marked as done, that is, with Done dates equal to or preceding the current date; or items that are marked as dependent upon some prerequisite items; or items that are assigned to parent categories because they have inherited this assignment through the assignment to one or more child categories. To hide items for any of these reasons, simply highlight the appropriate prompt and press the Spacebar to toggle the hiding instruction on or off, shown by Yes or No.

The last section of the View Preferences dialog box is labeled Other and provides for the editing or replacing of a view name and the inserting of a section separator (a line) between sections in the view. The view name can be typed over or edited using F2(Edit). Using F2(Edit) causes the now familiar edit functions to appear at the bottom of the screen. The section separator is simply a Yes or No toggle that you select by pressing the Spacebar when the highlight is on the prompt. Finally, pressing F9(Accept) closes the View Preferences dialog box with whatever settings you have input.

The View Manager

Although it might seem somewhat late to be bringing up the View Manager for discussion, we have already had quite a bit of exposure to it in this and earlier chapters. The purpose of this section is to review the functions available to you when you are looking at a View Manager screen.

First, to access the View Manager dialog box from an item view screen, press F8(Vw Mgr), as shown in Figure 5-12. A list of the available views will be presented, with the current view name appearing highlighted in the second line at the top of the dialog box and also highlighted at its position in the list. As you move the highlight up and down the list using the arrows, the name inserted in the second line will change. Therefore, to change views, all you have to do is move the highlight to the desired view name and press F9(Accept). Agenda will return you to the item view screen in the desired view.

Alternatively, if you wish to create a new view, press Ins or Insert to bring forth the New View dialog box as discussed at the beginning of this chapter and shown in Figure 5-3. If you wish to rename or edit the name of a highlighted view, press F2(Edit) and use the conventional edit functions to change the view name. If you wish to delete the highlighted view from the View Manager screen, press Del, Delete, F4(Delete), or Alt-F4(Delete). You are then asked if you are sure you want to delete the view. Answer yes and the view name disappears. Answer no and you are returned to the View Manager screen.

Figure 5-12.

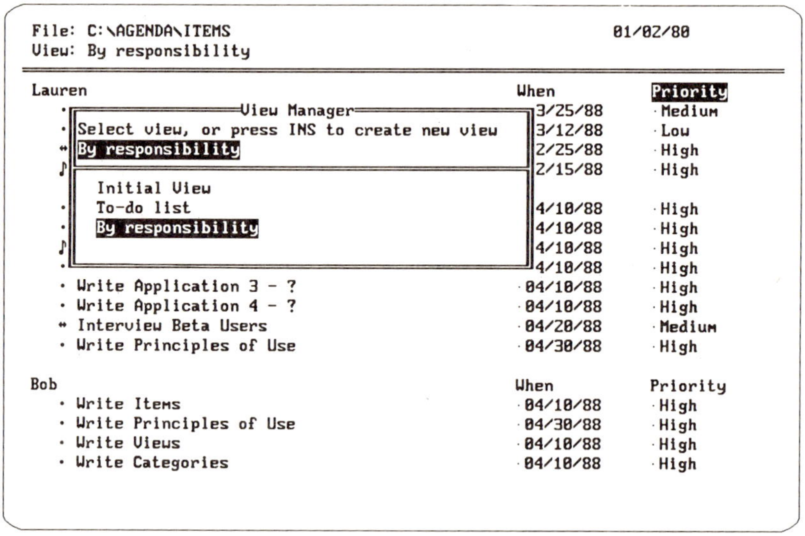

You can also move view names around the View Manager display either by sorting them in alphabetical order, or by moving them individually. To sort the view names in alphabetical order, press Alt-F9(Sort). To move a view name individually, first highlight the name and press F6(Move). Now move the highlight to the view name below which you wish to insert the view name being moved. Press Enter or F9(Accept) and the view name is moved.

Finally, you can copy a view definition to a new view so that you can adjust it without affecting the original view. To do so, highlight the view name you wish to copy and press F3(Copy). Agenda displays a New View dialog box, prompting you for the view name for the copy. Unlike the New View dialog box format we encountered earlier in the chapter, this New View dialog box does not prompt you for the initial category because it is copying it along with all the other category selections and filters to the new view name. After typing the new view name, press Enter and F9(Accept) to copy the view and leave you in the new view's item view screen.

Printing Functions

Having discussed all that there is to know about how you can customize your screen views of your database, it is appropriate to close this chapter by discussing the printing functions, that permit you to print views to paper or to files that can be manipulated by other programs. To initiate the printing function from an item view screen, press F10(Menu) and P for Print. A Print dialog box appears, as shown in Figure 5-13.

Figure 5-13.

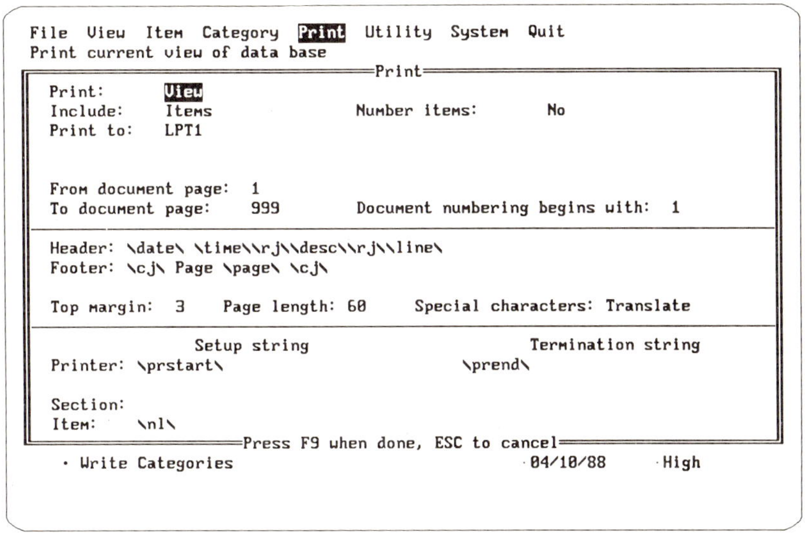

As with all the dialog boxes we have encountered, the choices for each prompt can be displayed by pressing the Spacebar to rotate through them or by pressing F2(Edit) or Grey + to see a window listing them. The first prompt asks what you want to print and includes the choices of the current item, the marked items in the view, the current section, the whole view, or an assignment profile, showing the category assignments for the highlighted item or the marked item.

The second prompt asks whether you wish to print the items, the item notes, or both. The *Number items:* prompt, which is suppressed if you are only printing item notes, requires a simple yes or no answer. Numbering the items, a feature that does not exist in the view screen, can be useful if you are discussing a printout of the items in the database. The *Print to:* prompt gives you the option of printing to any printer

(LPT1, 2, or 3), communications port (COM1 or 2) or to a file. If you select File, you must fill in both the *File:* prompt (to the right) by typing a filename, and the *Format:* prompt (below the filename) by selecting Text & printer codes or Text only. If you do not remember the filename, press Grey + to see a list of the available files, use the arrows to highlight the desired file, and F9(Accept) to return to the Print dialog box. The last prompts in this first section of the dialog box ask you for the page number range and at what number to begin numbering the pages. (These prompts will be reviewed in detail in Chapter 10.)

The next section in the Print dialog box concerns the formatting of the printed pages, including header, footer, margin, and page length settings, and whether or not to translate special characters. These fields can be edited to reflect your formatting preferences or any constraints such as the size of forms.

The last section provides for Setup and Termination strings, which need to be used with the printer or for printing items, notes, and sections. These setup strings are specific to your equipment and will also be discussed in Part IV, Chapter 10.

In addition to supporting the printing of item view screens, Agenda provides the capability of printing note screens and the Category Manager.

Whenever you are in either an item or category note screen, to access the printing features, press F10(Menu) and P for Print. Agenda displays a Print dialog box as shown in Figure 5-14.

The first prompt, *Print:*, asks whether you wish to print all the text in the note or just the text that you have previously marked using F7 (Mark) and the arrows. Choose the appropriate option by using the Spacebar, F2(Edit) or Grey + and F9(Accept), to identify your choice. The remaining prompts are identical to the item view screen printing prompts, including file or printer destination and formatting instructions. After you respond to the relevant prompts, press F9(Accept) to exit from the dialog box and begin the desired printing.

Whenever you are in the Category Manager, to access the printing features, press F10(Menu) and P for Print. Agenda displays a Print dialog box as shown in Figure 5-15.

Figure 5-14.

```
Print  Import  Export  Delete  Return
Print current note
═══════════════════════════════════Print═══════════════════════════════════
  Print:       All text in note

  Print to:    LPT1


  From document page:  1
  To document page:    999        Document numbering begins with:  1
───────────────────────────────────────────────────────────────────────────
  Header:
  Footer:

  Top margin:  3    Page length: 60     Special characters: Translate
───────────────────────────────────────────────────────────────────────────
                  Setup string                       Termination string
  Printer: \prstart\                          \prend\
  Note:    \mgn 5 74\
══════════════════════Press F9 when done, ESC to cancel═════════════════════
```

Figure 5-15.

```
Exclusive  Unindexed  Condition  Action  Print  Return
Print category hierarchy
═══════════════════════════════════Print═══════════════════════════════════
  Print:       Category hierarchy
  Include:     Categories
  Print to:    LPT1


  From document page:  1
  To document page:    999        Document numbering begins with:  1
───────────────────────────────────────────────────────────────────────────
  Header: \date\ \time\\rj\\desc\\rj\\line\
  Footer: \cj\ Page \page\ \cj\

  Top margin:  3    Page length: 60     Special characters: Translate
───────────────────────────────────────────────────────────────────────────
                  Setup string                       Termination string
  Printer: \prstart\                          \prend\

══════════════════════Press F9 when done, ESC to cancel═════════════════════
  TASKS
  "Untitled"
```

The first prompt, *Print:*, asks whether you wish to print the Category hierarchy or Database info. Choose the appropriate option by using the Spacebar, F2(Edit) or Grey + and F9(Accept), to identify your choice. If you choose category hierarchy for the first prompt, a second prompt, *Include:* appears, asking whether you wish to print categories, notes, or both. The remaining prompts are, as before, identical to the item view screen printing prompts, including file or printer destination and formatting instructions. After you respond to the relevant prompts, press F9(Accept) to exit from the dialog box and begin the desired printing.

SUMMARY

With this chapter, we have completed our review of the introductory concepts of Agenda, namely, the content or items, the structure or categories, and the display or views. This has set the stage for the applications chapters that follow.

Part III: Applications

6

Personal Contact File

One of the major responsibilities of a business person is to meet with various individuals as a representative of the company. The individuals may be co-workers, customers, vendors, competitors, press, service representatives, and so on. The quality of a business person's relationships with these individuals is crucial to his or her effectiveness on the job. Since meetings can take up much of a business person's time, the degree of productivity that he or she can achieve in these meetings also translates into greater effectiveness.

There are several ways to improve the productivity of a meeting. Among them is the ability to have the right material at hand and to have it organized in a meaningful way. Another less formal but crucial aspect of the dynamics of a meeting is the relationships among the participants. Mutual trust, respect, and a generally friendly atmosphere make people more open to new ideas. To help foster these relationships, many business people like to keep track of the backgrounds, personal preferences, idiosyncracies, and so on, of the people with whom they deal on a regular basis. For example, what their favorite restaurant is; what their children's names are; where they went to college; whether they are sports fans; and so on. Basically, any information that would permit the executive to make a meeting more pleasant, friendly, or interesting.

For a busy executive who meets many people each day, keeping track of all this information would be a job by itself, but Agenda makes it very simple. We can use Agenda to build a Personal Contact File into which all this information can be entered in anecdotal form for retrieval later. Then, before the executive meets with an individual, he or she can review the important details of the information.

HOW TO BUILD A PERSONAL CONTACT FILE

To create the Personal Contact File, first load Agenda. Then, when you are asked for the filename, type PERSONAL and press Enter. A New Database dialog box will appear. Type Personal Contact File, as shown in Figure 6-1. Next, press Enter and F9(Accept). A blank screen will appear, as in Figure 6-2.

Figure 6-1.

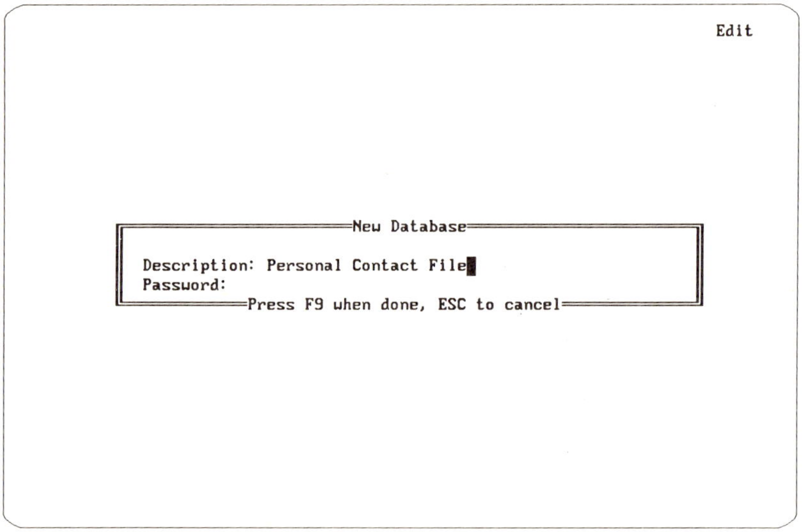

Figure 6-2.

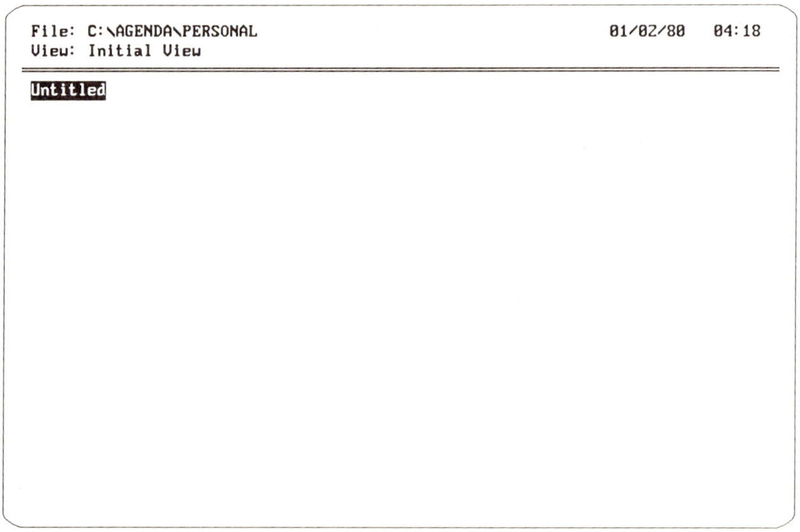

With the highlight on the word Untitled, type Meeting Anecdotes and press Enter. Press Ins to insert your first item and, when you have completed typing the item, press Enter. You can use arrows, Backspace, and Delete to correct typing errors. To type another item, press Ins and proceed as before. After completing an item, you may press Ins to insert the next item without first pressing Enter. Agenda enters the current item and moves you down to the next line where you may insert the next item. To create this illustration, type all the items shown in Figure 6-3. Remember to press Enter, not Ins, after typing the last item.

Figure 6-3.

```
File: C:\AGENDA\PERSONAL                                01/02/80   07:08
View: Initial View
========================================================================
Meeting Anecdotes
      • Met with Ken Morris 3/12/88, was his daughter's 8th b'day. Discussed
        Grayco. He's interviewing with Acme Co.
      • Spoke to Jane Hines re: Miller Plant. She thinks there will be a strike
        next month.
      • Jim Patrick is coming to town. Make dinner reservations for next friday.
        His favorite restaurant is La Cirque.
      • Sue mentioned her favorite flower is Iris. Her b'day is April 24.
      • Ken b'day is December 12.
      • Martin thinks Acme is in for big reorganization.
      • Sharon Frome signed R&D funding for Grayco.
      • Jim wrote "Rich Strike" 12 years ago. 28,000 copies sold. Out of print.
      • Sharon likes to eat at El Parador.
      • Sharon's husband works for Acme.
```

In reality this file would span years of meetings full of bits of information, but for the purposes of this example we will keep it small enough to fit on a single screen.

ADDING STRUCTURE

Now we need to add some categories so that the database can be manipulated. Press Home to go to the top of the database. To add a Who column:

Press: [F10] (MENU)
Type: C for Category
Type: C for Column
Type: N for New

You will see a New Column dialog box as shown in Figure 6-4.

Figure 6-4.

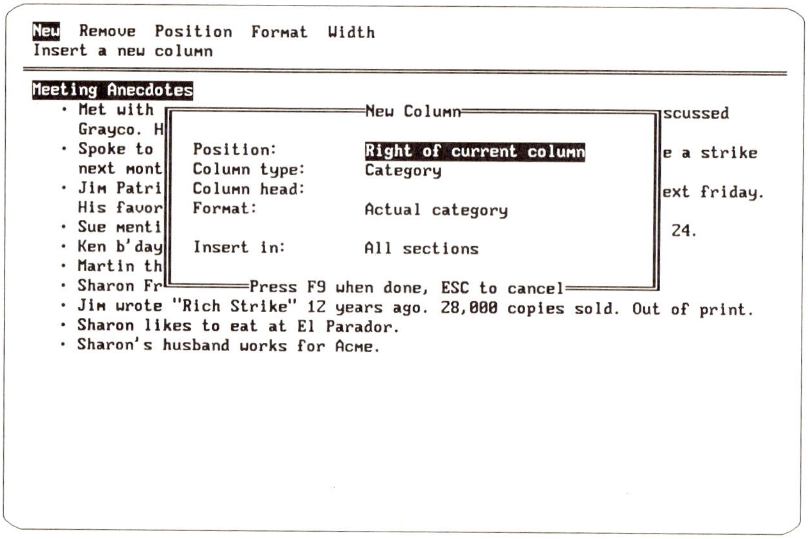

At the *Position:* and *Column type:* prompts, use the default choices. To see the other choices, use the arrows to place the highlight on the prompt line, and then either press the Spacebar to toggle through the choices or press F2(Edit) or Grey + to see a list of the choices. To the right of the *Column Head:* prompt, type Who and press Enter. At the *Format:* and *Insert in:* prompts, use the default categories again. Press F9(Accept) and a Who column will appear to the right of the items.

Placing the highlight to the right of the first item and under the Who column heading, type Ken Morris and press Enter. Use the arrows to move down to the Who column entry for the next item and type Jane Hines. As you proceed down the list of items, you need to type the name of the person referred to in the item only if that person has not been mentioned in a previous item. If the person has been mentioned in a previous item, leave the column blank.

You may have noticed that the column is not wide enough to accommodate all the names you have typed. To make all the names in the Who column visible, you can increase the column width. To do this, place the highlight on Who, and then:

Press: [F10] (MENU)
Type: C for Category
Type: C for Column
Type: W for Width
Type: 12
Press: [↵]

After entering the rest of the names in the Who column, your item view screen should look like the one shown in Figure 6-5.

Figure 6-5.

```
File: C:\AGENDA\PERSONAL                                  01/02/80   07:14
View: Initial View                                   When Date: 09/22/88
===========================================================================
Meeting Anecdotes                                              Who
  • Met with Ken Morris 3/12/88, was his daughter's 8th b'day.  ·Ken Morris
    Discussed Grayco. He's interviewing with Acme Co.
  • Spoke to Jane Hines re: Miller Plant. She thinks there will ·Jane Hines
    be a strike next month.
  • Jim Patrick is coming to town. Make dinner reservations for ·Jim Patrick
    next friday. His favorite restaurant is La Cirque.
  • Sue mentioned her favorite flower is Iris. Her b'day is     ·Sue
    April 24.
  • Ken b'day is December 12.
  » Martin thinks Acme is in for big reorganization.            ·Martin Bloom
  • Sharon Frome signed R&D funding for Grayco.                 ·Sharon Frome
  • Jim wrote "Rich Strike" 12 years ago. 28,000 copies sold.
    Out of print.
  • Sharon likes to eat at El Parador.
  • Sharon's husband works for Acme.
```

To complete the Who column, press Alt-X (with the Alt key depressed, press the X key) and Agenda completes the Who column for you.

To add a column called Topic, try a different method. Place the highlight on Who, and then:

Press: [ALT] - [R]
Type: Topic over the word Untitled
Press: [↵]

Now go down the column, entering the relevant topics. Note that the first anecdote mentions two topics, Grayco and Acme. To enter these two names:

Type: Grayco
Press: INS
Type: Acme
Press: ↵

The completed Topic column is shown in Figure 6-6.

Note in Figure 6-6 that birthdays and favorite restaurants have not been included in the Topic column. This information will be incorporated in notes attached to the entries in the Who column, which will be described later on in the application.

Figure 6-6.

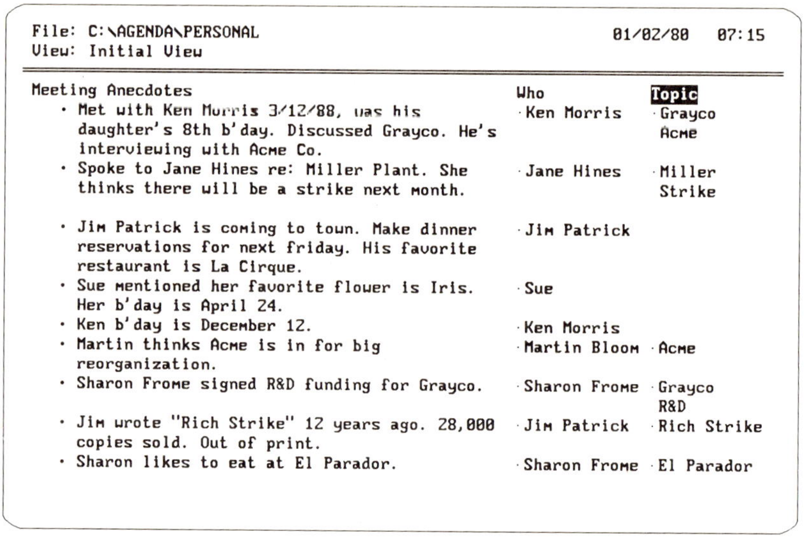

The next piece of useful information to add is the date associated with the item. To add a column to the left of the items column, place the highlight on Meeting Anecdotes and press Alt-L. If you type W, you will notice at the top of the screen that Agenda's automatic completion feature has suggested When for the column heading. Since this is what you wish to use for your column heading, press Enter to accept it. If you wanted to view the other automatic completion suggestions that Agenda tells you are available, press F8(NextSel) or Alt-N to see the other choices.

With When as your column heading, Agenda automatically fills in the column using the dates referred to in the items. Note the reference to next month in the second item. Since the item was entered in March, Agenda assigns the last day of the next month, April, as the When date. Since the third item was input on Friday, March 25, the reference to next Friday translates to an April 1 When date. If no date is mentioned in an item, Agenda leaves the When column blank. If you wish to add a date, you may insert one. For example, in the When column, next to the item "Martin thinks Acme is in for big reorganization," type, in 6 months, to the left of the item, in the form shown at the top of the screen in Figure 6-7. Agenda converts the verbal expression into a numeric date six months in the future. Note, in the last item, that Agenda can also calculate dates in the past.

Figure 6-7.

```
Date:                                                                 Edit
in six months

When          Meeting Anecdotes                       Who             Topic
 03/12/88   • Met with Ken Morris 3/12/88, was       Ken Morris      Grayco
              his daughter's 8th b'day.                               Acme
              Discussed Grayco. He's
              interviewing with Acme Co.
 04/30/88   • Spoke to Jane Hines re: Miller         Jane Hines      Miller
              Plant. She thinks there will be a                       Strike
              strike next month.
 04/01/88   • Jim Patrick is coming to town.         Jim Patrick
              Make dinner reservations for next
              friday. His favorite restaurant
              is La Cirque.
 04/24/88   • Sue mentioned her favorite flower      Sue
              is Iris. Her b'day is April 24.
 12/12/88   • Ken b'day is December 12.              Ken Morris
            » Martin thinks Acme is in for big       Martin Bloom    Acme
              reorganization.
            • Sharon Frome signed R&D funding        Sharon Frome    Grayco
              for Grayco.                                             R&D
 03/22/76   • Jim wrote "Rich Strike" 12 years       Jim Patrick     Rich Strike
```

You may want to attach some additional background data to the individuals in the Who column. To do this you can use the Note feature of Agenda. Place the highlight over the first name in the Who column and press F5(Note) to bring up the note screen as shown in Figure 6-8.

Figure 6-8.

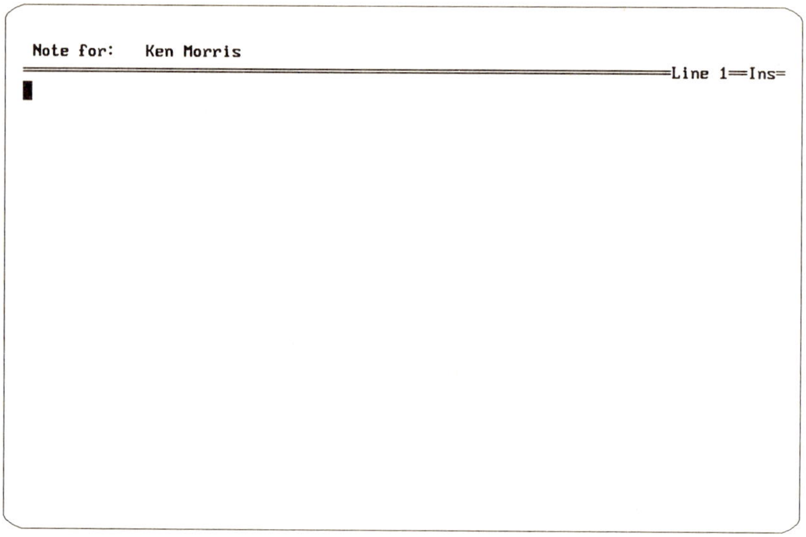

We will use this note screen to store personal data about Ken Morris. We will store the data in a consistent format for easy access later on. The form we will use is:

- Title
- Company Name
- Work Phone
- Birthday
- Favorite Restaurant
- Home Address
- Spouse
- Children
- Miscellaneous Information

These terms are labels for the corresponding lines in each note attached to a name. The terms themselves can be attached as a note to the Who category. By doing this, these terms will be displayed whenever you use the category note line format for a column, as explained in Chapter 4. Figures 6-9, 6-10, and 6-11 are note screens for Ken Morris, Jane Hines, and Jim Patrick, respectively.

Figure 6-9.

```
Note for:   Ken Morris
═══════════════════════════════════════════════════════Line 1══Ins═
UP Systems
Harcort Inc
303 287-3746
December 12
Brasserie 53rd St & Park Ave 373-8742
234 Gallagher Way, Boulder Colorado 80376 303 492-2834
Vivien
Mark & Carol-b'day 3-22
```

Figure 6-10.

```
Note for:   Jane Hines
═══════════════════════════════════════════════════════Line 1══Ins═
Plant Manager
Miller Plant
214 585-4956

Cafe de France 49 St W of 8th 392-2846
1 Waring Way, Plainview TX 39383
John
Janet & Megan
```

Figure 6-11.

```
 Note for:   Jim Patrick
══════════════════════════════════════════════════════════Line 1══Ins═
Manager Corp Human Resources
Hillerman Inc
316-276-2736
July 19
La Cirque
43 Main St  Pleasant Vally, IL
Lori
none
```

To enter the information, place the highlight over the name of the individual whose note you are going to enter. Press F5(Note) and enter the data. To return to the View, press F5(Return) again. When entering notes use the arrows, Backspace, and Delete to correct typing mistakes, just as you would when entering items.

DISPLAYING INFORMATION

To look at your data, you must create what is known as a view. Actually, when you entered the data into Agenda, you did this in a view that Agenda refers to as the Initial View. To fill a specific information need, you must create another view.

Let's say that you are having a meeting with Ken Morris and you want all the information related to him as well as all the information related to Acme Company because he is interviewing with them. What you want to do is to link information about Acme to Ken Morris. This can be done with a profile condition. To do this, place the highlight on Ken Morris in the Who column, and then:

Press: F9 (CAT MGR)
Press: F10 (MENU)
Type: C for Condition
Type: P for Profile
Move to: Acme
Press: F3 (INCLCAT)
Press: F9 (ACCEPT)

You will see the profile condition attached to Ken Morris as in Figure 6-12.

Figure 6-12.

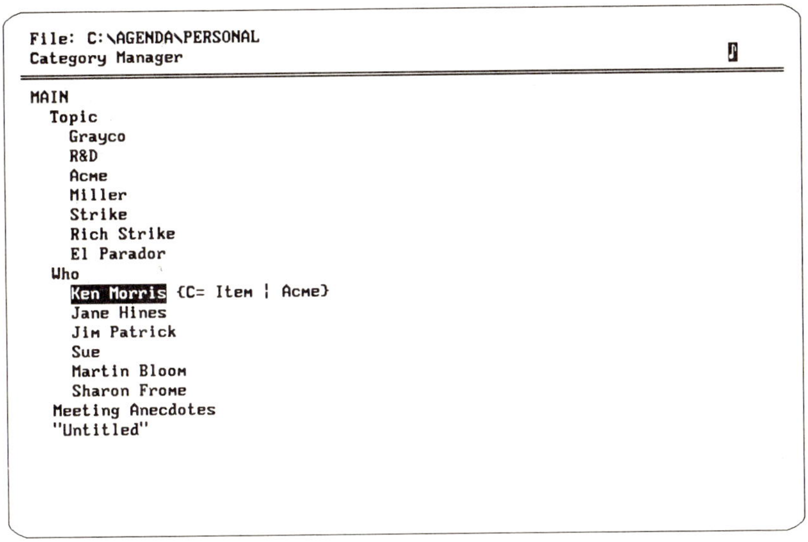

Having pressed F9(To View) to return to the view, create a new view consisting of Ken Morris. Because of the profile condition you have just attached to his name, this new view will include all the items about Acme Company as well. Press F8(Vw Mgr) and Ins to create a new view. Fill out the New View dialog box, as shown in Figure 6-13. Press F9(Accept) to see the view as it appears in Figure 6-14.

Figure 6-13.

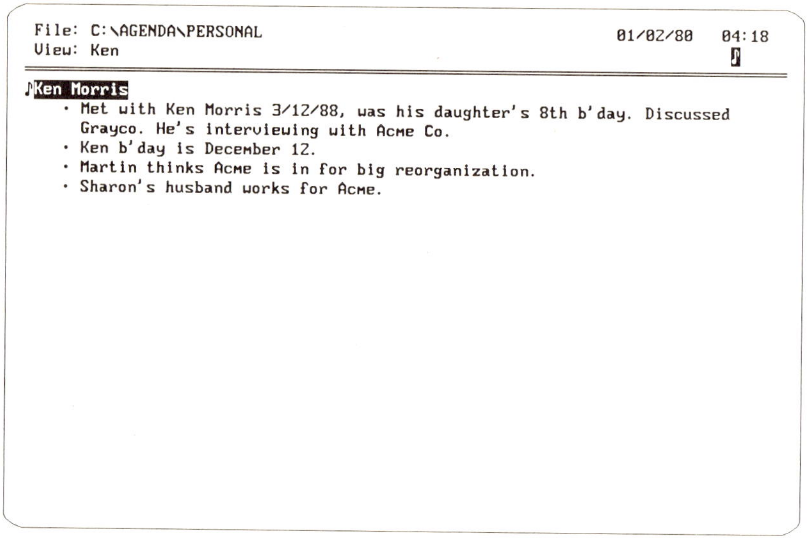

Figure 6 14.

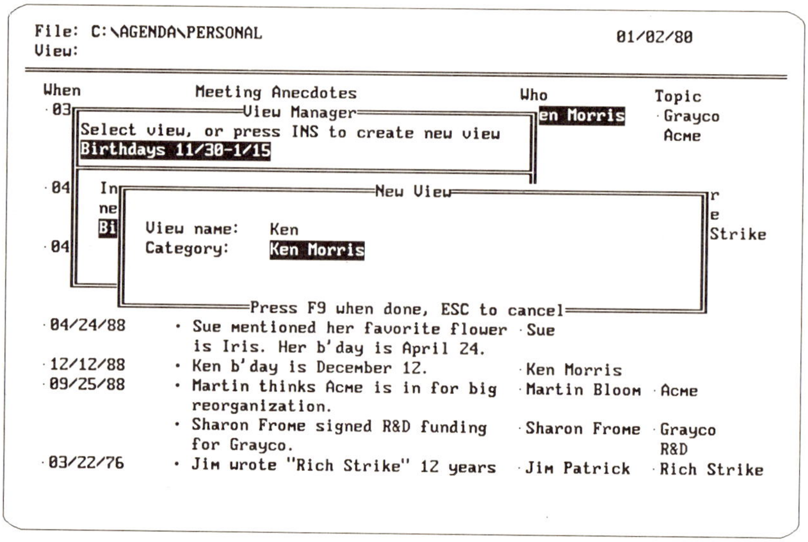

You may include the information about Ken that is stored in his note when you print the view by pressing F10(Menu) and P for Print. Move the highlight to the *Include:* prompt and change Items to Items & Notes by pressing the Spacebar once. Your screen will appear as shown in Figure 6-15. Press F9(Accept) and Agenda will print a report, as shown in Figure 6-16.

Figure 6-15.

```
File  View  Item  Category  Print  Utility  System  Quit
Print current view of data base
═══════════════════════════════Print═══════════════════════════════
 Print:       View
 Include:     Items & notes       Number items:        No
 Print to:    LPT1


 From document page:  1
 To document page:    999       Document numbering begins with:  1
───────────────────────────────────────────────────────────────────
 Header: \date\ \time\\rj\\desc\\rj\\line\
 Footer: \cj\ Page \page\ \cj\

 Top margin:  3    Page length: 60     Special characters: Translate
───────────────────────────────────────────────────────────────────
                 Setup string                    Termination string
 Printer:  \prstart\                       \prend\
 Note:     \mgn 10 69\
 Section:
 Item:     \nl\
══════════════════Press F9 when done, ESC to cancel═════════════════
```

Figure 6-16.

```
01/02/80 07:22                                    Personal Contact File
-----------------------------------------------------------------------
.Ken Morris
         VP Systems
         Harcort Inc
         303 287-3746
         December 12
         Brasserie 53rd & Park Ave 373-8742
         234 Gallagher Way, Boulder Colorado 80376 303 492-2834
         Vivien
         Mark & Carol-b'day 3-22




    . Met with Ken Morris 3/12/88, was his daughter's 8th b'day. Discussed
      Grayco. He's interviewing with Acme Co.

    . Ken b'day is December 12.

    . Martin thinks Acme is in for big reorganization.

    . Sharon's husband works for Acme.
```

SUGGESTIONS FOR OTHER REFINEMENTS

Over time your database will grow. There will be many entries about a given person, and before you went to meet an individual, you would find that looking through years of items on that individual was very cumbersome. To solve this problem, you could create a view of the Meeting Anecdotes about a specific individual and then sort the items by Entry date, the date on which the item was entered into the database, which Agenda records automatically. This permits you to look at your items according to their chronology.

Having added a column called Entry Date, to sort the view by Entry date:

Press: F10 (MENU)
Type: C for Category
Type: S for Section
Type: S for Sort

Then fill out the Sort dialog box, as shown in Figure 6-17. Change the *Sort on:* prompt for the Primary Sort to Entry Date, for the *Order:* prompt, choose Descending and press F9(Accept). Your items, which will now be listed from the most recent to the most dated, can be read as far back in time as you feel is appropriate.

Figure 6-17.

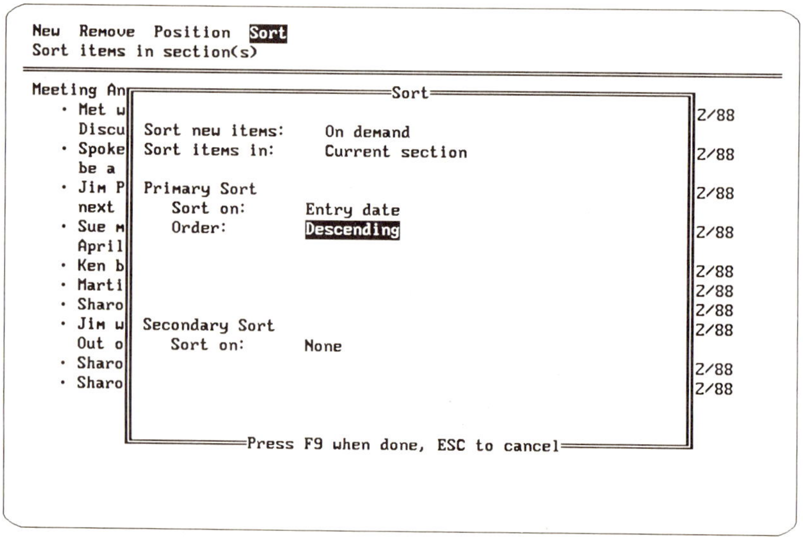

7

Quotation Reference

Public speakers frequently incorporate quotations from well-known individuals in their speeches. Most source materials are simple listings of these quotes organized by author or by topic, such as the following selected from

Peter Drucker

- My greatest strength as a consultant is to be ignorant and ask a few questions.
- The main impact of the computer has been the provision of unlimited jobs for clerks.

Henry Ford

- History is bunk!
- It is all one to me if a man comes from Sing Sing or Harvard. We hire a man, not his history.

Sidney Harris

- The time to relax is when you don't have time for it.
- Nobody can be so amusingly arrogant as a young man who has just discovered an old idea and thinks it is his own.
- The real danger is not that computers will begin to think like men, but that men will begin to think like computers.

Will Rogers

- We can't all be heroes because someone has to sit on the curb and clap as they go by.

- We don't know what we want, but we are ready to bite somebody to get it.
- Let advertisers spend the same amount of money improving their product that they do on advertising and they wouldn't have to advertise it.
- Even if you're on the right track, you'll get run over if you just sit there.

Generally, these listings have indexes in which you can look up each quote to determine its suitability for a particular speech, a particularly inefficient process. These guides are further limited in that you cannot look for a quote by more than one topic at a time. In addition, quotes often have meanings or associations for you that are not necessarily reflected in the reference guide you are using. Finally, you cannot easily add your own quotes to the guide book for future reference.

Agenda solves these problems by making it possible for you to store quotes as items, which can be organized both manually and automatically by topic, author, and so on, and which can be retrieved by any one or more categories or attributes. In addition, you can add new quotes to the database as you come across them, mark quotes with dates showing when they were last used, and even include the name of the speech and where it was given as a note for the quote.

HOW TO BUILD AN AUTOMATED QUOTATION REFERENCE

To create the Quotation Reference, load Agenda and, when you are asked for a filename, type QUOTES. A New Database dialog box will appear. Type Quotation Reference in response to the *Description:* prompt. Press Enter, skip the *Password:* prompt, and press F9(Accept). A blank screen will appear, with the view name Initial view.

Press F8(Vw Mgr) and F2(Edit) to retype the view name as By author. You can use the arrows, Backspace, and Delete to correct typing errors. Press Enter twice and you will be returned to the item view screen with the highlight on the Untitled section heading. Type Peter Drucker, press Enter, and the section heading will be changed. Press Ins to insert your first quote from those listed at the beginning of the chapter. When you have typed the quote, press Enter. Once again, you can use the arrows, Backspace, and Delete to correct typing errors.

To type Peter Drucker's second quote, press Ins and proceed as before. After entering the second quote, the item view screen should look like the one shown in Figure 7-1.

Figure 7-1.

```
File: C:\AGENDA\QUOTES                                      01/02/80   07:32
View: By author
================================================================================
Peter Drucker
     • My greatest strength as a consultant is to be ignorant and ask a few
       questions.
     • The main impact of the computer has been the provision of unlimited jobs
       for clerks.
```

To begin a new section with the name of another author,

Press: F10 (MENU)
Type: C for Category
Type: S for Section
Type: N for New

Agenda displays a New Section dialog box, which you should fill out as shown in Figure 7-2.

Press F9(Accept) to close the dialog box and insert the new section heading for Henry Ford's quotations. Now press Ins to insert a quotation and type the first of Henry Ford's two quotations. Press Enter and Ins again and enter the second quotation.

Repeat this process for the Sidney Harris and Will Rogers sections. The completed Quotation Reference is shown in Figure 7-3.

Figure 7-2.

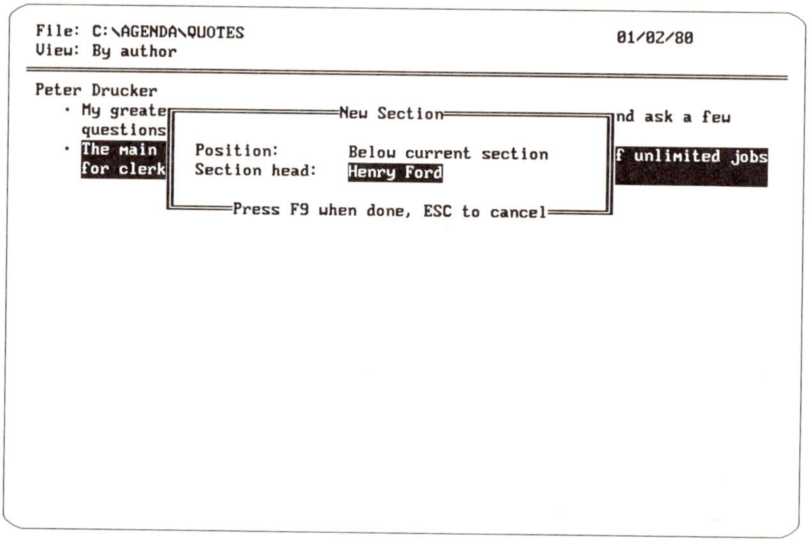

Figure 7-3.

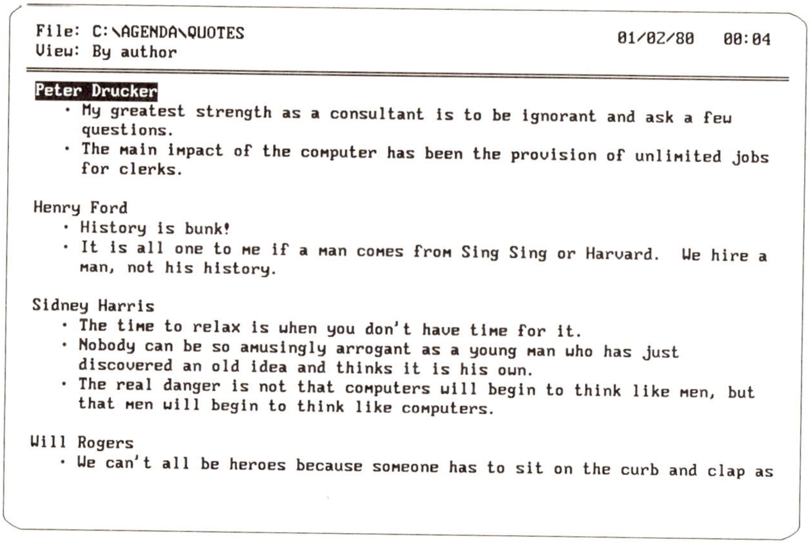

In reality, you would probably develop your file from your own source materials and memory, which would no doubt produce a very lengthy collection of quotes. We have tried to keep this example short enough so that most of the work can be demonstrated in the space of one screen.

ADDING STRUCTURE

Now, to develop the topics for classifying these quotes, let's work on the Category Manager. Press F9(Cat Mgr) and move the highlight to Peter Drucker. Press F2(Edit) and enclose his name in double quotes in order to suppress any automatic matching of Peter, Drucker, or both to item text. Do the same for Henry Ford, Sidney Harris, and Will Rogers.

Now we should insert a parent category, Authors, above the individual author names so that we can display quotes by the category Authors, without having to identify each and every author:

Move to: Peter Drucker
Press: [ALT]-[U]
Type: Authors
Press: [↵]
Move to: Peter Drucker
Press: [F8] (DEM →)

For each of the three other authors, highlight their names and press F8(Dem →) to make each of them a child category of Authors.

We should make Authors a mutually exclusive category by highlighting Authors and pressing F10(Menu) and E for Exclusive. This will ensure that a quote will not be assigned to more than one author.

With Authors still highlighted, press Alt-D to insert a new Category below and at the same level as Authors, type Topics, and press Enter. We can now add specific topics to this parent category for use in classifying the quotes:

Press: [INS]
Type: Advertising
Press: [↵]
Press: [F8] (DEM →)
Press: [INS]
Type: Banking
Press: [↵]
Press: [INS]

Type:	Computer
Press:	↵
Press:	INS
Type:	Consulting
Press:	↵
Press:	INS
Type:	Employment
Press:	↵
Press:	INS
Type:	Heroes
Press:	↵
Press:	INS
Type:	History
Press:	↵
Press:	INS
Type:	Relaxation
Press:	↵
Press	INS
Type:	Thought
Press:	↵
Press:	INS
Type:	Time
Press:	↵

The Category Manager should appear as shown in Figure 7-4. Note the bracketing to the left of the authors' names, indicating the mutual exclusivity of the category Authors.

Now let's return to the view by pressing F9(To View) and insert a new column for Topics to the right of the quotes. Place the highlight on the Peter Drucker section heading, and then:

Press:	F10 (MENU)
Type:	C for Category
Type:	C for Column
Type:	N for New

You will see a New Column dialog box, which you should fill out as shown in Figure 7-5.

Figure 7-4.

```
File: C:\AGENDA\QUOTES
Category Manager
════════════════════════════════════════════════════════════════
MAIN
  Quotes
  Authors
   ┌"Peter Drucker"
   ├"Henry Ford"
   ├"Sidney Harris"
   └"Will Rogers"
  Topics
    Advertising
    Banking
    Computers
    Consulting
    Employment
    Heroes
    History
    Relaxation
    Thought
    Time
```

Figure 7-5.

```
File: C:\AGENDA\QUOTES                                        01/02/88
View: By author
════════════════════════════════════════════════════════════════════
Peter Drucker
   • My greate╔═════════════════New Column══════════════════╗k a few
     questions║                                             ║
   • The main ║ Position:         Right of current column   ║imited jobs
     for clerk║ Column type:      Category                  ║
              ║ Column head:      Topics                    ║
Henry Ford    ║ Format:           Actual category           ║
   • History i║                                             ║
   • It is all║ Insert in:        All sections              ║  We hire a
     man, not ║                                             ║
              ╚═══════Press F9 when done, ESC to cancel═════╝
Sidney Harris
   • The time to relax is when you don't have time for it.
   • Nobody can be so amusingly arrogant as a young man who has just
     discovered an old idea and thinks it is his own.
   • The real danger is not that computers will begin to think like men, but
     that men will begin to think like computers.

Will Rogers
   • We can't all be heroes because someone has to sit on the curb and clap as
```

Press F9(Accept) to exit the dialog box and return to the item view screen, where you will see the Topics column heading without any column entries. To automatically assign the quotes to the topics, press Alt-X (with the Alt key depressed, press the X key). This will auto-assign all the items to the matching topics, based on the item text.

You will see an Execute window continuously reporting the percentage completion status of the auto-assignment. The item view will now appear as shown in Figure 7-6.

Figure 7-6.

```
File: C:\AGENDA\QUOTES                                       01/02/80   07:44
View: By author
=============================================================================
Peter Drucker                                                   Topics
   · My greatest strength as a consultant is to be ignorant and
     ask a few questions.
   · The main impact of the computer has been the provision of  ·Computers
     unlimited jobs for clerks.

Henry Ford                                                      Topics
   · History is bunk!                                           ·History
   · It is all one to me if a man comes from Sing Sing or       ·History
     Harvard.  We hire a man, not his history.

Sidney Harris                                                   Topics
   · The time to relax is when you don't have time for it.      ·Time
   · Nobody can be so amusingly arrogant as a young man who has
     just discovered an old idea and thinks it is his own.
   · The real danger is not that computers will begin to think  ·Computers
     like men, but that men will begin to think like computers.

Will Rogers                                                     Topics
   · We can't all be heroes because someone has to sit on the   ·Heroes
```

REFINING STRUCTURE

If you look closely you will see that Drucker's first quote, "My greatest strength as a consultant . . ." is not categorized under consulting. Therefore, it is time to start setting up text conditions or synonym-like words and phrases to categorize items that deal with consulting, even though they do not contain the word consulting. To do this, press F9(Cat Mgr), which takes you to the Category Manager. Move the highlight to Consulting, and then:

Press: F2 (Edit)
Press: END
Type: ;
Type: Consultant
Press: ↵

Now move the highlight to Employment and repeat the preceding steps to add the synonym Jobs. Finally, move the highlight to Thought and repeat the same steps to add the synonym Thinking. The Category Manager should appear as shown in Figure 7-7.

Figure 7-7.

```
File: C:\AGENDA\QUOTES
Category Manager
═══════════════════════════════════════════════
MAIN
  Quotes
  Authors
   ┌"Peter Drucker"
   ├"Henry Ford"
   ├"Sidney Harris"
   └"Will Rogers"
  Topics
    Advertising
    Banking
    Computers
    Consulting;Consultant
    Employment;Jobs
    Heroes
    History
    Relaxation
    Thought;Thinking
    Time
```

Now press F9(To View) to return to the item view, and press Alt-X again to auto-assign the items to the categories with their synonyms. Watch carefully and you will see Drucker's first quote assigned to Consulting, his second quote assigned to Employment, and so on, as shown in Figure 7-8.

Press F9(Cat Mgr) to return to the Category Manager so we can do some more work on refining our categories. Some of the topics have synonyms, which we have added as text conditions already. In other cases, although the categories may be strongly related to each other, they should still be identified separately so that they can appear as section headings, column headings, and column entries. A synonym as a text condition cannot appear this way; it is only useful in assigning an item to a category. Agenda provides profile conditions and profile actions, which permit you to categorize items in some categories based on their presence or absence in other categories.

Figure 7-8.

```
File: C:\AGENDA\QUOTES                                    01/02/80   07:46
View: By author
==========================================================================
Peter Drucker                                                 Topics
   • My greatest strength as a consultant is to be ignorant and ·Consulting
     ask a few questions.
   • The main impact of the computer has been the provision of  ·Computers
     unlimited jobs for clerks.                                  Employment

Henry Ford                                                    Topics
   • History is bunk!                                          ·History
   • It is all one to me if a man comes from Sing Sing or      ·History
     Harvard.  We hire a man, not his history.

Sidney Harris                                                 Topics
   • The time to relax is when you don't have time for it.     ·Time
   • Nobody can be so amusingly arrogant as a young man who has ·Thought
     just discovered an old idea and thinks it is his own.
   • The real danger is not that computers will begin to think ·Computers
     like men, but that men will begin to think like computers.  Thought

Will Rogers                                                   Topics
   • We can't all be heroes because someone has to sit on the  ·Heroes
```

For example, let us add the category Business as a new category between Banking and Computers. Business is a term that might appear in an item, and therefore it needs to be a separate category. However, references to Employment, which is already in a separate category, also have to do with Business, and we do not want to have to assign items to both Employment and Business. Therefore, we want to set up a profile action for the Employment category that will assign items to Business whenever they are assigned to Employment.

Place the highlight on Banking, and then:

Press:	INS
Type:	Business
Press:	↵
Move to:	Employment
Press:	F10 (MENU)
Press:	A for Action
Press:	P for Profile

You will see a Profile Action window with a listing of the Category Manager. Use the arrows to move the highlight to Business and press F3 (InclCat) or Tab to include Business in the Profile Action for Employment. An arrow pointing up appears to the left of the Business category name to indicate that any item assigned to Employment will also be assigned to Business. In the second line of the window, the Profile Action, as it appears in the Category Manager, will be displayed, as shown in Figure 7-9.

Figure 7-9.

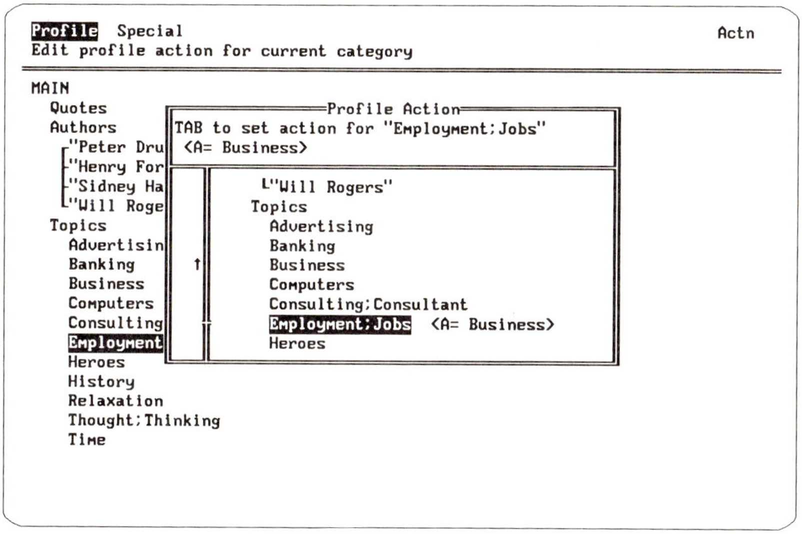

Press F9(Accept) to close the Profile Action window, and you will be returned to the Category Manager where the Business profile action will have been attached to the Employment category. Now you will see a Category Manager that should look like the one shown in Figure 7-10.

Another approach to linking categories would have been to attach a profile condition to the Business category and specify the other categories to which an item must be assigned (or not assigned) in order for it to be categorized as a Business item, too. If Employment were the only category that would trigger Business, this approach would work in the same way as the preceding profile action. However, if more than one category could trigger Business, a profile condition is not recommended because it assumes that all the categories that are marked in the profile condition must be present simultaneously for the assignment to take place. It is too strong a requirement to say that an item must belong to Employment, Advertising, Banking, and so on in order for it to be classified as being a Business item. Sometimes and-ing categories is appropriate, and profile conditions are the preferred method for dealing with them. Other times, or-ing categories is desired, and profile actions are the preferred method.

Figure 7-10.

```
File: C:\AGENDA\QUOTES
Category Manager
════════════════════════════════════════════════
MAIN
  Quotes
  Authors
   ┌"Peter Drucker"
   ├"Henry Ford"
   ├"Sidney Harris"
   └"Will Rogers"
  Topics
    Advertising
    Banking
    Business
    Computers
    Consulting;Consultant
    Employment;Jobs  <A= Business>
    Heroes
    History
    Relaxation
    Thought;Thinking
    Time
```

Now let us return to the item view screen:

Press: F9 (TO VIEW)
Press: F10 (MENU)
Type: U for Utility
Type: E for Execute

An Execute dialog box will be displayed. Move the highlight to the *Perform actions:* prompt, and press the Spacebar to select For new & old assignments, as shown in Figure 7-11.

Now press F9(Accept) to execute the profile action and to see what has happened to the classification of quotes. The item view screen should look like the one shown in Figure 7-12.

Figure 7-11.

```
Execute  Show  Questions  Trash  Compress  Preferences
Evaluate conditions/actions
================================================================================
Peter Drucker                                                         Topics
    · My greatest╔═══════════════════Execute══════════════════════╗Consulting
      ask a few q║                                                ║
    » The main im║ Evaluate conditions for:     All items         ║Computers
      unlimited j║ Categories to check:         Entire hierarchy  ║Employment
                 ║                                                ║
Henry Ford       ║                                                ║opics
    · History is ║ Perform actions:  For new & old assignments    ║History
    · It is all o║                                                ║History
      Harvard.  W╚══════Press F9 when done, ESC to cancel═════════╝

Sidney Harris                                                         Topics
    · The time to relax is when you don't have time for it.          ·Time
    · Nobody can be so amusingly arrogant as a young man who has     ·Thought
      just discovered an old idea and thinks it is his own.
    · The real danger is not that computers will begin to think      ·Computers
      like men, but that men will begin to think like computers.      Thought

Will Rogers                                                           Topics
    · We can't all be heroes because someone has to sit on the       ·Heroes
```

Figure 7-12.

```
File: C:\AGENDA\QUOTES                                        01/02/80   08:03
View: By author
================================================================================
Peter Drucker                                                         Topics
    · My greatest strength as a consultant is to be ignorant and     ·Consulting
      ask a few questions.
    » The main impact of the computer has been the provision of      »Computers
      unlimited jobs for clerks.                                     »Employment
                                                                     »Business

Henry Ford                                                            Topics
    · History is bunk!                                               ·History
    · It is all one to me if a man comes from Sing Sing or           ·History
      Harvard.  We hire a man, not his history.

Sidney Harris                                                         Topics
    · The time to relax is when you don't have time for it.          ·Time
    · Nobody can be so amusingly arrogant as a young man who has     ·Thought
      just discovered an old idea and thinks it is his own.
    · The real danger is not that computers will begin to think      ·Computers
      like men, but that men will begin to think like computers.      Thought

Will Rogers                                                           Topics
```

In addition to all this auto-categorizing, we can manually assign items to categories. For example, Sidney Harris' quote about young men with old ideas reminds us of consultants we have known, so let's assign that quote to consulting. First highlight the quote, then move right to the

Topics column over the category Thought, press Ins, and start typing the word Consulting. Agenda will beep at you to indicate that it has begun matching your typing to the stored category names and is ready to propose an automatic completion of the name Consulting for you to consider. You can accept this suggestion by pressing Enter, without having to complete your typing, and Agenda will insert Consulting directly below Thought.

Let's now add Intelligence as a category by assigning Drucker's "My greatest strength . . ." quote. Since Intelligence does not exist as a category, there will be no auto-completion suggestions. Locate Drucker's quote and move the highlight right over the Topics column heading. Press Insert, type Intelligence and press Enter. Agenda inserts Intelligence directly below Topics. Then do the same with the Harris quote about computers, assigning it to Intelligence. Because Intelligence has been added as a category, Agenda will propose an automatic completion as you type. At this point, your item view screen should look like the one shown in Figure 7-13.

Figure 7-13.

```
File: C:\AGENDA\QUOTES                                     01/02/80   08:05
View: By author
===========================================================================
Peter Drucker                                                 Topics
    • My greatest strength as a consultant is to be ignorant and  ·Intelligence
      ask a few questions.                                     Consulting
    • The main impact of the computer has been the provision of  ·Computers
      unlimited jobs for clerks.                               Employment
                                                               Business

Henry Ford                                                    Topics
    • History is bunk!                                        ·History
    • It is all one to me if a man comes from Sing Sing or    ·History
      Harvard.  We hire a man, not his history.

Sidney Harris                                                 Topics
    • The time to relax is when you don't have time for it.   ·Time
    • Nobody can be so amusingly arrogant as a young man who has ·Thought
      just discovered an old idea and thinks it is his own.    Consulting
    • The real danger is not that computers will begin to think ·Intelligence
      like men, but that men will begin to think like computers.  Thought
                                                               Computers
```

DISPLAYING INFORMATION

Now that we have assembled our content or items (quotes) and their structure or categories (topics and authors), it is time to start creating some views.

Suppose we have a speech coming up and we want to find some possible quotes to include on the topic of computers. We define a view that deals with computers by pressing F8(Vw Mgr), pressing Ins, and filling in the New View dialog box, as shown in Figure 7-14. Press F9(Accept) to see the result, as shown in Figure 7-15.

Figure 7-14.

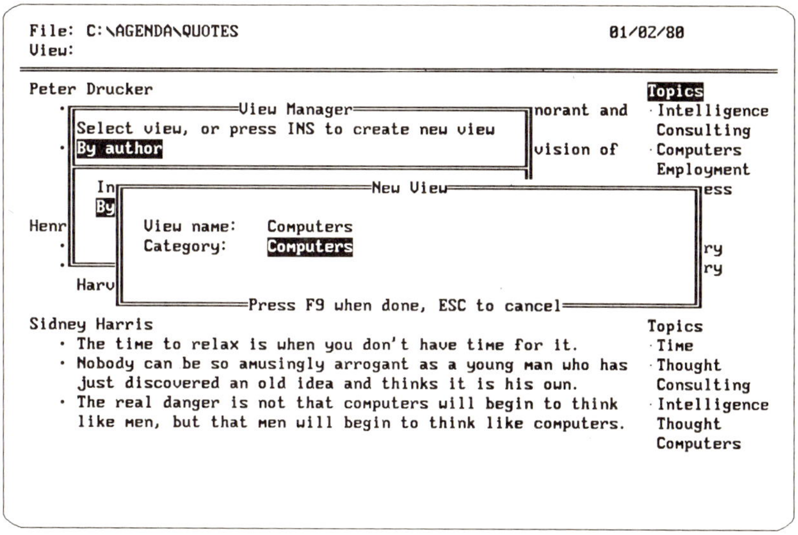

Figure 7-15.

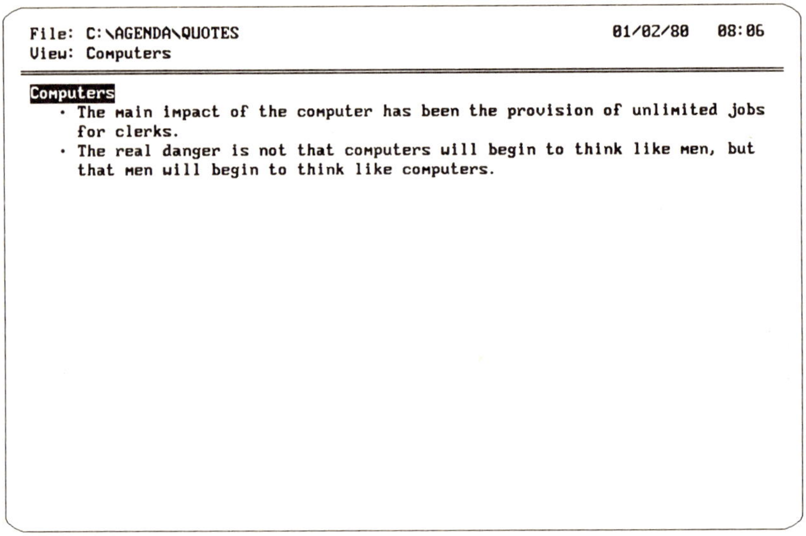

To add the Author column, place the highlight on Computers, and then:

Press: ALT - R
Type: Authors over Untitled
Press: F10 (MENU)
Type: C for Category
Type: C for Column
Type: W for Width
Press: → to widen the column until you can see the entire name
Press: ↵

The screen will appear as in Figure 7-16.

Figure 7-16.

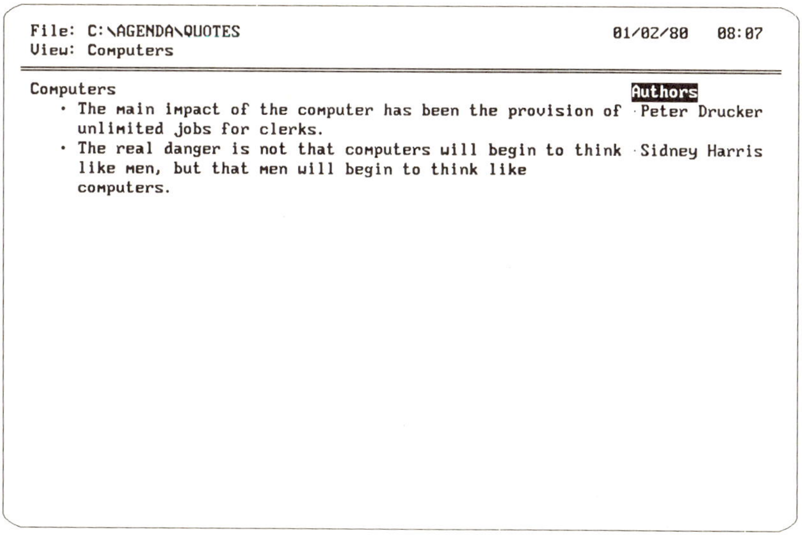

To identify quotes that we have used recently, so that we don't embarrass ourselves by using them again, we employ the Done feature in Agenda. Assume that we have used the first of the two computer quotes and we now want to mark it as done. Move the highlight over the first quote, press F4(Done), and the screen should appear as shown in Figure 7-17, with a double exclamation point (!!) to the left of the quote to indicate its "done" status.

Figure 7-17.

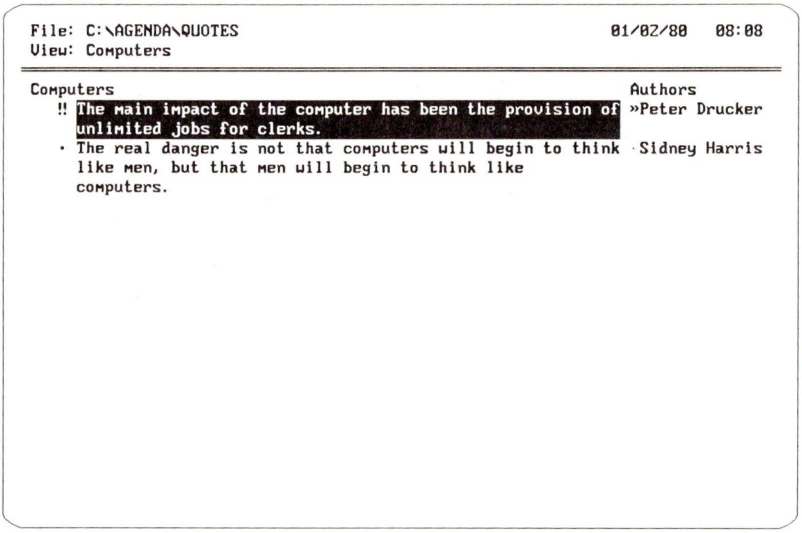

To hide the "done" items in subsequent references to this view, press F10(Menu), V for View, and P for Preferences, and then change the *Hide done items:* prompt to Yes as shown in Figure 7-18. Press F9 (Accept) and the first item, the one marked done, is removed from the view.

Figure 7-18.

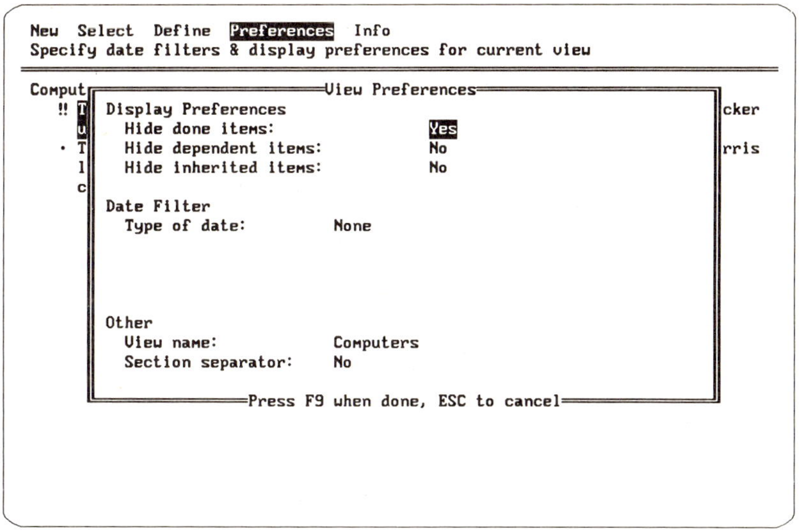

SUGGESTIONS FOR OTHER REFINEMENTS

Add some more actions for Banking and Advertising that will identify them with Business, just as we did with Employment.

Manually assign Henry Ford's "It is all one . . ." quote to Employment and Will Rogers' "We don't know . . ." quote to Ambition.

8

Project Evaluation

Everyone has to make decisions. Sometimes the alternatives are easily ranked from most to least desirable. For example, it is easy to decide which savings account to use if you base your decision simply on who is paying the highest interest on savings. However, multiple criteria or considerations usually influence decisions and it is not at all obvious how to rank the alternatives being considered. For example, if you really wanted to reap the best returns, you would probably not put your money in a regular savings account. You might consider CDs, money market funds, short-term bond funds, and other financial instruments as higher paying alternatives. Unfortunately, these alternatives involve other issues beyond the simple interest rate on your investment. You now need to consider risk and availability of your funds, neither of which are issues when you put your money in a savings account. Now that each alternative has three values—interest rate, risk, and availability—ranking them is more complicated than when you were dealing with just the single value of interest rate.

Multidimensional decision making is the rule rather than the exception, and Agenda can be an extraordinarily powerful tool for helping you evaluate alternatives when you have many dimensions to consider. One example of Agenda at work in such a setting involves the decisions that corporations have to make concerning which research and development (R&D) projects to fund.

Many corporations invest in research and development in order to experiment with products and processes that may improve or replace their current products and processes. Since these funds are typically limited, there are only so many projects that a corporation can afford to support in any one year. They may invite proposals from the employees as a means of generating a pool of proposals from which they can select the most promising. When the proposals come in, the company's management must evaluate the proposals in a number of different ways to determine which ones to fund. Ultimately, this leads to boiling the many dimensions down to a single dimension, namely, to fund or not to fund.

With Agenda, this process can be improved, both in form and content. As requests for funding are received, they are entered into Agenda as items with notes. Simple categorizations such as what area of interest would be served by the project, which division is submitting the proposal, how much money is being asked for, and so on can be done immediately. Having entered all the projects, we can begin looking for other ways to compare and contrast projects. For example, does this project from Division A duplicate that project from Division B? Should we ask the divisions involved to join forces and do the project only once? Although Agenda cannot ask those questions, these and other questions are easier to think about when you can look at or "view" the projects in many different ways. Agenda contributes by making this process of developing structure more efficient and effective.

HOW TO BUILD AN R&D PROJECT EVALUATION SYSTEM

Let's begin building an R&D project evaluation system by supposing that we received requests for funding for the twelve projects listed below:

- Umbrella voice technology fund
- Basic Research in Recognition
- Experiment with CASE tool
- Integrated Operating System
- Financial Planning Pilot
- Processing technologies
- Auditor's Expert System
- New Workstation
- AI/Image project
- Clerical Expert System
- Pattern recognition
- Evaluate connection machines

Our first step is to enter the projects in Agenda by loading the program and providing the filename R&D when prompted. In response to the New Database dialog box, enter a description of the file, for example, **1988 R&D Project Evaluations**, and a password to keep this material from prying eyes. After you press Enter, a blank screen appears, with an initial section labeled Untitled. Type **Projects** over the section heading and press Enter. Next press Ins or Insert to begin entering items or projects.

Type **Umbrella voice technology fund**, as the first project's name and press Ins or Insert. This enters the project and moves the highlight to the next item position on the screen, waiting for a new project name. You can use the arrows, Backspace, and Del or Delete to correct typing errors. When you finish typing each project name, press Ins or Insert to enter the project and move to the next. Continue entering projects until you come to the last one. After typing **Evaluate connection machines**, press Enter instead of Ins or Insert so that the last project name is entered but you are not prompted for another. After entering the twelve projects, the item view screen should look like the one shown in Figure 8-1.

Figure 8-1.

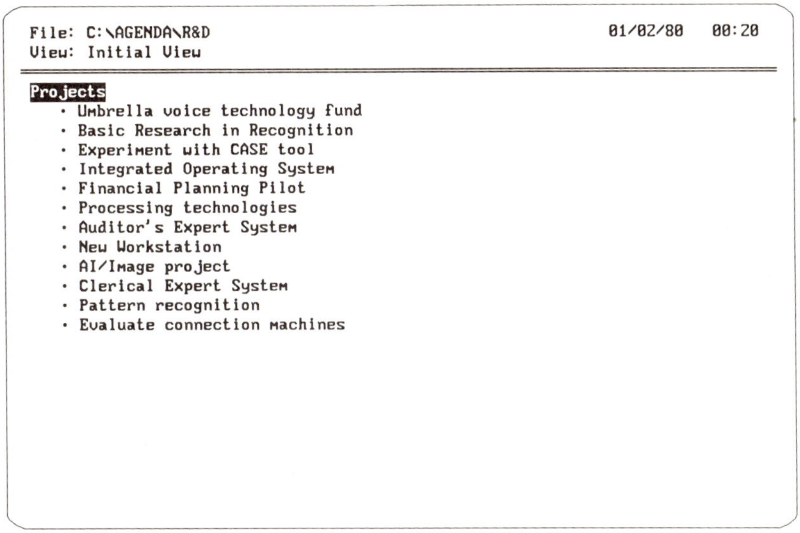

To each of these project items you can attach notes that describe the project in more detail. Executive summaries, abstracts, or even the complete project proposals, assuming that they are less than ten pages long (the limit for an item note), could be stored with the project names to help us reference the items when we classify them later. To attach a note to a project, first highlight the project name and then press F5(Note). Type up to ten pages of text in the item's note screen. When you are finished entering your note, press F5(Return) to return to the item view screen.

ADDING STRUCTURE

Now it is time to begin classifying the projects. Press Home to return to the Project section heading. To insert a new column to the right of the Project column:

Press: F10 (MENU)
Type: C for Category
Type: C for Column
Type: N for New

Agenda will display a New Column dialog box, as shown in Figure 8-2.

Figure 8-2.

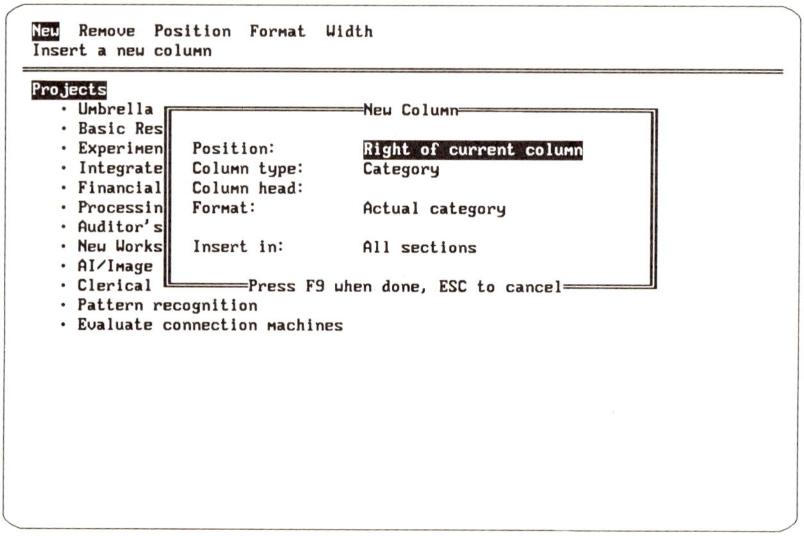

On the third line next to the *Column head:* prompt, type Division and press Enter. Press F9(Accept) to close the dialog box. Now move the highlight down to the first project's row under the Division column heading, type C Div., and press Enter. Move the highlight down to the next item's entry in the Division column and begin typing C Div. After you type the letter C, Agenda will beep to let you know that it is suggesting an automatic completion for the division you are entering. Obviously, the suggestion will be C Div., which you can accept by pressing Enter. Move to the next item and repeat the process. When you enter the division name for the first item in a division, Agenda does not suggest an automatic completion. However, after the first one, you can short cut the typing by responding to Agenda's suggestions of automatic completions.

To enter technologies and requested funds, repeat the process you followed for entering division names. The item view screen should look like the one shown in Figure 8-3.

Figure 8-3.

```
File: C:\AGENDA\R&D                                            01/02/80   00:22
View: Initial View

Projects                                   Division    Technology   Funding
  • Umbrella voice technology fund         C Div.      Telecom      450
  • Basic Research in Recognition          C Div.      Hardware     250
                                                       AI
                                                       Telecom
  • Experiment with CASE tool              A Div.      Software     150
  • Integrated Operating System            A Div.      Other        430
  • Financial Planning Pilot               A Div.      Other        150
  • Processing technologies                B Div.      Hardware     150
                                                       AI
                                                       Telecom
  • Auditor's Expert System                B Div.      AI           500
  • New Workstation                        B Div.      Hardware     100
  • AI/Image project                       C Div.      AI           500
  • Clerical Expert System                 C Div.      AI           200
  • Pattern recognition                    C Div.      Hardware     200
  • Evaluate connection machines           C Div.      Other        150
```

REFINING STRUCTURE

Now it is time to start identifying the attributes of the projects that should influence funding decisions. Let us go to the Category Manager to input a starter set of these attributes in a category we will call

Comments. Then, as we assign projects to these comments, we will find that we have to add others, and so the structure for evaluation will evolve.

To begin entering a category called Comments, which contains project attributes, into the Category Manager:

Press:	F9 (CAT MGR)
Press:	HOME
Press:	↓
Press:	INS
Type:	Comments
Press:	↵
Press:	INS
Type:	Fund by operating budgets
Press:	↵
Press:	F8 (DEM →)
Press:	INS
Type:	Minimal sharing
Press:	↵
Press:	INS
Type:	Enthusiastic champion
Press:	↵
Press:	INS
Type:	Off the shelf package
Press:	↵
Press:	INS
Type:	Not an emerging technology
Press:	↵
Press:	INS
Type:	Company-wide implications
Press:	↵

Now we are ready to start classifying projects. First, we return to the item view screen by pressing F9(To View). Next, press F8(Vw Mgr) to access the View Manager dialog box. Press Ins or Insert to create a new view and Agenda will display a New View dialog box, in which you should type "Comments by project" as the view name and Projects as the Category that will be used for the first section as shown in Figure 8-4. When you have made these selections, press F9(Accept) and Agenda will create a new view screen that lists the projects.

Figure 8-4.

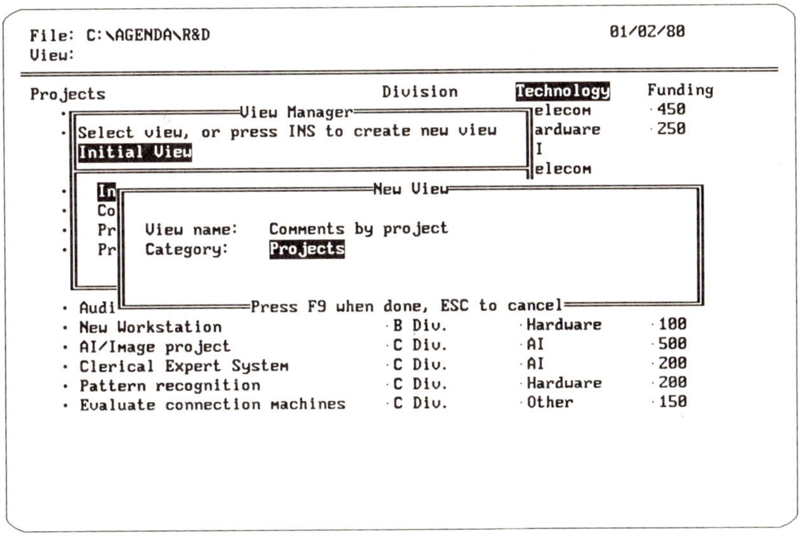

To insert a new column, with the heading Comments, to the right of the existing Projects column:

Press: ALT - R
Type: Comments over Untitled
Press: ↵

Now press the Down arrow to move the highlight to the first project row under the Comments column heading. Then start to type Fund by . . . . Agenda will beep to tell you that it has begun matching your typing to the category names already stored and has found a possible completion for your typing. If it is the correct completion, which it should be, just press Enter to accept it. If it is not the correct completion, continue typing or press F8(NextSel) or Alt-N to see the next possible completion that Agenda would propose. Press F7(PrevSel) or Alt-P to see the previous suggestion. At any time, you can simply finish typing the comment. If the comment does not already exist in the Category

Manager, Agenda will add it to the Comments category. Therefore, the Comments category will evolve as you decide what to say about each project. Continue assigning projects to Comments as shown in Figure 8-5.

Figure 8-5.

```
File: C:\AGENDA\R&D                                          01/02/80   00:38
View: Comments by Project

Projects                                 Comments
   · Umbrella voice technology fund      ·Fund by operating budgets
                                          Minimal sharing
                                          Enthusiastic champion
   · Basic Research in Recognition       ·Significant Cost Savings
   · Experiment with CASE tool           ·Off the shelf package
   · Integrated Operating System         ·Fund by operating budgets
                                          Not an emerging technology
                                          Minimal sharing
   · Financial Planning Pilot            ·Company-wide implications
   · Processing technologies             ·Fund by operating budgets
                                          Not an emerging technology
   · Auditor's Expert System             ·Don't Reinvent the Wheel
   · New Workstation                     ·Fund by operating budgets
                                          Not an emerging technology
                                          Minimal sharing
   · AI/Image project                    ·Investigate Synergy
   · Clerical Expert System               Enthusiastic champion
   · Pattern recognition                 ·Significant Cost Savings
   · Evaluate connection machines        ·Important New Technology
```

To change the width of the Comments column:

Press: F10 (MENU)
Type: C for Category
Type: C for Column
Type: W for Width
Press: ?

DISPLAYING INFORMATION

With these preliminaries behind us, we are now ready to create many views of the projects, each of which will give us a different perspective on whether a project should be funded.

First we should change the name of the Initial View to Project Entry Screen. To do this:

Press: F8 (VW MGR)
Move to: Initial View
Press: F2 (EDIT)
Type: Project Entry Screen
Press: ↵

Now, while we are still in the View Manager dialog box, let us create a view of projects by technology and ask to see the actual technologies displayed as section headings. To do this:

Press: INS
Type: Project by Technology
Press: ↵
Move to: *Category:* prompt
Type: Technology
Press: ↵
Move to: *Display child categories:* prompt
Type: Yes
Press: F9 (ACCEPT)

Figure 8-6 shows these selections.

Figure 8-6.

```
File: C:\AGENDA\R&D                                   01/02/80   00:40
View: Project by Technology
========================================================================
Software
    • Experiment with CASE tool

Other
    • Evaluate connection machines
    • Financial Planning Pilot
    • Integrated Operating System

Hardware
    • Basic Research in Recognition
    • Pattern recognition
    • New Workstation
    • Processing technologies

AI
    • Basic Research in Recognition
    • Clerical Expert System
    • AI/Image project
    • Auditor's Expert System
    • Processing technologies
```

Use Alt-R to add Division and Comments columns to the right. To adjust the width of the Comments column place the highlight anywhere in the column:

Press: F10 (MENU)
Press: C for Category
Press: C for Column
Press: W for Width
Press: → to increase the width
Press: F9 (ACCEPT)

The complete view by technology should look like the one shown in Figure 8-7.

Figure 8-7.

```
File: C:\AGENDA\R&D                                              01/02/80   00:41
View: Project by Technology
================================================================================
Software                                      Division      Comments
    • Experiment with CASE tool                A Div.        Off the shelf package

Other                                         Division      Comments
    • Evaluate connection machines             C Div.        Important New Tcchnology
    • Financial Planning Pilot                 A Div.        Company-wide implications
    • Integrated Operating System              A Div.        Fund by operating budgets
                                                             Not an emerging technology
                                                             Minimal sharing

Hardware                                      Division      Comments
    • Basic Research in Recognition            C Div.        Significant Cost Savings
    • Pattern recognition                      C Div.        Significant Cost Savings
    • New Workstation                          B Div.        Fund by operating budgets
                                                             Not an emerging technology
                                                             Minimal sharing
    • Processing technologies                  B Div.        Fund by operating budgets
                                                             Not an emerging technology

AI                                            Division      Comments
```

Now let's perform the same process to create a view of projects by division:

Press: F8 (VW MGR)
Press: INS
Type: Projects by Division
Press: ↵

Move to: *Category:* prompt
Type: Division
Press: [↵]
Type: Yes
Move to: *Display child categories:* prompt
Type: Yes
Press: [F9] (ACCEPT)

After creating the view by division, use Alt-R to add columns to the right by typing Technology and Comments over Untitled after inserting the columns. To adjust the width of the Comments column place the highlight anywhere in the column:

Press: [F10] (MENU)
Type: C for Category
Type: C for Column
Type: W for Width
Press: [→] to increase the width
Press: [F9] (ACCEPT)

The complete view by division should look like the one shown in Figure 8-8.

Figure 8-8.

```
File: C:\AGENDA\R&D                                          01/02/88   00:42
View: Project by Division
===============================================================================
A Div.                                   Technology      Comments
   • Financial Planning Pilot             Other           Company-wide implications
   • Integrated Operating System          Other           Fund by operating budgets
                                                          Not an emerging technology
                                                          Minimal sharing
   • Experiment with CASE tool            Software        Off the shelf package

B Div.                                   Technology      Comments
   • New Workstation                      Hardware        Fund by operating budgets
                                                          Not an emerging technology
                                                          Minimal sharing
   • Auditor's Expert System              AI              Don't Reinvent the Wheel
   • Processing technologies              Hardware        Fund by operating budgets
                                          AI              Not an emerging technology
                                          Telecom

C Div.                                   Technology      Comments
   • Basic Research in Recognition        Hardware        Significant Cost Savings
                                          AI
                                          Telecom
```

Now we are ready to begin evaluating projects for funding. To access the Projects by Technology view, press F8(Vw Mgr), move the highlight to Projects by Technology, and press F9(Accept). To insert a new column to the right of Comments, move the highlight to the Comments column heading and press Alt-R. Type Rec and press Enter to label the column as the place to store our recommendations.

To format the Rec column as a Yes/No column:

Press: F10 (MENU)
Type: C for Catgeory
Type: C for Column
Type: F for Format

Agenda will display a Column Format dialog box. Use the Spacebar to rotate through the format choices until you come to Yes/No, as in Figure 8-9. Press F9(Accept) to close the dialog box.

Figure 8-9.

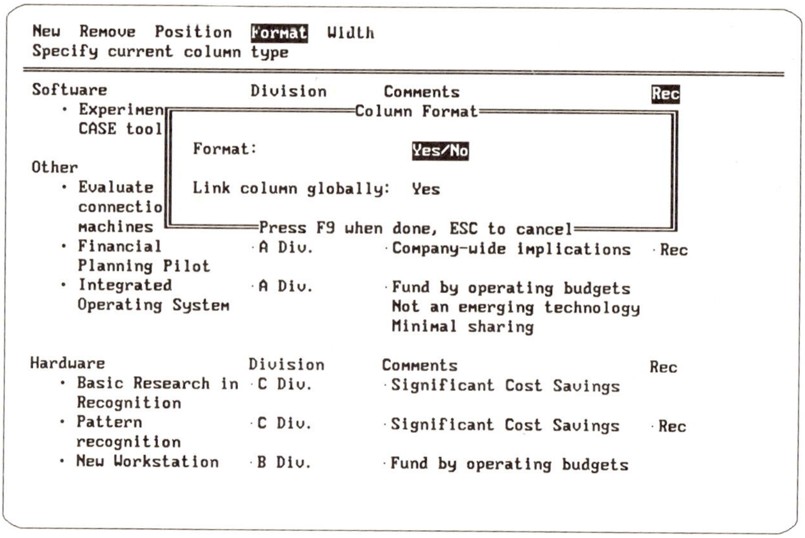

Now fill in the Rec column by moving to each row in the column and pressing the Spacebar to toggle back and forth between Y and N. You should enter the Y's and N's as they are shown in Figure 8-10.

Figure 8-10.

```
File: C:\AGENDA\R&D                                              01/02/80   00:44
View: Project by Technology
================================================================================
Software                 Division     Comments                        Rec
   · Experiment with     ·A Div.      ·Off the shelf package              N
     CASE tool

Other                    Division     Comments                        Rec
   · Evaluate            ·C Div.      ·Important New Technology           N
     connection
     machines
   · Financial           ·A Div.      ·Company-wide implications          Y
     Planning Pilot
   · Integrated          ·A Div.      ·Fund by operating budgets          N
     Operating System                  Not an emerging technology
                                       Minimal sharing

Hardware                 Division     Comments                        Rec
   · Basic Research in   ·C Div.      ·Significant Cost Savings           N
     Recognition
   · Pattern             ·C Div.      ·Significant Cost Savings           Y
     recognition
   · New Workstation     ·B Div.      ·Fund by operating budgets          N
```

Of course, in the real world you would not have someone to tell you where to place the Y's and N's. You would have to examine each of the projects and the associated comments to make these preliminary decisions.

Since you might want to make sure that each division is pursuing some R&D initiatives, you should now look at the Projects by Division view to see whose projects are being favored so far.

Press: F8 (VW MGR)
Move to: Projects by Division
Press: F9 (ACCEPT)

In the Projects by Division view, move the highlight to the Comments column heading and press Alt-R to insert a new column to the right of Comments. Type Rec and press Enter to insert the recommendations column. Format the column using the steps shown previously. Now we can see how our recommendations would affect the divisions. Of course, if we see any disparities, we can change the recommendations in this view by highlighting them and pressing the Spacebar to toggle between Y and N. Afterwards, if we were to return to the Projects by Technology view, the adjusted recommendations would be displayed.

When we are done assigning our projects to the recommendations categories, we can print the views of Projects by Technology and Division to communicate our recommendations to the company's management. For example, to print the view of Projects by Division:

Press: F8 (VW MGR)
Move to: Projects by Division
Press: F9 (ACCEPT)
Press: F10 (MENU)
Type: P for Print

Agenda will display a Print dialog box as shown in Figure 8-11.

Figure 8-11.

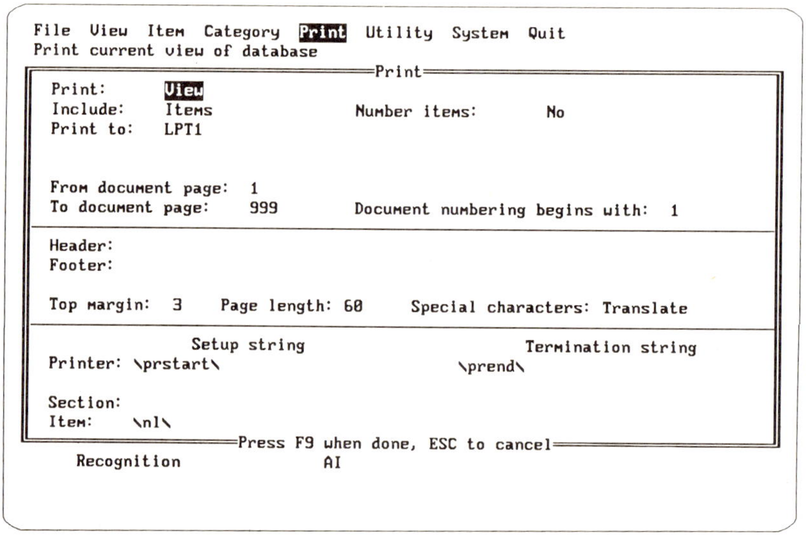

You can press F9(Accept) right away to obtain a straightforward printout of the items in the view. If you wish to see the notes as well, move the highlight to the second prompt, *Include:*, and press the Spacebar to rotate through the available options. If you wish to print the view to a file that you can then transfer to a word processing program for inclusion in a larger document, move the highlight to the *Print to:* prompt and press the Spacebar until you see the File option. To the right of the *Print to:* prompt, you will be prompted for the filename *(File:)*, which you must type, followed by pressing Enter. If you are not sure of the filename, press Grey + and use the arrows to highlight the desired file and press Enter. On the next line, you can choose a *Format:* by pressing the Spacebar. As you can see, there are page format and printer strings that can also be set using this dialog box. However, we will save a detailed discussion of these options until Chapter 10.

After selecting the options you prefer, press F9(Accept) to start the printing. The printed version of the view should look like the one shown in Figure 8-12.

Figure 8-12

```
A Div.                    Technology    Comments                          Rec

   . Financial            .Other        .Company-wide implications          Y
     Planning Pilot

   . Integrated           .Other        .Fund by operating budgets          N
     Operating System                    Not an emerging technology
                                         Minimal sharing

   . Experiment with      .Software     .Off the shelf package              N
     CASE tool
B Div.                    Technology    Comments                          Rec

   . New Workstation      .Hardware     .Fund by operating budgets          N
                                         Not an emerging technology
                                         Minimal sharing

   . Auditor's Expert     .AI           .Don't Reinvent the Wheel           Y
     System

   . Processing           .Hardware     .Fund by operating budgets          Y
     technologies          AI            Not an emerging technology
                           Telecom
C Div.                    Technology    Comments                          Rec

   . Basic Research in    .Hardware     .Significant Cost Savings           N
     Recognition           AI
                           Telecom

   . Umbrella voice       .Telecom      .Fund by operating budgets          N
     technology fund                     Minimal sharing
                                         Enthusiastic champion
                                         Important New Technology

   . Evaluate             .Other        .Important New Technology           N
     connection
     machines

   . Pattern              .Hardware     .Significant Cost Savings           Y
     recognition

   . Clerical Expert      .AI           .Enthusiastic champion              Y
     System

   . AI/Image project     .AI           .Investigate Synergy                Y
```

SUGGESTIONS FOR OTHER REFINEMENTS

Now that we have evaluated the projects overall, we might want to try a slightly different approach. We can rank the projects within division and technology separately, and then see if we can generate an overall ranking by combining these two specialized rankings.

To rank the projects within each division, return to the Projects by Division view and insert a column called Rank Within Division. Now go down the projects within each division and assign ranks from 1 to 3 or 6, depending on the division, with 1 being the highest rank and 3 or 6 being the lowest.

To rank the projects within each technology, return to the Projects by Technology view and insert a column called Rank Within Technology. Now go down the projects within each technology and assign ranks from 1 to 3 or 4, depending on the technology.

Now use the ranks by division and technology to evaluate the projects by creating a new view called Overall Rankings of Projects. This view should display the projects, the division, the division ranking, the technology, the technology ranking, and a new category column called Overall. Use this view to fill in Overall rankings based on the division and technology rankings. Then add the Rec category column to see how the Overall rankings correlate with the recommendations you entered previously. This might lead to some adjustments of the recommendations, which once again can be printed out for management review and discussion.

9

Executive Information System

Business executives typically have staffs who respond to ad hoc requests for information that has to be extracted from management control reports such as monthly budget documents. Sometimes these information requirements are bundled in book form and become the basis for board meetings, business reviews and informal information retrieval. Several pages from a hypothetical example of this type of executive briefing book are shown in Figure 9-1.

Figure 9-1

Executive Summary of 3rd Quarter Performance
($ millions)

Group	Actual	Last Year	% to Last Year
1 U.S. Division A	$59.6	$40.0	49.0
2 U.S. Division B	$5.9	$7.1	-17.2
3 Division C - Department A	$10.8	$7.4	46.2
4 Division C - Department B	$2.2	$2.0	9.6
5 Total U.S. Division C	$13.0	$9.4	38.4
6 U.S. Division D	$11.9	$6.5	82.8
7 U.S. Division E	$4.6	$14.1	-67.6
8 Total U.S.	$94.9	$77.1	23.1
9 Europe	$5.1	$4.5	13.1
10 Canada	$2.8	$1.9	47.1
11 Asia	$3.9	$2.1	85.9
12 Latin America	$4.0	$3.4	16.4
13 Japan	$2.0	$1.0	100.0
14 Headquarters	$0.1	$0.2	-49.9
15 Total International	$17.9	$13.1	36.1
16 Total Business Units	$112.8	$90.2	25.0
17 Other	$4.0	$5.0	-19.9
18 Total Operating Income	$116.8	$95.2	22.6
19 Investments	$5.0	$9.7	-47.9
20 Total Net Income	$121.8	$104.9	16.1

When it comes to using such information, executives tend to zero in on very specific pieces of information, according to their personal management style and whatever issues are most important at the time. The executive might ask how this year's actual revenues compare to budgeted revenues or how well the general managers meet their revenue budgets. Executives are less interested in the numbers as objects with which to calculate, than as objects to be referred to and annotated for follow-up and analysis. In other words, executives have highly personalized views, which they use to focus on specific information from the masses of data that are provided to them. If these executives or their staffs were able to create an Agenda database containing the briefing book data, the executives could look at the data in any way they wished.

One way to get data into Agenda is to simply type in the items by hand. Each number from the financial source document, for example, the monthly budget report, would be an item and the Type (Budget, Actual, or Variance), Group (Organizational Unit), and Period (Quarter, Semiannual, or Annual) columns would be the categories.

Another way to get the data into Agenda is to put the financial tables into a specially formatted 1-2-3 spreadsheet that we can then print to an ASCII text file called TRANSFER.PRN. Using the Agenda utility program called TXT2STF, we can then convert this text file into a structured text file (STF), which can be read into an Agenda database. With the information stored in this fashion, executives and their staffs can then create any views of the database that will satisfy their own personalized needs.

HOW TO BUILD AN EXECUTIVE INFORMATION SYSTEM

In this section we will first set up the specially formatted 1–2–3 spreadsheet that will be printed to a file and converted by TXT2STF into a structured text file (STF). We will then load Agenda, set up a new database for this Executive Information System, and import the STF file into the database. With the items and categories loaded, we can then begin developing views of the database that the executive might want to access on a regular basis. We will see that this electronic form of the briefing book can satisfy both the conventional display requirements as well as specialized requirements that executives may have from time to time.

Setting Up the 1–2–3 Spreadsheet

To begin, the 1-2-3 spreadsheet should have every numeric value in the A column and the relevant category labels in the C, E, and G columns. In formatting the spreadsheet, it is important to insert one-character-wide columns filled with a separator character (such as |) between each of the data columns, that is, in B, D, F, and H. TXT2STF will use this to break the text file input lines into columns for items and categories. The completed spreadsheet should look like the one shown in Figure 9-2.

Figure 9-2.

```
A1: 'Values                                                         READY


        A    B          C                   D   E   F       G        H
1   Values  |Group                          |Period |Type            |
2      $59.6 | 1 U.S. Division A            |3rd Qtr|Actual          |
3       $5.9 | 2 U.S. Division B            |3rd Qtr|Actual          |
4      $10.8 | 3 Division C - Department A|3rd Qtr|Actual            |
5       $2.2 | 4 Division C - Department B|3rd Qtr|Actual            |
6      $13.0 | 5 Total U.S. Division C     |3rd Qtr|Actual          |
7      $11.9 | 6 U.S. Division D            |3rd Qtr|Actual          |
8       $4.6 | 7 U.S. Division E            |3rd Qtr|Actual          |
9      $94.9 | 8 Total U.S.                 |3rd Qtr|Actual          |
10      $5.1 | 9 Europe                     |3rd Qtr|Actual          |
11      $2.8 |10 Canada                     |3rd Qtr|Actual          |
12      $3.9 |11 Asia                       |3rd Qtr|Actual          |
13      $4.0 |12 Latin America              |3rd Qtr|Actual          |
14      $2.0 |13 Japan                      |3rd Qtr|Actual          |
15      $0.1 |14 Headquarters               |3rd Qtr|Actual          |
16     $17.9 |15 Total International        |3rd Qtr|Actual          |
17    $112.8 |16 Total Business Units       |3rd Qtr|Actual          |
18      $4.0 |17 Other                      |3rd Qtr|Actual          |
19    $116.8 |18 Total Operating Income     |3rd Qtr|Actual          |
20      $5.0 |19 Investments                |3rd Qtr|Actual          |
02-Jan-80  12:26 AM
```

Figure 9-2.

```
A21: (C1) 121.829951611                                             READY


        A    B          C                   D   E   F       G        H
21    $121.8 |20 Total Net Income           |3rd Qtr|Actual          |
22     $79.7 | 1 U.S. Division A            |3rd Qtr|Budget          |
23      $5.2 | 2 U.S. Division B            |3rd Qtr|Budget          |
24      $7.0 | 3 Division C - Department A|3rd Qtr|Budget            |
25      $1.5 | 4 Division C - Department B|3rd Qtr|Budget            |
26      $8.5 | 5 Total U.S. Division C     |3rd Qtr|Budget          |
27     $13.4 | 6 U.S. Division D            |3rd Qtr|Budget          |
28      $8.2 | 7 U.S. Division E            |3rd Qtr|Budget          |
29    $115.0 | 8 Total U.S.                 |3rd Qtr|Budget          |
30      $4.3 | 9 Europe                     |3rd Qtr|Budget          |
31      $2.1 |10 Canada                     |3rd Qtr|Budget          |
32      $2.0 |11 Asia                       |3rd Qtr|Budget          |
33      $2.1 |12 Latin America              |3rd Qtr|Budget          |
34      $3.0 |13 Japan                      |3rd Qtr|Budget          |
35      $0.2 |14 Headquarters               |3rd Qtr|Budget          |
36     $13.6 |15 Total International        |3rd Qtr|Budget          |
37    $128.6 |16 Total Business Units       |3rd Qtr|Budget          |
38      $6.0 |17 Other                      |3rd Qtr|Budget          |
39    $134.6 |18 Total Operating Income     |3rd Qtr|Budget          |
40     $13.6 |19 Investments                |3rd Qtr|Budget          |
02-Jan-80  12:27 AM
```

Figure 9-2.

```
A41: (C1) 148.28413709                                                  READY

        A     B             C                  D   E   F       G        H
41    $148.3 |20 Total Net Income             |3rd Qtr|Budget
42     -25.1 | 1 U.S. Division A              |3rd Qtr|Pct to Budget    |
43      13.0 | 2 U.S. Division B              |3rd Qtr|Pct to Budget    |
44      54.7 | 3 Division C - Department A|3rd Qtr|Pct to Budget    |
45      46.2 | 4 Division C - Department B|3rd Qtr|Pct to Budget    |
46      53.2 | 5 Total U.S. Division C        |3rd Qtr|Pct to Budget    |
47     -11.5 | 6 U.S. Division D              |3rd Qtr|Pct to Budget    |
48     -44.5 | 7 U.S. Division E              |3rd Qtr|Pct to Budget    |
49     -17.4 | 8 Total U.S.                   |3rd Qtr|Pct to Budget    |
50      20.8 | 9 Europe                       |3rd Qtr|Pct to Budget    |
51      34.7 |10 Canada                       |3rd Qtr|Pct to Budget    |
52      94.5 |11 Asia                         |3rd Qtr|Pct to Budget    |
53      90.2 |12 Latin America                |3rd Qtr|Pct to Budget    |
54     -33.2 |13 Japan                        |3rd Qtr|Pct to Budget    |
55     -49.9 |14 Headquarters                 |3rd Qtr|Pct to Budget    |
56      31.4 |15 Total International          |3rd Qtr|Pct to Budget    |
57     -12.2 |16 Total Business Units         |3rd Qtr|Pct to Budget    |
58     -33.2 |17 Other                        |3rd Qtr|Pct to Budget    |
59     -13.1 |18 Total Operating Income       |3rd Qtr|Pct to Budget    |
60     -63.1 |19 Investments                  |3rd Qtr|Pct to Budget    |
02-Jan-80  12:28 AM
```

Figure 9-2.

```
A61: (F1) -17.7                                                         READY

        A     B             C                  D   E   F       G        H
61     -17.7 |20 Total Net Income             |3rd Qtr|Pct to Budget    |
62     $40.0 | 1 U.S. Division A              |3rd Qtr|Last year        |
63      $7.1 | 2 U.S. Division B              |3rd Qtr|Last year        |
64      $7.4 | 3 Division C - Department A|3rd Qtr|Last year        |
65      $2.0 | 4 Division C - Department B|3rd Qtr|Last year        |
66      $9.4 | 5 Total U.S. Division C        |3rd Qtr|Last year        |
67      $6.5 | 6 U.S. Division D              |3rd Qtr|Last year        |
68     $14.1 | 7 U.S. Division E              |3rd Qtr|Last year        |
69     $77.1 | 8 Total U.S.                   |3rd Qtr|Last year        |
70      $4.5 | 9 Europe                       |3rd Qtr|Last year        |
71      $1.9 |10 Canada                       |3rd Qtr|Last year        |
72      $2.1 |11 Asia                         |3rd Qtr|Last year        |
73      $3.4 |12 Latin America                |3rd Qtr|Last year        |
74      $1.0 |13 Japan                        |3rd Qtr|Last year        |
75      $0.2 |14 Headquarters                 |3rd Qtr|Last year        |
76     $13.1 |15 Total International          |3rd Qtr|Last year        |
77     $90.2 |16 Total Business Units         |3rd Qtr|Last year        |
78      $5.0 |17 Other                        |3rd Qtr|Last year        |
79     $95.2 |18 Total Operating Income       |3rd Qtr|Last year        |
80      $9.7 |19 Investments                  |3rd Qtr|Last year        |
02-Jan-80  12:28 AM
```

Figure 9-2.

```
A81: (C1) 104.903212323                                                    READY

        A    B              C               D   E   F       G        H
81    $104.9 |20 Total Net Income          |3rd Qtr|Last year         |
82      49.0 | 1 U.S. Division A           |3rd Qtr|Pct to Last Year|
83     -17.2 | 2 U.S. Division B           |3rd Qtr|Pct to Last Year|
84      46.2 | 3 Division C - Department A|3rd Qtr|Pct to Last Year|
85       9.6 | 4 Division C - Department B|3rd Qtr|Pct to Last Year|
86      38.4 | 5 Total U.S. Division C     |3rd Qtr|Pct to Last Year|
87      82.8 | 6 U.S. Division D           |3rd Qtr|Pct to Last Year|
88     -67.6 | 7 U.S. Division E           |3rd Qtr|Pct to Last Year|
89      23.1 | 8 Total U.S.                |3rd Qtr|Pct to Last Year|
90      13.1 | 9 Europe                    |3rd Qtr|Pct to Last Year|
91      47.1 |10 Canada                    |3rd Qtr|Pct to Last Year|
92      85.9 |11 Asia                      |3rd Qtr|Pct to Last Year|
93      16.4 |12 Latin America             |3rd Qtr|Pct to Last Year|
94     100.0 |13 Japan                     |3rd Qtr|Pct to Last Year|
95     -49.9 |14 Headquarters              |3rd Qtr|Pct to Last Year|
96      36.1 |15 Total International       |3rd Qtr|Pct to Last Year|
97      25.0 |16 Total Business Units      |3rd Qtr|Pct to Last Year|
98     -19.9 |17 Other                     |3rd Qtr|Pct to Last Year|
99      22.6 |18 Total Operating Income    |3rd Qtr|Pct to Last Year|
100    -47.9 |19 Investments               |3rd Qtr|Pct to Last Year|
02-Jan-80  12:28 AM
```

Figure 9-2.

```
A101: (F1) 16.1                                                            READY

        A    B              C               D   E   F       G        H
101     16.1 |20 Total Net Income          |3rd Qtr|Pct to Last Year|
102
103
104
105
106
107
108
109
110
111
112
113
114
115
116
117
118
119
120
02-Jan-80  12:28 AM
```

Converting the Spreadsheet to a Structured Text File

After setting up the spreadsheet as shown in Figure 9-2, we print it out as an ASCII text file and use the text file importing utility TXT2STF to convert the spreadsheet print file into a structured text file (STF) that Agenda can import to a database. To do this, use the /PF commands in 1-2-3 and the filename TRANSFER.PRN to format and print the 1-2-3 spreadsheet of Figure 9-2 to a file. Now exit from 1-2-3 and move to the Agenda directory, where the utility programs are stored. Type TXT2STF, followed by the name of the spreadsheet print file, which is TRANSFER.PRN, and the name of the DEF file that tells TXT2STF how to interpret the format of the TRANSFER.PRN file. The details of preparing DEF files will be covered in Chapter 12, but for this simple example, the DEF file consists of one record, which looks like this:

```
"^" @start( ) @table("\|",1, , ,) @end( )
```

This DEF file tells TXT2STF that, for each line read from TRANSFER.PRN, the columns of the underlying table will be separated by |'s and that the items will be found in the first column, the rest being used for categories. TXT2STF will apply this DEF file to the TRANSFER.PRN file and will use the name TRANSFER for the structured text file (STF) it creates. Your command should be typed as follows:

```
TXT2STF TRANSFER.PRN /D=TRANSFER.DEF
```

Once again, additional details about TXT2STF will be presented in the Advanced Concepts section of this book.

Importing the Structured Text File

Now that you have created the structured text file, load Agenda and select a name for your database. We called ours EIS, for Executive Information System, and input a password so that only our executive and his staff could have access to it. To continue with the loading of the STF file:

Type:	Values over Untitled
Press:	F10 (MENU)
Type:	F for File
Type:	T for Transfer
Type:	I for Import

The Import Structured File dialog box will be displayed as shown in Figure 9-3.

Figure 9-3.

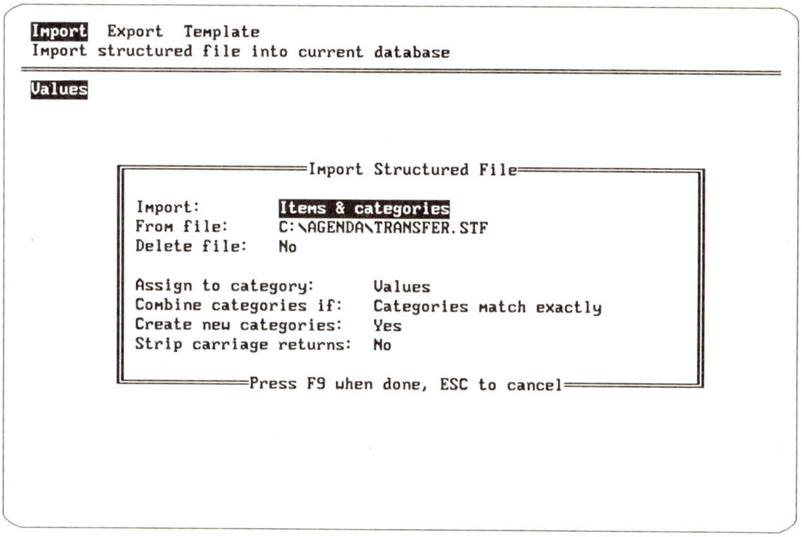

Press F9(Accept). You will have to wait for your file to be imported. Agenda will tell you how much of the file transfer has been completed as it works, as shown in Figure 9-4.

Figure 9-4.

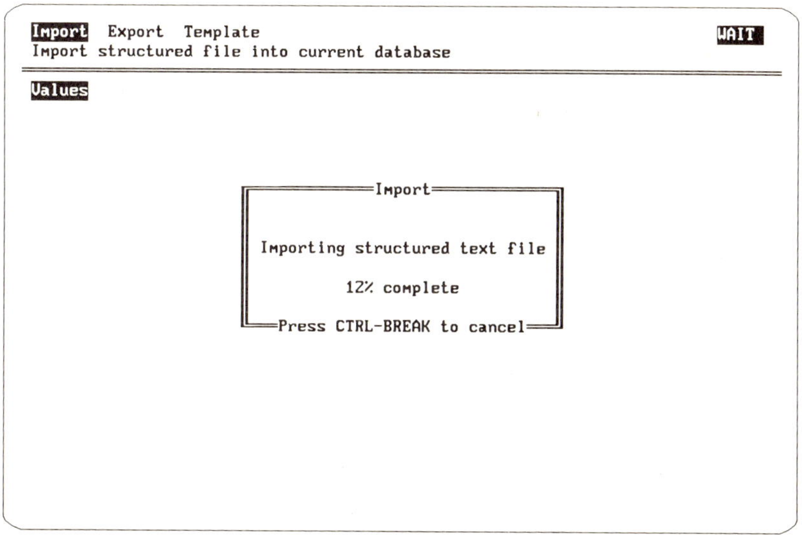

The numeric data will be imported automatically from column A of the 1-2-3 spreadsheet into Agenda's Values section and will appear as shown in Figure 9-5.

Figure 9-5.

```
File: C:\AGENDA\EIS                                01/02/80   05:23
View: Initial View
====================================================================
Values
   · $59.6
   · $5.9
   · $10.8
   · $2.2
   · $13.0
   · $11.9
   · $4.6
   · $94.9
   · $5.1
   · $2.8
   · $3.9
   · $4.0
   · $2.0
   · $0.1
   · $17.9
   · $112.8
   · $4.0
   · $116.8
   · $5.0
```

To complete the view, you will have to insert the three remaining categories:

Press: F10 (MENU)
Type: C for Category
Type: C for Column
Type: N for New

A dialog box will appear. Move the cursor to the blank area to the right of the *Column head:* prompt and type G. Since you have already used a word beginning with the letter G, Agenda will use its automatic completion feature to propose the completion of the word, Group, for you at the top of the screen. Press Enter to accept the word Group. The filled-in dialog box is shown in Figure 9-6.

Figure 9-6.

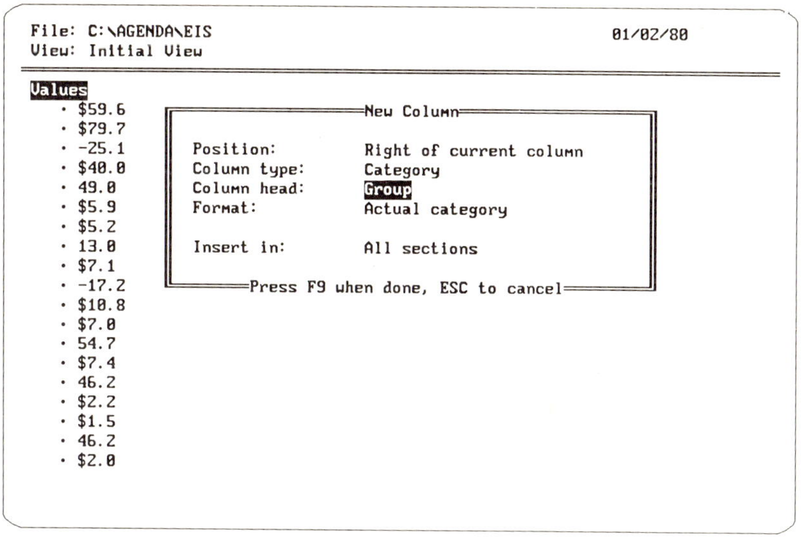

Press F9(Accept) and Agenda will insert the Group column to the right of Values. With the cursor on the heading for the new column, Group:

Press:	F10 (MENU)
Type:	C for Category
Type:	C for Column
Type:	W for Width
Type:	30
Press:	↵

To add the Period and Type columns, we will use the accelerator key method. Press Alt-R. This inserts a column to the right of the cursor. Its heading will read Untitled. Move the highlight to Untitled and begin typing the word Period. When you have typed Pe, the word Period will appear at the top of the screen. Press Enter and the new category will appear. Perform the same procedure to insert the Type column. You will only need to type the letter T for Agenda to match the word Type as the name of the column you wish to insert. As you did with the Group column, change the width of the Type column to 16 in order to display all the text. Your screen will appear as in Figure 9-7.

Figure 9-7.

File: C:\AGENDA\EIS 01/02/80 05:25
View: Initial View

Values	Group	Period	Type
$59.6	1 U.S. Division A	3rd Qtr	Actual
$5.9	2 U.S. Division B	3rd Qtr	Actual
$10.8	3 Division C - Department A	3rd Qtr	Actual
$2.2	4 Division C - Department B	3rd Qtr	Actual
$13.0	5 Total U.S. Division C	3rd Qtr	Actual
$11.9	6 U.S. Division D	3rd Qtr	Actual
$4.6	7 U.S. Division E	3rd Qtr	Actual
$94.9	8 Total U.S.	3rd Qtr	Actual
$5.1	9 Europe	3rd Qtr	Actual
$2.8	10 Canada	3rd Qtr	Actual
$3.9	11 Asia	3rd Qtr	Actual
$4.0	12 Latin America	3rd Qtr	Actual
$2.0	13 Japan	3rd Qtr	Actual
$0.1	14 Headquarters	3rd Qtr	Actual
$17.9	15 Total International	3rd Qtr	Actual
$112.8	16 Total Business Units	3rd Qtr	Actual
$4.0	17 Other	3rd Qtr	Actual
$116.8	18 Total Operating Income	3rd Qtr	Actual
$5.0	19 Investments	3rd Qtr	Actual

Since the table importing function creates unindexed categories, which cannot be used as section headings or in automatic completion of future typing entries, you must go to the Category Manager and index the unindexed categories. To index the categories, place the highlight on each column heading category name in turn, and then:

Press: F10 (MENU)
Type: C for Category
Type: M for Management
Type: U for Unindexed

CREATING VIEWS OF OUR EIS DATABASE

Our First View

Now imagine that the executive wants all the information about Division A, which is spread out across multiple pages of the briefing book. To create a new view with all the information concerning Division A in one place:

Press: F10 (Menu)
Press: V for View

Press: N for New
Type: Division A
Move to: *Category:* prompt
Type: 1 U.S. Division A
Press: ↵

Your screen will appear as in Figure 9-8.

Figure 9-8.

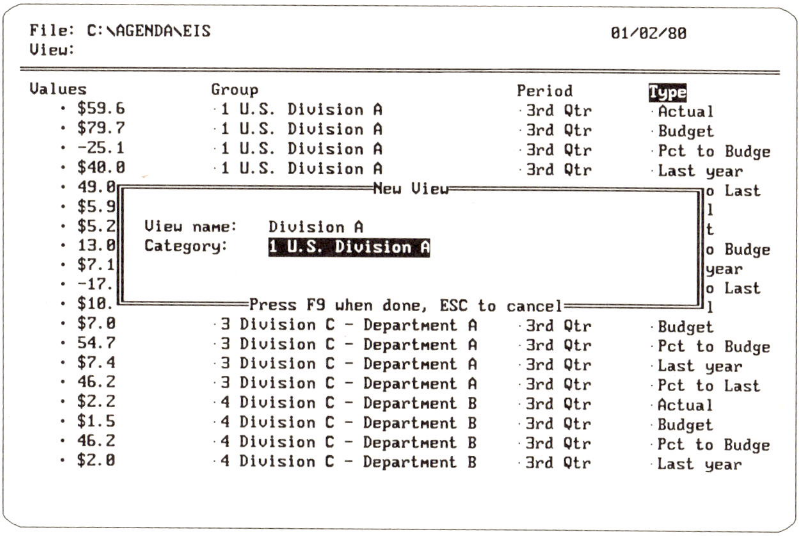

Press F9(Accept), and the new view will appear and be called Division A. To add the Period and Type columns, use the accelerator key method again:

Press: ALT - L
Type: Pe over Untitled
Press: ↵
Press: ALT - R
Type: T over Untitled
Press: ↵
Move to: Type
Press: F10 (MENU)
Type: C for Category
Type: C for Column

Type: W for Width
Type: 16
Press: ↵

The Division A view appears as in Figure 9-9.

Figure 9-9.

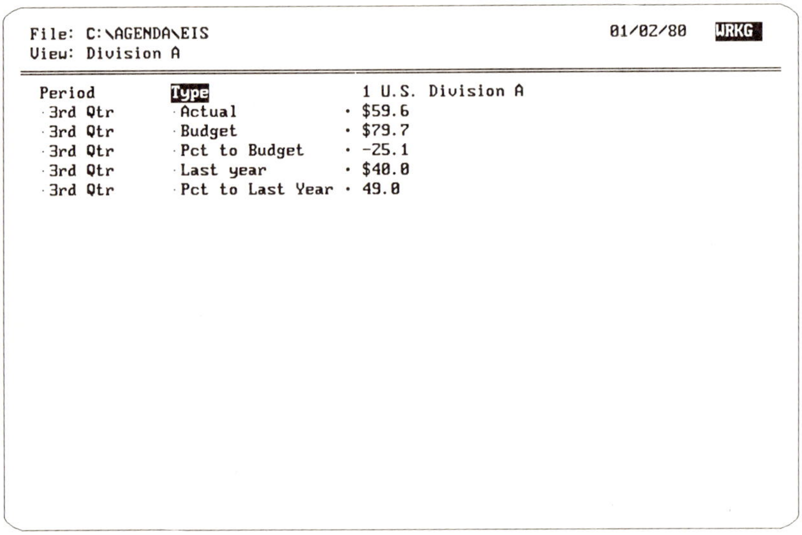

One of the most important features of Agenda as a personal information manager is the ability to input new material for Division A in this view. For example, if in her last review with you, the General Manager for Division A forecast that she would be 7% ahead of budget, you might want to add an item to this view to remind yourself of this commitment. All you need to do is place the cursor on the Pct to Budget item (–25.1) and press Ins to insert a new item. Then type whatever reminder will be relevant to you, for example, **Needs to explain why promised 7% turned out to be –25.1%?** This item will be assigned to the 1 U.S. Division A category along with the numeric values. With lots of reminders stored as items, a separate view of reminders by division could be prepared for handy reference at your next review meeting with your division General Managers.

This reminder could also be handled by another feature of Agenda, namely, the ability to attach notes to items or categories. In the EIS, in addition to the reminder just mentioned, you might want to attach explanations of variances as notes to the individual variance items. In our example, when you do have your review with the General Manager for Division A, you might want to enter her justification of the −25.1% as a note attached to the item. To do this, move the cursor to the item −25.1% and press F5(Note). The note entry screen will appear and you may type any text that is relevant to the explanation, for example, Strong dollar made imports suddenly more attractive. When you are done typing, press F5(Return) again to accept the note and you will be returned to your view. A musical note symbol will replace the item tag to the left of the −25.1 item to show that a note is attached to it.

Another View

An executive might also want to know how closely the divisions are sticking to their budgets. To display this information, you will want to create a view of the variance from budget percentages for all the divisions and then sort them from best to worst. To create this view:

Press:	F8 (VW MGR)
Press:	INS
Type:	Budget Variance
Move to:	*Category:* prompt
Type:	Pct to Budget
Press:	↵
Press:	F9 (ACCEPT).

The view will appear as in Figure 9-10.

Figure 9-10.

```
File: C:\AGENDA\EIS                                    01/02/80   WRKG
View: Budget Variance
================================================================
Pct to Budget
     ♪ -25.1
     · 13.0
     · 54.7
     · 46.2
     · 53.2
     · -11.5
     · -44.5
     · -17.4
     · 20.8
     · 34.7
     · 94.5
     · 90.2
     · -33.2
     · -49.9
     · 31.4
     · -12.2
     · -33.2
     · -13.1
     · -63.1
```

To add the Group names:

Press:	ALT - L
Type:	G over Untitled
Press:	↵
Press:	F10 (MENU)
Type:	C for Category
Type:	C for Column
Type:	W for Width
Type:	30
Press:	↵

To sort the values:

Press:	F10 (MENU)
Type:	C for Category
Type:	S for Section
Type:	S for Sort
Move to:	*Sort on:* prompt
Type:	Item text
Move to:	*Order:* prompt
Type:	Descending

Instead of typing the responses to the *Sort on:* and *Order:* prompts, you can use the Spacebar to rotate through the available options. After filling in the dialog box as shown in Figure 9-11, press F9(Accept), and the sorted view will appear as shown in Figure 9-12.

Our Last View

Finally, the executive might simply want to see a traditional list of the actual numbers by organizational unit. To display this information, you will want to create a view of the actuals for all the divisions. To create this view:

Press: F8 (VW MGR)
Press: INS
Type: Actuals
Move to: *Category name:* prompt
Type: A
Press: ↵

Figure 9-11.

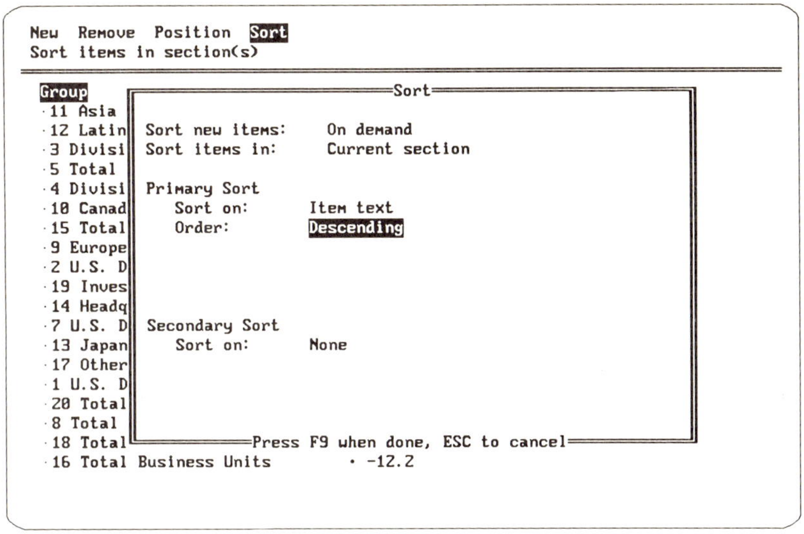

Figure 9-12.

```
File: C:\AGENDA\EIS                                             01/02/80   01:03
View: Budget Variance
================================================================================
Group                                 Pct to Budget
 11 Asia                            • 94.5
 12 Latin America                   • 90.2
 3 Division C - Department A        • 54.7
 5 Total U.S. Division C            • 53.2
 4 Division C - Department B        • 46.2
 10 Canada                          • 34.7
 15 Total International             • 31.4
 9 Europe                           • 20.8
 2 U.S. Division B                  • 13.0
 19 Investments                     • -63.1
 14 Headquarters                    • -49.9
 7 U.S. Division E                  • -44.5
 13 Japan                           • -33.2
 17 Other                           • -33.2
 1 U.S. Division A                  • -25.1
 20 Total Net Income                • -17.7
 8 Total U.S.                       • -17.4
 18 Total Operating Income          • -13.1
 16 Total Business Units            • -12.2
```

The completed dialog box will appear as in Figure 9-13. Press F9(Accept), and the view will appear.

Figure 9-13.

```
File: C:\AGENDA\EIS                                             01/02/80
View:
================================================================================
Group                                 Pct to Budget
 11 ================View Manager================
 12 Select view, or press INS to create new view
 3  Budget Variance
 5
 4    In=================================New View=================
 10   Sh
 15   Di   View name:   Actuals
 9    Bu   Category:    Actual
 2    Ac
 19
 14 ======================Press F9 when done, ESC to cancel=====
 7 U.S. Division E                  • -44.5
 13 Japan                           • -33.2
 17 Other                           • -33.2
 1 U.S. Division A                  • -25.1
 20 Total Net Income                • -17.7
 8 Total U.S.                       • -17.4
 18 Total Operating Income          • -13.1
 16 Total Business Units            • -12.2
```

To add the Group names:

Press: ALT - L
Type: G over Untitled
Press: ↵
Press: F10 (MENU)
Type: C for Category
Type: C for Column
Type: W for Width
Type: 30
Press: ↵

The view of actuals by group is shown in Figure 9-14.

SUGGESTIONS FOR OTHER REFINEMENTS

Now that you have developed three views of the EIS database, you might want to experiment with some of the following ideas.

Since you might want to occasionally remind yourself what the budgets are for the groups, develop a view of the budget figures similar to the "Actuals" view.

Figure 9-14.

```
File: C:\AGENDA\EIS                                    01/02/80   01:04
View: Actuals
========================================================================
Group                                   Actual
 1 U.S. Division A                    • $59.6
 2 U.S. Division B                    • $5.9
 3 Division C - Department A          • $10.8
 4 Division C - Department B          • $2.2
 5 Total U.S. Division C              • $13.0
 6 U.S. Division D                    • $11.9
 7 U.S. Division E                    • $4.6
 8 Total U.S.                         • $94.9
 9 Europe                             • $5.1
 10 Canada                            • $2.8
 11 Asia                              • $3.9
 12 Latin America                     • $4.0
 13 Japan                             • $2.0
 14 Headquarters                      • $0.1
 15 Total International               • $17.9
 16 Total Business Units              • $112.8
 17 Other                             • $4.0
 18 Total Operating Income            • $116.8
 19 Investments                       • $5.0
```

Do the same for last year's figures to which you may want to occasionally refer.

In the same spirit, you will certainly want focused views of organizations other than Division A. Develop views for Total U.S., Total International, Total Business Units, and Total Net Income.

Part IV: Advanced Concepts

10

Printing

The printing of item view screens, note screens, and the Category Manager was introduced in Chapter 5. To print these screens, you must choose a Printer Definition File identifying your printer to Agenda and you must respond to the prompts in the Print dialog boxes appropriate to each screen.

PRINTER DEFINITION FILES

Printer Definition Files, or PDFs, for the most popular printers are supplied by Lotus and are used by the print function in translating your print instructions to your specific printer. When you install Agenda, you choose the Printer Definition File that matches your printer. Alternatively, you can choose your PDF from the item view screen Utility/Preferences/Environment menu by pressing F10(Menu), U for Utility, P for Preferences, and E for Environment. Agenda will display an Environment Preferences dialog box as shown in Figure 10-1.

The fourth prompt, *Printer definition file:*, asks for the PDF to use for printing during this session. You can see the available options by pressing GREY +, and you can select one by moving the highlight to it and pressing Enter. Press F9(Accept) to close the dialog box.

Agenda will use this PDF for the remainder of this session unless you change it again. If you want this PDF permanently set up as the default, press F10(Menu), U for Utility, P for Preferences, and U for Update. Agenda asks if you are sure about updating the file preferences. Answer yes or no and press F9(Accept) to return to the item view screen.

Figure 10-1.

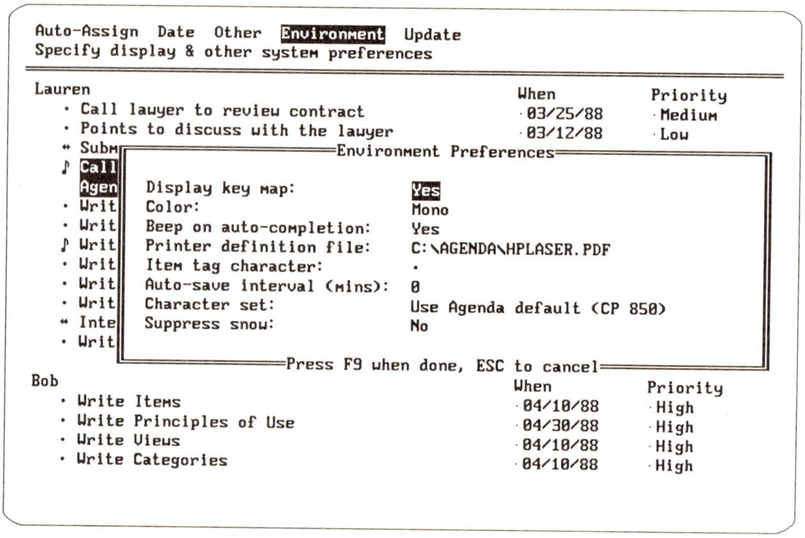

There is a default PDF called PRINTER.PDF, which you can use if your printer is not listed among the options provided by Lotus. You can customize any PDF, including the default, to tailor it to new printers or models or any other special requirements you may have. Customizing PDFs is described in the last section of this chapter.

PRINT DIALOG BOXES

Let's return to the Print dialog boxes, which are accessed from the item view, note, and Category Manager screens by pressing F10(Menu) and P for Print. The Print dialog boxes are shown in Figures 10-2, 10-3, and 10-4.

As you can see, each of the dialog boxes contains three similar sections. The first section has to do with printing options; the second, with page layout options; and the third, with formatting options.

Figure 10-2.

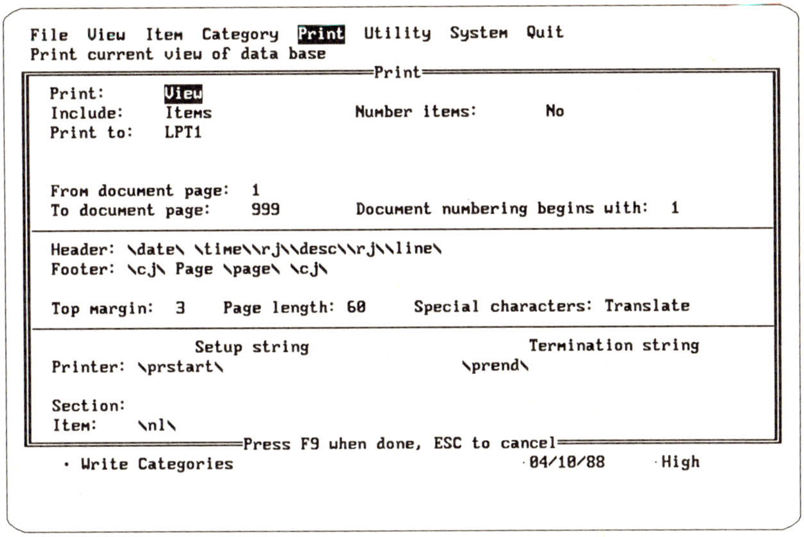

Figure 10-3.

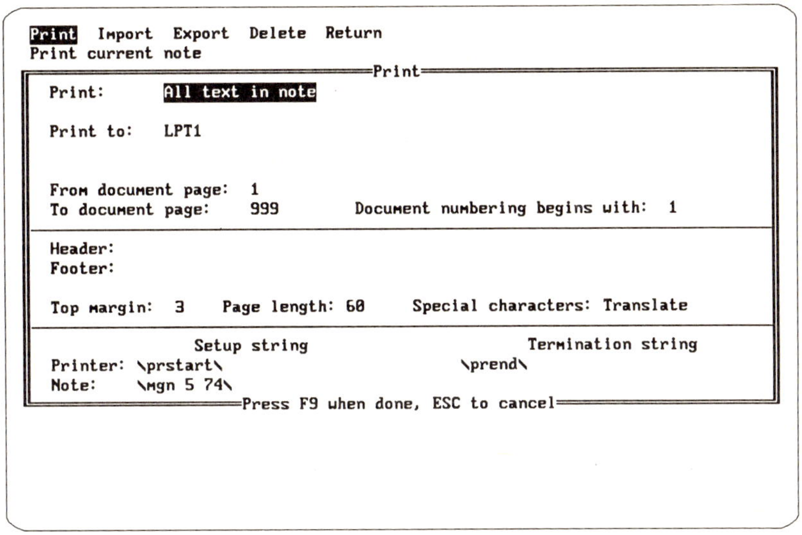

Figure 10-4.

```
Exclusive  Unindexed  Condition  Action  Print  Return
Print category hierarchy
═══════════════════════════════Print═══════════════════════════════
 Print:        Database info

 Print to:     LPT1


 From document page:   1
 To document page:     999        Document numbering begins with:  1
────────────────────────────────────────────────────────────────────
 Header:  \date\ \time\\rj\\desc\\rj\\line\
 Footer:  \cj\ Page \page\ \cj\

 Top margin:  3     Page length: 60     Special characters: Translate
────────────────────────────────────────────────────────────────────
                 Setup string                       Termination string
 Printer:  \prstart\                              \prend\
═══════════════════Press F9 when done, ESC to cancel═══════════════════
 TASKS
 "Untitled"
```

Printing Options

Let's begin with the first section, where the first prompt, *Print:*, asks what information you wish to have printed. In an item view screen, the options are the current item, the marked items in the view, the current section, the current view, or the assignment profile. The format for the first four options is the same because the information to be printed consists of items with or without their associated notes. The format for the assignment profile resembles the Category Manager, with a list of the categories and the asterisks or numbers to indicate whether and how many items are assigned to each category, as shown in Figure 10-5.

In a note screen, the options for *Print:* are either all text in the note or just the text marked by using F7(Mark). Finally, in the Category Manager, the options are to print either the entire hierarchy or a special display of database information, as shown in Figure 10-6. All these options can be selected using the Spacebar, F2(Edit), or Grey +.

Figure 10-5.

```
       MAIN
(11)     Quotes
         Authors
(2)       +"Peter Drucker"
(2)       +"Henry Ford"
(3)       +"Sidney Harris"
(4)       +"Will Rogers"
         Topics
(1)        Advertising
           Banking
(1)        Business
(2)        Computers
(2)        Consulting;Consultant
(2)        Intelligence
(1)        Employment;Jobs
(1)        Heroes
(2)        History
           Relaxation
(2)        Thought;Thinking
(1)        Time
```

Figure 10-6.

```
Database information for: C:\AGENDA\QUOTES

Description: Great Quotations

All files associated with this file are:
C:\AGENDA\QUOTES.AGA
C:\AGENDA\QUOTES.AGB


File Information

              Unused space: 3%
                     Items: 11
            Items in Trash: 0
          Items with notes: 0
                Categories: 20
    Average items/category: 1
   Average categories/item: 3
```

The next prompt, *Include:*, in the item view Print dialog box, if you are printing items, has three options: items, notes, or both. In the Category Manager Print dialog box, if you are printing the categories, *Include:* has similar options: categories, notes, or both. If you are printing an assignment profile, database information or a note screen, there will be no *Include:* prompt. The *Include:* options, too, can be selected using the Spacebar, F2(Edit), or Grey +.

In the item view Print dialog box, the next prompt to the right of the *Include:* prompt is *Number items:*. It asks whether or not you want the items numbered in the printout. This prompt does not appear if you are printing the assignment profile, or if you are printing categories or notes. Use the Spacebar to select either yes or no.

The remaining prompts in this section are the same regardless of whether you are printing items, notes, or categories. The next prompt, *Print to:*, asks for the device, communications port, or file to which you want the printing directed. There are three parallel ports (LPT1, LPT2, and LPT3), two serial ports (COM1 and COM2), and one response for printing to a file (File). Once again, the Spacebar, F2(Edit) or Grey + can be used to select one of these options.

If you select File for *Print to:*, two new prompts appear to the right, namely, *File:* and *Format:*. The *File:* prompt asks for the filename to which you want the output directed. Type the full filename, including directory identification if it is different from the directory in which you are working. If you just type the filename, Agenda automatically fills in the current directory and extension information. It is important to recognize that if the file you name already exists, Agenda will replace it with the new printed material, without any prompt to determine whether you are sure about the name. If you are not sure of the filename, press Grey + to see a list of available files. Either select one using the highlight or type a new name and press Enter.

The *Format:* prompt provides two options: print the text only or print the text with printer codes. If you are feeding the output from Agenda into some other analytic program or preparing it for someone with a different printer, you probably will want to print the text only. If you are sending the file to a word or text processing program or are storing it for later printing, you may want to leave the printer codes in the file.

The last three prompts in this section have to do with page numbering and selection. You can print the entire database or some subset of pages using the *From document page:* and *To document page:* prompts on the left side of the last two lines in the printing options section of the Print dialog box. If you are inserting the Agenda printout into a larger document such as one you are composing with a word processor, you have the option of numbering the pages with a starting page number of your choice using a combination of the *From document page:* and *Document numbering begins with:* prompts. To take advantage of this flexibility, you have to imagine the Agenda database starting at the page number that is relevant to its destination, either as a standalone document or as an insertion in a larger document. This page number is what you enter in response to the *Document numbering begins with:* prompt. Generally, this will be page one, or 1, but can be any page up to 999. Given this imaginary starting page for the Agenda database, you can then specify any range of pages between this starting page and 999 in response to the *From document page:* and *To document page:* prompts.

This may be easier to follow through a few examples:

Print Out	From Document Page:	To Document Page:	Document Numbering Begins with:
Entire database	1	999	1
First five pages	1	5	1
Pages 6 through 10	6	10	1
Entire database (start page numbering at 15)	15	999	15
First five pages (start page numbering at 15)	15	19	15
Pages 6 through 10 (start page numbering at 15)	20	24	15

Page Layout Options

The second section in the Print dialog box contains prompts for page layout options, including the top margin, the page length, and formatted lines to appear at the top and bottom of each page, which are also known as headers and footers. The last prompt tells Agenda how to print special characters.

The first two lines of the section are labeled *Header:* and *Footer:*. The formats for both of these are the same, and they provide for the printing of user-supplied text as well as system-controlled data such as page numbers, time, and date through a series of backslash commands. Each backslash command begins and ends with a backslash(\). Sometimes you must use the same command twice, before and after some text upon which the command is intended to act. For example, the backslash command for centering text, either in a header or in a footer, is \cj\. To center a title, you must precede and follow this title with the centering command. For example, to center the title To-Do List, you would specify:

```
\cj\ To-Do List \cj\
```

The other backslash commands that come in pairs are \rj\ and \lcj\. \rj\ is used the same as \cj\, but it moves the text that it surrounds to the right margin. \lcj\ is the command you use to center text and print a line from and to the left and right margins of the text. If you want to specify a line printing character other than the default hyphen (-), include the desired character following a space in the \lcj\ commands, for example, \lcj *\ for a line of asterisks or \lcj =\ for a line of equal signs.

The backslash commands that call for system information include \date\ for the current date in your default format, \fname\ and \desc\ for the display of the filename and description of the current Agenda database, \page\ for the page number, \view\ for the name of the current view, and \time\ for the current system time. \sect\ will cause the section and column headings to print. If you want these headings at the top of every page, include \sect\ in your header.

You can have multiline headers and footers if you include the new line, or \nl\, command in your series of backslash commands. You can insert a trailing line from the right of some text or system information to the right margin with the \line\ command. When it follows a new line, \nl\, command, the \line\ command prints a line of characters across the page. If you want to specify a line printing character other than the default hyphen (-), include the desired character following a space in the \line\ commands, for example, \line *\ or \line =\. With multiline headers and footers you may have to adjust the *Page length:* parameter.

If, for any reason, you want to enter a reminder or remark text along with the header or footer in the dialog box, but not have it print, include this reminder text in the \rem\ command and place them together at the end of the command line, for example, \rem this is a test\.

Finally, if you want to send a special printer control character to the printer from a header or footer, you can include a *nnn*\ command, where *nnn* is the ASCII number of the control character, ranging from 0 through 255. If the special character is a backslash, you can send it to the printer by typing it as a double backslash (\\) in your header or footer.

So far, the backslash commands that we have discussed are built in to Agenda and are not adjustable. Three more commands are stored in the PDFs, and they can be modified. Bracketing some text for the header or footer with \b\ causes the printer to make the text bold. If you want the text to be underlined, use \u\. Compressed print can be turned on and off with \c\. These three commands can be used in note text to control the display of individual words or phrases.

An example of these backslash commands at work might be to include a three-line header and a two-line footer. The first line of the header would start with the left-justified filename and description, separated by a hyphen, and the right-justified date. The second line would have the view name centered, and the third line would be a line of hyphens. The first line of the footer would be a labeled and centered page number in a line of hyphens and the second line would be a centered title, Confidential, which is printed bold. The commands to satisfy these specifications are shown in Figure 10-7, and a sample of the printed report is shown in Figure 10-8.

Figure 10-7.

```
File  View  Item  Category  Print  Utility  System  Quit                 Edit
Print current view of data base
══════════════════════════════Print══════════════════════════════
 Print:       View
 Include:     Items                  Number items:       No
 Print to:    LPT1


 From document page:   1
 To document page:     999        Document numbering begins with:  1
─────────────────────────────────────────────────────────────────
 Header: \fname\ - \desc\ \rj\ \date\ \rj\ \nl\ \cj\ \view\ \cj\ \nl\ \line\
 Footer: \lcj\ Page \page\ \lcj\ \nl\ \cj\ \b\ Confidential \b\ \cj\

 Top margin:  3    Page length: 60     Special characters: Translate
─────────────────────────────────────────────────────────────────
                 Setup string                        Termination string
 Printer: \prstart\                              \prend\

 Section:
 Item:     \nl\
═════════════════════Press F9 when done, ESC to cancel═════════════
   · Write Categories                          04/10/88      High
```

Figure 10-8.

```
C:\AGENDA\EIS - Executive Information System                        01/02/80
                                        Actuals
-----------------------------------------------------------------------------
Group                                   Actual
.1 U.S. Division A                    . $59.6
.2 U.S. Division B                    . $5.9
.3 Division C - Department A          . $10.8
.4 Division C - Department B          . $2.2
.5 Total U.S. Division C              . $13.0
.6 U.S. Division D                    . $11.9
.7 U.S. Division E                    . $4.6
.8 Total U.S.                         . $94.9
.9 Europe                             . $5.1
.10 Canada                            . $2.8
.11 Asia                              . $3.9
.12 Latin America                     . $4.0
.13 Japan                             . $2.0
.14 Headquarters                      . $0.1
.15 Total International               . $17.9
.16 Total Business Units              . $112.8
.17 Other                             . $4.0
.18 Total Operating Income            . $116.8
.19 Investments                       . $5.0
.20 Total Net Income                  . $121.8


----------------------------------- Page 1 -----------------------------------
                                  Confidential
```

After typing the header, which can be left or made blank to suppress any printing, press Enter, move the highlight to the *Footer:* prompt, and repeat the process that you used for the *Header:*.

Now move the highlight to the next prompt, *Top margin:*. Here you type the number of lines you want Agenda to skip from the top of the paper to the first line of the header. Press Enter and move the highlight to the next and related prompt, *Page length:*. Here you need to type the number of lines you wish to have printed on every page from the first line of the header to the last line of the footer. A default of 60 appears, which you can accept by pressing Enter.

The last prompt in this section, *Special characters:*, has three options—Translate, Do not translate, and Print as space—which can be selected using the Spacebar, F2(Edit) or Grey +. In sending text to the printer, the first option, Translate, causes Agenda to replace special characters that Lotus has specified, or that you have modified, as recorded in the PDF translation tables. The purpose of this translation is to avoid having the printer attempt to print characters that are not recognized or printable by the printer. Although translation tables for most common printers are included in the PDFs supplied with Agenda, you can change these translations to suit your preferences by following the directions in the last section of this chapter. The second option in the prompt, Do not translate, is self-explanatory and, although not generally suitable for output headed to your printer, may be useful for output to a file you intend to process in some other way. Finally, the third option, Print as space, replaces these unprintable characters with spaces or blank characters in the printout.

Formatting Options

The third and last section in the Print dialog boxes contains prompts for printer control characters that influence the overall printing of the information requested in the *Print:* prompt as well as individual items, notes, and sections, where applicable.

These printer control characters are referred to as setup and termination strings because they precede and follow the text whose format they are controlling. They are printer specific and certain obvious ones are already contained in the PDFs supplied by Lotus. The format of these strings is the same as the backslash commands described earlier. The ones supplied with Agenda include \prstart\, which initiates a printing session to the printer; \prend\, which terminates the printing session; and \reset\, which sends a reset command to the printer. In addition to these new backslash commands some of the backslash commands discussed in the previous section, \b\, \c\, \u\, \line\, \nl\, and *nnn*\, are also available for items, notes and section setup and termination strings.

Finally, a special format command is available for note text. It sets the left margin and the width of the printed note. The format for the command is \mgn *x y*\, where *x* is a number from 0 to 80 (or 0 to 160 in compressed mode), which you insert in the typed command to tell Agenda where to start printing the note relative to the left margin of the page, and *y* is a number indicating the width in characters (also limited to 0 to 80 or 160) of the note text for printing. \mgn\ can be used in place of the default settings \mgn 0 79\. If you insert the \mgn *x y*\ command in the setup and termination strings for the Note prompt, either in the item view or the note screen Print dialog boxes, this format will govern all note text printed. On the other hand, if you only want to apply this or any other \mgn *x y*\ format to one or more individual notes, you can insert these commands into the note texts themselves and Agenda will apply them only to the coded notes.

One other command that can be useful in a similarly selective fashion is \pgbk *x*\, which causes a page break to occur after *x* lines have been printed, where *x* can be any number, including 0, in which case the command is shown as \pgbk\. This command can be in the item, section, or note setup strings causing Agenda to skip to a new page for every item, section, and note respectively. Alternatively, this command can be inserted in text, for example, in an item's note text, to control the number of lines that must be printed together before a page break occurs. \pgbk 6\ inserted at the top of a paragraph in the text tells Agenda that if there are fewer than six lines of space available on the current page being printed, it should go to a new page to print this text.

Now that you are finished responding to the prompts in the Print dialog box, press F9(Accept) to close the box and begin printing.

CUSTOMIZING PDFs

Lotus supplies PDFs for most major printers. Using any text editor, EDLIN, for example, you can modify these files or create one of your own for a new printer by following the heavily commented form in the default or generic PRINTER.PDF file, which is shown in Figure 10-9.

Figure 10-9.

```
Generic printer
Agenda Printer Definition File

This pdf file assumes that the printer prints no special characters and is
unable to backspace.  For each translation where backspace would be used,  an
alternative is provided but commented out (preceded by REM), preventing the l
from being read as a legitimate translation.   If you wish to use these, remo
the REM and comment out the conflicting translation.

\pdfver\          "v1.00"
\pname\           "Generic Printer"

UTILITY DEFINITIONS

\reset\           ""                Resets printer to power on state
\prstart\         ""                No control before print
\prend\           ""                No control after print

ATTRIBUTE DEFINITIONS

\b\               "" ""                     Bold On / Off

\u\               "" ""                     Underline On / Off

\c\               "" ""                     Compressed On / Off

TRANSLATE TABLE

white happy face
# 1, 32
black happy face
# 2, 32
heart
# 3, 32
diamond.  In view used as mark character.
# 4, 255       See comment at the bottom of the file
club
# 5, 32
spade
# 6, 32
center dot
=\7\.
inverse center dot
# 8, 32
circle
=\9\o
inverse circle
# 10, 32
male
# 11, 32
female
# 12, 32
-- Carraige return can't be translated.  In view, note symbol is sent as 255.
-- Change the translation for 255 to change the way note symbol is printed.
```

Figure 10-9.

```
double note
# 14, 32
sun
=\15\*
right arrow
=\16\>
left arrow
=\17\<
up and down arrows
# 18, 32
double exclamation
=\19\!
paragraph
# 20, 32
section
# 21, 32
thick horizontal line
=\22\-
up and down arrows with underline
# 23, 32
up arrow
=\24\^
REM =\24\^\8\|
down arrow -- this is used as NOT in printing the category manager rules
=\25\~
REM =\25\v\8\|
right arrow
# 26, 32
REM =\26\>\8\-
ESC - left arrow
# 27, 32
REM =\27\<\8\-
right angle
# 28, 32
left and right arrows
# 29, 255          See the comment at the bottom of the file.
up triangle
# 30, 32
down triangle
# 31, 32

house
=\127\^
REM =\127\^\8\-

C cedille
=\128\C
u umlaute
=\129\u
e acute
=\130\e
a circumflex
=\131\a
REM =\131\a\8\^
```

Figure 10-9.

```
a umlaut
=\132\a
a grave
=\133\a
REM =\133\a\8\'
a ring
=\134\a
c cedille
=\135\c
e circumflex
=\136\e
REM =\136\e\8\^
e umlaut
=\137\e
e grave
=\138\e
REM =\138\e\8\'
i umlaut
=\139\i
i circumflex
=\140\i
REM =\140\i\8\^
i grave
=\141\i
REM =\141\i\8\'
A umlaut
=\142\A
A ring
=\143\A
E acute
=\144\E
ae dipthong
=\145\ae
AE dipthong
=\146\AE
o circumflex
=\147\o
REM =\147\o\8\^
o umlaut
=\148\o
o grave
=\149\o
REM =\149\o\8\'
u circumflex
=\150\u
REM =\150\u\8\^
u grave
=\151\u
y umlaut
=\152\y
O umlaut
=\153\O
U umlaut
=\154\U
```

Figure 10-9.

```
o slash
=\155\o
REM =\155\o\8\/
British pounds
=\156\L
REM =\156\L\8\=
O slash
=\157\O
REM =\157\O\8\/
times
=\158\x
Dutch guilders
=\159\f
a acute
=\160\a
i acute
=\161\i
o acute
=\162\o
u acute
=\163\u
n tilde
=\164\n
REM =\164\n\8\~
N tilde
=\165\N
a superscript and underscored (feminine ordinal)
=\166\a
REM =\166\a\8\_
o superscript and underscored (masculine ordinal)
=\167\o
REM =\167\o\8\_
inverted question mark
=\168\?
Registered trademark
=\169\r
abbreviated upper-right cornor
# 170, 32
one-half
=\171\1/2
one-fourth
=\172\1/4
inverted exclamation point
=\173\!
angle quotation left
=\174\<
angle quotation right
=\175\>
quarter dark
# 176, 32
half dark
# 177, 32
3/4 dark
# 178, 32
```

Figure 10-9.

```
vertical line
=\179\|
vertical w/ left
=\180\+
A acute
=\181\A
A circumflex
=\182\A
A grave
=\183\A
copyright
=\184\c
double vertical w/ left
=\185\+
double vertical
=\186\|
double upper right
=\187\+
double lower right
=\188\+
cents
=\189\c
REM =\189\c\8\|
Yen
=\190\Y
REM =\190\Y\8\=
upper right
=\191\+
lower left
=\192\+
horizontal w/ up
=\193\+
horizontal w/ down
=\194\+
vertical w/ right
=\195\+
horizontal
=\196\-
vertical and horizontal
=\197\+
a tilde
=\198\a
REM =\198\a\8\~
A tilde
=\199\A
double lower left
=\200\+
double upper left
=\201\+
double horizontal w/ up
=\202\+
double horizontal w/ down
=\203\+
double vertical w/ right
```

Figure 10-9.

```
=\204\+
double horizontal
=\205\-
double vertical and horizontal
=\206\+
General currency symbol
=\207\O
REM =\207\O\8\X
lowercase eth
=\208\d
REM =\208\d\8\-
uppercase eth
=\209\D
REM =\208\D\8\-
E circumflex
=\210\E
E umlaut
=\211\E
E grave
=\212\E
Dotless i
=\213\i
I acute
=\214\I
I circumflex
=\215\I
I umlaut
=\216\I
lower right
=\217\+
upper left
=\218\+
full dark
# 219, 32
bottom dark
=\220\_
elongated colon
=\221\|
I grave
=\222\I
upper dark
# 223, 32
O acute
=\224\O
Beta -- sharp S
=\225\ss
O circumflex
=\226\O
O grave
=\227\O
o tilde
=\228\o
REM =\228\o\8\~
O tilde
```

Figure 10-9.

```
=\229\O
mu
=\230\u
lowercase thorn
=\231\p
Uppercase thorn
=\232\P
U acute
=\233\U
U circumflex
=\234\U
U grave
=\235\U
y acute
=\236\y
Y acute
=\237\Y
breve
#238,32
acute
=\239\'
short horizontal line
=\240\-
plus minus
=\241\+
REM =\241\+\8\_
equals
=\242\=
three-fourths
=\243\3/4
paragraph
# 244, 32
section
# 245, 32
divided by
=\246\/
sideways apostrophe
# 247, 32
degrees
# 248, 32
umlaut
=\249\"
middle dot
=\250\.
superscript 1
=\251\1
superscript 3
=\252\3
superscript 2
=\253\2
middle block
# 254, 32

The character 255 is used for the note symbol in views (since note symbol is
```

Figure 10-9.

```
a carriage return), translate it in order to change printing of note symbol.
# 255, 255

If any character translates to 255, the translation for the current tag
character will be used.  This has the effect of eliminating the note symbols,
for example.  In order to print note symbols (or any character) as a space,
translate it to 32.

REM # 255, 32      Uncommented, this would print note symbols as space.
```

The first section of the PDF should begin with some text describing the PDF. On the next two lines, the PDF must contain the Agenda version number with which it will be used and the printer name, both enclosed in double quotes (" "), to the right of the backslash labels \pdfver\ and \pname\.

The next section contains utility definitions for the most common printer commands, namely, \reset\ for reset, \prstart\ for begin printing, and \prend\ for end printing. The commands appropriate to your printer should be inserted in double quotes to the right of each of these backslash labels. Any information that is not between either two backslash symbols or two double quotes will be ignored and, therefore, can be used as comment text.

The attribute definitions section contains translations for the bold or \b\, compressed or \c\, and underlined or \u\ commands. Once again, the character strings appropriate to your printer should be inserted in double quotes to the right of these backslash commands. There should be two character strings, each in double quotes, following the \b\, \u\, and \c\ commands, which require on and off settings. You can also add new backslash commands to this section by typing the formats which you will use in entering them, for example \italic\, and the one or two printer character strings which are needed to execute them.

The last section, or translate table, contains the substitutions or translations that Agenda will make prior to printing each of the possible 256 characters in the ASCII character set. Each line in the translation table consists of three components, first either an equal (=) or number (#) sign, then the ASCII code or character to be translated, and finally zero to eight characters that will be substituted as the result of the translation. If you want to replace one ASCII number with another, you can write the line beginning with the number sign, for example, #3, 32, which replaces the heart-shaped symbol with a blank space. Otherwise, if you are mixing ASCII numbers and actual characters, you must write the line beginning with the equal sign and any ASCII number must be typed in backslashes, for example, =\7\o, which replaces the circle symbol with a lowercase letter o. In both cases, you can use printer control characters in the substitution strings. For example, if you do not have an umlaut on your printer, you can backspace over a letter, for example, o, and print the double quote sign by entering either # 148, 111, 8, 34 or =\148\o\008\".

To fully appreciate the power of the PDFs, print them out, as we did in Figure 10-9, and examine the various definitions and substitutions. Be prepared to experiment with different settings until you have customized your PDF file to your liking.

SUMMARY

Although Agenda is not a word processing program, many of the printing capabilities commonly associated with word and/or text processing programs are provided through the various Print dialog boxes and Printer Definition Files. As we have seen, you have considerable flexibility in tailoring the printing of text to suit your preferences.

11

Macros

A macro is a stored sequence of characters, some of which are keystrokes that are meaningful to Agenda, for example Enter and Backspace, and others that are special advanced commands that are meaningful to macros, for example, {QUIT}. These stored sequences can be played back by simply pushing the proverbial button. Today, many software packages such as 1-2-3 provide macro capabilities, so this material may seem familiar to many readers. Although the basic concepts of macros are similar across these software packages, the details of using macros with Agenda are unique. Since macros can contribute to more efficient and effective work with Agenda, it pays to study this material closely.

The first of the two types of commands that can be stored in macros consists of sequences of keystrokes that are recorded as you type or press them while Agenda is in learn mode. These keystrokes are the ones that are meaningful in an Agenda session and include everything from alphabetic and numeric characters to special keys, function keys, and accelerator keys. To distinguish the function, special, and accelerator keys from ordinary typed characters in the stored macros, Agenda provides special formats enclosed in curly braces. For example, the first function key, F1(Help), is stored in macros as {F1}. Similarly, Alt-Q is stored as {AltQ}. The complete list of special formats is as follows:

Agenda key	As displayed in macro
Function keys	{F1}...{F10}
Alt-Function keys	{AltF1}...{AltF10}

Agenda key	As displayed in macro
Accelerator keys	{AltA}...{AltZ}
TAB	{TAB}
BACKSPACE	{BS}
ENTER	{ENTER}
CTRL-ENTER	{CtlENTER}
ESCAPE,HOME	{ESC},{HOME}
CTRL-HOME	{CtlHOME}
END,CTRL-END	{END},{CtlEND}
INSERT,DELETE	{INS},{DEL}
UP,DOWN	{UP},{DOWN}
LEFT,RIGHT	{LEFT},{RIGHT}
CTRL-LEFT	{CtlLEFT}
CTRL-RIGHT	{CtlRIGHT}
PAGE UP	{PgUp}
CTRL-PAGE UP	{CtlPgUp}
PAGE DOWN	{PgDn}
CTRL-PAGE DOWN	{CtlPgDn}
GREY– ,GREY+	{GREY– },{GREY+ }
SHIFT GREY– ,SHIFT GREY+	{ALT– },{ALT= }

The second type of macro command, or advanced command, is unique to the macro language, and directly exercises its influence over the execution of the macro. Examples of these types of commands, of which there are seventeen, include {QUIT}, which terminates a macro, and {LABEL;label name}, which establishes a named reference point in the macro. The complete list of macro commands is as follows:

ALERT	BRANCH	CLEAR	COMMENT
DEBUGON	DEBUGOFF	GETKEY	GOTO
IFEQ	IFNOTEQ	IFKEY	INPUT
LABEL	LET	QUIT	SPEED
TYPE			

In the rest of this chapter, we will review how macros are entered, stored, edited, and run in Agenda, beginning with the keystroke macros and concluding with the advanced macros.

KEYSTROKE MACROS

How Do Keystroke Macros Get into Agenda?

Before recording a macro, it is important to plan the steps you are interested in recording because, once the recorder is turned on, every key you press becomes part of the macro. For example, if you want to replace the six-keystroke sequence of changing a column's width (F10/C/C/W/?/Enter) with a three-key macro sequence (Alt-F10/W/F9), where W is the name you have given to this macro, you must begin recording the macro while in a category column because that is where Agenda correctly responds to the original six-keystroke sequence. Except for a feature in the advanced commands that allows you to do some minimal context checking to lessen the risk of executing a macro in the wrong setting, Agenda cannot tell whether you are executing the right macro in the right place. In other words, you have to be sure that the keystrokes that Agenda is going to record will accomplish the functional goal you intend for the macro.

To create a recorded keystroke macro, place your highlight in the appropriate starting location and press Alt-F10(Macro). If this is the first macro you are entering, Agenda prompts you for a name, up to 35 characters long, with which you will refer to the macro in the future, as shown in Figure 11-1.

If this is not your first macro, Agenda displays a list of previously entered macros in a Macros dialog box, as shown in Figure 11-2. To create a new macro based on recorded keystrokes, press Ins or Insert and Agenda will prompt you for the new macro name. When you select a name for your macro, try to make the first letters of the macro names different whenever possible. This will be helpful when you are using Agenda's automatic completion feature to quickly locate a macro for subsequent running or editing. After typing the macro name, press Enter.

To begin recording keystrokes, press F7(Learn). Agenda will close the Macros dialog box and return you to the item view, note, or Category Manager screen you left when you pressed Alt-F10(Macro). Now, every key you press will be recorded in the macro by Agenda. When you are finished pressing keys for the macro, press Alt-F10(Macro) again, and the recording will be turned off. You will be left in the Macros dialog box, where you can press F9(Run) to run the macro you just recorded.

Figure 11-1.

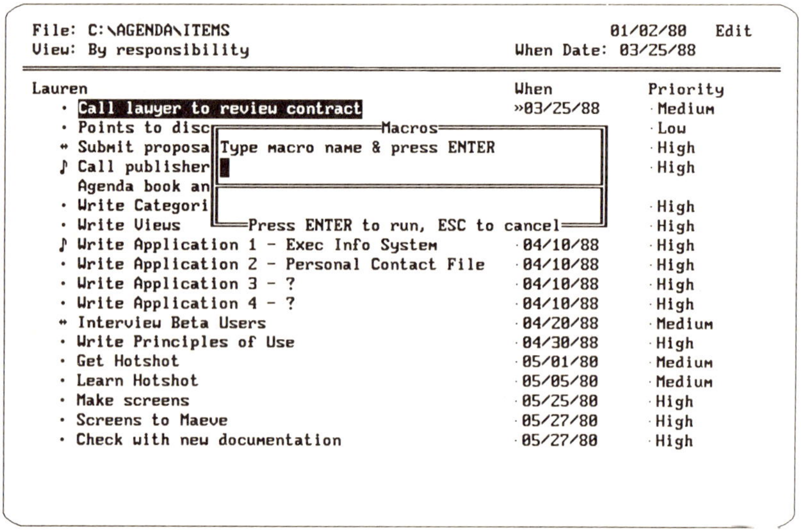

Figure 11-2.

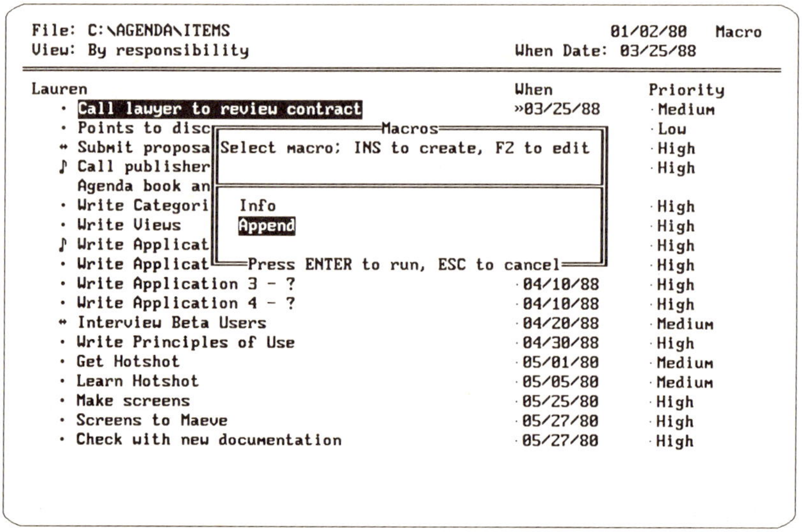

As an example, let's create the automatic column widening macro described earlier. Ordinarily, if you wanted to widen a column to the width suggested by Agenda based on the column's heading and entries, you would position the highlight on the column heading and press F10(Menu), C for Category, C for Column, W for Width, ? for automatic sizing, and Enter to complete the process. Assuming that this is the first macro you are entering and that the highlight is on any column heading, this six-keystroke sequence can be replaced by a three-key macro-driven sequence as follows:

Press:	ALT - F10 (MACRO)
Type:	W as the macro name to stand for widen
Press:	↵
Press:	F7 (LEARN) to return to the item view screen
Press:	F10 (MENU)
Type:	C for Category
Type:	C for Column
Type:	W for Width
Press:	? for letting Agenda propose width
Press:	↵ to accept proposed width
Press:	ALT - F10 (MACRO) to turn off learning
Press:	Any key to continue

Now, to test the macro, move the highlight to any column heading in the item view screen, and then press Alt-F10(Macro), W for the widen macro, and F9(Run) to execute it. You have accomplished the same thing with three keystrokes that formerly would have taken six. Although not as efficient as the one-key accelerator alternatives, you can save significant amounts of time with multikey command sequences by developing macros to accomplish the same functions in half or fewer keystrokes.

Following the previous example, you can easily develop macros to automatically format a column in any of the standard formats, using names like Star(*), Y/N, Actual, Parent:child, Ancestor, and Category note. Since the first letters of most of these are distinct, you will be able to invoke the macro with just three keystrokes instead of six. In the case of Actual and Ancestor, where it takes the first two characters to distinguish the names using auto-completion, it will sometimes take four keystrokes to identify and execute the format macros.

How to Use Macros

To run an existing macro, be sure that the highlight is positioned in your item view, note, or Category Manager screen at the appropriate place for the macro to execute. A keystroke macro does not know that it was created in an item view screen, but that you are attempting to use it in a note screen. Therefore, since {F3} in a macro means different things depending on whether you are in an item view or note screen, it is important to be sure that you call the macro from the context in which it was developed. As mentioned earlier, certain advanced commands provide limited context checking. With the highlight properly positioned, press Alt-F10(Macro) and Agenda will display the Macros dialog box. Use the arrows to highlight the desired macro name, or start typing the name. Agenda uses automatic completion to locate the name you are typing. As we saw earlier, to run the highlighted macro, press F9(Run).

As with other functions in Agenda, there is an accelerator key with which you can rerun the last macro executed. This can be helpful if you use the same macro over and over again, for example, in a complicated item and category input routine. To rerun the last macro, press Alt-Z.

There is still another automated technique for running a macro, in this case, one you want to have executed every time you open the database. Since this is similar in concept to the idea of an AUTOEXEC.BAT file in DOS, it is recognized by the name AUTOEXEC. If you want a particular macro to execute every time you enter the database, save the macro under the name AUTOEXEC.

If after running the macro you find that it does not do what you wanted it to do or you want to otherwise modify it, you must return to the Macros dialog box where you can use F7(Learn) to append to or replace the highlighted macro, or you can use F2(EditMac) to edit the stored text version of the macro. Unless the macro is very long and complicated, it is usually easier to replace it by relearning than to attempt to edit it. However, the choice is yours, and Agenda makes it possible for you to correct a macro either way.

With the macros dialog box displayed and the desired macro highlighted, press F7(Learn), Agenda once again changes to learn mode, prompts you to determine whether you want to append or replace the macro, and returns you to the screen that you left when you pressed Alt-F10 (Macro). Any keystrokes you now make will either be added to the end of the existing macro or replace it. When you are done with the learning process, press Alt-F10(Macro) to terminate learning.

If you press F2(EditMac) to edit the stored text version of the macro, Agenda displays an Edit macro screen, with the name of the macro as the first line of macro text. The format of this screen is shown in Figure 11-3.

Figure 11-3.

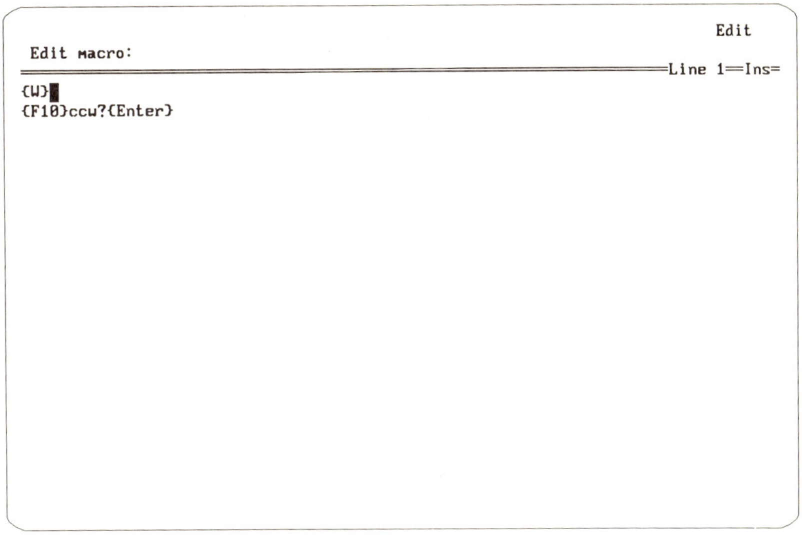

You can edit the macro text using any of the function key commands at the bottom of the screen including F2(Paste), F3(Copy), F4(Cut), F7(Mark), Alt-F4 (Delete), and Alt-F5(Search). These commands function the same way as the note edit functions that we have encountered in the items and categories chapters. Since you might find the continuous string of macro commands hard to decipher, you might want to edit long macros to insert carriage returns by pressing Enter in selected locations of the macro text to break it up into meaningful chunks. The W macro of Figure 11-3 has been edited along these lines, and the revised macro appears in a more readable format in Figure 11-4.

Figure 11-4.

In the Edit macro screen, if you press F10(Menu), a menu will appear at the top of the screen giving you the options of Importing or Exporting a macro as a named text file, Printing the macro, or Deleting the macro. You may find over time that you are creating a series of macros that are useful in many of your Agenda databases. For example, you might have some standard headers and footers that you want to apply in all Print dialog boxes in all your databases. You can develop macros for the item view screen, note screen, and Category Manager Print dialog boxes, that automatically access the dialog box and fill in the *Header:* and *Footer:* prompts, waiting for you to respond to the remaining prompts. However, since macros are only associated with the databases in which they were created, it is up to you to export and import them between databases.

To export a macro to a named text file so that it can in turn be imported into any other Agenda database, you must be in the Edit macro screen for that macro. If you press F10(Menu) and E for Export, Agenda prompts you for a filename to be used in storing the macro. After typing the filename, press Enter and F9(Accept). If Agenda finds that the filename is a new one, it will write the macro out to the named file. If this file already exists, Agenda will ask whether you want to replace the old file or append the new information to it.

Now, whenever you are in a different database and you need to have this header/footer macro, import it by pressing Alt-F10(Macro) and Ins or Insert, followed by typing the name for the macro and pressing Enter. Now press F2(EditMac) to access the blank Edit macro screen. Press F10(Menu) and I for Import and then type the filename under which you previously stored the macro. If you cannot remember the name, press GREY + to see a list of all files in your directory, select one with the arrow keys, and press Enter and F9(Accept). When Agenda imports the file, the old macro name will still be in the macro text, alongside the new name you just created for the purpose of importing the macro. You can use your edit keys to remove the old macro name in the first line of the macro text.

If you want to transfer all your macros from one database to a new database, use the F10/File/Transfer/Template commands, which will copy not only the macros, but the Category Manager, view definitions, and stored conditions and actions as well.

You can delete a macro in either of two ways. First, in the Macros dialog box, you can use F4(Delete), Delete, or Del to remove the highlighted macro name. Alternatively, in the Edit macro screen, you can use Alt-F4(Delete) to remove some or all of the macro from the screen. In the first three cases, Agenda double checks to ensure that you really do want to delete the macro.

Another Example

Suppose that you wanted to develop a macro that will undiscard all items in the Trash, set up a new category to which you can selectively move items to be recovered, and re-discard the remaining items. Using the keystroke macro recording feature, you can accomplish this with two macros, which we will call Begin Undiscard and End Undiscard. Before recording these macros, plan out and test the keystrokes that you intend to incorporate in these macros.

Basically, you may expect to be in an item view screen and for there to be items in the Trash, though with keystroke macros there is no way for the macro to verify any of this. You want Begin Undiscard to create a new view, to be called Recover lost items, with its first and only section called Trashed items. Then undiscard the items currently in the Trash and insert them into this new section. Next create a new section, to be called Recovered items and leave the macro. This allows you to selectively move items from the Trashed items section to the new Recovered items section. Finally, initiate the End Undiscard macro, which will re-discard the items left in the Trashed items section and leave you in the Recover lost items view with just the Recovered items, ready to be assigned to categories, printed, and so on.

With this basic plan, which you will test as you develop the macros, you can start out in a view screen. You first need to put some items in the Trash by marking them using F7(Mark) and discarding them by pressing F10(Menu), I for Items, and D for Discard. For the purposes of this example, discard the four Write application items from the view that you saw in Figure 11-1. To create the Begin Undiscard macro, press Alt-F10(Macro) and Ins or Insert. Type **B** as the macro name and press Enter. Next press F7(Learn) and Agenda will be in keystroke macro learning mode. Now follow the basic plan we described:

Press: F8 (VW MGR)
Press: INS
Type: Recover lost items
Press: ↵
Press: ↓
Type: Trashed items
Press: ↵
Press: F9 (ACCEPT)
Press: F10 (MENU)
Type: I for Items
Type: U for Undiscard
Type: A for All items
Press: ↵
Press: F10 (MENU)
Type: C for Category
Type: S for Section
Type: N for New
Press: ↓
Type: Recovered items
Press: ↵

Press: F9 (ACCEPT)
Press: ALT - F10 (MACRO) to turn off learning mode
Press: Any key to continue

You will be left in the Recover lost items view, as shown in Figure 11-5.

Figure 11-5.

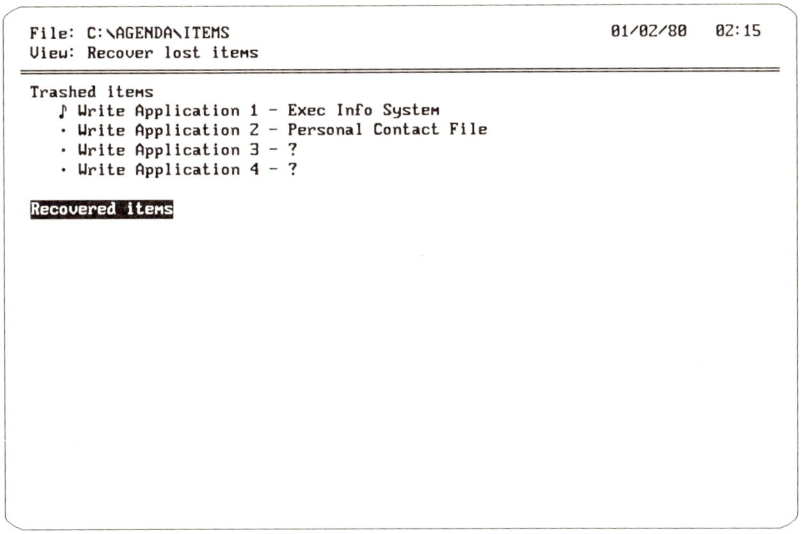

To see the stored macro text, press Alt-F10(Macro), place the highlight on B and press F2(EditMac). The Edit macro screen shown in Figure 11-6 should appear. You can now edit the macro to break up the one long line of text into meaningful chunks, by using the arrows and Enter to insert carriage returns in the text. The reformatted macro is shown in Figure 11-7.

To return to the Macros dialog box, press F9(Accept). To return to the item view screen, press Esc.

While we tested the macro logic as we recorded it, if we wanted to test it again, we would have to make sure that there were some items in the trash. If so, and only if you are back in the view screen, you can press Alt-F10(Macro), type B, and press F9(Run) to see if the macro performs correctly. If the macro is not executing correctly, return to the Edit macro screen and verify that you typed the macro text exactly as shown in Figure 11-6 or Figure 11-7.

Figure 11-6.

```
                                                                        Edit
Edit macro:
═══════════════════════════════════════════════════════════════════Line 1═Ins═
{B}█
{F8}{INS}Recover lost items{Enter}{DOWN}Trashed
items{Enter}{F9}{F10}iua{Enter}{F10}csn{DOWN}Recovered Items{Enter}{F9}
```

Figure 11-7.

```
                                                                        Edit
Edit macro:
═══════════════════════════════════════════════════════════════════Line 1═Ins═
{B}█
{F8}{INS}Recover lost items{Enter}
{DOWN}Trashed items{Enter}{F9}
{F10}iua{Enter}
{F10}csn{DOWN}Recovered Items{Enter}{F9}
```

When you are ready to create the End Undiscard macro, first move some items into the Recovered items section from the Trashed items section, by marking them with F7(Mark) and moving them by pressing

F6(Move) and selecting Recovered items as the destination section. If as your items you moved the Write applications 1 and 2, the item view screen should look like the one shown in Figure 11-8.

Figure 11-8.

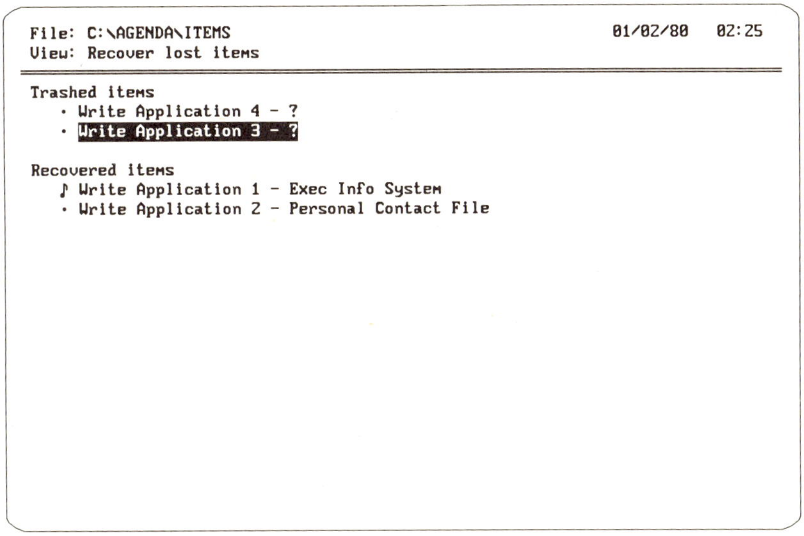

Press Alt-F10(Macro) to access the Macros dialog box, and press Ins or Insert to create a new macro. Type E and press Enter. Now press F7(Learn) to return to the item view screen where you can re-discard the items left in the Trashed items section. To do this:

Press:	ALT - F6 (GO TO)
Type:	Trashed items
Press:	↵
Press:	F7 (MARK)
Press:	F10 (MENU)
Type:	I for Items
Type:	D for Discard
Type:	M for marked items
Press:	↵
Press:	ALT - F4 (DISCARD) to discard the category
Press:	F8 (VW MGR)
Press:	F4 (DELETE)

Type: Y for Yes
Press: ↵
Press: ALT - F10 (MACRO) to turn off learning mode
Press: Any key to continue

You will be left in the view manager, where you can select the highlighted view by pressing Enter or F9(Accept). To see the stored macro text, press Alt-F10(Macro), place the highlight on E and press F2(EditMac). The Edit macro screen shown in Figure 11-9 should appear.

Figure 11-9.

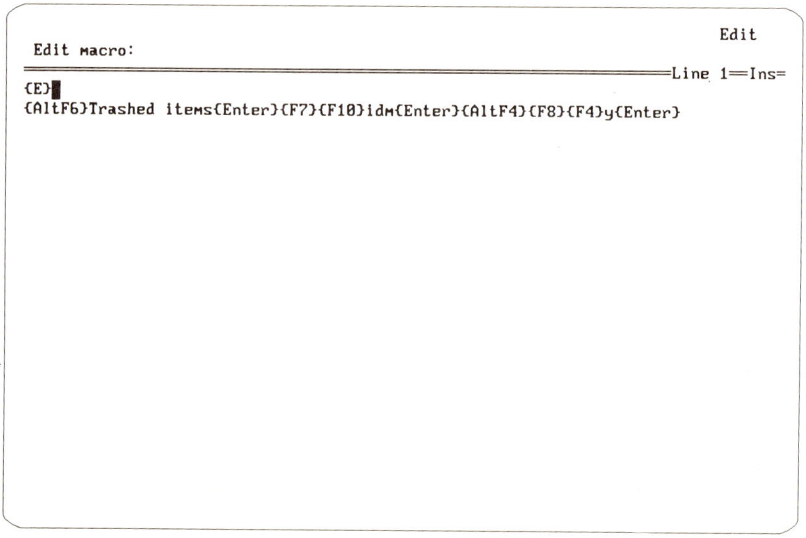

You can then edit the macro to break up the one long line of text into meaningful chunks, by using the arrows and Enter to insert carriage returns in the text. The reformatted macro is shown in Figure 11-10. Press F9(Accept) to return to the macros dialog box and Esc to return to the view screen.

As the macro was entered, the functions were being performed. Therefore, the Recover lost items view has been deleted, and the recovered items can only be seen by adding their section to any view. To display the recovered items in the current view, press F10(Menu), C for Category, S for Section, N for New, and A for inserting the new section above the current one in the view. Then move the highlight down, type Recovered items, press Enter and F9(Accept), and the view should appear like the one shown in Figure 11-11. If your results are different from those shown here, you should compare your macro to the one shown in Figure 11-10, and make any necessary corrections.

Figure 11-10.

```
                                                                    Edit
 Edit macro:
==================================================================Line 7==Ins=
{E}
{AltF6}Trashed items{Enter}
{F7}
{F10}idm{Enter}
{AltF4}
{F8}{F4}
y{Enter}
```

Figure 11-11.

```
File: C:\AGENDA\ITEMS                                      01/02/80   02:27
View: By responsibility
============================================================================
Recovered items                                     When          Priority
    ♪ Write Application 1 - Exec Info System
    • Write Application 2 - Personal Contact File

Lauren                                              When          Priority
    • Call lawyer to review contract                03/25/88      Medium
    • Points to discuss with the lawyer             03/12/88      Low
    •• Submit proposals                             02/25/88      High
    ♪ Call publishers to see if they are doing an   02/15/88      High
      Agenda book and to get author guidelines
    • Write Categories                              04/10/88      High
    • Write Views                                   04/10/88      High
    • Interview Beta Users                          04/20/88      Medium
    • Write Principles of Use                       04/30/88      High
    • Check with new documentation                  05/27/80      High

Bob                                                 When          Priority
    • Write Items                                   04/10/88      High
    • Write Principles of Use                       04/30/88      High
    • Write Views                                   04/10/88      High
```

ADVANCED COMMANDS

Advanced commands add another dimension to the building of macros. For example, suppose that you typically find yourself using the same item entry macro, and you are tired of inputting the same macro initiation instructions item after item. The idea of a macro that causes Agenda to automatically loop through the item entry macro requires what are called advanced commands in Agenda. These are commands that control macros as opposed to commands that control Agenda. Other examples include commands to pause and prompt the user for input or to change the speed of macro execution.

Most advanced commands have arguments, shown in lowercase in the following definitions. All arguments are separated from each other and from the command name by semicolons. The whole command, including its name and arguments, must be enclosed in curly braces, for example, {TYPE;Items}. There can be no spaces within the braces unless they are part of some text that is serving as an argument. If a single command with its arguments requires more than one screen line to display, do not insert a carriage return in the middle of the text. Just keep on typing and let Agenda wrap the text around to the next line.

Generally, command arguments can be specific text strings or variables representing such strings, up to 80 characters in length, unless otherwise specified. There can be up to 26 macro variables, each of whose names must consist of a % and a letter ranging from a through z, or %a through %z. All macros in a database can access any variable that has been initialized or changed in any other macro in the database. Finally, there are seven special arguments that can be used in supplying system values such as date and time and in testing variables. These include #DATE and #TIME in the default date and HH:MM formats; #NULL or empty; #TRUE and #FALSE for comparisons of variables; #KEYHIT, which is TRUE or FALSE depending on whether a key has been pressed; and #MODE, which carries Agenda's current mode, namely, VIEW, CATMGR, NOTE, or OTHER. This last argument can be used to test that the user is in the correct mode before executing a macro.

Since advanced macro commands are used for programming macros, it is reasonable to categorize them according to the functions they serve, as shown in the following table.

Function	Command	Description
Controlling the screen	{TYPE;text}	Types text to the screen.
Allowing keyboard interaction:	{ALERT;box name;message}	Displays a box with a name in the top line and a message inside (up to 76 characters or a variable name), waiting for a key to be pressed. If the box is not to have a name, use the format {ALERT;;message}.
	{GETKEY;variable name}	Causes macro execution to pause, waiting for a key to be pressed. The pressed key is stored in the named variable. Unlike INPUT, GETKEY does not prompt the user for the keystroke; another command must handle this.
	{INPUT;message;variable}	Displays an unnamed box and causes macro execution to pause, waiting for typed text in response to the message, which can be a constant or a variable, up to 38 characters long. The text response, up to 79 characters in length, can be edited while it is being entered, and is stored in the named variable. The box is closed by pressing Enter or Esc.
Controlling the sequence of macro command execution	{BRANCH;label name}	Transfers control to (that is, continues execution at) the section of the same macro that begins with the matched {LABEL;label name} command.
	{GOTO;macro name}	Transfers control to the beginning of another macro with the argument's name, which can be a variable or a constant.

Function	Command	Description
	{IFEQ;value1;value2;label name}	If value1 equals value2 (either of which can be constants, variables, or special arguments) this command transfers control to the section of the same macro that begins with the matched {LABEL;label name} command. Otherwise, the macro continues with the next command.
	{IFKEY;label name}	If a key is pressed, this command transfers control to the section of the same macro that begins with the matched {LABEL;label name} command. The value of the keystroke is not saved, but, if this command is followed by a GETKEY or INPUT command, the keystroke's value can be stored and tested.
	{IFNOTEQ;value1;value2;label name}	If value1 does not equal value2 (either of which can be constants, variables, or special arguments) this command transfers control to the section of the same macro that begins with the matched {LABEL;label name} command. Otherwise the macro continues with the next command.
	{LABEL;label name}	Identifies a named section of the macro to which other commands refer. The label name can be a constant or a variable.
	{QUIT}	Stops macro execution.

Function	Command	Description
	{SPEED;argument}	Slows down or restores the speed of macro execution. The argument can be SLOW, MED, or FAST, all of which are slower than the normal setting, which can be restored with an argument of MAX.
Manipulating variables	{CLEAR;variable} or {CLEAR;ALL}	Is used to reset the named variable or all variables to the initial value, null, or blank.
	{LET;variable;value}	Is the basic assignment command that sets the named variable equal to the text string (value).
Helping to write and test macros	{COMMENT;text}	Is not executed by the macro and can be used for storing notes throughout the macro that explain the logic being used.
	{DEBUGON}	Turns on a step and trace mode of operation whereby the macro is executed one keystroke or command at a time in response to the user pressing any key. This can be useful in debugging or testing a macro that does not seem to be doing what you expected.
	{DEBUGOFF}	Turns off the step and trace mode of operation and returns the macro to normal, automated operation. With {DEBUGON}, these commands can be inserted at the beginning and end of a macro to test the whole macro or selectively to bracket certain sections of a macro you want to test.

An Example

Suppose you wanted to make the column widening macro interactive. That is, if users wanted to execute it again on an adjacent column, instead of having to use the three-key sequence, they could tell the macro to move right or left and to automatically execute the column widening macro again. This would continue, until the users signaled that they were done.

With this basic plan in mind, you would access the W macro that was created earlier by pressing Alt-F10(Macro), W for the auto-widen macro, and F2(EditMac) to access the Edit macro screen. The screen should look like the one in Figure 11-4. Now edit the macro as shown below:

```
{W}
{COMMENT;make sure user is in a view}
 {LET;%a;VIEW}
 {IFNOTEQ;#MODE;%a;wrong-mode}
{COMMENT;original routine}
 {LABEL;auto-widen}
 {F10}
 c
 c
 w
 ?
 {Enter}
{COMMENT;prompt user to continue}
 {LET;%a;Q}
 {ALERT;Move to new column or quit;Press — >, < — or
    Esc twice}
 {GETKEY;%a}
{COMMENT;test users response}
 {IFEQ;%a;{ESC};end}
 {IFEQ;%a;{LEFT};move-left}
 {IFEQ;%a;{RIGHT};move-right}
{COMMENT;this moves highlight to the right and recalls
   auto-widen}
 {LABEL;move-right}
 {RIGHT}
 {BRANCH;auto-widen}
```

```
{COMMENT;this moves highlight to the left and recalls auto-widen}
  {LABEL;move-left}
  {LEFT}
  {BRANCH;auto-widen}
{COMMENT;this alerts user to need to be in a view}
  {LABEL;wrong-mode}
  {ALERT;ERROR;Start macro in a view}
{COMMENT;this ends the macro altogether}
  {LABEL;end}
  {QUIT}
```

Notice how comments and indenting are used throughout the macro to provide structure and clarity. Basically, the macro checks to make sure that the user is at least in an item view screen. The macro does not know if the user has the highlight positioned in a category column, which is the only place that you would want to perform the auto-widening macro. If the user is not in a view screen, the macro executes the wrong-mode section and exits with an error message. If the user is in a view screen, the macro executes the auto-widen section, which is the original routine. Then the macro prompts the user for a RIGHT or LEFT Arrow or Esc. The right and left arrows cause Agenda to move right or left and execute the auto-widen section again. The Esc causes the macro to perform the end section, where the macro quits. If you study this macro and the samples provided in the *Agenda User's Guide*, you will develop a better sense of how to plan, design, and develop advanced macros.

How Do Advanced Command Macros Get into Agenda?

To create macros with advanced commands requires a good deal of planning because they are equivalent to programs with which you control both Agenda and your PC. The design phase might include outlining the major functions of the macro in English as we have just done. Then go back and further define each of the major functions into subfunctions. Continue this redefinition of smaller subfunctions until the subfunctions seem to be small enough to be coded as macros or labeled sections of macros. In this fashion, you will be coding from top to bottom and grouping related functions, which are generally considered to be good programming practices. It is also important to exit or quit the macro carefully and, if at all possible, at one labeled location in the macro.

Finally, it is important to practice executing the macro by hand and thoroughly proofreading it to minimize the chances of subtle errors in logic.

To enter the macro you have designed, be sure that the highlight is positioned in an area appropriate to the function that the macro will perform. Press Alt-F10(Macro) and press Ins or Insert. Agenda prompts you for a name, which you should type. Then press Enter. Now, instead of pressing F7(Learn) to start recording keystrokes, press F2(EditMac). This causes the Edit macro screen to be displayed with just the macro name as the first line of text. Move the highlight to the second line on the screen and begin typing your macro commands, as previously specified and as represented in your design. Remember, keystroke and advanced commands can be interspersed.

If, on the other hand, you intend to add advanced commands to an existing keystroke macro, press Alt-F10(Macro), select the desired macro with the highlight or by typing its name, and press F2(EditMac) to access the Edit macro screen, where you can begin inserting the advanced commands in the planned locations to accomplish the intended function.

How To Use Macros

When you are done entering a macro, press F9(Accept) to return to the Macros dialog box and press F9(Run) to run and test the macro.

If you want to test the macro on some limited collection of information, you can transfer a template of your database to a new database set up for test purposes. Your macros, categories, conditions, actions, and views will be copied into the new database. You will have to separately export some items to the new database for test purposes. Then open the new database and perform the testing and debugging of your macros. When you are satisfied with the performance of the macros, you can export them to text files and import them back into the original database, where they can be expected to perform correctly.

If a macro does not perform as expected, you will have to discover the problem and edit the macro to correct the necessary commands. Discovering the problem can be a very complicated task, which will be discussed in the next section on debugging. As far as correcting the macro is concerned, return to the Macros dialog box and select the macro you want to correct. Press F2(EditMac) and you will be returned to the Edit macro screen, where you can add, change, and delete any macro text using the standard edit function and special keys as described earlier in the Keystroke Macros section.

DEBUGGING MACROS

As mentioned in the Advanced Commands section, you should use {COMMENT;text}, {DEBUGON}, and {DEBUGOFF} to test and debug macros that are not performing according to your expectations. If you use comments liberally, it will be easier to track down commands that are not implementing the functional descriptions in the comments. Also, by turning the debug commands on and off selectively within your macro, you can isolate the sections of commands that you suspect are giving you the trouble. One other tip that can help you avoid problems with macros is to use the first letters of menu and list selections for selecting options, rather than attempting to move the highlight to the desired choices. The chances that the macro will choose the desired option are increased, and the amount and complexity of the macro code are decreased, both of which are very desirable outcomes. Experience, intuition, and a bit of luck will help in the art of debugging.

SUMMARY

You have seen how macros can increase the efficiency and effectiveness of your work with Agenda. You can and should experiment with macros. You will find the time savings to be significant, especially in long, complicated, or repetitive sequences of Agenda menu commands; dialog box entries; function, special, and accelerator keystrokes.

12

Structured Text Files

Structured text files or STFs are the formatted files that Agenda uses to import and export information between Agenda databases and between Agenda databases and other applications such as e-mail, time-sharing services, database products, spreadsheets, word processors, and project management software. For readers familiar with spreadsheet products, the STF concept is similar in spirit to the Data Interchange Format or DIF associated with VisiCalc, in that they both represent conventions with which the suppliers and users of information attempt to ensure complete and accurate exchanges of data. The ability to communicate with Agenda from other PC software opens up the potential for a whole line of Agenda add-on products.

For our purposes, the actual format of structured text files is not terribly important. However, so that you can claim passing familiarity with the details of STF format and show the scars to prove it, in Figure 12-1, we have listed the first page of the STF file that was produced in Chapter 9 for the Executive Information System application. Figure 12-2 shows the 1–2–3 print file that was the source for the STF file shown in Figure 12-1.

The data content of the STF begins on the second line with the header information labeled {STF001} . . . . The next eight lines contain the first item and its associated categories from the TRANSFER.PRN file. These eight lines form a repeating pattern that starts with a line signaling the beginning of an item with its label {I}. This is followed by five lines of category assignments, each beginning with {C} and ending with {.}, where the category name, for example, Group, is followed by the category value for the item, for example, 1 U.S. Division A. The category assignments are followed by the item text itself, labeled {T}, and the item closes with the symbol {!}. In other STFs, you might see labels such as {E}, {W}, and {D}, indicating Entry, When, and Done dates, respectively; {N}, indicating the beginning of item note text and so on. These coded lines represent the conventions established by Lotus for communicating with Agenda.

Figure 12-1.

```
"^"  @start()  @table("\|",1,,,)   @end()
{STF001}06/22/88;12:54:46
{I}
{C}Values     |    $59.6 {.}
{C}Group                          |1 U.S. Division A          {.}
{C}Period |3rd Qtr{.}
{C}Type              |Actual            {.}
{C}|{.}
{T}   $59.6
{!}
{I}
{C}Values     |     $5.9 {.}
{C}Group                          |2 U.S. Division B          {.}
{C}Period |3rd Qtr{.}
{C}Type              |Actual            {.}
{C}|{.}
{T}    $5.9
{!}
{I}
{C}Values     |    $10.8 {.}
{C}Group                          |3 Division C - Department A{.}
{C}Period |3rd Qtr{.}
{C}Type              |Actual            {.}
{C}|{.}
{T}   $10.8
{!}
{I}
{C}Values     |     $2.2 {.}
{C}Group                          |4 Division C - Department B{.}
{C}Period |3rd Qtr{.}
{C}Type              |Actual            {.}
{C}|{.}
{T}    $2.2
{!}
{I}
{C}Values     |    $13.0 {.}
{C}Group                          |5 Total U.S. Division C    {.}
{C}Period |3rd Qtr{.}
{C}Type              |Actual            {.}
{C}|{.}
{T}   $13.0
{!}
{I}
{C}Values     |    $11.9 {.}
{C}Group                          |6 U.S. Division D          {.}
{C}Period |3rd Qtr{.}
{C}Type              |Actual            {.}
{C}|{.}
{T}   $11.9
```

Figure 12-2.

Values	Group	Period	Type
$59.6	1 U.S. Division A	3rd Qtr	Actual
$5.9	2 U.S. Division B	3rd Qtr	Actual
$10.8	3 Division C - Department A	3rd Qtr	Actual
$2.2	4 Division C - Department B	3rd Qtr	Actual
$13.0	5 Total U.S. Division C	3rd Qtr	Actual
$11.9	6 U.S. Division D	3rd Qtr	Actual
$4.6	7 U.S. Division E	3rd Qtr	Actual
$94.9	8 Total U.S.	3rd Qtr	Actual
$5.1	9 Europe	3rd Qtr	Actual
$2.8	10 Canada	3rd Qtr	Actual
$3.9	11 Asia	3rd Qtr	Actual
$4.0	12 Latin America	3rd Qtr	Actual
$2.0	13 Japan	3rd Qtr	Actual
$0.1	14 Headquarters	3rd Qtr	Actual
$17.9	15 Total International	3rd Qtr	Actual
$112.8	16 Total Business Units	3rd Qtr	Actual
$4.0	17 Other	3rd Qtr	Actual
$116.8	18 Total Operating Income	3rd Qtr	Actual
$5.0	19 Investments	3rd Qtr	Actual
$121.8	20 Total Net Income	3rd Qtr	Actual
$79.7	1 U.S. Division A	3rd Qtr	Budget
$5.2	2 U.S. Division B	3rd Qtr	Budget
$7.0	3 Division C - Department A	3rd Qtr	Budget
$1.5	4 Division C - Department B	3rd Qtr	Budget
$8.5	5 Total U.S. Division C	3rd Qtr	Budget
$13.4	6 U.S. Division D	3rd Qtr	Budget
$8.2	7 U.S. Division E	3rd Qtr	Budget
$115.0	8 Total U.S.	3rd Qtr	Budget
$4.3	9 Europe	3rd Qtr	Budget
$2.1	10 Canada	3rd Qtr	Budget
$2.0	11 Asia	3rd Qtr	Budget
$2.1	12 Latin America	3rd Qtr	Budget

HOW TO CREATE STRUCTURED TEXT FILES

You can create STFs in seven ways:

1. By using the Items Accesory, described in Chapter 13.
2. By creating a Special Action for a category, as described in Chapter 4. This sends items off to a STF if they happen to get assigned to the category with the Special Action.
3. By choosing to process done items by exporting them to a STF as described in Chapter 3.
4. By using the F10(Menu)/File/Transfer/Export menu commands to export some or all of one Agenda database to an STF, as explained in this chapter.
5. By using the TXT2STF utility that Lotus supplies with Agenda, which converts external files to the STF format.

6. By using the LM2STF utility that Lotus supplies with Agenda, which converts external files to the STF format.

7. By writing a program yourself, conforming to the STF standard, to create a file that can be read into an Agenda database.

Since we have covered the first three approaches in other chapters of this book, we will concentrate in this chapter on the last four methods.

From Agenda

Let's begin with the File/Transfer/Export method of creating STFs. Assume that you are in an Agenda database item view screen and you decide that you want to export some or all of the items, categories, notes, and dates to another database. Press F10(Menu), F for File, T for Transfer, and E for Export. Agenda then displays the Export Structured File dialog box shown in Figure 12-3.

Figure 12-3.

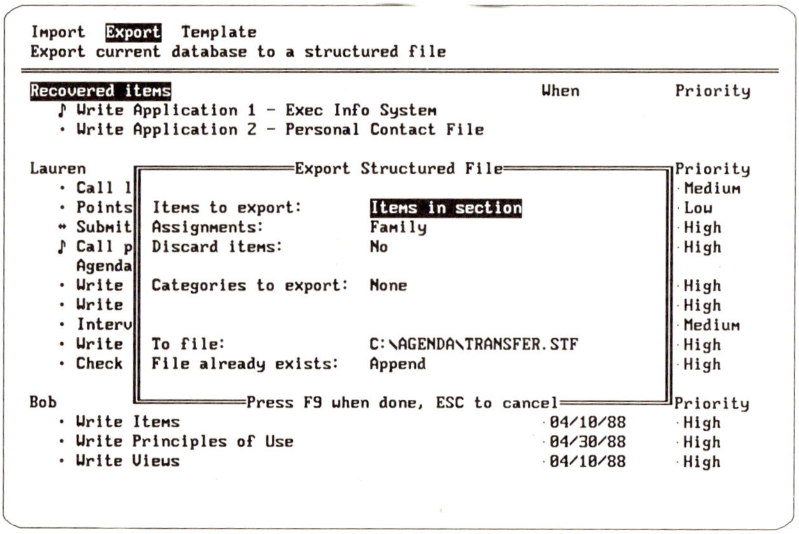

The first prompt, *Items to export:*, has the following familiar options: none, current item, all items, marked items, section, and view, which you can select by using the Spacebar or F2(Edit) or Grey +. The next prompt, *Assignments:*, asks whether or not you want to export the category assignments for your items. If you do, it asks whether you want the assignments to include the families of categories associated with each item or just the categories to which the item was explicity assigned. If you have some categories where identically named child categories mean different things under their respective parents, it will be important to export the family assignments to disambiguate these categories in the destination database. An example of this situation might be the category Leader, which in one family might mean the person who stays behind directing activities, and in another family might mean the person who leads the charge. If you only export the explicit category assignments to Leader, there will be ambiguities in the destination database.

The third prompt, *Discard items:*, asks whether or not you want to discard the items from your current database after they have been exported. The next prompt, *Categories to export:*, gives you the choice of exporting no categories at all or the entire Category Manager hierarchy or a single category, which can be a parent, an ancestor, or a child. If you just want to export a single category, choose the Partial hierarchy option for this prompt, and a new prompt will appear on the next line, *Parent category:*. You can type a category name or press F2(Edit) or Grey + to see a list of the Category Manager in which you can move the highlight to the desired name. In either case, press F9(Accept) or Enter to accept the category name and move the highlight down to the next prompt, *To file:*.

The default setting for the name of the file to which you will be exporting is TRANSFER.STF, and the default directory is the one in which you are running Agenda. You can enter any filename in response to this prompt. If the file already exists, Agenda will add another prompt, *File already exists:*, with two options, Append and Replace. If you are unsure of the filename press Grey + to see a list of available files and select one by moving the highlight to it and pressing Enter. If you are accumulating items from many different databases, you might want to append the information you are exporting from the current database to a growing STF. On the other hand, if you are simply adding new information to your destination database, you will probably select the Replace option. When you are finished responding to the prompts, press F9(Accept) to exit from the dialog box and to begin the file exporting.

The one constraint that you might encounter in exporting a database is that this process does not transfer conditions, actions, and views. If you need to transfer conditions, actions, and views as well as items, categories, notes, and dates, you should copy the database to another one with a different name using the F10(Menu)/File/Copy procedure described in Chapter 2.

A related function called Transfer/Template, is provided in the File menu options. This is a means of transferring categories, conditions, actions, views, and macros, but not items, from one database to another. To transfer a template, press F10(Menu), F for File, T for Transfer, and T for Template. Since this is such a restricted form of transfer, there is only one prompt, the filename for the destination database. A Select File window appears in which you can type a name or move the highlight to an existing name, as shown in Figure 12-4.

Figure 12-4.

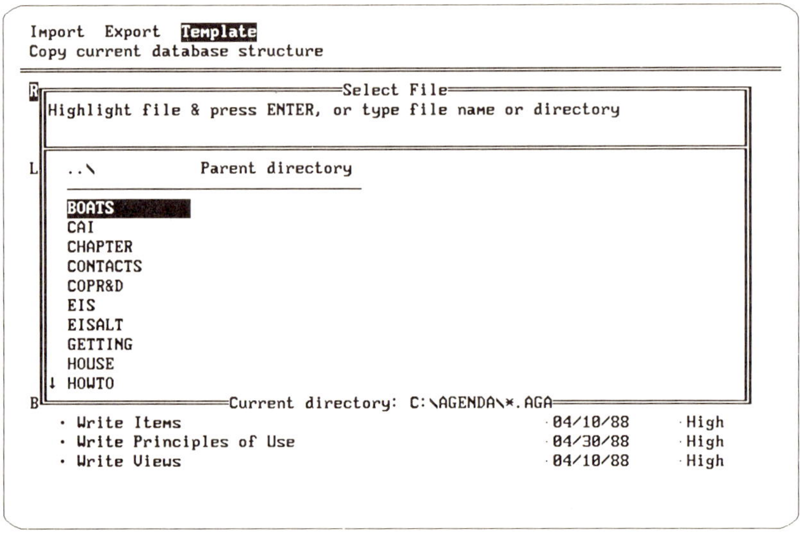

In either case, press Enter and the transfer takes place. Then open this new database and start entering items. The value of the transfer template process is that it permits you to export structure without content. For example, if you were building a hotel guide for different cities, the structure of the database would likely be the same, even though the content, the hotels, would be different. Using the transfer template commands, you could duplicate the structure for one city as many times as was necessary to develop hotel guides for other cities.

From Agenda Utilities

The next method of creating structured text files is by using the two utility programs supplied with Agenda, namely, TXT2STF and LM2STF.

TXT2STF

TXT2STF, which is referred to as "text to stuff," converts a text file into a structured text file. It performs this conversion using a set of default translation rules or a set of user-supplied rules contained in what is called a DEF or definition file.

To run TXT2STF, you need to be in the directory where it is stored, which is probably the Agenda directory, where you type TXT2STF followed by at least one or more parameters.

The first parameter must be the filename and extension of the text file you want to translate into STF format. This filename will be used as the filename for the STF, unless you override it with the optional output filename parameter (/O=). If you use an asterisk (*) in place of the filename, *.ext, then TXT2STF will read, translate, and combine all the files with the same extension. However, if you use the *.ext format for the input file, you must specify the output filename in the form /O=filename (no extension).

The rest of the parameters for TXT2STF, if they are required, must be typed following the filename and must be separated with spaces. Besides /O=, the next optional parameter is /S=, which tells TXT2STF that there is a special separator character other than the default carriage return character which marks the separation of item and note text. Two separation characters together separate adjacent items. If you are using a text file with some special line separator, such as *,

| or a special ASCII character code, type this parameter as /S=*, /S=|, or /S=\nnn, where *nnn* is the ASCII code for the separator character. The most significant optional parameter is the name of the user-supplied DEF or definition file you want TXT2STF to use in translating the text file to STF format. This parameter is typed as /D=filename.DEF, where DEF should be the extension for the definition file.

If you are using a DEF file for translation, you may want to consider three other parameters, /p, /u, and /l. If you include /p in the list of parameters, TXT2STF will display on the screen each line being translated into STF format and a summary of its processing. /u displays the pattern being matched to each item as the file is being translated. /l shows how an input line in your text file is being skipped, stripped, or trimmed in the course of translation. Since these displays are useful for debugging and since they are usually displayed too quickly to work with on the screen, you can direct their output to a file for subsequent printing or scanning. To do so, type >filename at the end of the TXT2STF command line.

The last parameter makes TXT2STF case sensitive in matching patterns of text for the purpose of applying translation rules. As TXT2STF is set up, it ignores case differences, that is lowercase versus uppercase, in pattern matching. If you want TXT2STF to be case sensitive, type /c as the last parameter.

Two examples of TXT2STF command lines are as follows:

- TXT2STF myfile.ext

  This is the simplest form of TXT2STF, which converts myfile using the default rules built into TXT2STF.

- TXT2STF myfile.ext /O=newfile.STF /D=rules.DEF /p

  Here we are translating myfile, using the rules contained in rules.DEF, producing a file called newfile.STF, and monitoring the whole process

TXT2STF works by reading your input text file one line at a time; applying each of its default rules, or your own DEF file rules, if supplied, to the line completely; and writing the specified output line to the STF. Then it reads the next input line and repeats the rule testing and output line generation. It proceeds with this read, test, and write sequence until it exhausts the input file.

Default Rules

The default rules built into TXT2STF include:

1. Unless you override it with a /S=option, TXT2STF assumes that a double carriage return or blank line in your text file is the separator between items and that a single carriage return is the separator between items and their notes.

2. TXT2STF begins capturing text for the first item at the top of the text file and continues until it reaches a single carriage return separator or the 350th character, whichever comes first.

3. If the 350 character limit for an item comes in the middle of a sentence, TXT2STF backs up to the previous terminal punctuation mark (. ? ! ; :), or blank space if there is no punctuation mark, and ends the item. All remaining text up to 10K characters or the next item, whichever comes first, is stored as a note for the item.

4. If a double carriage return is encountered, Agenda terminates the item or note and starts a new item.

5. If the 10K character limit for a note comes before a double carriage return separator signaling the next item, TXT2STF backs up to the previous terminal punctuation or space, ends the note, and begins a new item.

DEF Files

Let's briefly look at the form and content of DEF files. Detailed technical specifications for DEF files are contained in the *Agenda Definition Files* booklet which accompanies the software. Therefore, the purpose of this section will be to introduce the concepts behind DEF rules, not to provide step-by-step procedures for constructing and using DEF files. If you wish to write complex DEF files, you should consult the *Agenda Definition Files* booklet.

DEF or definition files are the means with which we communicate the structure of external text files so that TXT2STF can correctly translate them into the desired structured text files. These STFs in turn can be imported into Agenda. An example of a DEF file is shown in Figure 12-5.

Figure 12-5.

```
C>type email.def
#This is the template for e-mail letters received using Lotus Express
"^via\:"          @start()
\                 @custom_category("E-Mail","Mail",)
"^To\: "          @skip("\: ", 1)
\                 @category(",","To",)
"^From\:"         @skip("\: ", 1)
\                 @category("$" , "From",)
"^cc\:"           @skip("\: ",1)
\                 @category("$","cc",)
"^Subj(ect)*\:" @skip("\: ", 1)
\                 @item("^Date", 80, N)
"^Date\:"         @skip("\: ", 1)
\                 @date( W )
"Message-Id\:"  @skip_lines(1)
\                 @note("^via\:")
\                 @end()
"!^via\:"         @note("^via\:")
\                 @end()

C>
```

This is a DEF file, called EMAIL.DEF, which is used in translating e-mail letters received from MCI Mail using Lotus Express. There are a number of important features to notice about this file. Each rule begins with a pattern, enclosed in double quotes (" "), which TXT2STF uses to try to match the rule to each input line in your text file. If the pattern matches, the second part of the rule, consisting of one or more actions, preceded with @ symbols, is executed. To follow the formatting convention discussed in the *Agenda User's Guide*, each rule in this example spans two lines, which is indicated by the \ in the first position of the second line in each pair. This format permits the patterns and actions to line up vertically as you scan down the DEF file listing. The first action in the file must be @start( ) and the last action must be @end( ). Comment lines, which are recognized by the # symbol in the first character position, can and should be used to describe the DEF file and to "explain" the patterns and actions. In this example, there is only one comment explaining the purpose of EMAIL.DEF.

To better understand the functioning of some of these rules, a sample e-mail letter from MCI Mail is shown in Figure 12-6.

Figure 12-6.

```
C>type email.txt
via: mailbox 1, emitchell on VAX at Lotus (LDC) ** Message Received OK
To:       @SHOTGUN_LIST ! To All Employees in ALL_VAX_USERS
From:     YOGI::PRDept
Subj:     LOTUS THIRD QUARTER EARNINGS
Date:     19-OCT-1987 12:52

                              FOR IMMEDIATE RELEASE

                         Lotus Development Corporation Reports
Record Revenues and Earnings for Third Quarter

     CAMBRIDGE, Mass., October 19 -- Lotus Development Corporation
(NASDAQ:LOTS) today announced record revenues and earnings for the third
quarter ended October 3.  Revenues for the quarter rose 54% to $101.2 million
as compared to the previous year's third-quarter revenues of $65.6 million. Net
income for the quarter was $19.1 million, an increase of 101% over the $9.5
million for the previous year's third quarter.  Earnings per share rose 100% to
42 cents per share versus 21 cents per share for the third quarter of 1986.


C>
```

As you can see, the e-mail letter begins with the word via:, so the first rule in the DEF file must identify a pattern containing via:, namely, "^via\:", where the ^ means that this pattern must be looked for at the beginning of a line in the text file and the \: is the way special symbols like colons can be recognized as text as opposed to DEF commands. The \ preceding a special symbol means that the symbol is to be taken literally as a piece of text. Therefore, the first rule begins with a pattern that directs TXT2STF to find a line beginning with via: before testing the rest of the rules in the DEF file.

The actions in the first rule are @start( ), which always has to be the first action in a group that processes one or more text file statements, and @custom_category("E-Mail","Mail",), which assigns the item created by applying EMAIL.DEF to the child category E-Mail and the parent category Mail. This @custom_category command is used to assign items to categories automatically, in addition to whatever assignments take place in applying the other rules to the text lines.

The next rule's pattern looks for the word To:, and once a text line beginning with To: is found, the first action skips past the To: to find the addressees of the letter and assign the item created by applying EMAIL.DEF to the parent category To and the child categories consisting of the addressees. The following rules handle the sender's name and cc's, which become children of the From and cc categories, respectively.

The next rule looks for the line beginning with the word Subj:, skips the Subj: and makes the following text, up to the word Date:, into the item for this e-mail letter, with an added constraint of 80 characters. The rule looking for the Date: uses the date of the e-mail letter to assign the item's When date, and the last rules place everything up to the next via: into a note for this item.

The STF resulting from applying EMAIL.DEF to the e-mail letter in Figure 12-6 is shown in Figure 12-7.

Figure 12-7.

```
#This is the template for e-mail letters received using Lotus Express
{STF001}01/02/80;01:28:09
{I}
{C}Mail\E-Mail{.}
{.}To\@SHOTGUN_LIST ! To All Employees in ALL_VAX_USERS
{.}From\YOGI::PRDept
{W}  19-OCT-1987 12:52

{T}  LOTUS THIRD QUARTER EARNINGS

{N}                           FOR IMMEDIATE RELEASE

                     Lotus Development Corporation Reports
Record Revenues and Earnings for Third Quarter

     CAMBRIDGE, Mass., October 19 -- Lotus Development Corporation
(NASDAQ:LOTS) today announced record revenues and earnings for the third
quarter ended October 3.  Revenues for the quarter rose 54% to $101.2 million
as compared to the previous year's third-quarter revenues of $65.6 million. Net
income for the quarter was $19.1 million, an increase of 101% over the $9.5
million for the previous year's third quarter.  Earnings per share rose 100% to
42 cents per share versus 21 cents per share for the third quarter of 1986.
{!}

C>
```

You can now see the familiar item labeled {I}, categories labeled {C}, and When date labeled {W} in the STF produced by TXT2STF while applying EMAIL.DEF. You can also see where the body of the letter was treated as a note.

Another example of a very simple DEF file at work is the TRANSFER.DEF file, which we created to import the Executive Information System data into Agenda in Chapter 9. That file consisted of just one rule:

```
"^" @start( ) @table("\|",1,,,) @end( )
```

This rule utilizes a very useful action called @table, which translates data formatted as tables into STF format. The rule's only pattern says that at the beginning of every line (remember ^), start and end a @table action. The format for the @table action is:

```
@table(separator,item-col,entry-col,when-col,done-col)
```

where separator stands for a text string that you use to divide columns of data; and item-col, entry-col, when-col, and done-col refer to the column positions, counting from 1 at the left of the table, where the item values, and the Entry, When and Done dates, respectively, can be found. If any of these data are not provided for in the table, the comma in the @table action must still be there to mark the empty place, as in the previous example. The @table action makes items out of the values in the designated column and categories out of the corresponding values in the adjacent columns, separated by the separator character or string. In other words, each row, except the first, becomes an item whose value is found in the item column and whose category assignments are found in the other column values on the same row. The parent category names, or column headers in Agenda, need to be placed in their respective columns of the first row. All the categories are imported as unindexed. TXT2STF assumes that the first blank row in the table marks the end of data.

The reason that we have gone into the @table action in such detail is that it can be very useful in importing tabular data from lots of other applications, including spreadsheets, databases, and financial software.

The TRANSFER.DEF file was used to produce the TRANSFER.STF file shown in Figure 12-1 from the TRANSFER.PRN file shown in Figure 12-2.

In developing DEF files, you have to study your input text file carefully to discover the recurring patterns of text lines that you intend to capture with TXT2STF. Once these patterns have been identified, you can start thinking about the ways to describe them as patterns and actions. The next step is to convert this plan into an actual DEF file that you can test on your input file. By examining the /u, /p, and /l displays as well as by printing out the resulting STF, you can see if the DEF file is working. If not, you can debug and fix it as much as you need to before actually importing anything to an Agenda database. Once you are satisfied with the DEF file's performance, use it to generate a final STF, which you can import to Agenda.

Once again, if you need to go beyond the simple examples discussed here, refer to the *Agenda Definition Files* booklet.

LM2STF

A utility that is similar to TXT2STF, but simpler, is LM2STF, which you use to convert Lotus Metro List Manager files to STF format. To perform the conversion, you need to be in DOS, in the directory where LM2STF is located. Type LM2STF followed by the filename of the List Manager file to be converted. If the file is in a different directory, you will have to include the pathname with the filename. When LM2STF is finished, you can import the STF with the matching filename into your Agenda database, just like you would with any other STF. For more details about this process, consult the *Agenda User's Guide*, Chapter 19, and the Lotus Metro List Manager documentation.

From Other Programs

Just as TXT2STF and LM2STF are programs that produce structured text files, it is not difficult to imagine building STF's from other application programs as well. In these situations, you will have to determine the relative effort involved in producing a straightforward text file from the application program and writing the appropriate DEF file, versus writing your own routine to create the STF format directly. Your choice will probably depend on how often you would use this formatting program and on how much easier or more difficult it would be to code it versus setting up the DEF file required by TXT2STF.

HOW TO USE STRUCTURED TEXT FILES

Now that you have a structured text file to import to Agenda, you need to open up the database into which you want to import the STF. Before importing the STF, you should disable text condition processing because Agenda will attempt to match text conditions as it imports your STF. This will considerably slow down the importing process. To disable text condition processing, press F10(Menu), U for Utility, P for Preferences, and A for Auto-Assign. Agenda displays the Auto-Assignment Preferences dialog box, where the first prompt, *Enable text conditions:*, should be answered no. Press F9(Accept) to return to the view. From the item view screen in the destination database, press F10(Menu), F for File, T for Transfer, and I for Import. Agenda displays the Import Structured File dialog box shown in Figure 12-8.

Figure 12-8.

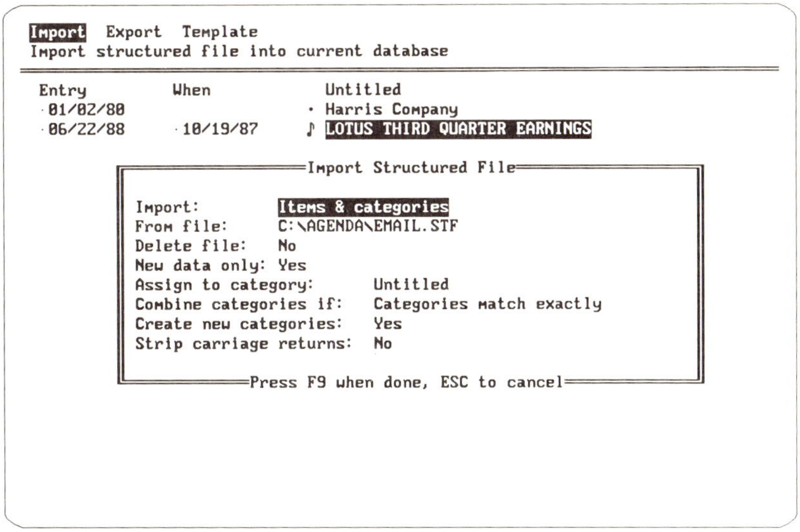

The first line, *Import:*, prompts you for your choice of items, categories, or both to import. Choose the appropriate option using the Spacebar, F2(Edit), or Grey +. The next prompt, *From file:*, asks for the STF filename and path, if different from the current one. You can type the name or press GREY + and highlight the desired name in the displayed list of files. Then press Enter and move the highlight down to the next prompt, *Delete file:*, which asks whether or not you want to delete the STF file after it has been imported. Answer yes or no, and move the highlight to the fourth line if a prompt appears. The fourth prompt line *New data only:* appears only when the file you are importing is the file you used the last time you imported information into this database. Agenda recognizes the file it last accessed and the data which it imported during the last session. The prompt asks if you wish to import only new data from that file (that is, items and categories) or everything including the data you imported during the previous session. The default is Yes, which is generally the correct choice. As with the first line in the dialog box, you can use the Spacebar, F2(Edit), or Grey + to make your choice. Next, move down to the *Assign to category:* prompt, which asks you to name the category in the destination database to which items should be initially assigned when they are imported. You can type the name of the desired category or press GREY + and move the highlight to the name in the Category Manager listing. Press Enter to accept the category name, and move down to the next prompt, *Combine categories if:*.

If you are importing categories, Agenda avoids importing categories from the STF if they match existing categories in the destination database. This matching is controlled by the *Combine categories if:* prompt, where the options are to combine categories, thereby avoiding the importing of the STF categories, when any expression in the two categories in question is identical, when only the first expression or category name is identical, or when the categories are completely identical. The next prompt, *Create new categories:*, is related to the preceding one in that it specifies how to deal with categories in the STF, when they cannot be combined through the matching. If you want new categories found in the STF to be added to the destination database, answer yes; otherwise, no.

Finally, the last prompt, *Strip carriage returns:*, asks whether or not you want carriage returns in note text removed, so that Agenda can format them and wrap them according to the requirements of your view and note screens and your printing preferences. Answer yes or no to this last prompt and press F9(Accept) to close the dialog box. Agenda now imports the named structured text file and continuously reports the percentage completion of the transfer in a window on the screen.

When the transfer is complete, you will be left in the item view screen, in a section whose heading is the category name you typed in response to the *Assign to category:* prompt.

If you would like to automatically import a certain structured text file each time you access a specific database, Agenda provides a method for accomplishing this. For example, you might use the Items Accessory regularly to capture items while you are working in other application programs. Although we will not be discussing the Items Accessory until Chapter 13, you store these captured items in a structured text file. In the example we are considering here, you might want to automatically import your latest collection of captured items as the first activity upon opening your database. To instruct Agenda to perform this auto-importing, be sure to be in an item view screen of the database into which you want to automatically import these captured items and press F10(Menu), U for Utility, P for Preferences, and O for Other. Agenda displays the Other Preferences dialog box shown in Figure 12-9.

Figure 12-9.

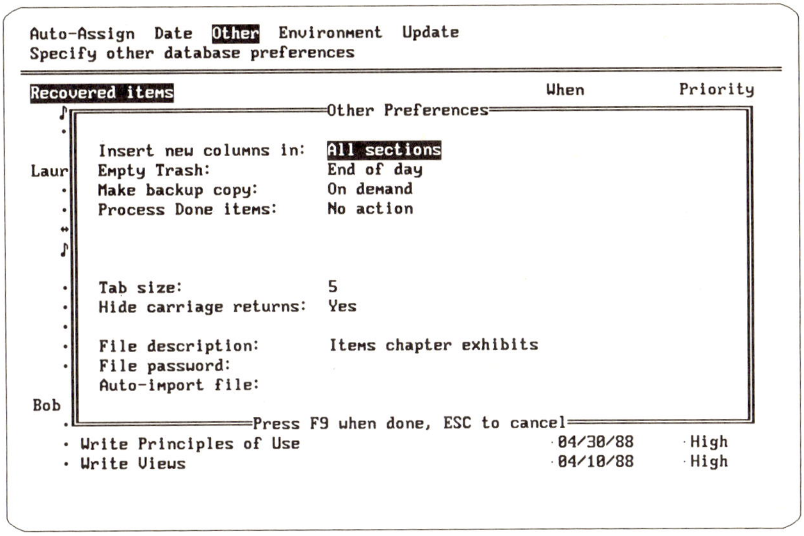

The last prompt, *Auto-import file:*, asks you which STF file you want to automatically import upon opening this database. Type the appropriate filename or press GREY + and highlight the desired filename. Press Enter and F9(Accept) to close the dialog box. The next time you open this database, Agenda automatically imports any previously nonimported items from the named STF file. Agenda avoids the duplication of items in imported STFs by keeping track of the STFs from which it has imported data.

SUMMARY

Agenda comes equipped with some powerful tools for exchanging data with other applications as well as across Agenda databases. We have examined the file transfer tools in this chapter and will review the special accessory tools capturing chunks of text in other applications in the next chapter. The combination of these tools can help reduce the effort involved in getting the text of items, categories, and notes into Agenda, where they can be easily and flexibly managed.

13

Items and Clipboard Accessories

Four Metro accessory programs and the Metro kernel are delivered with Agenda. This software is part of a larger set of applications, which are available in another Lotus product, Metro. Two of the programs, the Items and Clipboard accessories, deal directly with the "pop-up" capturing of items and notes from other applications such as spreadsheets, database packages, word processors, and project management packages. The Items Accessory is a text editor that you can use to record ideas you have while using another piece of software but which you would like to save for subsequent inclusion in an Agenda database. The Clipboard Accessory lets you save a piece of a 1-2-3 spreadsheet, for example, and paste it into an Agenda database.

The two other accessory programs, the Kaleidoscope and Configuration Accessories, are used in customizing the Items and Clipboard Accessories with respect to the memory that is used, the colors on the screen, and so on.

The installation of the accessory and kernel software supplied with Agenda is covered in Chapter 2 of the *Agenda User's Guide*. The customizing possibilities with the Kaleidoscope and Configuration Accessories are covered in Appendix A of the *Agenda User's Guide*.

Our purpose in this chapter is to show you how to use the Items and Clipboard Accessories, assuming that they, the Metro kernel, and Agenda have been successfully installed.

HOW TO USE THE ITEMS AND CLIPBOARD ACCESSORIES

Before starting any other programs and while you are still in the root directory where Metro has been installed, type Metro and press Enter. Metro should be the last background, pop-up, or terminate and stay resident program that you load.

We will use 1-2-3 as the sample application during which you might want to save some ideas for later importing to Agenda. Load 1-2-3 and enter the spreadsheet from the EIS application in Chapter 9 as shown in Figure 13-1.

Figure 13-1.

```
A1: [W29]                                                              READY

                A                              B          C          D
1
2               Executive Summary of 3rd Quarter Performance
3                                ($ millions)
4
5    Group                                  Actual    Budget     % to Budget
6    ----------------------------         --------  --------   ---------------
7     1 U.S. Division A                    $59.6     $79.7            -25.1
8     2 U.S. Division B                     $5.9      $5.2             13.0
9     3 Division C - Department A          $10.8      $7.0             54.7
10    4 Division C - Department B           $2.2      $1.5             46.2
11    5 Total U.S. Division C              $13.0      $8.5             53.2
12    6 U.S. Division D                    $11.9     $13.4            -11.5
13    7 U.S. Division E                     $4.6      $8.2            -44.5
14    8 Total U.S.                         $94.9    $115.0            -17.4
15    9 Europe                              $5.1      $4.3             20.8
16   10 Canada                              $2.8      $2.1             34.7
17   11 Asia                                $3.9      $2.0             94.5
18   12 Latin America                       $4.0      $2.1             90.2
19   13 Japan                               $2.0      $3.0            -33.2
20   14 Headquarters                        $0.1      $0.2            -49.9
02-Jan-80  12:24 AM
```

Using the Items Accessory

As you are using 1-2-3, you have some ideas that you want to save to be added later to an Agenda database. To access the Items Accessory press Alt-Shift-I. A pop-up screen appears as shown in Figure 13-2.

In the upper right-hand corner of the screen, the Items Accessory tells you this is the screen for Item 1. Type your item on the blank screen as shown in Figure 13-3. You can enter up to 10 items, each on their own numbered screen. Each item may be as long as the 350 character limit for item text in Agenda. To move to the next screen press PgDn. To move to the previous screen press PgUp.

Figure 13-2.

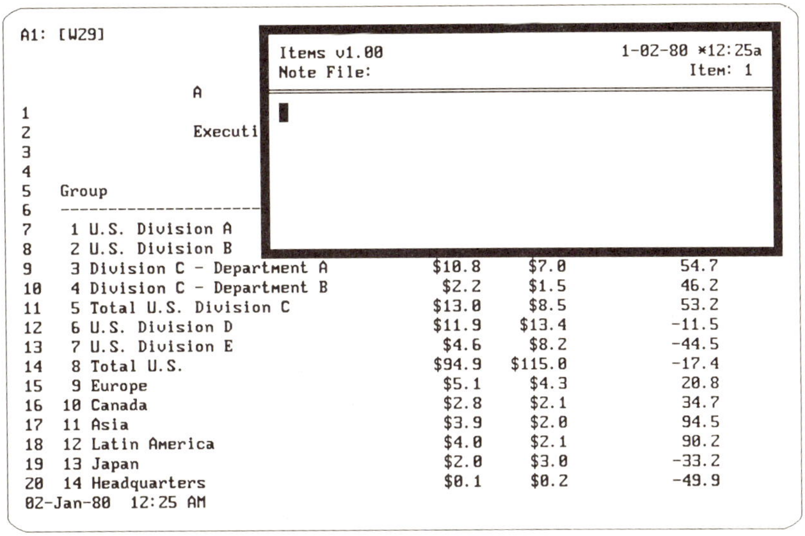

Figure 13-3.

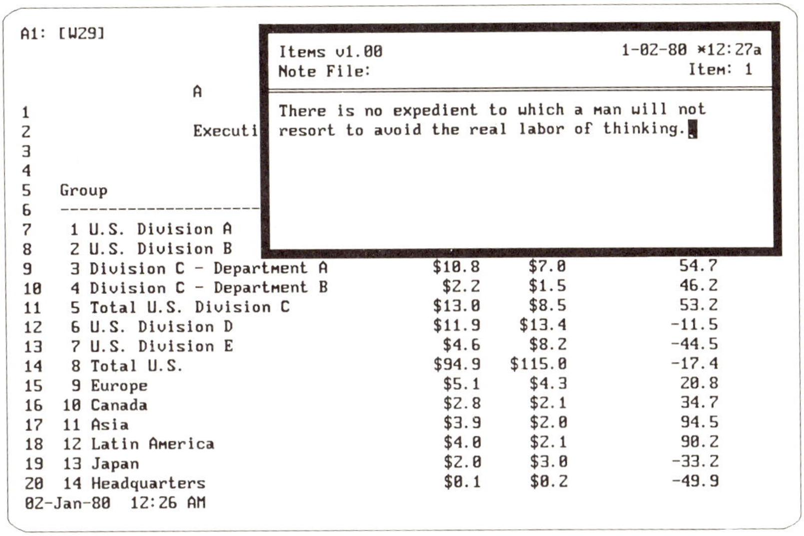

You can specify one category for all the items you entered. To do this press F10(Menu) and C for Category. Type a category name when prompted, as shown in Figure 13-4, and press Enter.

Figure 13-4.

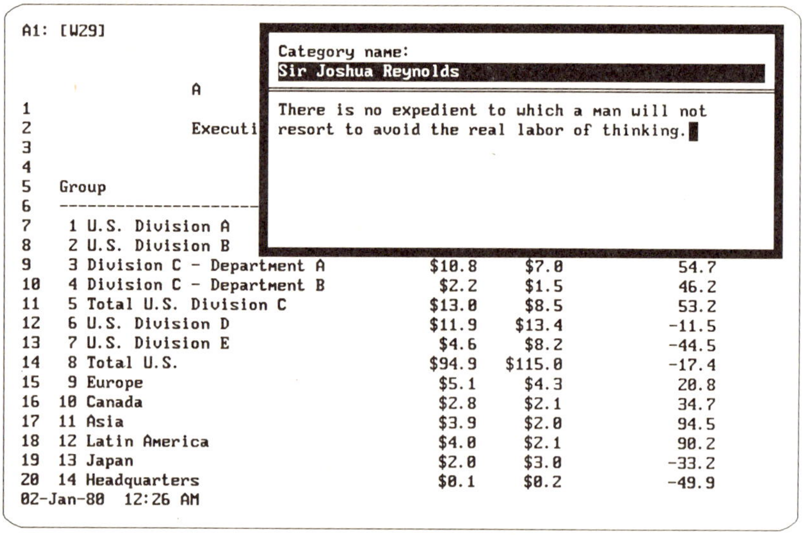

Using the Items Accessory you can specify a text file as an external note file attached to an item. You can do this for each item in the Items Accessory. Press F10(Menu) and N for Note. Type the filename of the text file you want to use as an external note file and press Enter. The Items Accessory will not check to see if the file is a valid one.

You can Print or Delete either the Current or All items by pressing F10(Menu) and P for Print or D for Delete. You will then be given the choice of printing or deleting the Current item or All items.

The next step in the process is to transfer the items in the Items Accessory to a structured text file. Press F10(Menu) and T for Transfer. You may transfer the Current item or All items. Type a name for the structured text file and press Enter. If you use the name of an existing file, you have the option to Replace or Append the file. The Items Accessory uses a default filename of TRANSFER.STF if you do not specify one. Alt-T is the accelerator key method for transferring All the items to a structured file.

Before you import the items to Agenda, you must put away the Items Accessory by pressing F10(Menu) and Q for Quit. After loading Agenda, select the database into which you want to import the items from the Items Accessory. Press F10(Menu), F for File, T for Transfer, and I for Import. Type the name of the structured file you created as shown in Figure 13-5. Press F9(Accept) to import the file.

Figure 13-5.

```
Import  Export  Template
Import structured file into current database

Untitled-2

              ═══════════Import Structured File═══════════

              Import:         Items & categories
              From file:      C:\AGENDA\TRANSFER.STF
              Delete file:    No
              New data only:  Yes
              Assign to category:        Untitled-2
              Combine categories if:     Categories match exactly
              Create new categories:     Yes
              Strip carriage returns:    No

              ═════════Press F9 when done, ESC to cancel═════════
```

Using the Clipboard Accessory

If you are using 1–2–3 and decide you want to move a part of your spreadsheet (such as the one shown earlier in Figure 13-1) into Agenda, press Alt-Shift-D. Your screen will appear as in Figure 13-6.

Figure 13-6.

```
A1: [W29]                                                           READY

                  A                      B             C            D
1
2                 Executive Summary of 3rd Quarter Performance

  Clipboard v1.10         Fast                          1-02-80 *12:37a
                                 unformatted column=0    Prefix=none

15    9 Europe                          $5.1        $4.3          20.8
16   10 Canada                          $2.8        $2.1          34.7
17   11 Asia                            $3.9        $2.0          94.5
18   12 Latin America                   $4.0        $2.1          90.2
19   13 Japan                           $2.0        $3.0         -33.2
20   14 Headquarters                    $0.1        $0.2         -49.9
02-Jan-80  12:37 AM
```

Press F10(Menu) and C for Copy. You will have the option of copying the whole screen, specific lines of text without any trailing spaces, or a rectangular block as shown in Figure 13-7.

Figure 13-7.

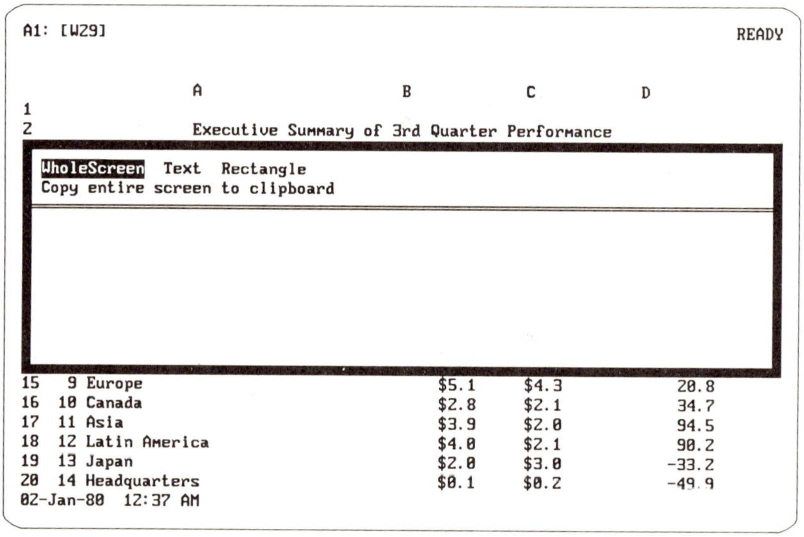

If you select the Whole Screen option, the Clipboard saves it for you. If you choose Text or Rectangle, the Clipboard disappears and the cursor appears in the upper left-hand corner of the screen. You must place the cursor on the first character to be copied. Press F7 to mark the beginning of the text to be copied, move the cursor using the arrows to highlight the rest of the text to be copied, and press Enter. The Clipboard reappears displaying the text to be copied as shown in Figure 13-8.

To format the text, press F10(Menu) and F for Format. If you want the text to be included as an item, select the Word Processor option. If you want the text to be included as a Note, select the default option Normal. The spreadsheet option formats text for a spreadsheet and should be ignored.

To put the Clipboard away, automatically saving its contents as long as the machine remains on, press F10(Menu) and Q for Quit.

Figure 13-8.

```
A1: [W29]                                                            READY

                  A                    B             C            D
1
2                 Executive Summary of 3rd Quarter Performance
  Clipboard v1.10          Fast                            1-02-80 *12:38a
                                 unformatted column=0    Prefix=none

  1 U.S. Division A                     $59.6
  2 U.S. Division B                      $5.9
  3 Division C - Department A           $10.8
  4 Division C - Department B            $2.2

15    9 Europe                              $5.1     $4.3            20.8
16   10 Canada                              $2.8     $2.1            34.7
17   11 Asia                                $3.9     $2.0            94.5
18   12 Latin America                       $4.0     $2.1            90.2
19   13 Japan                               $2.0     $3.0           -33.2
20   14 Headquarters                        $0.1     $0.2           -49.9
02-Jan-80   12:37 AM
```

To paste the contents of the Clipboard into Agenda, load Agenda, open your database, place the cursor on the item or in the note where you would like the text to appear, and press Alt-Shift-Enter. In Figure 13-9 the contents of the Clipboard are being pasted into a note. To unload Metro from memory press Alt-Shift-End.

Figure 13-9.

```
 Note for:   Acme
=====================================================Line 5==Ins=
1 U.S. Division A                     $59.6
2 U.S. Division B                      $5.9
3 Division C - Department A           $10.8
4 Division C - Department B            $2.2
█
```

14

Tips and Tricks

By this point you should be quite familiar with Agenda and, as with anything new, increasing comfort will come with time and practice. Ted Levitt, the well-known marketing professor at Harvard Business School tells classes of graduating MBA's, "You don't have to know what you know to know it." Whether you know it, or feel it, or not, having read and worked through the Agenda tutorial and this book, you are probably among the most knowledgable users of Agenda.

ABOUT LEARNING AGENDA

Our intention in writing this book was to help you learn and become adept with a piece of software that truly is in a class by itself. To preserve our sense of what it takes to master Agenda, we deliberately waited to learn the product until we began to write. In addition to empathizing with our readers, we have tried to provide practical examples of the uses of Agenda that, through their familiarity, can narrow the gap between a conceptual understanding of what Agenda is versus how to use it. Also, we interviewed as many beta users as we could to gain further insight into how we could help our readers learn Agenda.

In our interviews, we found that most new users tried to develop a working definition or real-life metaphor for Agenda. For example, spreadsheet software has the familiar green accounting form as its metaphor; word processing software has the blank page and the typewriter as its metaphors. However, there is not an obvious metaphor for Agenda.

The closest we came to finding such a metaphor for Agenda was the description given to us by one of the beta users. He thought of Agenda as a model of the workings of the human mind when it is trying to solve a problem. When you are working on a problem, ideas come to mind. You may not quite know how they fit together, so you leave the problem for a while. With Agenda, you would input these ideas as items and then leave them until a later time. As your mind continues to work on the problem, you come up with more ideas that you can input to Agenda as items. At this point, perhaps you begin to see some way to relate the ideas you have had. With Agenda, you begin to categorize your items. The more you ponder the problem, the more relationships you will see among the items. You will also begin to see new categories (and categories of categories), and perhaps you will fit your ideas (items) into categories where previously you had not thought they belonged. This is how structure evolves, both in your mind and with Agenda.

Although this metaphor may be helpful in beginning to understand Agenda, we should not let it constrain our ability to capitalize on Agenda's flexibility. The tendency to look for structure, especially when trying to understand something new, is very natural. However, Agenda neither provides nor forces its user to develop structure at the outset. In Agenda, structure can be an evolutionary process. It molds itself to your analysis of the problem in question and changes as your viewpoint changes. You do not have to adjust your data or your thinking to a structure that Agenda imposes on you. The data you enter, the way you think about it, and the nature of the problem you are trying to solve dictate the structure that evolves.

APPLICATIONS

Because of its flexibility, Agenda can be used in many different ways. The beta users we interviewed had some interesting ideas about how to use Agenda.

To-Do list	A collection of tasks, priorities and responsibilities.
Project manager	Sort tasks by dates and dependencies.

Write a book	Usc the items as pieces of text, the notes to augment them when you run out of space, and the categories to describe where the items go within the book.
Plan a seminar	Schedule paper sessions and panel discussions; plan for facility availability; coordinate accommodations; and so on.
Attend a seminar	Select paper sessions and panel discussions you wish to attend. Include their days and times, prioritize them, and then schedule yourself to attend as many as possible.
Personnel manager	Keep track of facts and figures on personnel.
Idea manager	Brainstorming.
Scheduler	A Congressman's assistant has to know where the Congressman is every minute of the day. With Agenda, the assistant can enter all engagements as items, attaching When dates to them. Changes can be made very easily, and the scheduled meeting can be looked at in any number of ways.
Records management	The Iran Contra files fill 200 boxes. To try to find a particular piece of information would be a monumental task if done manually. Agenda can keep the facts as items and categorize them for easy retrieval.
Media manager	Agenda can keep track of the various features of different advertising media. For a given advertisement, it can select the best medium, based on the audience, the frequency of publications, the cost, and any other relevant parameters.

E-mail message	Agenda can capture important pieces of e-mail based on keywords. Views can be created for the appropriate person, based on the content of the message. One person may want to see the messages according to product, another according to vendor, another by geography, and still another by client.
System design	Progammers can use Agenda as a brainstorming and outlining tool to develop the structure of a system, and later to document the system.
Study tool	Instead of taking notes on paper as you read, you can enter the information as items, categorize them, and then, create views to study by topic.

In addition to the preceding applications Lotus has collected hundreds of examples from their extensive beta user population, including the following:

User Population	Uses Agenda to
Government workers	▪ Track legislation ▪ Store and organize constituent priorities ▪ Monitor compliance with federal regulations
Legal professionals	▪ Track litigation ▪ Record, organize, and analyze client notes, contract terms, and other legal details.
Manufacturing professionals	▪ Schedule production ▪ Monitor customer feedback ▪ Maintain interactive technical support references
Scientists	▪ Make decisions on funding research projects ▪ Catalog research report abstracts
Financial professionals	▪ Track expense reports ▪ Analyze portfolio information ▪ Monitor news wire data ▪ Collect and organize audit findings

User Population	Uses Agenda to
Sales professionals	▪ Collect client and product information ▪ Maintain telephone, address, and schedule data
Medical professionals	▪ Collect and organize patient histories ▪ Store and retrieve medical symptoms and potential diagnoses ▪ Schedule resources such as conference rooms, X-ray machines, and photographic equipment
Consultants	▪ Plan projects ▪ Collect and organize data about current and prospective customers ▪ Organize project findings ▪ Analyze competitors ▪ Record billable time ▪ Outline proposals ▪ Develop presentations
Public Relations professionals	▪ Plan events ▪ Maintain a dynamic PR media list that can be used not only as a scheduling tool but as an automatic reporting structure (meeting summaries and press clips can be added as you go along) ▪ Develop strategy
Advertising professionals	▪ Track program results ▪ Plan media placements ▪ Control agency traffic ▪ Plan articles ▪ Storyboard concepts for television spots
Insurance professionals	▪ Update legal issues online ▪ Maintain policy coverage information
Travel professionals	▪ Track travel itineraries ▪ Plan trips ▪ Organize package tours ▪ Maintain interactive directories of restaurants, hotels, flights, sights, and so on
Educational professionals	▪ Analyze historical events ▪ Organize and analyze case studies ▪ Develop-course syllabi and study guides

User Population	Uses Agenda to
Library professionals	▪ Analyze and distribute research findings ▪ Index articles, abstracts, and other reference material
Real estate professionals	▪ Maintain lease data on large properties ▪ Store and organize properties according to client criteria
Software development professionals	▪ Track bugs and application backlogs ▪ Catalog source code
Executive search and recruiting professionals	▪ Track open positions and potential candidates
Service professionals	▪ Schedule and track repair orders

DESIGN ISSUES

In spite of Agenda's considerable flexibility, some choices, once made, are relatively difficult to undo. These include what information should be represented as items; what information should be represented as categories; what information should be represented as notes; how to structure the Category Manager; how best to take advantage of the limited real estate available in the view screen; and when to suppress the functioning of the entry date so that an extra date field will be available. In addition to these topics, there are still other design considerations, for example, when to use the various types of conditions, actions, prerequisites, and dependencies. These were thoroughly covered in the chapters on items and categories.

Items

If we agree that for the purposes of our problem, an item is an irreducible element of content, then what we want to do with items is to aggregate, chain, sequence, assemble, organize, classify, prioritize, and assemble them. You do not want to dissect them. Therefore, when thinking about the problem you are approaching with Agenda, if it is not clear whether or not some information should be considered an item, you should apply the preceding criteria by asking yourself what you intend to do with the information.

Categories

If categories represent the stucture of your information, then what we want to do with them is to aggregate, organize, classify, prioritize, and assemble the elements of information or items. If you are not sure whether or not some piece of information is a category, you should ask whether or not it can be used to do the previously mentioned tasks.

Notes

The proper way to think about notes is as extensions of items and categories, not as replacements for them. In all computer applications, size constraints are unavoidable and so it is with the 350-character limit for items and the 69-character limit for categories. Thus it is important to condense as much meaning as possible into your items and categories, leaving the note capability for unavoidable excess and additional explanatory material. However, it is important to realize that item notes can be used in applying text conditions and searching for text, which make them a somewhat more useful extension to items than to categories. With categories, notes can provide additional information concerning the types of items that should be assigned to the categories and alternative representation for categories as column entries.

The Category Manager

Unless there is some compelling reason to do otherwise, it probably pays to alphabetize every level in the Category Manager. Unfortunately, you have to do this one family at a time using Alt-F9(Sort). However, it will make referencing the Category Manager that much more efficient if the organization of the material is a familiar one.

The concept of inheritance as represented in the promoting and demoting capabilities is a powerful organizational tool. Frequently it is much easier to reference and manipulate a group of items that belong to a family of categories than it is to deal with each of the family member categories individually. This is not just an issue of efficiency but also of clear thinking, and it enhances the comprehension of the relationships among the items in your database.

Beyond the vertical organization of the Category Manager are the decisions concerning indexing and mutual exclusivity. These are tools that can help in efficiency in the former case and accurate classification in the latter. Therefore, it pays to consider the merits of using these attributes of categories opportunistically.

Views

With 25 rows and 80 columns on the typical PC screen, only so much information can be displayed. You should keep this constraint in mind when entering category names, especially long ones, and narrower alternate headings for categories should be included wherever possible. You should also organize categories so they can appear as column entries in a single column rather than as column headings in multiple columns. Finally, make use of the Star (*) and Y/N formatting options whenever possible. When all else fails and you cannot display all your information in the 80-column width, start thinking about using sections to communicate category information vertically.

Suppressing the Entry Date

As we mentioned in Chapter 3, Agenda provides the capability of turning off the automatic assignment of entry dates. This date field is then free to be used for some other date-related purpose. However, in taking advantage of this option, you lose the value that entry dates provide such as the ability to track the length of time that an item has been in the database for the purpose of purging old items.

THE TIPS

After working with Agenda, talking to the users, and going through the *Agenda User's Guide*, we have put together a collection of notes, tips, and tricks concerned with using Agenda. The list is quite long, and any given tip may apply to more than one topic. Ironically, this makes a perfect application for Agenda. What we have done is to make every tip an item in Agenda. Then we attached as many categories as we could think of to each topic. Figure 14-1, which is at the end of the chapter, displays a copy of that listing by subject.

We suggest that you use this listing as the beginning of your own tips file. Enter all the items and adjust or add categories so that they are meaningful to you. When you come across a new tip, either discovering it yourself or perhaps from another user you can add it to the file along with any other little reminders to help you use Agenda. When you need some help you can create a view on the subject or subjects of interest. This will be your own personalized Help File.

CROSS-REFERENCE

In addition to the index appearing at the end of this guide, we have prepared a cross-reference database of the material in the previous chapters, based on the types of goals you might have or problems you are trying to solve. For example, your goal might be to copy an Agenda database or to enter an item. You can look these types of goals up in the cross-reference shown in Figure 14-2, also at the end of this chapter.

After you locate the desired goal, the chapter and section heading where this goal is addressed can be found in the Chap/Sect column, and the keystrokes needed to accomplish this goal can be found in the then Press column. These section headings are referenced in Figure 14.3.

IN CLOSING

We hope that you have as much fun and excitement learning and productively using Agenda as we did. If you would like to purchase a diskette containing the examples used in this guide, including the Tips & Tricks and Cross-reference Agenda databases, rather than typing them into Agenda yourself, or if you would like to share your thoughts and experiences, please refer to the coupon at the back of the book.

Figure 14-1.

@end	▪ If your input group sometimes ends with a given structure and sometimes the structure is omitted, you may find that the only way to tell where an input group ends is to match on the beginning of the next input group. Make @end the First action in the statement group, followed by the @start action. To write the very last formatted input group to the structured file; you must include a statement of the form ''END @end( )'' in your definition file.
@equate	▪ To save space, you can use the @equate action in advance to define a short variable name and equate it to a long pattern.
@reset	▪ When you use an @reset action, reset-string replaces your current input line. If you need to use the current input line as well, use an @set action before the @reset action to save the current input line as a variable. ▪ To make multiple passes on one input line, use the @set action as the first action in the statement that matches the input line. This saves the input line as a variable. You can use @skip to change the line; to reuse it, use @reset action, which restores it to original form.
@set	▪ When you use an @reset action, reset-string replaces your current input line. If you need to use the current input line as well, use an @set action before the @reset action to save the current input line as a variable. ▪ To make multiple passes on one input line, use the @set action as the first action in the statement that matches the input line. This saves the input line as a variable. You can use @skip to change the line; to reuse it, use @reset action, which restores it to original form.
Reset-string	▪ When you use an @reset action, reset-string replaces your current input line. If you need to use the current input line as well, use an @set action before the @reset action to save the current input line as a variable.
@skip_lines	▪ If related parts for a single item or category are separated by intervening material, use the @skip_lines action to skip over the irrelevant material. You can delete unwanted lines and use another @item or @note action to append the rest of the text. ▪ There are two circumstances in which you might use @skip_lines with a pattern: either you know the pattern for the start of the

text you want to format or you know the pattern for the end of the text you want to skip over. In both cases, you use that pattern as the termination point. In the first case, the line with the pattern you are looking for will be in memory, so you should include the formatting actions (@item,@note,etc) in the same statement. In the second case, you want to discard the last line read into memory and find the next line. You can use an @skip_lines(1) action in the same statement to read the next line into memory. Do not use a pattern as the termination point and then as the pattern to search for at the start of the next statement. Once the line that matches the pattern has been read into memory to match the termination point, it will no longer be available to match the pattern at the start of the next statement. (Note that this is different from the @item action, where the line that matches the termination point is available to match another statement.)

- Do not specify as your termination point the same pattern you specify in the statement that matches the first line of each input group. @skip_lines reads the line containing the termination point into memory, leaving it available as the current input line. TXT2STF does not attempt to find a definition file statement that matches the line containing the termination point. Thus, if you used the same pattern both to match the first input line in the group, and as the location to skip to, your definition file will skip over every second input group.

@start

- If your input group sometimes ends with a given structure and sometimes the structure is omitted, you may find that the only way to tell where an input group ends is to match on the beginning of the next input group. Make @end the First action in the statement group, followed by the @start action.

  To write the very last formatted input group to the structured file; you must include a statement of the form ''END @end( )'' in your definition file.

Actions

- If your input group sometimes ends with a given structure and sometimes the structure is omitted, you may find that the only way to tell where an input group ends is to match on the beginning of the next input group. Make @end the First action in the statement group, followed by the @start action.

Figure 14-1.
Continued.

To write the very last formatted input group to the structured file; you must include a statement of the form "END @end( )" in your definition file.

- To save space, you can use the @equate action in advance to define a short variable name and equate it to a long pattern.
- When you use an @reset action, reset-string replaces your current input line. If you need to use the current input line as well, use an *@set action before the* @reset action to save the current input line as a variable.
- If related parts for a single item or category are separated by intervening material, use the @skip_lines action to skip over the irrelevant material. You can delete unwanted lines and use another @item or @note action to append the rest of the text.
- If you do not want to use the entire input line, use the @skip, @strip, @replace, or @trim actions to remove unwanted text.
- If you want to build a new database from part of an existing database, you can preserve views, macros, conditions, and actions by following these basic steps: Use the File Transfer Template command to export the items (and their assignments) from your database to a structured file. Use the File Transfer Export command to export the items (and their assignments) from your database to a structured file.

  Open the database you created in step one.

  Use the File Transfer Import command to import the structure file you created.

  Discard the categories in the category hierarchy that you do not want.
- Profile actions can trigger other profile actions for 16 levels. In other words, an action can assign an item to a category with another action, which assigns an item to a category with another action, up to 16 times. After that, the actions will not be executed.
- If you want to remove only a profile action, press Tab or F3(InclCat) until all arrows have been removed from all categories. This removes the profile action.
- If you copy an action to a category that already has one, the new action (whether a profile action or a special action or both) replaces the entire action that was attached to the category.

- If an item is removed from a category with an action, the action is not ''undone''; rather, the effect of the action remains.
- When you unindex a category, all conditions and actions are lost.
- If the related parts for a single item or category are separated by intervening material in your input file, you should use the pattern to locate the start of the item, category, or note. Use the appropriate action to format.
- To make multiple passes on one input line, use the @set action as the first action in the statement that matches the input line. This saves the input line as a variable. You can use @skip to change the line; to reuse it, use @reset action, which restores it to original form.

Ancestor

- The root category, Main is the ancestor of all categories in the Database. Thus all items are assigned to Main by inheritance and can be viewed by selecting a view with Main as the category selected.

Backup

- If you cannot access your backup file from F10(Menu), File, Use-Backup, then go to DOS and copy the .BKA & .BKB files to .AGA & .AGB files.
- If there is a power loss during an Agenda session, your database files can become damaged. If Agenda is set to make backups when you open your database, it will overwrite your good backup (.BKA and .BKB) with a new backup made from the damaged database. If you believe your database has been damaged do not open it. Instead, create a new database by using your operating system to make a copy of your good backup files with a new name and the extensions .AGA and .AGB.
- If you want to keep a copy of an earlier version of your database as well as a copy of your current database, do not make a backup of your database. Instead, use the File Copy command to make an additional copy.
- You cannot copy or make backups of your Agenda disks until you have validated your copy of Agenda (which you do by using the install program).
- Even if you set Agenda to automatically save your work at specified intervals you should still make backups of your database, because as soon as you enter new information, your database files are no longer up-to-date.
- Do not replace a damaged database using the File Use-Backup command if you have Make Backup copy set to When file is opened,

Figure 14-1.
Continued.

as Agenda will overwrite your good backup with a damaged backup. Instead you can make a new database from the backup files using operating system commands.

Beep

- Agenda beeps if you press Insert in a column where the categories are mutually exclusive. An item cannot be assigned to two mutually exclusive categories.
- If Agenda beeps when you select F10(Menu), Category, Column, New, you don't have enough space on the screen and you have to shrink or remove existing columns.

Categorization

- If Agenda is making matches you don't want, increase the Required Match Strength under Utility Preferences Auto-Assign or set Confirm assignments to Sometimes or Always.
- If Agenda makes matches you don't want, use other special characters to specify more clearly the kind of text that should match the expression.
- If Agenda is not assigning items to categories where you expect, make sure your category names do not include commas as punctuation.
- If Agenda is not assigning items to categories where you think there should be a match, check to see whether there is a question mark in the upper right corner of the screen. Agenda is suggesting matches for you to confirm.
- If you want Agenda to search the database for items that match a new category, use the Utility Other Execute command or Alt-X.
- If a word is three letters or fewer Agenda does not ignore the suffixes, even if you select Yes. Thus panes does not match pan, even though es is considered a suffix.
- If Agenda is making matches that you don't want, enclose all or part of the category in double quotation marks to avoid matching irrelevant words.
- If Agenda is not assigning items to categories where you think there is a match, make sure Text condition Match on under Condition Settings for the category in question is not set to Disable.
- If Agenda is not assigning items to categories where you think there is a match, and the category is not a proper name, make sure you have not used initial capital letters (Sales Planning) in the category name.

- If you select Text condition for the Syntax setting you can experiment with the text strings that you may want to use as category expressions. Doing so lets you see what items will match different combinations of special characters.
- As you type an item you may notice that it includes text that appears in a category that you do not want the item to match. You can enclose that in double quotation marks (or whatever characters you have selected for the Skip text enclosed by setting) and Agenda will ignore the text within the quotation marks when searching for matches.
- Avoid using all capital letters or initial capital letters in expressions that are not proper names. Agenda treats all words that begin with capital letters as names; if it considers a category to be a name, it may not make matches that you expect.
- For best results in matching proper names, use initial caps in the category (Bob Thomas). Agenda treats two or more words that begin with capital letters as names and applies special rules that increase the number of correct matches on names.
- To experiment with how items match particular expressions, use the Utility Show Match command and enter the expression you want to test. Set Syntax to Text Condition. This creates a Show View of the items that match the expression you specify according to the logic used in interpreting text conditions.
- If Agenda is not assigning items to categories where you think there is a match, make sure Enable text conditions under Utility Preferences Auto-Assign is set to Yes.
- If Agenda is not assigning items to categories where you think there is a match, check the Match on setting under Utility Preferences Auto-Assign to make sure Agenda is searching for text where you expect.
- If Agenda is not assigning items to categories where you think there is a match, decrease the Required match strength under Utility Preferences Auto-Assign.

Category, Category Hierarchy

- If related parts for a single item or category are separated by intervening material, use the @skip_lines action to skip over the irrelevant material. You can delete unwanted lines and use another @item or @note action to append the rest of the text.
- If you want to remove only a profile action, press Tab or F3(InclCat) until all arrows have been removed from all categories. This removes the profile action.

Figure 14-1.
Continued.

- If an item is removed from a category with an action, the action is not "undone"; rather, the effect of the action remains.
- If you copy a condition to a category that already has one, the new condition (whether a profile condition or a date condition or both) replaces the entire condition that was attached to the category.
- Profile actions can trigger other profile actions for 16 levels. In other words, an action can assign an item to a category with another action, which assigns an item to a category with another action, up to 16 times. After that, the actions will not be executed.
- If you copy an action to a category that already has one, the new action (whether a profile action or a special action or both) replaces the entire action that was attached to the category.
- Agenda beeps if you press Insert in a column where the categories are mutually exclusive. An item cannot be assigned to two mutually exclusive categories.
- If Agenda is not assigning items to categories where you expect, make sure your category names do not include commas as punctuation.
- If Agenda is not assigning items to categories where you think there should be a match, check to see whether there is a question mark in the upper right corner of the screen. Agenda is suggesting matches for you to confirm.
- If you want Agenda to search the database for items that match a new category, use the Utility Other Execute command or Alt-X.
- When you unindex a category, all conditions and actions are lost.
- If Agenda is not assigning items to categories where you think there is a match and the category is not a proper name, make sure you have not used initial capital letters (Sales Planning) in the category name.
- If Agenda is not assigning items to categories where you think there is a match, make sure Text condition Match on under Condition Settings for the category in question is not set to Disable.
- If Agenda is making matches that you don't want, enclose all or part of the category in double quotation marks to avoid matching irrelevant words.

- If the related parts for a single item or category are separated by intervening material in your input file, you should use the pattern to locate the start of the item, category, or note. Use the appropriate action to format.
- If you copy an item from one mutually exclusive category to another, Agenda removes the item from the original section, since an item cannot be assigned to two mutually exclusive categories at the same time.
- You can display Entry, When, and Done dates in date columns. These date column heads and column entries are not categories and cannot be used as section heads.
- Editing a category name is different from replacing one category with another.
- If you remove all of the sections in a view, Agenda does not delete the view. Instead it replaces the last category with an untitled category.
- You cannot enter a category at the same level as Main.
- Discarding a parent category also discards any child categories it might have.
- If you select Text condition for the Syntax setting you can experiment with the text strings that you may want to use as category expressions. Doing so lets you see what items will match different combinations of special characters.
- If an item was assigned to a category because of a condition, and it no longer meets that condition, it will be removed from the category the next time Agenda tests items against conditions.
- When specifying a category, you must specify the first expression for that category or the assignment may not be made.
- If your computer does not recognize Shift Grey +, use Alt = to expand one or all families in the category hierarchy.
- If you do not see what is causing the circular reference, you may want to look at the assignment profile for all the items involved. This lets you see whether all the items are assigned to one or more of the same categories. You can mark all of the items and then press Alt-F9(Profile) to see the assignment profile for all the items involved.
- If Agenda beeps when you select F10(Menu), Category, Column, New, you don't have enough space on the screen and you have to shrink or remove existing columns.

Figure 14-1.
Continued.

- If you want to remove only a profile condition, press F3(InclCat) as many times as you need to in order to remove the arrows from all categories involved, thereby removing the profile condition.
- As you type an item you may notice that it includes text that appears in a category that you do not want the item to match. You can enclose that in double quotation marks (or whatever characters you have selected for the Skip text enclosed by setting) and Agenda will ignore the text within the quotation marks when searching for matches.
- For best results in matching proper names, use initial caps in the category (Bob Thomas). Agenda treats two or more words that begin with capital letters as names and applies special rules that increase the number of correct matches on names.
- Avoid using all capital letters or initial capital letters in expressions that are not proper names. Agenda treats all words that begin with capital letters as names; if it considers a category to be a name, it may not make matches that you expect.
- If you find that you have included a number of expressions for a category, you may want to refine your category hierarchy to make each expression a category. For instance, you could make Atlantic, Pacific, and Indian, into child categories of Ocean.
- When you import a structured file, Agenda also assigns the items in the structured file to all categories whose text conditions they meet. You can prevent this by disabling the text conditions before you import the file.
- Discarding a parent category discards the children.
- Discarded categories are not placed in the trash and therefore cannot be undiscarded; however, if items have been discarded with the category, they can be recovered.
- The root category, Main is the ancestor of all categories in the Database. Thus all items are assigned to Main by inheritance and can be viewed by selecting a view with Main as the category selected.
- If Agenda is not assigning items to categories where you think there is a match, decrease the Required match strength under Utility Preferences Auto-Assign.
- If Agenda is not assigning items to categories where you think there is a match, make sure Enable text conditions under Utility Preferences Auto-Assign is set to Yes.

- If Agenda is not assigning items to categories where you think there is a match, check the Match on setting under Utility Preferences Auto-Assign to make sure Agenda is searching for text where you expect.
- If the appended text and current text together exceed 350 characters in the case of an item, or 69 in the case of a category, Agenda leaves the remaining text in the note.

Assignment

- When specifying a category, you must specify the first expression for that category or the assignment may not be made.
- The root category, Main, is the ancestor of all categories in the Database. Thus all items are assigned to Main by inheritance and can be viewed by selecting a view with Main as the category selected.
- If you set a When date for an item using the When(Alt-F2) key, or by entering the date in the When Date column instead of letting Agenda assign the date in the When Date column you create, then editing the date in the item will not change the When Date for the item.
- If Agenda is not assigning items to categories where you think there is a match, make sure Enable text conditions under Utility Preferences Auto-Assign is set to Yes.
- If Agenda is not assigning items to categories where you think there is a match, check the Match on setting under Utility Preferences Auto-Assign to make sure Agenda is searching for text where you expect.
- If Agenda is not assigning items to categories where you think there is a match, make sure Text condition Match on under Condition Settings for the category in question is not set to Disable.
- If Agenda is not assigning items to categories where you think there is a match and the category is not a proper name, make sure you have not used initial capital letters (Sales Planning) in the category name.
- If Agenda is not assigning items to categories where you think there is a match, decrease the Required Match Strength under Utility Preferences Auto-Assign.
- If Agenda is making matches you don't want, increase the Required Match Strength under Utility Preferences Auto-Assign or set Confirm assignments to Sometimes or Always.

Figure 14-1.
Continued.

- When you import a structured file, Agenda also assigns the items in the structured file to all categories whose text conditions they meet. You can prevent this by disabling the text conditions before you import the file.
- If you do not see what is causing the circular reference, you may want to look at the assignment profile for all the items involved. This lets you see whether all the items are assigned to one or more of the same categories. You can mark all of the items and then press Alt-F9(Profile) to see the assignment profile for all the items involved.
- If you copy an item from one mutually exclusive category to another Agenda removes the item from the original section, since an item cannot be assigned to two mutually exclusive categories at the same time.
- Agenda beeps if you press Insert in a column where the categories are mutually exclusive. An item cannot be assigned to two mutually exclusive categories.
- If Agenda is not assigning items to categories where you think there should be a match, check to see whether there is a question mark in the upper right corner of the screen. Agenda is suggesting matches for you to confirm.
- If Agenda is not assigning items to categories where you expect, make sure your category names do not include commas as punctuation.
- If an item was assigned to a category because of a condition, and it no longer meets that condition, it will be removed from the category the next time Agenda tests items against conditions.
- Profile actions can trigger other profile actions for 16 levels. In other words, an action can assign an item to a category with another action, which assigns an item to a category with another action, up to 16 times. After that, the actions will not be executed.
- If you want to build a new database from part of an existing database, you can preserve views, macros, conditions, and actions by following these basic steps: Use the File Transfer Template command to export the items (and their assignments) from your database to a structured file. Use the File Transfer Export command to export the items (and their assignments) from your database to a structured file.

Open the database you created in step one.

Use the File Transfer Import command to import the structure file you created.

Discard the categories in the category hierarchy that you do not want.

Child

- Discarding a parent category also discards any child categories it might have.
- If you find that you have included a number of expressions for a category, you may want to refine your category hierarchy to make each expression a category. For instance, you could make Atlantic, Pacific, and Indian, into child categories of Ocean.
- Discarding a parent category discards the children.

Circular Reference

- If you do not see what is causing the circular reference, you may want to look at the assignment profile for all the items involved. This lets you see whether all the items are assigned to one or more of the same categories. You can mark all of the items and then press Alt-F9(Profile) to see the assignment profile for all the items involved.

Clipboard

- If you unload Metro, the contents of the Clipboard will be lost.

Collapse

- If your computer does not recognize Shift Grey –, use Alt – to collapse one or all sections in a view.

Column

- Agenda beeps if you press Insert in a column where the categories are mutually exclusive. An item cannot be assigned to two mutually exclusive categories.
- You can display Entry, When, and Done dates in date columns. These date column heads and column entries are not categories and cannot be used as section heads.
- If you want to move a column that appears in many sections it may be easier to remove the column and then insert it where you want it.
- If Agenda beeps when you select F10(Menu), Category, Column, New, you don't have enough space on the screen and you have to shrink or remove existing columns.
- If you discover a mistake in a column entry after you enter it, highlight the entry and press Alt-F4(Discard); then type Y and press Enter. Enter it again.

Figure 14-1.
Continued

- You cannot adjust the column width of the item column.
- If you set a When date for an item using the When(Alt-F2) key, or by entering the date in the When Date column instead of letting Agenda assign the date in the When Date column you create, then editing the date in the item will not change the When Date for the item.

Column width

- You cannot adjust the column width of the item column.

Conditions

- If you want to build a new database from part of an existing database, you can preserve views, macros, conditions, and actions by following these basic steps: Use the File Transfer Template command to export the items (and their assignments) from your database to a structured file. Use the File Transfer Export command to export the items (and their assignments) from your database to a structured file.

  Open the database you created in step one.

  Use the File Transfer Import command to import the structure file you created.

  Discard the categories in the category hierarchy that you do not want.
- If you copy a condition to a category that already has one, the new condition (whether a profile condition or a date condition or both) replaces the entire condition that was attached to the category.
- If Agenda is not assigning items to categories where you expect, make sure your category names do not include commas as punctuation.
- If a word is three or fewer letters, Agenda does not ignore the suffixes, even if you select Yes. Panes does not match pan.
- If Agenda is not assigning items to categories where you think there should be a match, check to see whether there is a question mark in the upper right corner of the screen. Agenda is suggesting matches for you to confirm.
- If Agenda is not assigning items to categories where you think there is a match, make sure Text condition Match on under Condition Settings for the category in question is not set to Disable.

- If you select Text condition for the Syntax setting you can experiment with the text strings that you may want to use as category expressions. Doing so lets you see what items will match different combinations of special characters.
- If Agenda is not assigning items to categories where you think there is a match, and the category is not a proper name, make sure you have not used initial capital letters (Sales Planning) in the category name.
- If an item was assigned to a category because of a condition, and it no longer meets that condition, it will be removed from the category the next time Agenda tests items against conditions.
- When you unindex a category, all conditions and actions are lost.
- If you do not see what is causing the circular reference, you may want to look at the assignment profile for all the items involved. This lets you see whether all the items are assigned to one or more of the same categories. You can mark all of the items and then press Alt-F9(Profile) to see the assignment profile for all the items involved.
- If you want to remove only a profile condition, press F3(InclCat) as many times as you need to in order to remove the arrows from all categories involved, thereby removing the profile condition.
- To experiment with how items match particular expressions, use the Utility Show Match command and enter the expression you want to test. Set Syntax to Text Condition. This creates a Show View of the items that match the expression you specify, according to the logic used in interpreting text conditions.
- As you type an item you may notice that it includes text that appears in a category that you do not want the item to match. You can enclose that in double quotation marks (or whatever characters you have selected for the Skip text enclosed by setting). Agenda will ignore the text within the quotation marks when searching for matches.
- For best results in matching proper names, use initial caps in the category (Bob Thomas). Agenda treats two or more words that begin with capital letters as names and applies special rules that increase the number of correct matches on names.
- Avoid using all capital letters or initial capital letters in expressions that are not proper names. Agenda treats all words that begin with capital letters as names; if it considers a category to be a name, it may not make matches that you expect.

Figure 14-1.
Continued.

- If you find that you have included a number of expressions for a category, you may want to refine your category hierarchy to make each expression a category. For instance, you could make Atlantic, Pacific, and Indian, into child categories of Ocean.
- When you import a structured file, Agenda also assigns the items in the structured file to all categories whose text conditions they meet. You can prevent this by disabling the text conditions before you import the file.
- If Agenda is not assigning items to categories where you think there is a match, make sure Enable text conditions under Utility Preferences Auto-Assign is set to Yes.
- If Agenda is not assigning items to categories where you think there is a match, check the Match on setting under Utility Preferences Auto-Assign to make sure Agenda is searching for text where you expect.
- If Agenda is not assigning items to categories where you think there is a match, decrease the Required match strength under Utility Preferences Auto-Assign.

Copy

- If you want to build a new database from part of an existing database, you can preserve views, macros, conditions, and actions by following these basic steps: Use the File Transfer Template command to export the items (and their assignments) from your database to a structured file. Use the File Transfer Export command to export the items (and their assignments) from your database to a structured file.

  Open the database you created in step one.

  Use the File Transfer Import command to import the structure file you created.

  Discard the categories in the category hierarchy that you do not want.
- If you copy a condition to a category that already has one, the new condition (whether a profile condition or a date condition or both) replaces the entire condition that was attached to the category.
- If you copy an action to a category that already has one, the new action (whether a profile action or a special action or both) replaces the entire action that was attached to the category.

- If you want to keep a copy of an earlier version of your database as well as a copy of your current database, do not make a backup of your database. Instead, use the File Copy command to make an additional copy.
- If you cannot access your backup file from F10(Menu), File, Use-Backup, then go to DOS and copy the .BKA & .BKB files to .AGA & .AGB files.
- You cannot copy or make backups of your Agenda disks until you have validated your copy of Agenda (which you do by using the install program).
- Do not replace a damaged database using the File Use-Backup command if you have Make Backup copy set to When file is opened, as Agenda will overwrite your good backup with a damaged backup. Instead you can make a new database from the backup files using operating system commands.
- If you copy an item from one mutually exclusive category to another, Agenda removes the item from the original section since an item cannot be assigned to two mutually exclusive categories at the same time.
- Do not select an existing database unless you want to replace it with a copy of the current database when you do a File Copy.
- After pasting text, it remains in the temporary file until you cut or copy other text.
- If you are printing to a file and select text only, make sure that the special characters setting is set to Do not translate, unless you plan to copy the file to your printer. Otherwise, all characters in your printer-specific translation table will be translated.

Special Action

- If you copy an action to a category that already has one, the new action (whether a profile action or a special action or both) replaces the entire action that was attached to the category.

Cut

- After pasting text, it remains in the temporary file until you cut or copy other text.

Database

- If you want to build a new database from part of an existing database, you can preserve views, macros, conditions, and actions by following these basic steps: Use the File Transfer Template command to export the items (and their assignments) from your database to a structured file. Use the File Transfer Export command to export the items (and their assignments) from your database to a structured file.

Figure 14-1.
Continued.

Open the database you created in step one.

Use the File Transfer Import command to import the structure file you created.

Discard the categories in the category hierarchy that you do not want.

- If there is a power loss during an Agenda session, your database files can become damaged. If Agenda is set to make backups when you open your database, it will overwrite your good backup (.BKA and .BKB) with a new backup made from the damaged database. If you believe your database has been damaged do not open it.

  Instead, create a new database by using your operating system to make a copy of your good backup files with a new name and the extensions .AGA and .AGB.

- If you want to keep a copy of an earlier version of your database as well as a copy of your current database, do not make a backup of your database. Instead, use the File Copy command to make an additional copy.
- Even if you set Agenda to automatically save your work at specified intervals you should still make backups of your database, because as soon as you enter new information, your database files are no longer up-to-date.
- Do not replace a damaged database using the File Use-Backup command if you have Make Backup copy set to When file is opened, as Agenda will overwrite your good backup with a damaged backup. Instead you can make a new database from the backup files using operating system commands.
- If you want Agenda to search the database for items that match a new category, use the Utility Other Execute command or Alt-X.
- Do not select an existing database unless you want to replace it with a copy of the current database when you do a File Copy.
- Agenda uses the term File when referring to a database.
- You must quit Agenda before you reboot your computer or turn it off. Failing to do so may damage your database and/or result in loss of data.
- All users on a LAN can see any note files referenced by an Agenda database. Only one user at a time can modify the note.

- If your database is on a diskette or other removable media, do not take it out of your computer until you close the current database.
- TXT2STF does not check whether the file exists. If the file does not exist, Agenda asks whether you want to create it when you attempt to look at the note in the Agenda database.
- If you delete a database through the operating system, you should delete all the database files (ex: Sales.*).
- You may be able to open a damaged database and recover most of your items by exporting them to a structured file and importing them to a new database.
- The root category, Main, is the ancestor of all categories in the Database. Thus all items are assigned to Main by inheritance and can be viewed by selecting a view with Main as the category selected.

Dates

- If you copy a condition to a category that already has one, the new condition (whether a profile condition or a date condition or both) replaces the entire condition that was attached to the category.
- You can display Entry, When, and Done dates in date columns. These date column heads and column entries are not categories and cannot be used as section heads.
- Always enter dates in the default date format since 10-8 will be read differently by mm-dd-yy or dd-mm-yy.
- The relative format applies only to dates within the current two weeks.
- If you set a When date for an item using the When(Alt-F2) key, or by entering the date in the When Date column instead if letting Agenda assign the date in the When Date column you create, then editing the date in the item will not change the When Date for the item.

Delete

- If related parts for a single item or category are separated by intervening material, use the @skip_lines action to skip over the irrelevant material. You can delete unwanted lines and use another @item or @note action to append the rest of the text.
- If you remove all of the section in a view, Agenda does not delete the view. Instead it replaces the last category with an untitled category.
- If you delete a database through the operating system, you should delete all the database files (ex: Sales.*).

Figure 14-1.
Continued.

- All of the Agenda printer definition files are copied onto your system during installation. If you are concerned about disk space, you may want to delete those printer definition files that you do not plan to use.
- TXT2STF assumes that the first blank line in the input file indicates the end of the table. If your table includes blank lines before the end, delete them. If your table includes empty cells, put 0 or the word ''blank'' in the empty cells.

Dependent

- Agenda does not prevent you from designating as done or discarding dependent items.

Discard

- Discarding a parent category also discards any child categories it might have.
- If you discover a mistake in a column entry after you enter it, highlight the entry and press Alt-F4(Discard); then type Y and press Enter. Enter it again.
- Keep in mind that some operations affect marked items regardless of which sections they are marked in. For example, if you discard a marked item that appears in more than one section, Agenda will discard that item from all sections in which it appears.
- Discarding a parent category discards the children.
- Agenda does not prevent you from designating as done or discarding dependent items.
- Discarded categories are not placed in the trash and therefore cannot be undiscarded; however, if items have been discarded with the category, they can be recovered.

Documentation

- Including many lines of comments can significantly lengthen the run time of TXT2STF with your definition file. Try keeping any lengthy documentation in a separate file.

Expand

- If your computer does not recognize Shift Grey +, use Alt = to expand one or all families in the category hierarchy.

Export

- If you want to build a new database from part of an existing database, you can preserve views, macros, conditions, and actions by following these basic steps: Use the File Transfer Template command to export the items (and their assignments) from your database to a structured file. Use the File Transfer Export command to export the items (and their assignments) from your database to a structured file.

Open the database you created in step one.

Use the File Transfer Import command to import the structure file you created.

Discard the categories in the category hierarchy that you do not want.

- You may be able to open a damaged database and recover most of your items by exporting them to a structured file and importing them to a new database.

Files

- If you want to build a new database from part of an existing database, you can preserve views, macros, conditions, and actions by following these basic steps: Use the File Transfer Template command to export the items (and their assignments) from your database to a structured file. Use the File Transfer Export command to export the items (and their assignments) from your database to a structured file.

  Open the database you created in step one.

  Use the File Transfer Import command to import the structure file you created.

  Discard the categories in the category hierarchy that you do not want.

- If there is a power loss during an Agenda session, your database files can become damaged. If Agenda is set to make backups when you open your database, it will overwrite your good backup (.BKA and .BKB) with a new backup made from the damaged database. If you believe your database has been damaged do not open it.

  Instead, create a new database by using your operating system to make a copy of your good backup files with a new name and the extensions .AGA and .AGB.

- Even if you set Agenda to automatically save your work at specified intervals, you should still make backups of your database, because as soon as you enter new information your database files are no longer up-to-date.

- If you cannot access your backup file from F10(Menu), File, Use-Backup, then go to DOS and copy the .BKA & .BKB files to .AGA & .AGB files.

Figure 14-1.
Continued.

- If you want to keep a copy of an earlier version of your database as well as a copy of your current database, do not make a backup of your database. Instead, use the File Copy command to make an additional copy.
- Do not replace a damaged database using the File Use-Backup command if you have Make Backup copy set to When file is opened, as Agenda will overwrite your good backup with a damaged backup. Instead you can make a new database from the backup files using operating system commands.
- When you import a structured file, Agenda also assigns the items in the structured file to all categories whose text conditions they meet. You can prevent this by disabling the text conditions before you import the file.
- Do not select an existing database unless you want to replace it with a copy of the current database when you do a File Copy.
- All users on a LAN can see any note files referenced by an Agenda database. Only one user at a time can modify the note.
- Agenda uses the term File when referring to a database.
- TXT2STF does not check whether the file exists. If the file does not exist, Agenda asks whether you want to create it when you attempt to look at the note in the Agenda database.
- Files created in many word processing applications contain formatting codes, as well as text. See your word processing documentation for information about creating files without embedded codes.
- If you delete a database through the operating system, you should delete all the database files (ex: Sales.*).
- Including many lines of comments can significantly lengthen the run time of TXT2STF with your definition file. Try keeping any lengthy documentation in a separate file.
- You may be able to open a damaged database and recover most of your items by exporting them to a structured file and importing them to a new database.
- All of the Agenda printer definition files are copied onto your system during installation. If you are concerned about disk space, you may want to delete those printer definition files that you do not plan to use.

- If you use a backslash command as justification or for a text attribute (for example, \rj\ or\b\), that feature will be in effect until the next occurrence of the command. For example, you might turn on the compressed text attribute in the Printer setup string, using the \c\ command defined in the Agenda printer definition files. You may also want to print all your Agenda notes in compressed mode. But if you specify in the Note setup string as well as in the printer setup string, the second occurrence will turn off this feature. You may need to experiment with your setup and termination strings until you are satisfied with the output.
- The generic printer definition file, PRINTER.PDF, does not include these commands because some printers do not support these features. They are: \prstart\, \prend\, and \reset\.
- The printer definition files assume that the translated character prints to a single space. You may see unexpected line wrapping if the translated character prints to two or more spaces.
- If you supply the name of an existing file, Agenda overwrites that file with the new one.
- If the notes in your structured file contain paragraphs that are not separated by at least one blank line and you want to preserve the paragraph divisions, do not strip carriage returns when you import the structured file.
- If the file that you are importing is larger than 10k, Agenda imports only the first 10K characters.
- An item may reference only one external note file at a time.
- You can only use text files as note files. To reference other types of information such as spreadsheet data you must first print to a text file.
- After pasting text, it remains in the temporary file until you cut or copy other text.
- If you are printing to a file and select text only, make sure that the special characters setting is set to Do not translate, unless you plan to copy the file to your printer. Otherwise, all characters in your printer-specific translation table will be translated.
- When printing to a file (unless you plan to send the file to the printer without modifying it), you should select either Do not translate or Print as space for this setting.
- TXT2STF assumes that the first blank line in the input file indicates the end of the table. If your table includes blank lines before the end, delete them. If your table includes empty cells, put 0 or the word ''blank'' in the empty cells.

Figure 14-1.
Continued.

Overwrite	▪ If you supply the name of an existing file, Agenda overwrites that file with the new one. ▪ If there is a power loss during an Agenda session, your database files can become damaged. If Agenda is set to make backups when you open your database, it will overwrite your good backup (.BKA and .BKB) with a new backup made from the damaged database. If you believe your database has been damaged do not open it. Instead, create a new database by using your operating system to make a copy of your good backup files with a new name and the extensions .AGA and .AGB. ▪ Do not replace a damaged database using the File Use-Backup command if you have Make Backup copy set to When file is opened, as Agenda will overwrite your good backup with a damaged backup. Instead you can make a new database from the backup files using operating system commands.
Damaged	▪ Do not replace a damaged database using the File Use-Backup command if you have Make Backup copy set to When file is opened, as Agenda will overwrite your good backup with a damaged backup. Instead you can make a new database from the backup files using operating system commands. ▪ You must quit Agenda before you reboot your computer or turn it off. Failing to do so may damage your database and/or result in loss of data. ▪ If there is a power loss during an Agenda session, your database files can become damaged. If Agenda is set to make backups when you open your database, it will overwrite your good backup (.BKA and .BKB) with a new backup made from the damaged database. If you believe your database has been damaged do not open it. Instead, create a new database by using your operating system to make a copy of your good backup files with a new name and the extensions .AGA and .AGB. ▪ You may be able to open a damaged database and recover most of your items by exporting them to a structured file and importing them to a new database.
Word-processor	▪ Files created in many word processing applications contain formatting codes, as well as text. See your word processing documentation for information about creating files without embedded codes.

Function Keys

- If you want to remove only a profile action, press Tab or F3(InclCat) until all arrows have been removed from all categories. This removes the profile action.
- If you do not see what is causing the circular reference, you may want to look at the assignment profile for all the items involved. This lets you see whether all the items are assigned to one or more of the same categories. You can mark all of the items and then press Alt-F9(Profile) to see the assignment profile for all the items involved.
- If you want to remove only a profile condition, press F3(InclCat) as many times as you need to in order to remove the arrows from all categories involved, thereby removing the profile condition.
- If you set a When date for an item using the When(Alt-F2) key, or by entering the date in the When Date column instead if letting Agenda assign the date in the When Date column you create, then editing the date in the item will not change the When Date for the item.

Import

- If you want to build a new database from part of an existing database, you can preserve views, macros, conditions, and actions by following these basic steps: Use the File Transfer Template command to export the items (and their assignments) from your database to a structured file. Use the File Transfer Export command to export the items (and their assignments) from your database to a structured file.

  Open the database you created in step one.

  Use the File Transfer Import command to import the structure file you created.

  Discard the categories in the category hierarchy that you do not want.
- When you import a structured file, Agenda also assigns the items in the structured file to all categories whose text conditions they meet. You can prevent this by disabling the text conditions before you import the file.
- You may be able to open a damaged database and recover most of your items by exporting them to a structured file and importing them to a new database.
- If the notes in your structured file contain paragraphs that are not separated by at least one blank line and you want to preserve the paragraph divisions, do not strip carriage returns when you import the structured file.

Figure 14-1.
Continued.

- If the file that you are importing is larger than 10k, Agenda imports only the first 10K characters.

Index

- When you unindex a category, all conditions and actions are lost.

Items

- If related parts for a single item or category are separated by intervening material, use the @skip_lines action to skip over the irrelevant material. You can delete unwanted lines and use another @item or @note action to append the rest of the text.
- If you want to build a new database from part of an existing database, you can preserve views, macros, conditions, and actions by following these basic steps: Use the File Transfer Template command to export the items (and their assignments) from your database to a structured file. Use the File Transfer Export command to export the items (and their assignments) from your database to a structured file.

  Open the database you created in step one.

  Use the File Transfer Import command to import the structure file you created.

  Discard the categories in the category hierarchy that you do not want.
- If an item is removed from a category with an action, the action is not ''undone''; rather, the effect of the action remains.
- Profile actions can trigger other profile actions for 16 levels. In other words, an action can assign an item to a category with another action, which assigns an item to a category with another action, up to 16 times. After that, the actions will not be executed.
- Agenda beeps if you press Insert in a column where the categories are mutually exclusive. An item cannot be assigned to two mutually exclusive categories.
- If Agenda is not assigning items to categories where you expect, make sure your category names do not include commas as punctuation.
- To use only the first matching input line as the item, specify ^ as the termination string. This causes TXT2STF to terminate the item at the start of the second line. You cannot use $ because TXT2STF does not search the first line of the item for the termination string. It begins searching on the second line, so using $ as the termination-string causes TXT2STF to use the first two lines as the item.

- If Agenda is not assigning items to categories where you think there should be a match, check to see whether there is a question mark in the upper right corner of the screen. Agenda is suggesting matches for you to confirm.
- If you want Agenda to search the database for items that match a new category, use the Utility Other Execute command or Alt-X.
- If Agenda is not assigning items to categories where you think there is a match, make sure Text condition Match on under Condition Settings for the category in question is not set to Disable.
- If Agenda is not assigning items to categories where you think there is a match and the category is not a proper name, make sure you have not used initial capital letters (Sales Planning) in the category name.
- If the related parts for a single item or category are separated by intervening material in your input file, you should use the pattern to locate the start of the item, category, or note. Use the appropriate action to format.
- If you copy an item from one mutually exclusive category to another, Agenda removes the item from the original section since an item cannot be assigned to two mutually exclusive categories at the same time.
- If you select Text condition for the Syntax setting you can experiment with the text strings that you may want to use as category expressions. Doing so lets you see what items will match different combinations of special characters.
- If an item was assigned to a category because of a condition, and it no longer meets that condition, it will be removed from the category the next time Agenda tests items against conditions.
- If you do not see what is causing the circular reference, you may want to look at the assignment profile for all the items involved. This lets you see whether all the items are assigned to one or more of the same categories. You can mark all of the items and then press Alt-F9(Profile) to see the assignment profile for all the items involved.
- To experiment with how items match particular expressions, use the Utility Show Match command and enter the expression you want to test. Set Syntax to Text Condition. This creates a Show View of the items that match the expression you specify, according to the logic used in interpreting text conditions.
- As you type an item you may notice that it includes text that appears in a category that you do not want the item to match. You can enclose that in double quotation marks (or whatever characters you

Figure 14-1.
Continued.

have selected for the Skip text enclosed by setting). Agenda will ignore the text within the quotation marks when searching for matches.

- When you import a structured file, Agenda also assigns the items in the structured file to all categories whose text conditions they meet. You can prevent this by disabling the text conditions before you import the file.
- Keep in mind that some operations affect marked items regardless of which sections they are marked in. For example, if you discard a marked item that appears in more than one section, Agenda will discard that item from all sections in which it appears.
- Agenda does not prevent you from designating as done or discarding dependent items.
- You may be able to open a damaged database and recover most of your items by exporting them to a structured file and importing them to a new database.
- To see all items in the trash, create a new section and use the item undiscard command.
- Agenda only keeps track of a single removed item, the last one, which you can recover using Alt-Y.
- Discarded categories are not placed in the trash and therefore cannot be undiscarded; however, if items have been discarded with the category, they can be recovered.
- You cannot adjust the column width of the item column.
- The root category, Main is the ancestor of all categories in the Database. Thus all items are assigned to Main by inheritance and can be viewed by selecting a view with Main as the category selected.
- If you set a When date for an item using the When(Alt-F2) key, or by entering the date in the When Date column instead of letting Agenda assign the date in the When Date column you create, then editing the date in the item will not change the When Date for the item.
- If Agenda is not assigning items to categories where you think there is a match, decrease the Required match strength under Utility Preferences Auto-Assign.

- If Agenda is not assigning items to categories where you think there is a match, check the Match on setting under Utility Preferences Auto-Assign to make sure Agenda is searching for text where you expect.
- Marking text is different from marking complete items.
- An item can only be 350 characters long. Any text over 350 characters becomes a note attached to the item.
- You can use F6(Move) to put items in a specific position within the current section or within another section in the view. To do this, first mark the items and then move the highlight above the place in the section where you want to position them. Press F6(Move); then press Enter twice. Agenda inserts the marked items below the highlight.
- An item may reference only one external note file at a time.
- If the appended text and current text together exceed 350 characters in the case of an item or 69 in the case of a category, Agenda leaves the remaining text in the note.

Text strings

- If you select Text condition for the Syntax setting, you can experiment with the text strings that you may want to use as category expressions. Doing so lets you see what items will match different combinations of special characters.

Syntax

- If you select Text condition for the Syntax setting, you can experiment with the text strings that you may want to use as category expressions. Doing so lets you see what items will match different combinations of special characters.
- When a macro types unwanted characters, check the syntax and length of each macro command to make sure it is correct.
- To experiment with how items match particular expressions, use the Utility Show Match command and enter the expression you want to test. Set Syntax to Text Condition. This creates a Show View of the items that match the expression you specify, according to the logic used in interpreting text conditions.

LAN

- All users on a LAN can see any note files referenced by an Agenda database. Only one user at a time can modify the note.

Macros

- If you want to build a new database from part of an existing database, you can preserve views, macros, conditions, and actions

Figure 14-1.
Continued.

by following these basic steps: Use the File Transfer Template command to export the items (and their assignments) from your database to a structured file. Use the File Transfer Export command to export the items (and their assignments) from your database to a structured file.

Open the database you created in step one.

Use the File Transfer Import command to import the structure file you created.

Discard the categories in the category hierarchy that you do not want.

- When a macro types unwanted characters, check the syntax and length of each macro command to make sure it is correct.
- Character strings used as arguments in commands in a macro cannot exceed 256 characters in length.
- Leaving a semicolon out of a statement that uses multiple arguments will cause the macro to malfunction.
- If the macro types characters that look like incomplete macro commands, this usually means that there are curly braces missing.
- If a macro types unexpected keys, this usually means that the macro was recorded in one mode and run in another mode.

Main

- You cannot enter a category at the same level as Main.
- The root category, Main, is the ancestor of all categories in the Database. Thus all items are assigned to Main by inheritance and can be viewed by selecting a view with Main as the category selected.

Marking items

- If you do not see what is causing the circular reference, you may want to look at the assignment profile for all the items involved. This lets you see whether all the items are assigned to one or more of the same categories. You can mark all of the items and then press Alt-F9(Profile) to see the assignment profile for all the items involved.
- Keep in mind that some operations affect marked items regardless of which sections they are marked in. For example, if you discard a marked item that appears in more than one section, Agenda will discard that item from all sections in which it appears.

- Keep in mind that some operations affect marked items regardless of which sections they are marked in. For example, if you discard a marked item that appears in more than one section, Agenda will discard that item from all sections in which it appears.
- Marking text is different from marking complete items.
- You can use F6(Move) to put items in a specific position within the current section or within another section in the view. To do this, first mark the items and then move the highlight above the place in the section where you want to position them. Press F6(Move); then press Enter twice. Agenda inserts the marked items below the highlight.

Marking text

- Marking text is different from marking complete items.

Metro

- Metro should be loaded last of any terminate and stay resident applications that you have.
- If you unload Metro the contents of the Clipboard will be lost.

Mutually exclusive

- Agenda beeps if you press Insert in a column where the categories are mutually exclusive. An item cannot be assigned to two mutually exclusive categories.
- If you copy an item from one mutually exclusive category to another, Agenda removes the item from the original section since an item cannot be assigned to two mutually exclusive categories at the same time.

Notes

- If related parts for a single item or category are separated by intervening material, use the @skip_lines action to skip over the irrelevant material. You can delete unwanted lines and use another @item or @note action to append the rest of the text.
- If the related parts for a single item or category are separated by intervening material in your input file, you should use the pattern to locate the start of the item, category, or note. Use the appropriate action to format.
- All users on a LAN can see any note files referenced by an Agenda database. Only one user at a time can modify the note.
- TXT2STF does not check whether the file exists. If the file does not exist, Agenda asks whether you want to create it when you attempt to look at the note in the Agenda database.

Figure 14-1.
Continued.

- Two of the backslash commands that you can insert in notes (\pgbk\ and \mgn\) should be placed on a separate line within the note to work correctly.
- If the notes in your structured file contain paragraphs that are not separated by at least one blank line, and you want to preserve the paragraph divisions, do not strip carriage returns when you import the structured file.
- An item can only be 350 characters long. Any text over 350 characters becomes a note attached to the item.
- An item may reference only one external note file at a time.
- If the appended text and current text together exceed 350 characters in the case of an item or 69 in the case of a category, Agenda leaves the remaining text in the note.
- You can only use text files as note files. To reference other types of information such as spreadsheet data you must first print to a text file.

External note file

- An item may reference only one external note file at a time.

Parent

- Discarding a parent category also discards any child categories it might have.
- Discarding a parent category discards the children.

Password

- If you use a password, write it down since you will not be able to get back into the DB without it.

Paste

- After pasting text, it remains in the temporary file until you cut or copy other text.

Printing

- All of the Agenda printer definition files are copied onto your system during installation. If you are concerned about disk space, you may want to delete those printer definition files that you do not plan to use.
- If you use a backslash command as justification or for a text attribute (for example, \rj\ or\b\), that feature will be in effect until the next occurrence of the command. For example, you might turn on the compressed text attribute in the Printer setup string, using the \c\ command defined in the Agenda printer definition files.

You may also want to print all your Agenda notes in compressed mode. But if you specify in the Note setup string as well as in the printer setup string, the second occurrence will turn off this feature. You may need to experiment with your setup and termination strings until you are satisfied with the output.

- The generic printer definition file, PRINTER.PDF, does not include these commands because some printers do not support these features. They are: \prstart\, \prend\, and \reset\.
- The printer definition files assume that the translated character prints to a single space. You may see unexpected line wrapping if the translated character prints to two or more spaces.
- You can only use text files as note files. To reference other types of information such as spreadsheet data you must first print to a text file.
- If you are printing to a file and select text only, make sure that the special characters setting is set to Do not translate, unless you plan to copy the file to your printer. Otherwise, all characters in your printer-specific translation table will be translated.
- When printing to a file (unless you plan to send the file to the printer without modifying it), you should select either Do not translate or Print as space for this setting.

Translate

- The printer definition files assume that the translated character prints to a single space. You may see unexpected line wrapping if the translated character prints to two or more spaces.
- If you are printing to a file and select text only, make sure that the special characters setting is set to Do not translate, unless you plan to copy the file to your printer. Otherwise, all characters in your printer-specific translation table will be translated.
- When printing to a file (unless you plan to send the file to the printer without modifying it), you should select either Do not translate or Print as space for this setting.

Proper names

- If Agenda is not assigning items to categories where you think there is a match, and the category is not a proper name, make sure you have not used initial capital letters (Sales Planning) in the category name.
- For best results in matching proper names, use initial caps in the category (Bob Thomas). Agenda treats two or more words that begin with capital letters as names and applies special rules that increase the number of correct matches on names.

Figure 14-1.
Continued.

- Avoid using all capital letters or initial capital letters in expressions that are not proper names. Agenda treats all words that begin with capital letters as names; if it considers a category to be a name, it may not make matches that you expect.

Running out of space

- If Agenda beeps when you select F10(Menu), Category, Column, New you don't have enough space on the screen and you have to shrink or remove existing columns.
- All of the Agenda printer definition files are copied onto your system during installation. If you are concerned about disk space, you may want to delete those printer definition files that you do not plan to use.

Save

- To save space, you can use the @equate action in advance to define a short variable name and equate it to a long pattern.
- When you use an @reset action, reset-string replaces your current input line. If you need to use the current input line as well, use an @set action before the @reset action to save the current input line as a variable.
- Even if you set Agenda to automatically save your work at specified intervals you should still make backups of your database, because as soon as you enter new information, your database files are no longer up-to-date.
- Never turn off or reboot Agenda during session.
- To make multiple passes on one input line, use the @set action as the first action in the statement that matches the input line. This saves the input line as a variable. You can use @skip to change the line; to reuse it, use @reset action, which restores it to original form.

Section

- If you copy an item from one mutually exclusive category to another, Agenda removes the item from the original section since an item cannot be assigned to two mutually exclusive categories at the same time.
- You can display Entry, When, and Done dates in date columns. These date column heads and column entries are not categories and cannot be used as section heads.
- If you remove all of the section in a view, Agenda does not delete the view. Instead it replaces the last category with an untitled category.

- If you want to move a column that appears in many sections, it may be easier to remove the column and then insert it where you want it.
- Keep in mind that some operations affect marked items regardless of which sections they are marked in. For example, if you discard a marked item that appears in more than one section, Agenda will discard that item from all sections in which it appears.
- To see all items in the trash, create a new section and use the item undiscard command.
- You can use F6(Move) to put items in a specific position within the current section or within another section in the view. To do this, first mark the items and then move the highlight above the place in the section where you want to position them. Press F6(Move); then press Enter twice. Agenda inserts the marked items below the highlight.
- If your computer does not recognize Shift Grey –, use Alt – to collapse one or all sections in a view.

Structure

- If your input group sometimes ends with a given structure and sometimes the structure is omitted, you may find that the only way to tell where an input group ends is to match on the beginning of the next input group. Make @end the First action in the statement group, followed by the @start action.

  To write the very last formatted input group to the structured file; you must include a statement of the form ''END @end( )'' in your definition file.

Tab

- If you want to remove only a profile action, press Tab or F3(InclCat) until all arrows have been removed from all categories. This removes the profile action.

Trash

- To see all items in the trash, create a new section and use the item undiscard command.
- Discarded categories are not placed in the trash and therefore cannot be undiscarded; however, if items have been discarded with the category, they can be recovered.

TXT2STF

- Do not specify as your termination point the same pattern you specify in the statement that matches the first line of each input group. @skip_lines reads the line containing the termination point into memory, leaving it available as the current input line. TXT2STF does not attempt to find a definition file statement that

Figure 14-1.
Continued.

matches the line containing the termination-point. Thus, if you used the same pattern both to match the first input line in the group, and as the location to skip to, your definition file will skip over every second input group.

- To use only the first matching input line as the item, specify ^ as the termination string. This causes TXT2STF to terminate the item at the start of the second line. You cannot use $ because TXT2STF does not search the first line of the item for the termination string. It begins searching on the second line, so using $ as the termination-string causes TXT2STF to use the first two lines as the item.
- TXT2STF does not check whether the file exists. If the file does not exist, Agenda asks whether you want to create it when you attempt to look at the note in the Agenda database.
- Including many lines of comments can significantly lengthen the run time of TXT2STF with your definition file. Try keeping any lengthy documentation in a separate file.
- TXT2STF assumes that the first blank line in the input file indicates the end of the table. If your table includes blank lines before the end, delete them. If your table includes empty cells, put 0 or the word ''blank'' in the empty cells.

Undiscard

- To see all items in the trash, create a new section and use the item undiscard command.
- Discarded categories are not placed in the trash and therefore cannot be undiscarded; however, if items have been discarded with the category, they can be recovered.

Utility

- If Agenda is making matches you don't want, increase the Required Match Strength under Utility Preferences Auto-Assign or set Confirm assignments to Sometimes or Always.
- If you want Agenda to search the database for items that match a new category, use the Utility Other Execute command or Alt-X.
- To experiment with how items match particular expressions, use the Utility Show Match command and enter the expression you want to test. Set Syntax to Text Condition. This creates a Show View of the items that match the expression you specify, according to the logic used in interpreting text conditions.

- If Agenda is not assigning items to categories where you think there is a match, check the Match on setting under Utility Preferences Auto-Assign to make sure Agenda is searching for text where you expect.
- If Agenda is not assigning items to categories where you think there is a match, make sure Enable text conditions under Utility Preferences Auto-Assign is set to Yes.
- If Agenda is not assigning items to categories where you think there is a match, decrease the Required match strength under Utility Preferences Auto-Assign.

View

- If you want to build a new database from part of an existing database, you can preserve views, macros, conditions, and actions by following these basic steps: Use the File Transfer Template command to export the items (and their assignments) from your database to a structured file. Use the File Transfer Export command to export the items (and their assignments) from your database to a structured file.

  Open the database you created in step one.

  Use the File Transfer Import command to import the structure file you created.

  Discard the categories in the category hierarchy that you do not want.
- If you remove all of the section in a view, Agenda does not delete the view. Instead it replaces the last category with an untitled category.
- To experiment with how items match particular expressions, use the Utility Show Match command and enter the expression you want to test. Set Syntax to Text Condition. This creates a Show View of the items that match the expression you specify, according to the logic used in interpreting text conditions.
- The root category, Main, is the ancestor of all categories in the Database. Thus all items are assigned to Main by inheritance and can be viewed by selecting a view with Main as the category selected.
- If your computer does not recognize Shift Grey –, use Alt – to collapse one or all sections in a view.

Figure 14-2.
Cross Reference

You are in	and you would like to	then press	Chap/Sect
Anywhere	accept a proposed automatic completion for your typing	Enter	4.1.1 8.3
Cat Mgr Note View	access the Macros dialog box, with the highlight in the appropriate starting location for running the desired macro	Alt-F10(Macro)	11.1.2
View	access the note screen for the highlighted item	F5(Note)	3.1.2
View	access the View Define window for the purpose of specifying filters	F10(Menu)/V/D F8(Vw Mgr)/F8(Define)	5.2.4
Cat Mgr	add a synonymous but shorter alternate name for a category when it appears as a column heading, and to be used in text matching	separate w/semicolon	4.2.9 7.3
Cat Mgr	add additional text conditions to a category to assist in automatic classification	separate w/semicolon	4.2.9
Macro	add macro control commands to an existing keystroke macro	F2(Edit)	11.2 11.3
Cat Mgr	alphabetically sort the child categories, or siblings, within a highlighted parent category	Alt-F9(Sort)	4.2.2.1
Vw Mgr	alphabetically sort the view names	Alt-F9(Sort)	5.2.7
View Cat Mgr	annotate the highlighted category with up to ten pages of associated text	F5(Note)	4.1.5
Cat note	append the current word or line, the entire note text or just some marked note text to the current category	Alt-F8(Append)	4.1.5.2 4.2.4.2

You are in	and you would like to	then press	Chap/Sect
Item Note	append the current word or line, the entire note text, or just some marked note text to the current item	Alt-F8(Append)	3.2.8.2 3.1.2
View	apply actions to only those items whose assignments have changed due to reevaluated conditions	F10(Menu)/U/E	4.2.17
View	apply the current conditions and actions for all categories to all the items in the database	Alt-X	4.2.9.1 4.2.17 6.2 7.2 7.3
View	apply the current conditions and actions for all categories to the highlighted item	Alt-E	4.2.9.1 4.2.17
Profile	assign a group of marked items to a category listed in the item profile	F7(Assign)	3.2.10 4.2.17.1
View	assign a When date to each item in a group of marked items	Alt-F2(When)	3.2.4.3
View	assign a When date to the highlighted item	Alt-F2(When)	3.2.4.3
View	assign items to a category by adding or inserting them in a section; copying or moving them to a section; or by changing column entries		4.2.17.2 6.2 7.3 8.2 8.3
View	assign items to Yes/No format categories as column entries	Spacebar	8.4
Profile	assign the highlighted item to a category listed in the item profile	F7(Assign)	3.2.10 4.2.17.1

Figure 14-2.
Cross Reference
Continued

You are in	and you would like to	then press	Chap/Sect
View	attach an external ASCII text file as a note to the highlighted category	F10(Menu)/F/N	4.1.5.1
View	attach an external ASCII text file as a note to the highlighted item	F10(Menu)/F/N	3.1.3
View	automatically import a structured text file each time you open or access the current database	F10(Menu)/U/P/O	12.2
DOS	automatically run a macro called AUTOEXEC every time the database is opened		11.1.2
Anywhere	back up or undo your last keystrokes or commands	Esc	2.1.1
View	backup your files now to BKA and BKB files	F10(Menu)/F/B	2.4
Macro	begin recording keystrokes for a macro just named in the Macros dialog box	F7(Learn)	11.1.1 11.1.3
DOS	build structured text files from other application programs		12.1.3
View	change item text while in edit mode	Arrows, Bkspc, or Del	3.2.1 6.1 7.1 8.1
View	change the character set to accomodate or suppress international characters	F10(Menu)/U/P/E	2.5
View	change the file description for the database	F10(Menu)/U/P/O	2.5

You are in	and you would like to	then press	Chap/Sect
View	change the format with which column entries are displayed	F10(Menu)/C/C/F	5.2.3.1 8.4
View	change the hiding of hard carriage returns	F10(Menu)/U/P/O	2.5
View	change the item tag character	F10(Menu)/U/P/E	2.5
View	change the member sections in a view	F10(Menu)/V/D F8(Vw Mgr)/F8(Define)	5.2.1.1
View	change the password for the database	F10(Menu)/U/P/O	2.5
View	change the Printer Definition File (PDF) which you installed with Agenda or subsequently changed	F10(Menu)/U/P/E	10.1
View	change the screen colors	F10(Menu)/U/P/E	2.5
View	change the strength of text matching	F10(Menu)/U/P/A	4.2.9.1
View	change the tab size used in notes	F10(Menu)/U/P/O	2.5
View	change the text matching suppression characters from double quotes to some other special characters	F10(Menu)/U/P/A	4.2.9.1
View	change the width of the column with the highlight by entering a specific number of characters, or by using the arrow keys to adjust the displayed width	F10(Menu)/C/C/W Arrows Enter	5.2.3.1 4.1.3 6.2 7.4 8.4 9.1.3 9.2.2 9.2.3
View	change the width of the column with the highlight to the minimum required as determined by Agenda	F10(Menu)/C/C/W/?	5.2.3.1 8.3 11.1.1

Figure 14-2.
Cross Reference
Continued

You are in	and you would like to	then press	Chap/Sect
View	change when Agenda validates its proposed category assignments based on text conditions	F10(Menu)/U/P/A	4.2.9.1
Prof Act	clear all profile action indicators; that is, up and down arrows	F4(ClrCats)	4.2.13.1
Prof Cond	clear all profile condition indicators; that is, up and down arrows	F4(ClrCats)	4.2.10
View	collapse all the sections, thus hiding or suppressing the display of all items	Alt- twice Shift Grey – twice	5.2.1.3
View	collapse the section in which the highlight appears, thus hiding or suppressing the display of its items	Alt- Shift Grey –	5.2.1.3
View	conserve space by emptying the Trash on demand	F10(Menu)/U/T	3.2.7
View	conserve space by emptying the Trash periodically	F10(Menu)/U/P/O	3.2.7
DOS	convert a text file into a structured text file using either a set of default translation rules or a set of user supplied rules contained in a DEF file	TXT2STF plus parameters	12.1.2.1
DOS	convert an ASCII text file produced by printing a 1–2–3 spreadsheet to a file into a structured text file (STF) for importing to Agenda	TXT2STF	9.1.2

You are in	and you would like to	then press	Chap/Sect
DOS	convert Lotus Metro List Manager files to structured text files	LM2STF plus filename Metro	12.1.2.4
View	copy a database to another file name	F10(Menu)/F/C	2.3
View	copy a group of marked items to another section within the same view	F3(Copy)/Arrows	3.2.3
Cat Edit	copy a single word or line, a marked section, or the entire text of a category while in edit mode, and store the copied text in the edit buffer	F3(Copy)	4.2.1.1
Note edit	copy a single word or line, a marked section, or the entire text of a note while in edit mode, and store the copied text in the edit buffer	F3(Copy)	3.2.8 4.1.5
Item edit	copy a single word or line, a marked section, or the entire text of an item while in edit mode	F3(Copy)	3.2.1.1
Cat Mgr	copy conditions or actions from the highlighted category to another category	F3(Cpy C/A)/Arrows	4.2.15
Macro edit	copy highlighted macro text while in edit mode	F3(Copy)	11.1.2
DOS	copy text from another application into Agenda using the Clipboard Accessory	Alt-Shift-D	13.1.2
Vw Mgr	copy the definition for the highlighted view to a new view	F3(Copy)	5.2.7
View	copy the highlighted item to another section within the same view	F3(Copy)/Arrows	3.2.3

Figure 14-2.
Cross Reference
Continued

You are in	and you would like to	then press	Chap/Sect
Clip Acc	copy the whole screen, specific lines, or a rectangular block of text into the Clipboard Accessory	F10(Menu)/C	13.1.2
View	correct or reset the Done indicator and Done date for a highlighted item	F4(Done)	3.2.4.2
View	correct or reset the Done indicators and Done dates for a group of marked items	F4(Done)	3.2.4.2
Item edit	create a new category from the current item, or a marked portion of it, while in edit mode	F6(MakeCat)	3.2.1.4
View	create a new view	F8(Vw Mgr)/Ins(ert)	5.2.7 6.3 7.4 8.3 8.4 9.2.2 9.2.3 3.1.1 5.1 9.2.1
DOS	create a simple Definition (DEF) file with the @table action which reads text files in tabular format, such as printed spreadsheet files		12.1.2.3
Item edit	cut a single word or line, a marked section, or the entire text of an item while in edit mode	F4(Cut)	3.2.1.1
Macro edit	cut highlighted macro text while in edit mode	F4(Cut)	11.1.2

You are in	and you would like to	then press	Chap/Sect
View	delete a database from your system	F10(Menu)/F/D	2.3
Item Acc	delete either the current item or all the items being saved in the Items Accessory	F10(Menu)/D	13.1.1
Macro edit	delete highlighted macro text while in edit mode	Alt-F4(Delete)	11.1.2
Note	delete or erase the current note	F10(Menu)/D	3.2.9.4 4.2.5.4
Note	delete or erase the current word or line of a note, or just some marked note text	Alt-F4(Delete)	3.2.9.2 4.2.5.2
Note	delete or erase the entire note text	Alt-F4(Delete) F10(Menu)/D	3.2.9.2 4.2.5.2
Macro	delete the current macro	Alt-F4(Delete)	11.1.2
Sel File	delete the highlighted file	F4(Delete)	2.3
Vw Mgr	delete the highlighted view	Del(ete) F4(Delete) Alt-F4(Delete)	5.2.7 3.2.4.2
Dialog	delete the macro with the highlight in the Macros dialog box	F4(Delete) Del(ete)	11.1.2
Cat Mgr	demote the highlighted category by moving it one level to the right	F8(Dem →)	4.2.2.2 7.2 8.3
Macro	develop a macro that controls its own execution by looping, testing conditions, and so on		11.2 11.3
View	develop a macro to recover selected items from the Trash		11.1.3
Cat Mgr	develop a profile action for the highlighted category in the Category Manager	F10(Menu)/A/P Alt-A	4.2.13.1 7.3

Figure 14-2.
Cross Reference
Continued

You are in	and you would like to	then press	Chap/Sect
View	develop a profile action for the highlighted category in the item view screen	F10(Menu)/C/M/A/P	4.2.13.1
Cat Mgr	develop a profile condition for the highlighted category in the Category Manager	F10(Menu)/C/P Alt-C	4.2.10 6.3
View	develop a profile condition for the highlighted category in the item view screen	F10(Menu)/C/M/C/P	4.2.10
Cat Mgr	develop a special action to discard items, mark them as done, set their When dates, or export them to files if they are assigned to the highlighted category in the Category Manager	F10(Menu)/A/S	4.2.13.2
View	develop a special action to discard items, mark them as done, set their When dates, or export them to files if they are assigned to the highlighted category in the item view screen	F10(Menu)/C/M/A/S	4.2.13.2
View	disable text condition processing in preparation for importing a structured text file	F10(Menu)/U/P/A	12.2
View	disable the automatic display of the function key map	F10(Menu)/U/P/E	2.5
View	disable the automatic setting of the Entry date, so that the date field can be used for some other purpose	F10(Menu)/U/P/D	3.2.4.1

You are in	and you would like to	then press	Chap/Sect
View	disable the automatic setting of When dates for all items	F10(Menu)/U/P/D	3.2.4.3
View	disable the beep sound which signals automatic completion	F10(Menu)/U/P/E	2.5
View	discard done items in the Trash	F10(Menu)/U/P/O	3.2.4.2
Anywhere	display a context sensitive menu at the top of the screen	F10(Menu)	2.1.1
View	display a view of the completed or done items only	F10(Menu)/U/S/I	3.2.4.2
View	display all circular references, to which you have been alerted by the small circle in the upper right hand corner of the screen	F10(Menu)/U/S/C	4.2.16
View	display all items in the database, regardless whether they are included in any view or not	F10(Menu)/U/S/A	3.2.11
View	display information about the highlighted category, including the number of items, children, section headings, conditions, actions, and view filters	F10(Menu)/C/I	4.2.6
View	display statistics about the current database, such as numbers of items, categories and assignments	F10(Menu)/F/I	2.3
View	display statistics about the items and categories in the current view	F10(Menu)/V/I	2.3

Figure 14-2.
Cross Reference
Continued

You are in	and you would like to	then press	Chap/Sect
Anywhere	display the function key map at the bottom of the screen	Alt-K	2.1.1
View	display the number of items assigned to each category for a group of marked items	Alt-F9(Profile)	3.2.10 4.2.17.1
View	edit a highlighted item	F2(Edit)	3.2.1
Cat Mgr View	edit a note for the highlighted category	F5(Note)	4.2.4
View	edit a note for the highlighted item	F5(Note)	3.2.8
Cat Mgr	edit a profile condition for the highlighted category	F10(Menu)/C/P	4.2.10
View	edit a When, Entry or Done date using words		3.2.4.3
View	edit or replace the current view name	F10(Menu)/V/P F8(Vw Mgr)/F2(Edit) F8(Vw Mgr)/F5(Prefs)	5.2.6 5.2.7 7.1 8.4
Vw Mgr	edit or replace the highlighted view name	F2(Edit) F5(Prefs)	5.2.7
Anywhere	edit the highlighted category	F2(Edit)	4.2.1 7.2 7.3
Macro	edit the macro with the highlight in the Macros dialog box by appending new keystrokes to the end	F7(Learn)	11.1.2
Macro	edit the macro with the highlight in the Macros dialog box by changing the stored commands with standard edit keys	F2(EditMac)	11.1.2 11.1.3
View	enable or disable actions for all categories	F10(Menu)/U/P/A	4.2.14

You are in	and you would like to	then press	Chap/Sect
View	enable or disable the automatic matching of date conditions for all categories	F10(Menu)/U/P/A	4.2.12
View	enable or disable the automatic matching of profile conditions for all categories	F10(Menu)/U/P/A	4.2.12
View	enable or disable the automatic matching of text conditions for all categories	F10(Menu)/U/P/A	4.2.9.1
Cat Mgr	enable, disable, or control the application of conditions for the highlighted category in the Category Manager	F10(Menu)/C/S	4.2.12
View	enable, disable, or control the application of conditions for the highlighted category in the item view screen	F10(Menu)/C/M/C/S	4.2.12
Cat Mgr Note View	end or turn off recording of keystrokes for a macro	Alt-F10(Macro)	11.1.1 11.1.3
View	enter a category for the highlighted or marked items under a specific column heading	F10(Menu)/I/A Alt-A Enter	4.1.3
View	enter a date in words such as today, next Tuesday, etc.		3.2.4.3
Cat Mgr View	enter a note for the highlighted category	F5(Note)	4.2.4 6.2
View	enter a note for the highlighted item	F5(Note)	3.2.8 8.1 9.2.1
View	enter an item below the highlighted section heading or item	Ins(ert) F10(Menu)/I/N	3.1.1 6.1 7.1 8.1 9.2.1

Figure 14-2.
Cross Reference
Continued

You are in	and you would like to	then press	Chap/Sect
View	enter another item below the current item regardless of what column you are in	Alt-I Enter	3.1.1 6.1 7.1 8.1
View	enter or remove a date filter which includes or excludes items in the view based on their Entry, When or Done dates, relative to specified date ranges	F10(Menu)/V/P F8(Vw Mgr)/F5(Prefs) Enter	5.2.5
View	enter the item that you just typed and move to an adjacent category column	Tab Shift-Tab	3.1.1
Cat Mgr	erase or clear the conditions and actions attached to the highlighted category	F4(Clr C/A)	4.2.15
Anywhere	examine all the options for a highlighted dialog box field at one time	F2(Edit) Grey +	2.2
Anywhere	examine the options for a highlighted dialog box field one by one	Spacebar	2.2
Macro	export a macro to a named text file	F10(Menu)/E	11.1.2
Note	export a note to a text file	F10(Menu)/E	3.2.9.4 4.2.5.4
View	export done items to a Done file	F10(Menu)/U/P/O	3.2.4.2
View	export some or all of the items, categories, notes, and dates; but not conditions, actions, and view definitions, to another database	F10(Menu)/F/T/E	12.1.1
Anywhere	find out what accelerator keys do	F1(Help)	2.1.3

You are in	and you would like to	then press	Chap/Sect
Anywhere	find out what function keys do	F1(Help)	2.1.1
Anywhere	find out what special keys do	F1(Help)	2.1.2
Clip Acc	format the text being saved in the Clipboard Accessory for use as an item (Word Processor format), or a note (Normal format)	F10(Menu)/F	13.1.2
View	go to the Category Manager screen	F9(Cat Mgr)	4.1.4 7.3
View	hide items marked as done	F10(Menu)/V/P F8(Vw Mgr)/F5(Prefs)	5.2.6 7.4
View	hide items which are dependent on marked prerequisite items	F10(Menu)/V/P F8(Vw Mgr)/F5(Prefs)	5.2.6
View	hide items which are not explicitly assigned to their categories, that is items which inherit their assignments	F10(Menu)/V/P F8(Vw Mgr)/F5(Prefs)	5.2.6
Cat Mgr	hide or suppress the display of child categories for the entire Category Manager	Alt- twice	4.2.7
Cat Mgr	hide or suppress the display of child categories for the highlighted parent category	Alt-	4.2.7
Cat Mgr	hide or suppress the display of conditions and actions	Alt-F3(HideC/A)	4.2.15
View	identify marked items as prerequisites for the highlighted item	Alt-F3(DpndsOn)	3.2.5

Figure 14-2.
Cross Reference
Continued

You are in	and you would like to	then press	Chap/Sect
View	identify the categories to which the highlighted item has been assigned when there are marked items	Grey+	3.2.10 4.2.17.1
View	identify the categories to which the highlighted item has been assigned when there are no marked items	Alt-F9(Profile)	3.2.10 4.2.17.1
View	ignore accents in matching all text conditions	F10(Menu)/U/P/A	4.2.9.1
Cat Mgr	ignore one character exactly in matching a text condition	replace with an *	4.2.9
View	ignore suffixes in matching all text conditions	F10(Menu)/U/P/A	4.2.9.1
Cat Mgr	ignore the special significance of characters such as the carat, tilde, and exclamation point	precede with backslash	4.2.9
Cat Mgr	ignore zero or more letters in matching a text condition	replace with an *	4.2.9
Macro	import a macro saved as a named text file	F10(Menu)/I	11.1.2
View	import a STF to your Agenda database and insert the imported data below the highlighted item	F10(Menu)/F/T/I	9.1.3
View	import a STF, having disabled text condition processing	F10(Menu)/F/T/I	12.2
Note	import a text file into a note	F10(Menu)/I	3.2.9.4 4.2.5.4

You are in	and you would like to	then press	Chap/Sect
Note	import note text from an external ASCII text file for the highlighted category's note	F10(Menu)/I	4.1.5.1
Note	import note text from an external ASCII text file for the highlighted item's note	F10(Menu)/I	3.1.3
View	import or transfer categories saved in a specially formatted external file with a STF extension to the current database	F10(Menu)/F/T/I	3.1.5 4.1.6
View	import or transfer items saved in a specially formatted external file with a STF extension to the current database	F10(Menu)/F/T/I	3.1.5 4.1.6
View	import the items saved in the STF created by the Items Accessory	F10(Menu)/F/T/I	13.1.1
Cat Mgr	index the highlighted category	F10(Menu)/U	4.2.2.4
View	index the highlighted category	F10(Menu)/C/M/U	4.2.2.4
Cat Mgr	index the unindexed categories that TXT2STF creates when converting table data into a STF	F10(Menu)/U	9.1.3
View	indicate that the highlighted task item has been completed or done, and set the Done date	F4(Done)	3.2.4.2 7.4
View	indicate that the marked task items have been completed or done, and set the Done dates	F4(Done)	3.2.4.2

Figure 14-2.
Cross Reference
Continued

You are in	and you would like to	then press	Chap/Sect
Cat Mgr Note View	Initiate recording, or edit a keystroke macro, with the highlight on the appropriate starting location	Alt-F10(Macro)	11.1.1 11.1.3
Item edit Note edit	insert ''hard'' carriage returns in text while it is being typed	Alt-M	3.1.4 3.2.8
Cat Mgr	insert a new child category below and to the right of the highlighted category	Alt-R	4.1.4
View	insert a new column heading to the left of the highlighted, current column heading	F10(Menu)/C/C/N Alt-L	4.1.2 5.2.2.1 6.2 9.2.1 9.2.2 9.2.3
View	insert a new column heading to the right of the highlighted current column heading	F10(Menu)/C/C/N Alt-R	4.1.2 5.2.2.1 6.2 7.2 7.4 8.2 8.3 8.4 9.1.3 9.2.1
Cat Mgr	insert a new parent category above and to the left of the highlighted category	Alt-L	4.1.4
Cat Mgr	insert a new sibling category below and at the same level as the highlighted category	Ins(ert) Alt-D Alt-I	4.1.4 7.2 8.3
Cat Mgr	insert a new sibling category above and at the same level as the highlighted category	Alt-U	4.1.4 7.2

You are in	and you would like to	then press	Chap/Sect
View	insert a section above the section with the highlighted heading or item	F10(Menu)/C/S/N Alt-U	5.2.1.1
View	insert a separator between sections in the current view	F10(Menu)/V/P F8(Vw Mgr)/F5(Prefs)	5.2.6
View	insert an untitled section below the section with the highlighted heading or item	F10(Menu)/C/S/N Alt-D	5.2.1.1 4.1.1 7.1
View	instruct Agenda when to automatically backup your database (BKA and BKB files not AGA and AGB files)	F10(Menu)/U/P/O	2.4
View	interrupt the importing or transfer of items or categories using a STF	Ctrl-Break	3.1.5 4.1.6
Cat Mgr	know database statistics such as numbers of items, categories, assignments, and unused space	F10(Menu)/P/D	2.3
Anywhere	know how to respond to a dialog box	F1(Help)	2.2
Cat Mgr	know what files are attached to your database	F10(Menu)/P/D	2.3
View	leave Done items in the database	F10(Menu)/U/P/O	3.2.4.2
Any edit Any dialog	leave edit mode or dialog box and return to the previous screen	F9(Accept)	3.2.1 4.2.1.3
Clip Acc	leave the Clipboard Accessory before pasting the saved text into an Agenda database (Do NOT turn off or re-boot the computer)	F10(Menu)/Q	13.1.2

Figure 14-2.
Cross Reference
Continued

You are in	and you would like to	then press	Chap/Sect
Item Acc	leave the Item Accessory before importing the structured text file to Agenda	F10(Menu)/Q	13.1.1
Cat Mgr	make text matching sensitive to case for the enclosed text preceded by a tilde symbol	enclose text in ( )	4.2.9
Cat Mgr	make text matching sensitive to suffixes for the enclosed text preceded by a carat symbol	enclose text in ( )	4.2.9
View	make the changed settings in the Auto-Assign, Date and Other Preferences dialog boxes the permanent defaults	F10(Menu)/U/P/U	10.1 2.5
Cat Mgr	make the child categories of the highlighted parent category mutually exclusive from within the Category Manager	F10(Menu)/E	4.2.2.3 7.2
View	make the child categories of the highlighted parent category mutually exclusive from within the item view screen	F10(Menu)/C/M/E	4.2.2.3
Note	make the current word or line, the entire note text, or just some marked note text, into a category	F6(MakeCat)	4.1.5.2 4.2.4.1 3.2.8.1 3.1.2
Note	make the current word or line, the entire note text, or just some marked note text, into an item	F8(MakeItm)	3.2.8.1 4.1.5.2 4.2.4.1 3.1.2

You are in	and you would like to	then press	Chap/Sect
Macro edit	mark macro text for copying, cutting, or deleting while in edit mode	F7(Mark)/Arrows	11.1.2
Cat Edit	mark some category text beginning with the highlighted character	F7(Mark)/Arrows	4.2.1.1
Item edit	mark some item text beginning with the highlighted character	F7(Mark)/Arrows	3.2.1.1
Note edit	mark some note text beginning with the highlighted character	F7(Mark)/Arrows	3.1.2 3.2.8.1 4.1.5.2 4.2.4.1
View	mark the highlighted item for moving or copying	F7(Mark)	3.2.3
View	mark the highlighted section heading for moving or copying the items in the section to another section in the same view	F7(Mark)	3.2.3
Clip Acc	mark the specific lines or rectangular block of text to be copied into the Clipboard Accessory	F7(Mark)/Arrows	13.1.2
View	match text based on item text, note text, or both	F10(Menu)/U/P/A	4.2.9.1
Cat Mgr	match text if it is not the same as the enclosed text preceded by an exclamation point	enclose text in ( )	4.2.9
View	move a group of marked items to another section within the same view	F6(Move)/Arrows	3.2.3
View	move the column with the highlighted heading	F10(Menu)/C/C/P/Arrows	5.2.2.2
Cat Mgr	move the highlighted category to another location	F6(Move)/Arrows	4.2.2

Figure 14-2.
Cross Reference
Continued

You are in	and you would like to	then press	Chap/Sect
View	move the highlighted item to another position within the same section	F10(Menu)/I/P/Arrows	3.2.2
View	move the highlighted item to another section within the same view	F6(Move)/Arrows	3.2.3
Vw Mgr	move the highlighted view name elsewhere in the View Manager	F6(Move)/Arrows	5.2.7
View	move the section with the highlighted heading	F6(Move)/Arrows	5.2.1.4
View	move the section with the highlighted heading or item	F10(Menu)/C/S/P/Arrows	5.2.1.4
Item Acc	move to another item being saved in the Items Accessory	PgDn PgUp	13.1.1
Item edit Item note	move to the next item while in edit mode	Alt-N	3.2.1
Note	move to the next item's note while working in the current item's note	Alt-N	3.2.8
View	move to the next selection among those proposed for automatic completion	F8(NextSel) Alt-N	8.3 6.2
Item edit Item note	move to the previous item while in edit mode	Alt-P	3.2.1
Note	move to the previous item's note while working in the current item's note	Alt-P	3.2.8
View	move to the previous selection among those proposed for automatic completion	F7(PrevSel) Alt-P	8.3
DOS	open a database from DOS	type Agenda and file name	2.3 3.1.1 6.1 7.1 8.1 9.1.3

You are in	and you would like to	then press	Chap/Sect
View	open a database from within an Agenda session	F10(Menu)/F/O	2.3
View	override the automatic setting of a specific item's When date based on the item text	Alt-F2(When)	3.2.4.3
Macro edit	paste saved macro text at the highlighted character location while in edit mode	F2(Paste)	11.1.2
View	paste the Clipboard Accessory contents into the current screen at the location of the highlight	Alt-Shift-Enter	13.1.2
Item edit	paste, cut, or copy text into another item or into another location in the current item while in edit mode	F2(Paste)	3.2.1.2
Note edit	paste, cut, or copy text stored in the edit buffer into a note while in edit mode	F2(Paste)	3.2.8 4.1.5
Cat Edit	paste, cut, or copy text, stored in the edit buffer into another category, or into another location in the current category while in edit mode	F2(Paste)	4.2.1.2
DOS	prepare to use the Items and/or Clipboard Accessories by loading the Metro kernel	Metro	13.1
Cat Mgr	print a collection of facts about your database and its associated files to a printer or to a file	F10(Menu)/P	5.2.8 10.2 10.2.1

Figure 14-2.
Cross Reference
Continued

You are in	and you would like to	then press	Chap/Sect
Cat Mgr	print a listing of the category hierarchy to a printer or to a file	F10(Menu)/P	5.2.8 10.2 10.2.1
Note	print all or just some marked text from either an item or category note to a printer or to a file	F10(Menu)/P	5.2.8 10.2 10.2.1 3.2.9.4 4.2.5.4
View	print all or some of a view's items and/or notes to a printer or to a file	F10(Menu)/P	5.2.8 6.3 8.4 10.2 10.2.1
Item Acc	print either the current item, or all the items being saved, in the Items Accessory	F10(Menu)/P	13.1.1
Macro	print the current macro	F10(Menu)/P	11.1.2
View	print the item profile for all items to a printer or to a file	F10(Menu)/P	5.2.8 10.2 10.2.1
Cat Mgr	promote the highlighted category by moving it one level to the left	F7(Prm ←)	4.2.2.2
View	quit from Agenda, saving all files correctly	F10(Menu)/Q	2.7
View	reclaim reserved but unused space due to removing or discarding	F10(Menu)/U/C	2.3
View	recover backup files within DOS by copying BKA and BKB files to AGA and AGB files	F10(Menu)/S	2.4
View	recover BKA and BKB backup files within Agenda, and delete the current database	F10(Menu)/F/U	2.4
Cat Mgr	redisplay previously hidden conditions and actions	Alt-F3(HideC/A)	4.2.15

You are in	and you would like to	then press	Chap/Sect
Anywhere	refer to the online help system	F1(Help)	2.1.1
Profile	remove a group of marked items from a category to which they have been assigned in the item profile	F7(Assign)	3.2.10 4.2.17.1
View	remove a group of marked items from the database and store them in the Trash	Alt-F4(Discard) F10(Menu)/I/D	3.2.7
Cat Edit	remove a single word or line, a marked section, or the entire text of a category, while in edit mode, without storing the removed text in the edit buffer	Alt-F4(Delete)	4.2.1.3
Vw define	remove all filters	F4(ClrFltr)	5.2.4
View	remove an item's assignment to the highlighted column entry, and remove the category from the database	Alt-F4(Discard)	4.2.17.2
View	remove an item's assignment to the highlighted column entry, leaving the category in the database	Del(ete)	4.2.17.2
Cat Edit	remove or cut a single word or line, a marked section, or the entire text of a category, while in edit mode, and store the cut text in the edit buffer	F4(Cut)	4.2.1.1

Figure 14-2.
Cross Reference
Continued

You are in	and you would like to	then press	Chap/Sect
Note edit	remove or cut a single word or line, a marked section, or the entire text of a note, while in edit mode, and store the cut text in the edit buffer	F4(Cut)	3.2.8 4.1.5
View	remove the column with the highlight from the current view, without removing its category from the database	F10(Menu)/C/C/R	4.2.3 5.2.2.3
View	remove the column with the highlighted heading from the view, and remove its category from the database	Alt-F4(Discard)	5.2.2.3
View	remove the column with the highlighted heading from the view, without removing its category from the database	Del(ete)	5.2.2.3
Cat Mgr	remove the highlighted category, along with any items exclusively assigned to it, from the database	Del(ete)	4.2.3
View	remove the highlighted category, along with any items exclusively assigned to it, from the database	Alt-F4(Discard)	4.2.3
Profile	remove the highlighted item from a category to which it has been assigned in the item profile	F7(Assign)	3.2.10 4.2.17.1
View	remove the highlighted item from the database and store it in the Trash	Alt-F4(Discard) F10(Menu)/I/D	3.2.7

You are in	and you would like to	then press	Chap/Sect
View	remove the highlighted item from the section in which it is being displayed	F10(Menu)/I/R Del(ete)	3.2.7
View	remove the section with the highlighted heading from the view and the database, along with any items exclusively assigned to it	Alt-F4(Discard)	5.2.1.2
View	remove the section with the highlighted heading from the view, but not from the database	Del(ete)	5.2.1.2 4.2.3
View	remove the section with the highlighted heading or item from the view, but not from the database	F10(Menu)/C/S/R	5.2.1.2 4.2.3
Sel File	rename the highlighted file	F6(Rename)	2.3
View	replace an Untitled section heading	Type over and press Enter Grey +	4.1.1 6.1 7.1 8.1 9.1.3
Note	replace text within a note	Alt-F5(Search)	3.2.9.3 4.2.5.3
Anywhere	request the next suggestion for automatic completion of your typing	F8(NextSel)	6.2 8.3
Cat Mgr Note View	rerun the last macro which was executed	Alt-Z	11.1.2
View	reset When dates automatically for items which recur on a periodic basis	F10(Menu)/U/P/D	3.2.4.3

Figure 14-2.
Cross Reference
Continued

You are in	and you would like to	then press	Chap/Sect
Cat Mgr View	resolve a potential conflict caused by attempting to assign an item to both a parent category, and one of its child categories		4.2.2.2
Cat Mgr View	resolve a potential conflict caused by attempting to make mutually exclusive categories which have one or more items assigned to two or more of them		4.2.2.3
View	restore a collapsed and highlighted section, thus redisplaying its items	Alt= Shift Grey +	5.2.1.3
View	restore all collapsed sections, thus redisplaying their items	Alt= twice Shift Grey + twice	5.2.1.3
CatMgr	restore the display of child categories for the entire Category Manager	Alt= twice Shift Grey + twice	4.2.7
Cat Mgr	restore the display of child categories for the highlighted parent category	Alt= Shift Grey +	4.2.7
View	retrieve discarded items from the Trash (as long as it has not been emptied)	F10(Menu)/I/U	3.2.7
Note	retrieve marked items from the current view, and insert them into the current note	Alt-F3(GetItms)	3.2.9.1 4.2.5.1
View	retrieve the last item discarded in the Trash (as long as it has not been emptied)	Alt-Y	3.2.7

You are in	and you would like to	then press	Chap/Sect
DOS	return to Agenda from a temporary session in DOS	EXIT in DOS	2.6
Cat Mgr Note View	return to Macros dialog box after appending new keystrokes to a macro	Alt-F10(Macro)	11.1.2
Note	return to the highlighted category from the associated note screen	F5(Return)	4.1.5 6.2
Note	return to the highlighted item from the associated note screen	F5(Return)	8.1 9.2.1
View	return to the last view from the current view	Alt-F8(Last Vw)	3.2.4.2 3.2.5
Cat Mgr	return to the view screen	F9(To View)	4.1.4 7.2 7.3
Note	return to the view screen or Category Manager from the current note screen	F10(Menu)/R	3.2.9.4 4.2.5.4
Cat Mgr	reverse the mutually exclusive setting for the highlighted category from within the Category Manager	F10(Menu)/E	4.2.2.3
View	reverse the mutually exclusive setting for the highlighted category from within the item view screen	F10(Menu)/C/M/E	4.2.2.3
Dialog	run the macro with the highlight in the Macros dialog box	F9(Run)	11.1.1 11.1.2 11.1.3
View	search for an item based on some portion of its content, or the content of its associated note	Alt-F5(Search)	3.2.6

Figure 14-2.
Cross Reference
Continued

You are in	and you would like to	then press	Chap/Sect
Macro	search for specific macro text while in edit mode	Alt-F5(Search)	11.1.2
Note	search with new parameters for text within a note	Alt-F5(Search)	3.2.9.3 4.2.5.3
Note	search with the previous parameters for text within a note	Alt-S	3.2.9.3 4.2.5.3
View Note	see a list of file names for use as an external note file, or for note importing and exporting	Grey +	3.1.3 4.1.5.1
View	see all items matching your item or note text search criteria in a special *Show View*	F10(Menu)/U/S/M	3.2.6
View	see all items which are prerequisites for other items; in other words, all items with dependencies	F10(Menu)/U/S/D	3.2.5
View	see all items which depend on the highlighted item	F10(Menu)/U/S/D	3.2.5
View	see all items which depend upon other items; in other words, all items with prerequisites	F10(Menu)/U/S/P	3.2.5
View	see what prerequisite items have been identified for the highlighted item	F10(Menu)/U/S/P	3.2.5
Window	select a category in the View Define window as an exclusive filter for the view, so that items assigned to it will not appear in the view	F3(Filter) twice	5.2.4

You are in	and you would like to	then press	Chap/Sect
Window	select a category in the View Define window as an inclusive filter for the view, so that only items assigned to it will appear in the view	F3(Filter)	5.2.4
Anywhere	select a menu option by moving the highlight	Arrows	2.1.1
Anywhere	select a menu option by typing the first letter of the option name	Letter key	2.1.1
View	select or change to an existing view	F8(Vw Mgr)/Arrows F10(Menu)/V/S/Arrows	5.1 3.2.5 5.2.7 8.4
Window	select or unselect the children of the highlighted parent category as section headings in the View Define window	F8(Chldrn)	5.2.1.1
Window	select or unselect the highlighted category as a section heading in the View Define window	F7(Section) Spacebar	5.2.1.1
Anywhere	select the default value for a highlighted dialog box field	F8(Default)	2.2
Anywhere	select the defaults for all the fields in a dialog box	Alt-F8(DfltAll)	2.2
View	set a When date based on word or number format dates appearing in item text		3.2.4.3 6.2
View	set Entry dates when items are edited, reassigned, or entered	F10(Menu)/U/P/D Enter	3.2.4.1

Figure 14-2.
Cross Reference
Continued

You are in	and you would like to	then press	Chap/Sect
View	set the default date format for Entry, Done, and When dates	F10(Menu)/U/P/D	3.2.4.1
View	set the default for column insertion to either all sections, or just the current section	F10(Menu)/U/P/O	4.1.2 5.2.2.1
View	set the length of time between automatic saving of the current database (AGA and AGB files-not BKA and BKB files)	F10(Menu)/U/P/E	2.4
DOS	set up a definition (DEF) file for TXT2STF to use in converting a table of numbers in an ASCII text file into a STF	TXT2STF	9.1.2
View	sort items in either the current section, or all sections, by item text, category, category note, or date	F10(Menu)/C/S/S	3.2.12 5.2.1.5 6.4 9.2.2
View	sort items in the current section by the most recently set criteria	Alt-S	3.2.12 5.2.1.5
Item Acc	specify a text file to be used as an external note file for the current item being edited in the Items Accessory	F10(Menu)/N	13.1.1
Cat Mgr	specify a When, Entry or Done date condition for the highlighted category in the Category Manager	F10(Menu)/C/D	4.2.11
View	specify a When, Entry or Done date condition for the highlighted category in the item view screen	F10(Menu)/C/M/C/D	4.2.11

You are in	and you would like to	then press	Chap/Sect
Item Acc	specify one category to which all of the items being saved in the Items Accessory will be assigned	F10(Menu)/C	13.1.1
Cat Mgr Note View	specify printer control characters to influence the overall printing, as well as the printing of individual items, notes, and sections	F10(Menu)/P	10.2.3
Dialog	specify that an item is to be assigned to the highlighted category in the Profile Action dialog box, if it is assigned to the current category	F3(InclCat) Tab	4.2.13.1 7.3
Dialog	specify that an item is to be removed from the highlighted category in the Profile Action dialog box, if it is assigned to the current category	F3(InclCat) twice Tab/Tab	4.2.13.1
Dialog	specify that an item must be absent from the highlighted category in the Profile Condition dialog box for the condition to be satisfied	F3(InclCat) twice Tab/Tab	4.2.10
Dialog	specify that an item must be present in the highlighted category in the Profile Condition dialog box for the condition to be satisfied	F3(InclCat) Tab	4.2.10 6.3

Figure 14-2.
Cross Reference
Continued

You are in	and you would like to	then press	Chap/Sect
Cat Mgr Note View	specify the top margin, page length, headers and footers, and special character handling for printing items, notes, the Category Manager, an Item Profile or Database Info	F10(Menu)/P	10.2.2
Item edit	split the current item into two items while in edit mode, with the highlighted character and everything to the right becoming the new item	F8(Split)	3.2.1.3
Cat Mgr	suppress matching of a text enclosed in double quotes	enclose text in ( )	4.2.9 7.2
View	suppress snow which may appear on monitors with CGA cards	F10(Menu)/U/P/E	2.5
Cat Mgr	suppress synonymous but shorter alternate category name	separate w/2 semicolons	4.2.9
Anywhere	suppress the function key map at the bottom of the screen	Alt-K	2.1.1
View	suspend Agenda and temporarily return to DOS to run another application	F10(Menu)/S	2.6
View	test a single category's conditions and actions on a limited number of items in the database	F10(Menu)/U/E	4.2.17
View	test all conditions and actions on a limited number of items in the database	F10(Menu)/U/E	4.2.17 7.3

You are in	and you would like to	then press	Chap/Sect
View	transfer a template consisting of categories, conditions, actions, and view definitions; but not items, to another database	F10(Menu)/F/T/T	12.1.1 4.1.6
Item Acc	transfer all of the items being saved in the Items Accessory to a new or existing structured text file	F10(Menu)/T Alt-T	13.1.1
View	transfer all your macros from the current database to a new database (along with the current database's Category Manager, view definitions, stored conditions, and actions)	F10(Menu)/F/T/T	11.1.2
View	transfer conditions, actions, and view definitions; as well as items, categories, notes and dates	F10(Menu)/F/C	12.1.1
1-2-3	transfer numeric information to Agenda by setting up a specially formatted 1-2-3 spreadsheet		9.1.1
Item Acc	transfer the current item being saved in the Items Accessory to a new or existing structured text file	F10(Menu)/T	13.1.1
DOS	understand how to develop and use DEF files		12.1.2.3
DOS	understand the default translation rules		12.1.2.2
DOS	understand what AGA, AGB, BKA, BKB, STF, and note files are		2.3

Figure 14-2.
Cross Reference
Continued

You are in	and you would like to	then press	Chap/Sect
Cat Mgr	unindex the highlighted and indexed category	F10(Menu)/U	4.2.2.4
View	unindex the highlighted and indexed category	F10(Menu)/C/M/U	4.2.2.4
Item Acc Clip Acc	unload Metro from memory	Alt-Shift-End	13.1.2
Macro edit	unmark macro text for copying, cutting, or deleting while in edit mode	F7(Mark)	11.1.2
Cat Edit	unmark some category text beginning with the highlighted character	F7(Mark)	4.2.1.1
Item edit	unmark some item text beginning with the highlighted character	F7(Mark)	3.2.1.1
Note edit	unmark some note text beginning with the highlighted character	F7(Mark)	3.2.8
Clip Acc	unmark the specific lines or rectangular block of text to be copied into the Clipboard Accessory	F7(Mark)	13.1.2
View	unmark, or remove the marking from the highlighted item	F7(Mark)	3.2.3
View	unmark, or remove the markings from all marked items in the database	Alt-F7(UnmkAll)	3.2.3
View	unmark, or remove the markings from the items under the highlighted section heading	F7(Mark)	3.2.3
Note	update, replace, or refresh an external ASCII note text file with the current note text	F10(Menu)/E	3.1.3 4.1.5.1

You are in	and you would like to	then press	Chap/Sect
Cat Mgr	use a Special Action to create a STF		12.1
DOS	use any text editor to modify an existing PDF or create a new PDF to control the printer's behavior in response to print commands from Agenda		10.3
View	use the done item processing to create a STF	F10(Menu)/U/P/O	12.1
View	use the file export feature to create a STF	F10(Menu)/F/T/E	12.1
DOS	use the Items Accessory to create a STF	Alt-Shift-I	12.1
DOS	use the LM2STF utility to create a STF	LM2STF	12.1
DOS	use the TXT2STF utility to create a STF	TXT2STF	12.1
DOS	use your own external program to create a STF		12.1
View	validate a proposed category assignment by responding to a question mark prompt in the upper right hand corner of the screen	F10(Menu)/U/Q Alt-Q	4.2.9.1

Figure 14-3.

Chap/Sect Code	Chapter and Section Headings
1	Introduction
1.1	Why do we need Agenda
1.1.1	How we Work Today
1.1.2	How we might Work Tomorrow—with Agenda
1.2	Why are these AI Techniques so Important
1.3	How does Agenda Compare with other PC Products
1.4	In Closing
2	Getting Around Agenda
2.1	Types of Keys
2.1.1	Function Keys
2.1.2	Special Keys
2.1.3	Accelerator Keys
2.2	Dialog Boxes
2.3	Files in Agenda
2.4	Saving and Backing Up Your Work
2.5	Other Customizing Settings
2.6	Exiting to DOS
2.7	Quitting Agenda
3	Items
3.1	How Do Items Get into Agenda
3.1.1	Manual Entry of Items
3.1.2	Notes Attached to Items
3.1.3	Notes as External Files
3.1.4	Item Format
3.1.5	File Transfer of Items
3.2	How do I use Items
3.2.1	Editing
3.2.1.1	Copy and Cut
3.2.1.2	Paste
3.2.1.3	Split
3.2.1.4	Making Categories from Items
3.2.1.5	Delete
3.2.2	Moving Items within a Section
3.2.3	Moving or Copying Items between Sections
3.2.4	Dates
3.2.4.1	Entry Dates
3.2.4.2	Done Dates
3.2.4.3	When Dates

Chap/Sect Code	Chapter and Section Headings
3.2.5	Dependencies
3.2.6	Searching for Item or Note Text
3.2.7	Removing Items from the Section or Database
3.2.8	Notes Attached to Items
3.2.8.1	Making Note Text into Items and Categories
3.2.8.2	Appending Note Text to an Item
3.2.9	Other Note Functions
3.2.9.1	Retrieving Marked Items into a Note
3.2.9.2	Deleting Marked Text from a Note
3.2.9.3	Searching for Text within a Note
3.2.9.4	More about Notes
3.2.10	Assignment Profile
3.2.11	Show All Items
3.2.12	Sort Items in a Section
4	Categories
4.1	How do Categories get into Agenda
4.1.1	Categories as Section Headings
4.1.2	Categories as Column Headings
4.1.3	Categories as Column Entries
4.1.4	The Category Manager
4.1.5	Notes in Categories
4.1.5.1	Notes as External Files
4.1.5.2	Making Note text into a Category or an Item
4.1.6	File Transfer of Categories
4.2	How do I use Categories
4.2.1	Edit
4.2.1.1	Copy/Cut
4.2.1.2	Paste
4.2.1.3	Delete
4.2.2	The Category Manager
4.2.2.1	Sorting Categories in the Category Manager
4.2.2.2	Promoting and Demoting Categories
4.2.2.3	Mutual Exclusivity
4.2.2.4	Indexing Categories
4.2.3	Removing Categories
4.2.4	Notes in Categories
4.2.4.1	Making Note Text into Items and Categories
4.2.4.2	Appending Note Text to a Category
4.2.5	Other Note Functions
4.2.5.1	Retrieving Marked Items into a Note

Figure 14-3.
Continued

Chap/Sect Code	Chapter and Section Headings
4.2.5.2	Deleting Marked Text from a Note
4.2.5.3	Searching for Text within a Note
4.2.5.4	More about Notes
4.2.6	Category Info
4.2.7	Hide Display of Child Categories
4.2.8	Conditions/Actions
4.2.9	Text Conditions
4.2.9.1	Controlling Text Matching for All Categories
4.2.9.2	Controlling Text Matching for a Single Category
4.2.10	Profile Condition
4.2.11	Date Condition
4.2.12	Controlling Conditions
4.2.13	Actions
4.2.13.1	Profile Actions
4.2.13.2	Special Actions
4.2.14	Controlling Actions
4.2.15	Other Processes with Conditions and Actions
4.2.16	Issues in the Use of Conditions and Actions
4.2.17	Assigning Items to Categories
4.2.17.1	Assignment Profile
4.2.17.2	Manual Techniques for Assigning Items to Categories
5	Views
5.1	How do Views get into Agenda
5.2	How do I use Views
5.2.1	Sections
5.2.1.1	Adding a Section to a View
5.2.1.2	Removing Sections from a View
5.2.1.3	Collapsing a Section
5.2.1.4	Repositioning a Section
5.2.1.5	Sorting Items in a Section
5.2.2	Columns
5.2.2.1	Adding a Column to a View
5.2.2.2	Changing the Position of a Column
5.2.2.3	Removing a Column from a View
5.2.3	Other Column Functions
5.2.3.1	Changing Column Format
5.2.4	Filtering Items in a View

Chap/Sect Code	Chapter and Section Headings
5.2.5	Date Filters
5.2.6	Hiding Items
5.2.7	The View Manager
5.2.8	Printing Functions
6	Personal Contact File
6.1	How to Build a Personal Contact File
6.2	Adding Structure
6.3	Displaying Information
6.4	Suggestions for Other Refinements
7	Quotation Reference
7.1	How to Build an Automated Quotation Reference
7.2	Adding Structure
7.3	Refining Structure
7.4	Displaying Information
8	Project Evaluation
8.1	How to Build an R&D Project Evaluation System
8.2	Adding Structure
8.3	Refining Structure
8.4	Displaying Information
9	Executive Information System
9.1	How to Build an Executive Information System
9.1.1	Setting up the 1-2-3 Spreadsheet
9.1.2	Converting the Spreadsheet to a Structured Text File
9.1.3	Importing the Structured Text File
9.2	Creating Views of Our EIS Database
9.2.1	Creating Our First View
9.2.2	Creating Another View
9.2.3	Creating Our Last View
10	Printing
10.1	Printer Definition Files
10.2	Print Dialog Boxes
10.2.1	Printing Options
10.2.2	Page Layout Options
10.2.3	Formatting Options

Figure 14-3.
Continued

Chap/Sect Code	Chapter and Section Headings
10.3	Customizing PDFs
11	Macros
11.1	Keystroke Macros
11.1.1	How do Keystroke Macros get into Agenda?
11.1.2	How to use Macros
11.1.3	Another Example
11.2	Advanced Commands
11.2.1	An Example
11.2.2	How do Advanced Command Macros get into Agenda
11.2.3	How to Use Macros
11.3	Debugging Macros
12	Structured Text Files
12.1	How to Create Structured Text Files
12.1.1	From Agenda
12.1.2	From Agenda Utilities
12.1.2.1	TXT2STF
12.1.2.2	Default Rules
12.1.2.3	DEF Files
12.1.2.4	LM2STF
12.1.3	From other programs
12.2	How to use Structured Text Files
13	Items and Clipboard Accessories
13.1	How to Use the Items and Clipboard Accessories
13.1.1	Using the Items Accessory
13.1.2	Using the Clipboard Accessory
14	Tips and Tricks
14.1	About Learning Agenda
14.2	Applications
14.3	Design Issues
14.3.1	Items
14.3.2	Categories
14.3.3	Notes
14.3.4	The Category Manager
14.3.5	Views
14.3.6	Suppressing the Entry Date
14.4	The Tips
14.5	Cross-reference
14.6	In Closing

Glossary

absolute date A date that Agenda sets without referring to the system date. For example, "September 14" is an absolute date.

accelerator keys Keystroke combinations using the Alt key with an alphabetical key.

accessory A pop-up program that you can call up on the screen without quitting the program you are currently running. Agenda supplies two accessories that let you enter information: the Items accessory (for storing information to use as items in Agenda), and the Clipboard accessory (for copying text from another application to paste into an Agenda item or note). Two other accessories (Kaleidoscope and Configuration) allow you to customize these accessories.

action An instruction you attach to category. An action tells Agenda to do something with items when they are assigned to the category with the action. There are two kinds of actions: *profile* and *special*.

action statement The statement that appears beside a category in the category hierarchy when you establish an action for that category. The action statement is a description of the action you established, enclosed within angle brackets (< >). For example, <A= Accountant> is an action statement.

Agenda database A collection of text (items) with a structure (categories). An Agenda database consists of two files with the extensions .AGA and .AGB.

ancestor A category at a higher level in the category hierarchy within the same family. For example, in the following family of categories, Company is the ancestor of all the other categories in the family; Staff is the ancestor of Sales and its child categories, Robert, Teresa, and Douglas:

Company
Staff
Sales
Robert
Teresa
Douglas

assignment The linking of an item and a category. Some of the ways to assign an item to a category include inserting the item in a section, entering a category in a column beside the item, using an *assignment profile,* and establishing conditions and actions.

assignment profile The list of categories to which the current item or marked items are assigned. You can assign the current or marked items to additional categories, or remove the current or marked items from categories, using the Assignment Profile box.

auto-import file A structured file that Agenda imports each time you open a database.

automatic assignment The process by which Agenda assigns an item to a category based on the *conditions* and *actions* in the category hierarchy. By default, Agenda automatically assigns an item to a category if the item's text includes the category name (*text condition*).

automatic completion The process by which Agenda tries to match what you type with existing category names. Automatic completion takes place when you are entering categories in a view or making selections from a list.

backslash command A command you enclose in backslashes (\ \) that sends control codes or other information to your printer. You can use backslash commands in a note or in the Print box.

backup A copy of your database as it exists at a certain point in time. Making backups allows you to experiment with your database. You can open the backup if you want to return your database to the way it was before you made the changes. You should also make backups regularly so you can use them if your database becomes damaged. When you make a backup, Agenda gives the backup files the same name as the current database with the extensions .BKA and .BKB. These backup files are stored in the same directory as the current database.

category One or more words used to group related items. Categories provide structure for a database. Items are assigned to categories.

category column A column in a view that displays categories or other information about assignment.

category filter A restriction that allows a view to display only those items that are assigned (or not assigned) to one or more specified categories.

category hierarchy A list of all the categories in a database that shows you how the categories are related to each other.

category manager A screen display that allows you to work with the *category hierarchy.*

child category In a *family* of categories, a category that belongs to a *parent category.* In the category hierarchy, child categories (also called children) are indented under their parent. For example, in the following family of categories, Loretta, Sam, and Nicholas are child categories:

People
- Loretta
- Sam
- Nicholas

circular reference A conflict that occurs when a combination of conditions and/or actions assigns an item to a category and removes it from the same category. The item in question would be caught in an endless loop. When a circular reference occurs, Agenda displays a circle in the upper right corner of the current view. You can see the item(s) caught in a circular reference using the Utility Show Circular command.

Clipboard accessory A pop-up accessory that allows you to copy text from another application and paste it into an Agenda item or note.

column A column head and one or more column entries. Columns can display categories (or other information about assignment) and dates.

column entry The information in a column. Column entries can be categories (or other information about assignment) or dates.

column head The category or type of date (Entry, When, or Done) that heads a column in a view.

compose sequence Two characters that you type after you press Compose (Alt=F1) in order to produce a character that does not appear on the keyboard.

compress Recover unused space in a database with the Utility Compress command.

condition An instruction you attach to a category. A condition tells Agenda to assign items to a category if they meet the condition attached to that category. There are three kinds of conditions: *text condition*, *profile condition*, and *data condition*.

condition statement The statement that appears next to a category in the category hierarchy when you establish a condition for that category. The condition statement is a description of the condition you established, enclosed within curly braces ({ }). For example, {C= ¦ Mary} is a condition statement.

control panel The top two lines of the screen, where Agenda displays status information.

cursor Reverse video square in a note or when editing an item.

cut Remove text so you can paste it elsewhere. Agenda stores the cut text in a temporary file. You can cut text when editing a note, item, or category.

date column A column in a view that displays *Entry, When*, or *Done dates*.

data condition A condition that tells Agenda to assign items to a category if they have a certain Entry, When, or Done date. For example, you can establish a date condition for the category Promotion that tells Agenda to assign items to that category if they have When dates within the week your company plans to do a major promotion.

date filter A restriction that allows a view to display only those items that have Entry, When, or Done dates within (or outside) a specified range.

definition file A set of statements that tells the TXT2STF utility how to convert a text file to a structure file. You use a definition file to control what TXT2STF converts into items, categories, and notes. For example, you might use a definition file to convert electronic mail files, program source code, text with headings, or news items with headlines.

delete Remove text without saving it to paste elsewhere. See also *remove*, *discard*.

demote Move a category to the right of its current position in the category hierarchy, which moves it down one level. For example, a category that is demoted may become the child of a former sibling.

dependent item An item that you indicate depends on the completion of one or more other items. You can choose to hide (not display) dependent items until their *prerequisite* items are either designated as done or discarded.

descendent A category at a lower level in the category hierarchy within the same family. For example, in the following family of categories, Robert, Teresa, and Douglas are descendents of all the categories at a higher level (Sales, Staff, and Company):

Company
    Staff
        Sales
            Robert
            Teresa
            Douglas

dialog box A box that contains settings for a particular command (for example, the box that is displayed when you select the Utility Preferences Environment command). You can change any of the settings in the box (for example, the color setting). When you are finished, press Accept(F9) to accept the changed setting(s).

discard Eliminate an item or category from the database. When you discard an item, it goes into the *Trash*; if the Trash has not been emptied, it can be recovered. When you discard a category, it cannot be recovered.

Done date The date Agenda records when you designate an item as done. For example, if you designate an item as done on July 19, the Done date for that item is July 19.

Done file A structured file for storing items that have been designated as done.

Done items Items that have been designated as done (that is, that have a Done date set for them).

Entry date The date Agenda records when you enter an item. For example, if you enter an item on July 12, the Entry date for that item is July 12.

exclusive categories See *mutually exclusive categories*.

execute Test items against existing conditions, and perform existing actions.

export (1) For a database, store items, categories and other information in a structured file that can be imported into an Agenda database. (2) For a note, create a text file from text in a note.

expression A word or phrase you add to a category as part of a text condition. Agenda assigns items that contain the expression to the category. (Agenda also displays the second expression in a column if the first expression is too wide.) To add an expression to a category, you edit that category. Each expression must be separated by a semi-colon as in the example, Deborah;Manager.

family A group of related categories in the category hierarchy consisting of a *parent category* and one or more *child categories*.

filter A view option you set to display only items that meet certain criteria. See *date filter, category filter.*

function key map The display at the bottom of the screen that tells you the meaning of each function key in the part of Agenda you are in. You can turn the function key map on and off by pressing Alt=K.

highlight The reverse video bar.

import (1) Bring a structured file into a database. (2) Bring a text file into a note.

indicators Symbols and words that provide information about the status of your database. Indicators can be displayed beside items or categories, or in the upper right corner of the control panel.

inheritance The process by which items assigned to a *child category* in a *family* are also assigned to the *parent category*. For example, in the following family of categories, the parent category, People, inherits the items assigned to Loretta, Sam, or Nicholas:

People
  Loretta
  Sam
  Nicholas

Initial View The view that Agenda automatically creates for you when you open a new database.

item A piece of text up to 350 characters long; the basic unit of information in Agenda.

item tag The symbol used to designate the beginning of an item.

LM2STF Utility supplied with Agenda that allows you to convert a Lotus Metro List Manager file to a structured file that you can import into an Agenda database.

macro A stored series of commands and keystrokes that you can execute quickly. Macros provide shortcuts for complicated or frequently used procedures.

MAIN The root category of the database, which includes all of the other categories. Because MAIN is the parent of all the other categories, it automatically *inherits* all the items in those categories.

marked items Items that have been selected for procedures such as copying, removing, discarding, or moving. Marking items allows you to perform a procedure on more than one item at a time. Agenda displays a diamond beside a marked item.

marked text Text in a note or item that has been selected for procedures such as copying, cutting, deleting, making the text into a category, appending the text to an item, and creating a new item from the marked text.

match strength The ratio of the words in an item that appear in a category expression to the total number of words in that expression. Agenda calculates a match strength to determine whether to assign an item to a category based on the text condition.

menu commands The commands available on the three Agenda menus (which appear in a view, a note, and the category manager). Agenda menus have several levels, and you select commands in a sequence from these levels. For example: Category Column New is a menu command sequence.

mutually exclusive family A family (made up of a *parent category* and one or more *child categories*) in which an item can be assigned to only one of the child categories. For example, suppose you have a mutually exclusive family in which the parent category is Priority and the child categories are High, Medium, and Low. Items can be assigned to High or Medium or Low, but not to High and Medium, or High and Low.

note Text attached to an item or a category to provide additional information. A note can be as long as 10K (about seven pages of double spaced text). A note can be stored as part of your database, or it can be stored in an external note file.

note file A text file external to the database that Agenda references as a note for an item or category. Storing notes in note files saves space in your database, and/or allows you to maintain an ongoing exchange between Agenda and another application.

options Choices for settings; similar to field values in other programs.

parent category In a *family* of categories, the category that includes the *child categories* under it. In the following family of categories, the category People is the parent:

People
    Loretta
    Sam
    Nicholas

pointer-movement keys The keys you use to move the highlight or cursor in a view, a note, the category manager, or a dialog box. For example, Up, Down, and Home are pointer-movement keys.

preferences A group of Agenda settings that allow you to configure certain behavior. For example, View Preferences determine how information is displayed in a particular view.

prerequisite item An item that you indicate must be completed before another item (the *dependent* item).

printer definition file A file that maps *backslash commands* to control codes for a specific printer. The printer definition file also includes a translation table that provides substitutes for characters your printer cannot print. The control codes determine printer behavior and output characteristics. Printer definition files have the extension .PDF.

profile A set of categories. See also *assignment profile, profile condition, profile action*.

profile action An action that directs Agenda to assign an item to (or remove an item from) one or more specified categories. You provide a *profile* of the categories to which you want to assign or remove items. For example, if Gina is in charge of Sales, you can attach a profile action to Sales that automatically assigns all items to Gina.

profile condition A condition that lets you tell Agenda to assign items to a category if they are assigned to (or not assigned to) one or more specified categories. You provide a *profile* of the categories to which the item must (or must not) be assigned. For example, if budget matters are high priority, you can establish a profile condition for the High category (under Priority) that assigns items to that category if they are assigned to the Budget category.

promote Move a category to the left of its current position which moves it up one level in the category hierarchy. For example, you can promote a category so that it becomes the parent of its former siblings.

questions Suggestions for assigning an item to a category that Agenda makes based on the text of that item. When Agenda has questions, it displays a question mark in the upper right corner of the screen. To confirm or reject the suggested assignments, use the Utility Questions command.

recurring date A date that recurs regularly, such as ''every Monday'' or ''each Thursday.'' Agenda interprets any date that includes the words ''each'' or ''every'' as a recurring date. When the original data passes, or the item is marked as done, Agenda gives the item the next date.

relative date A date that Agenda interprets based on the current system data. For example, ''next Monday'' is a relative date because Agenda uses the system date to calculate the date for next Monday.

relative date format A format for a *date column*. A relative format displays dates that occur within a three week span—the current week, the past week, and the coming week—in words (for example, ''today or ''nxt Mon'').

remove Take an item out of a section, or take sections or columns out of a view. Unlike *discarding*, removing does not delete information from the database. When you remove an item from a section, it remains in the database but is no longer assigned to the category that is the section head. When you remove a section from a view, both the category that is the section head and the items in the section remain in the category hierarchy. When you remove a column from a view, the categories, or dates contained in the column remain in the database.

section A category and the items assigned to that category.

section head The category displayed at the top of a section.

selection box A box that allows you to select from user-defined choices (such as views and databases) and from options for a setting in a dialog box.

settings The fields of a dialog box; settings allow you to determine the behavior of Agenda operations.

Show View A view Agenda creates to show summary information about a database. Agenda creates a show view when you use any of the Utility Show commands. The Show View can display the following types of information: all items that contain a specific word or phrase; all items that are *prerequisites* for the current item; all items that are *dependent* on the current item; all items that have been designated as Done; all items caught in *circular references*; all items in the database.

sibling categories *Child categories* with the same *parent* on the same family level. For example, in the following family of categories, Loretta, Sam, and Nicholas are all siblings of each other:

People
    Loretta
    Sam
    Nicholas

special actions Actions that allow you to discard items, designate items as done, set When dates for items, or export items to a structured file. For example, you can establish a special action for the category Outdated that automatically discards items when they are assigned to that category.

strong assignments Assignments made through actions or explicit user instructions. Strong assignments do not change when conditions are re-evaluated.

structured file A file that contains text plus formatting commands that break up the text into items, categories, and notes. Structured files have the extension .STF. You can create a structured file from all or part of a database with the File Transfer Export command. You also create a structured file when you export done items to a Done file. You can create a structured file from information outside Agenda with the utilities TXT2STF and LM2STF. You can import a structured file into Agenda with the File Transfer Import command.

sub-expression A unit within an *expression* attached to a category. When an expression includes sub-expressions, Agenda assigns an item to the category only if the item's text matches *all* the sub-expressions. Each sub-expression must be separated by a comma, which represents a logical AND, as in the example, Dave.Sales. Dave and Sales are sub-expressions; an item must match both words to be assigned to the category.

text condition A condition that tells Agenda to assign items to a category if the item text includes certain words or phrases. For example, you can establish a text condition that assigns items that include the word ''taxes'' to the category IRS. A category name is also a text condition; Agenda assigns items to a category if the item text includes the category name.

Trash The place where Agenda puts discarded items. Until the Trash has been emptied, you can recover discarded items with the Item Undiscard command.

TXT2STF A utility supplied with Agenda that converts a text file to a structured file. If the text file has a format that you want to capture (for instance, electronic mail that you want to make into items, notes and categories), you can use a *definition file.*

undiscard Get a single item or all items from the Trash, and insert them in the current section.

unindexed category A category that does not appear in the category hierarchy and cannot be used as a section head. You can use unindexed categories to store unique information such as a person's address or phone number (if the person's name is an item).

Untitled category A "blank" category Agenda inserts as the first section head in a new database, or as the section head or column head if you create the section or column with an accelerator key.

view A screen display that lets you enter and display information. Views are similar to reports in a traditional database in that you can create as many as you want and each view displays the information that you choose. Views differ from reports in that they allow you to enter as well as display information.

view manager A selection box that displays a list of all the views in your database. You use the view manager to change views or create new views.

weak assignments Assignments made through a condition. When Agenda re-evaluates conditions, all weak assignments are re-tested. If an item no longer meets a condition, it is removed from the category with the condition.

When date A date you set for an item yourself. It can be a due date for a report, a start date for a project, or any crucial date you want to keep track of.

work area The main part of the screen in a view, a note, or the category manager; the area below the control panel.

Index

SPECIAL OFFER

We have prepared 5 1/4" double-sided/double-density diskettes for the IBM® PC and compatibles to save you the time it takes to type in the examples shown in this book.

These diskettes contain, in addition to the various examples and applications in chapters 1 to 13, the complete Tips and Tricks and Cross Reference databases shown in chapter 14.

If you are interested in obtaining the diskettes described above or in other Agenda applications, please photocopy or clip out the coupon below, fill it out completely and mail it to:

Lauren M. Flast
660 Fairmont Avenue
Westfield, NJ 07090

or call (201) 232-4674

File: Agendaware™ 08/10/88 03:22
View: From the authors of the LOTUS GUIDE TO AGENDA® , Addison-Wesley, 1988

Items for sale	Categories covered (and examples)
• Ready to run Agenda® applications:	. Agenda® (interactive guide to the software)
	. Travel (restaurant guides for major cities)
	. Government (U.S. Senate database)
	. Management (HR policy and appraisal tools)
• starter databases	. Education (curriculum and counseling tools)
	. Programming (software documentation tools)
• prototypical examples of Agenda® at its best	. Interviewing (analysis and comparison tools)
	. Small business (startup checklist and audits)
	. Research (newswire analysis & bibliographic tools)

For more information, fill out the spaces below, and forward this card by return mail to the address shown above.

Name : ____________________

Address : ____________________

City, State and Zip : ____________________